T0331804

Secure Communicating Systems

More and more working computer professionals are actively confronted with the use, maintenance, or customization of cryptographic components and program certification mechanisms for local or remote (mobile) code. This text, meant for advanced undergraduate and beginning graduate students, tells what every computer scientist ought to know about cryptographic systems, security protocols, and secure information flow in programs. In addition to the standard material on public-key cryptosystems, stream and block ciphers, and certain secure communication protocols, the author presents several important topics not treated in most other texts:

- a detailed description of the new advanced encryption standard (AES) of NIST, the cipher Rijndael, announced as winner of the AES design competition on October 2, 2000;
- a complete description of an optimal public-key encryption using RSA that turns "textbook RSA" into a practical implementation whose semantic security is supported by a theoretical analysis conducted in the random oracle model;
- a current, formal discussion of standard security models for information flow in computer programs or human organizations;
- a presentation of a formal method for specifying and debugging security protocols; and
- a current discussion of the moral, legal, and political ramifications of cryptology and an overview of recent legislative efforts.

In addition, the text has WWW support and contains numerous implementation projects, a rigorous analysis of the Miller–Rabin algorithm, and a proof of the existence of primitive roots for prime powers.

Michael Huth is a Senior Lecturer in the Department of Computing at the Imperial College of Science, Technology and Medicine (London). He has also held positions at Kansas State University (Manhattan), the Technical University of Darmstadt, and the University of Birmingham. He has given numerous invited lectures and seminars and is the author of more than twenty papers on computer science and mathematics in international journals and conference proceedings. Together with Mark Ryan he wrote the textbook *Logic in Computer Science: Reasoning and Modelling about Systems,* recently published by Cambridge University Press.

Secure Communicating Systems

Design, Analysis, and Implementation

Michael R A Huth

Imperial College of Science, Technology and Medicine

CAMBRIDGE
UNIVERSITY PRESS

CAMBRIDGE
UNIVERSITY PRESS

University Printing House, Cambridge CB2 8BS, United Kingdom

One Liberty Plaza, 20th Floor, New York, NY 10006, USA

477 Williamstown Road, Port Melbourne, VIC 3207, Australia

4843/24, 2nd Floor, Ansari Road, Daryaganj, Delhi - 110002, India

79 Anson Road, #06-04/06, Singapore 079906

Cambridge University Press is part of the University of Cambridge.

It furthers the University's mission by disseminating knowledge in the pursuit of
education, learning and research at the highest international levels of excellence.

www.cambridge.org
Information on this title: www.cambridge.org/9780521807319

First published 2001

A catalogue record for this publication is available from the British Library

Library of Congress Cataloging in Publication data
Huth, Michael, 1962–
Secure communicating systems : design, analysis, and implementation / Michael R A Huth.
p. cm.
Includes bibliographical references and index.
ISBN 0-521-80731-X
1. Telecommunication – Security measures.
TK5102.85.H88   2001
005.8 – dc21   2001025484

ISBN 978-0-521-80731-9 Hardback

Contents

Preface

In the past ten years, the dramatic growth of the Internet has had a profound and lasting impact on the way in which organizations and individuals communicate and conduct their public and private affairs. Tax forms are available online, students may submit their exams electronically to a (possibly remote) campus network, and companies may use the Internet as a public channel for linking up internal computing facilities or processes. For example, an employee may dial into a company's intranet from a hotel room or her home via a public Internet service provider. Since the Internet protocol does not provide sufficient mechanisms for ensuring the privacy, authenticity, integrity, and (if desired) anonymity of data that are processed through a usually dynamically determined chain of computers, there is a need for tools that guarantee the confidentiality and authenticity of data and of their communication sources and targets. Cautious consumers of mobile or foreign code prefer to verify that downloaded programs (e.g., Java applets) abide by a formal set of safety rules, possibly defined by the individual consumer. These needs appear to be even more pressing in the recent evolution of *electronic commerce,* where the act of selecting and purchasing a product occurs online. Although online companies are still waiting to reap their first real profits, it is evident that companies in general need to offer this mode of business in order to survive in a new economy that is global and at the same time strengthens regional identity.

The design and analysis of cryptographic systems, security protocols, and programs that process secret or confidential information – together with the safety analysis of (possibly foreign) code – are important tools for establishing a sufficient level of security and confidentiality between human agents, social groups, and machines that communicate over a public, and therefore untrusted, medium. Alas, current computer science and information technology degree programs typically only touch upon these topics in a course on operation systems or telecommunication systems within the larger context of "computer security". As more and more working computer professionals are actively confronted with the use, maintenance, or customization of cryptographic components and program certification mechanisms, I see a pressing need for a textbook, aimed at the advanced undergraduate and beginning graduate level, that teaches "what every computer scientist ought to know about cryptographic systems, security protocols, and secure information flow in programs". This book presents public-key cryptosystems, stream and block ciphers, certain secure communication protocols, and so forth that are usually covered in similar texts. However, this text distinguishes itself, and goes beyond most existing books, in several important ways.

1. It contains several topics that are quite novel and mostly absent from current textbooks:
   - a detailed description of the new advanced encryption standard (AES) of NIST, the cipher Rijndael, announced as the winner of the AES design competition on 2 October 2000;
   - a complete description of an optimal public-key encryption system using RSA that turns "textbook RSA" into a practical implementation whose semantic security is supported by a theoretical analysis conducted in the random oracle model;
   - a current and formal discussion of standard security models for information flow in computer programs or human organizations;
   - the presentation of a formal method for specifying and debugging security protocols;
   - log-in protocols based on zero-knowledge proofs;
   - the basics of elliptic curve public-key and signature systems;
   - the subtleties in meaning of terms used in the informal or formal specification of security protocols, exemplified by the term "authentication"; and
   - a discussion of the moral, legal, and political ramifications of cryptology and an overview of recent legislative efforts.
2. It provides a *cohesive text* with a *vast number of carefully designed and stated exercises,* many of which explore variations or extensions of material covered in this text at multiple levels of difficulty.
3. It features small *programming projects* that help clarify the nature and potential complexity of the number-theoretic concepts used in this text (e.g., how decryption and encryption work for RSA).
4. It animates each topic with substantial *implementation exercises* that are ideally assigned to *teams* of students.
5. It proves *in full detail* the correctness of the Miller–Rabin algorithm for primality testing, thereby making an important educational contribution to the analysis and design of (probabilistic) algorithms.
6. It includes a mathematically rigorous appendix on primitive roots, which allows for additional reading and course work by mathematics majors and makes this book appropriate and useful for a mathematics course in applied number theory.
7. It is supported by a website that contains ancillary material, such as Java source code for some of the programs featured in this text. This website features links to all the sites mentioned in the book as well as links to online papers and tutorials that complement or deepen the presented topics.

The cipher Rijndael will certainly become a global standard for symmetric encryption software and hardware, and it will be found in a full range of computational objects – from smartcards to mainframes. At the time of publication, this text is likely among the first to include a full exposition of this cipher.

The inclusion of an optimal public-key cryptosystem using RSA transforms RSA from its textbook version to a practical implementation that is rigorous and secure. To my knowledge, the discussion of such an important practical realization of RSA is absent from other textbooks on this subject.[1] This practical discussion is complemented by a proof of exact security results in the random oracle model.

---

[1] I acknowledge an anonymous reviewer who brought this to my attention and suggested that I include this material.

Another principal contribution that sets this text apart from existing ones is its elementary description and well-motivated design of tools built for formally reasoning about security protocols. As their analysis component, most texts consider mathematical and often sophisticated techniques for assessing the strength of, say, a particular block cipher encryption algorithm. Although these techniques are important, they are meant for the specialist whose task it is to design new – and attack existing – cryptographic algorithms. This text therefore delegates such specialized topics to the references, but it emphasizes the analysis of specified security protocols as a major task in avoiding the corruption of secrecy, integrity, and anonymity in a communication network. I base this choice on the fact that inherent design flaws in protocols are, next to implementation flaws and compromises, the most likely cause for a cryptographic system to be broken. Moreover, the detection of such design errors is typically as difficult as the discovery of bugs in ordinary synchronous or asynchronous concurrent systems. For the latter, automated (e.g., the model checker SMV) and semi-automated (e.g., the theorem prover PVS) tools and specification frameworks have been developed and are already being embraced by research and development labs. The tool I feature is a model checker combined with a natural deduction engine modeling an attacker, due to W. Marrero, E. Clarke, and S. Jha.

As another applied component, I discuss D. Denning's (1976, 1977) classical work on program certification for secure information flow but present it in a contemporary and rigorous framework of a type inference system. This treatment allows for a formal proof that this analysis of secure information flow in programs satisfies a noninterference property that can be used to guarantee secrecy or integrity of information flow. I then present a semantic approach to secure information flow in programs, due to R. Joshi and K. R. M. Leino, that uses weakest predicate transformers and partial correctness proofs for its refutation and validation of program security. This material, as well as the analysis part of the optimal RSA encryption, constitutes the more advanced part of this text and is likely to be covered in a graduate course or presented by talented undergraduate students in class.

Formal methods for the analysis of cryptographic systems and the secure flow of information in programs, or their secure execution, are currently a vibrant research area, and their fruitful development should be a vital step toward the establishment of sound methodologies for "cryptographic engineering", just as such working standards have already emerged in conventional software engineering. The education of future security engineers in such tools may also help to address the next set of challenges in security engineering on the Internet. For example: How can one establish and reason about a dynamically evolving "network of trusted nodes"? What are sound methodologies for the verification of complex specifications within multiparty protocols (electronic cash flow between consumers, merchants, and banks; broadcasting and multicasting communication sessions; etc.)? How can we realize efficient but reliable platforms for the definition, verification, and certification of safety policies for mobile code?

Cryptography and the certification of (mobile) code are certainly only two requirements for the establishment and maintenance of a reliably functioning digital society. Yet, considering that an alarming percentage of the current cryptographic products make poor or even unprofessional design decisions (choice of algorithm, key length, protocol, etc.), it seems evident that students ought to know the "dos and don'ts" of this area. Although this text is not meant to become a standard monograph or a standard reference text, I believe that it can well become the preferred choice of instructors who – while not necessarily being experts in this field themselves – mean to effectively teach students whose backgrounds necessitate a delicate and careful presentation and development of nontrivial mathematical concepts and who need to see these concepts applied in a concrete context they can relate to; this I hope to accomplish through the inclusion of small programming exercises and larger implementation projects. Although competing texts present more cryptographic topics and at a more advanced level, instructors may decide to use this text because it reasons also about the secure behavior of programs, noting that a framework for trusted (mobile) code cannot be implemented with cryptographic techniques alone: We can use cryptography to authenticate the origin of mobile code or to ensure that this code has not been tampered with in transit; but even establishing all of that tells us nothing about the actual behavior of the program when it is executed locally.

This text contains more material than one could cover in a 12–15-week course. Beyond a common backbone of fundamentally important sections, instructors should feel free to omit or emphasize certain topics as they see fit for their individual course objectives. I took great care in presenting almost all the key issues, even though some may be condensed or confined to the exercises. At the same time, I strove for the creation of a relatively compact text that is highly interconnected and reasonably self-contained. The provided links to online research papers, tutorials, and cited references should enable instructors and students alike to extend appropriately the breadth and depth of the material presented here.

I have taken care to write this text without creating deep dependencies between any of its chapters. It is possible to read any of these chapters in isolation, as long as one has a "black-box understanding" of the concepts discussed in each chapter. Some dependencies, however, are inescapable. In particular, most topics discussed in Chapter 4 rely on material from the first three chapters.

So far, I have taught two interdisciplinary courses based on a draft of this text in three phases. The first phase was conducted in a "traditional" lecture style, where I made heavy use of this text in discussing the basics of symmetric and public cryptosystems and security protocols. During that time, I assigned additional reading and exercises from drafts of this book. In the second phase, I let student teams "implement" various standards (e.g., SHS, DSS, and triple DES) in a programming language of their choice. In the third phase, students made use of the more advanced part of this text or consulted online resources in order to identify papers and/or tools they chose to present in class. Feedback regarding these three phases, their mode, and their contents was extremely positive. Generally, students felt that the implementation work helped them solidify the mathematical underpinnings of the utilized techniques.

The supplementary material of this text is collected on the website

www.doc.ic.ac.uk/~mrh/scs

and includes the Java source code of some of the featured programs. Also included are links to research papers, repositories, tutorials, public and private standards, articles, and companies that promote their security products. The site features a current list of errata for this book; readers are kindly asked to report errors not found in that list to m.huth@doc.ic.ac.uk.

Acknowledgments

Many people have, directly or indirectly, assisted in writing and certainly improving this book. K. Rustan M. Leino made several critical suggestions on how to improve Section 6.3. Jason Lamm, Corina Păsăreanu, Guillaume Ravanas, and Matthew Zimmer pointed out several embarrassing typographical and conceptual errors. Wendy Bohnenkamp kept me informed on the current popular pulse in cryptography. Mark Ryan has provided substantial LATEX support through consulting and the writing of style files. I made use of Paul Taylor's LATEX style file for proof trees. The search engine www.google.com has been an effective tool that facilitated the writing of this text. I held illuminating conversations with David Schmidt on abstraction and weakest precondition semantics. I thank the numerous anonymous reviewers of various drafts of this text for their constructive and most helpful criticism; in fact, one of them encouraged me to write the chapter on optimal public-key encryption with RSA. My editor Lauren Cowles helped shape the vision of this text. I am also grateful for the enthusiasm and support of students at Kansas State University who made it challenging and rewarding to teach this material. Notwithstanding all this kind support, I am expressly and solely responsible for all errors of fact or presentation that this text may well include.

CHAPTER 1

Secure Communication in Modern Information Societies

1.1 ELECTRONIC COMMERCE: THE MANTRA OF Y2K+

We are presently witnessing mergers and takeovers of unprecedented speed and extent between companies once thought to have national identities, or at least clearly identifiable lines of products or services. On the day this paragraph was written, the British Vodaphone AirTouch announced an Internet alliance with the French conglomerate Vivendi. The deal was conditional on Vodaphone's hostile takeover of Germany's Mannesmann and, in the end, did establish a branded multi-access portal in Europe. About a week later, the takeover of Mannesmann was official – the biggest ever, and friendly. MCI's attempted takeover of Sprint is another example of a strategically advantageous combination of different information technologies. January 2000 saw CNN, NTV, and the *Deutsche Handelsblatt* (a direct competitor to the *Financial Times*) launch a multimedia product for stock market news that is accessible via television, printed newspapers, and the World Wide Web. And so it goes. Although many differing views are held regarding the causes and consequences of these phenomena, we would probably all agree that they reflect a certain shift of emphasis from production-based economics to one grounded in the processing, marketing, and *access* of information. Whether the products themselves are merely "information" or systems for managing and processing vast amounts of data, information systems are seen as a crucial strategic means for organizing, improving, and maintaining more traditional production cycles.

Such a shift could not have been achieved without the creation of reliable, dense, and global electronic information networks that offer the full spectrum of accessibility modes that conventional information carriers allow. This spectrum ranges from being open to the general public (e.g., a public library) to being open only to members of a very well-defined community (e.g., the NASA engineers who develop the next generation of shuttle thrusters). The Internet and the World Wide Web have become a key medium for the storage, transmission, transformation, and analysis of information of any kind: textual, visual, or auditory. Recently, we even witnessed the release of a device that "interprets" olfactory information transmitted over the Internet! Apparently, we increasingly participate in – and depend on – electronically networked communities. This raises societal and managerial questions pertaining to the rights and responsibilities of network participants. However, it is not clear a priori whether standard practices from offline communities adequately transfer to so-called virtual communities and electronic communication networks. For example, children's bookstores and pornographic shops are typically found at disjoint locations in real cities, whereas such an exclusion principle is hardly implementable on the Internet; this renders online protection and guidance of minors an unresolved issue.

Regulatory efforts, which are mostly confined to sovereign states and trade unions, have little hope of success in a truly global environment unless their legal and moral force is recognized, and enforced, worldwide.

Today's digital networks are adopting an abundance of newly developed information technology tools that facilitate the gathering and creation of meaningful information needed for successful business ventures; yet these tools also provide a platform for *conducting* business. The fashionable term "electronic commerce" denotes any kind of commercial activity that occurs over the World Wide Web, the Internet, intranets, facsimile, telephone, and so forth. Electronic commerce is believed to have the greatest growth rates in any economic sector. E-commerce start-ups are enthusiastically received, and almost indiscriminately so, by investors. As a result, individuals who can install or maintain information systems for e-commerce are much in demand. However, the promises of electronic commerce must be weighed against their possible dangers and inherent challenges.

1. The *locality* and *authenticity* of electronically communicating agents is dubious at best; electronic business interactions make it harder to guarantee that potential business partners are honest about who and where they are.
2. Sensitive information or other private data may be transmitted through unreliable or otherwise *unsecure communication channels*. Not only does this pose a threat in that competitors may be able to access and use confidential strategic or technical information, it also raises grave concerns about the *privacy of individuals* who use those very channels for noncommercial (yet still nonpublic) communications.
3. Even if electronic transactions came equipped with a mechanism of authenticating agents, one needs to ensure that agents cannot subsequently deny any of their properly authenticated actions. We speak of *nonrepudiation* if an authentication scheme has this desirable property.
4. The right to anonymous actions has held an important role in securing free speech and unhindered political discourse. Although mechanisms that implement anonymous interaction may also be subject to serious abuse, they are an important component of democratic processes. Most patents on digital cash realize such electronic cash in an anonymous way. However, the financial services sector (including tax agencies) are quite interested in removing this anonymity feature of such cash, at which point the issue becomes not merely technical but also one of politics, policies, and laws.
5. "The devil is in the implementation" – this means that a secure specification of a cryptographic system (or security-handling computer program) is still a long way from its actual secure implementation.
6. Mobile code, active networks, and extensible operation system kernels require: novel methodologies for specifying safety rules for executing programs that are foreign to the local system; provably correct algorithms for verifying that programs meet such safety specifications; and mechanisms that attach certificates to mobile code so that these certificates can quickly be evaluated locally.

These are only a few (and by no means the most critical) problems that electronic commerce faces. Even if all had acceptable solutions, a host of other pressing questions would remain unanswered. For example, how should businesses protect the integrity, existence, and control of their information systems? – given that they may be distributed globally and have plenty of interfaces to publicly accessible resources. There is also the daunting task of designing working frameworks for the taxation of Internet sales, given the conflicting interests of stakeholders: local counties, states in a federation, sovereign states, e-commerce companies, and consumers. Guaranteeing privacy of communication and authenticity of agents may be of little use if unauthorized and presumably hostile network agents are able to penetrate the heart of a company's information system. Federal agents recently managed to enter, without proper authorization, sites that are vital to the security of U.S. national infrastructures. We all have read stories of the so-called hackers who gained access to computers of the U.S. Department of Defense and thereby downloaded huge amounts of sensitive data during the initial phase of Operation Desert Storm. Computer security cases in the military sector are not out of place in this section, for defense agencies rely on electronic purchasing and ordering procedures that are increasingly required to interface with the nonmilitary commercial world. At present, it is unclear what the psychological and sociological effects and implications will be of making electronic commerce a main mode of entrepreneurial activity, but the events of May 2000 have already demonstrated the threat that e-mail viruses and worms pose to an economy that depends more and more on the Internet and the World Wide Web. It is not the objective of this text to address these pressing issues; rather, it focuses solely on the six points previously listed. Specifically, we give an introduction to *secure communicating systems* by studying the design, analysis, and implementation of systems that are built to provide solutions to the practical problems of (a) certifying the safety rules of programs, (b) realizing the authentication of secure and perhaps anonymous communication along an open channel, and (c) the nonrepudiation of committed (trans)actions.

1.2 CRYPTOGRAPHIC SYSTEMS

Although cryptology has a rather long history and is a thriving field of sophisticated research, in this text we give only a selective overview by choosing representative designs of cryptographic systems and some forms of their analysis that are accessible to senior undergraduate and beginning graduate students. To be up-front about it, there is an inherent and deplorable tradeoff between the degree to which cryptographic systems realize their stated security goals and the computational overhead they impose on information networks.[1] More often than not, such security goals are left implicit or are formulated with insufficient precision, as the discussion of authentication in Section 4.3 illustrates. Perfectly secure mechanisms for ensuring private communication along a channel are possible; the one-time pad (see page 86), while being perfectly secure, requires an encryption key that is as long as the actual message to be communicated. This burden hardly justifies its use unless perfect security is a minimum requirement, as for the "hotline" between the White House and the Kremlin. More efficient systems don't have such perfect security, so one needs to assess just how secure they are. In concrete terms, such security is often measured in how much money, or time, one would have to spend in order to "break"[2] a cryptographic system; unfortunately, such estimates may only be meaningful

---

[1] There is an even more disconcerting tradeoff between the security of a communicating system and the convenience of its user-level functionality.

[2] Breaking a system can mean a variety of things: obtaining access to a single message (or fragment thereof) with or without control over which message that should be; corrupting the entire security of the system for an extended period of time, with or without its legal users noticing the break-in; being able to assume someone else's identity; etc.

for a specific method of breaking a system. A useful measure should thus provide cost predictions for *all possible attacks,* independent of whether they are known to the analyst. Evidently, this can only be realized in a very limited manner. This also entails a reasonably clear understanding of how secure the respective communication and authentication components *must be.* Such a quantitative requirement analysis is usually quite difficult; for example, the monetary value of a company's customer database is typically hard to assess and may be a function of who would gain access to it. And how would *you* quantify the loss of privacy if your medical records were to be posted on the World Wide Web?

We mention these issues in passing but more often assess the *computational effort* needed to break certain cryptographic systems. A fundamental difficulty with such analyses is that they must consider some (mathematical) model of the cryptographic system under consideration, or even a specific implementation thereof. Any positive security results drawn from such an analysis are therefore only valid *within the given model or implementation.* Alas, this does not rule out an attack *outside the given model*; the well-publicized attack of RSA encryption implemented on a smartcard is one such alarming example (see pages 68 and 204). In an extreme view, one may even consider such results as helping potential attackers by pointing out to them what sorts of things *won't* succeed; it is wise to assume that attackers read the relevant technical literature.

You may be surprised to hear that the bulk of cryptographic systems make use of rather astonishing facts about natural numbers and some of their computational problems. Thus we need to study a certain amount of number theory and get to know a few important number-theoretic algorithms that form fundamental components of real cryptographic systems. We hasten to point out that we aim to develop such material at a graceful pace and at an accessible level.[3] In this chapter, we mention the role of number theory in cryptography because all the cryptographic systems that use certain "hard" number-theoretical problems – for realizing secure communication, authentication, or nonrepudiation – rest their security on the premise that such hard problems don't have easy solutions. The point is that this premise's validity is still an open (and most difficult) research problem and moreover that even its validity would usually not *ensure* security.

Because this text will not develop the rather advanced concepts required for a precise definition of what "hard" and "easy" problems are, we mean to illustrate this via example. Integer factorization is believed to be a hard problem, and the security of the RSA cryptosystem relies on this belief (see Section 2.5). More specifically, it is believed to be computationally infeasible to find a factor of an integer with 1024 binary digits if that number is the product of two randomly generated primes of about equal size. (Improvements in processor speed and cheaper computer parts, such as memory, may require a future increase in the number of bits needed.) Yet to this day, nobody has put forward any proof of this belief. It is conceivable that somebody will eventually devise an efficient procedure for factoring such large numbers. Similar concerns (and lack of proof) prevail for other "hard" problems used in building cryptographic systems, whether they are grounded in number theory or some other computational structures.

---

[3] Appendix A may be skipped entirely without compromising the appreciation of our cryptographic designs, but it does fill the explanatory gap of proving the correctness of the Miller–Rabin algorithm for primality testing, one of the "workhorses" in our cryptographic toolbox.

Even if such (unlikely) proofs were to be found, they could only be carried out *relative to a computational model,* such as a conventional personal computer. This means that their resulting safeguards would only apply to that very same computational model. However, various computing paradigms may be vastly different in nature from each other. Some, admittedly small, instances of certain "hard" problems have been solved using chemical reactions based on the processing of DNA. We already have seen computers with up to four states, where computation is driven by the laws of quantum mechanics. If – and that is a big "if" – the development of such machines is scalable in the number of states, then this will provide an efficient engine for factoring large integers. It is debatable whether any of these approaches might pose a real threat to existing cryptographic systems, but only time can tell. In June 2000, a Swiss research team used entanglement of photons[4] to transport an encrypted message from one town to another through ordinary fiber-optic lines. A U.S. team is currently investigating how one can make it harder for eavesdroppers to alter the properties of photons. A German–Austrian team has used such techniques to encrypt an image. This news is exciting, but it also suggests that new technology may only provide new instantiations for familiar players, such as eavesdroppers. It is also unclear whether such technology can be used on large networks that intend to reach ordinary households. It seems rather disturbing (perhaps pleasing, to some) that the realization of electronic commerce and the protection of vital national infrastructures – which rely on secured information systems – may depend on facts about number theory, microbiology, and quantum physics.

Cryptographic components, even if assumed to be perfectly secure as isolated components, raise novel security questions if placed within the context of *interacting networks.* For example, can a *security protocol* be successfully attacked even though none of its cryptographic primitives can be broken in isolation? Indeed, quite a few published protocols were found to have undergone such attacks. Such insights gave rise to research activity similar to that in the design and analysis of concurrency protocols. We therefore present a customized framework for "debugging" security protocols in Section 4.5. Again, such tools are certainly needed by implementors and designers of security protocols; if *they* don't do their homework then attackers will do it for them – and let them know by attacking weaknesses discovered with the aid of those tools.

This point illustrates another peculiarity in the study of cryptographic systems. Historically, such designs (say, a particular encryption algorithm) were kept secret, and knowing the design was often coextensive to knowing how to break it. All such early systems were broken eventually. A conceptual breakthrough was the idea of *key-dependent cryptosystems.* Ideally, such systems are secure even if one knows all the intricate details of their design – as long as one does not know the concrete key with which the system was instantiated. This idea made it possible to publish designs so that the entire scientific community could study and attack them. Although this development can only improve the strength of emerging designs, it takes time for such studies to be of any substantial value. It is fair to

---

[4] Quantum computing rests on three principles: (i) *superposition* of quantum bits allows for an exponential speed-up factor for certain computations (including the factorization of integers); (ii) *quantum entanglement* enables a reliable and instantaneous communication of quantum bits over arbitrarily long distances; and (iii) *quantum interference* poses the challenge of engineering a system of quantum bits that does not interfere with its environment (decoherence).

say that the Data Encryption Algorithm (featured in Section 3.2.1) and the RSA encryption system (presented in Section 2.2) underwent more than twenty years of public analysis and scrutiny without revealing any fundamental design weaknesses. More recent crypto-systems and cryptographic algorithms, such as the new Advanced Encryption Standard *Rijndael,* may well be far superior to the previous ones, but again only time can tell because we have no single sound and coherent mathematical theory or methodology for reasoning about the strength of such systems. This places consumers and standards committees alike in an awkward position. When and why should one abandon a given cryptographic system in favor of another? If a cryptographic standard is fully implemented and integrated into other network standards, what can be done if the cryptographic design turns out to have serious flaws? Note that this is not just an engineering problem of replacing one system with a different (and, it is hoped, more secure) one, since sensitive data will have been stored in an unsecure manner. This raises several thorny issues, not the least of which is liability.

At the time of this writing, it is anticipated that the Data Encryption Standard (DES) will be replaced by the Advanced Encryption Standard (AES), the cipher Rijndael, which is featured in Section 3.2.2. On 2 October 2000, the U.S. Department of Commerce announced Rijndael as the winner of a worldwide design contest. Pending a period of public comment and final approval, this cipher will become a standard of the U.S. National Institute of Standards and Technology. That the submissions came from all over the world already suggests that national standards and their overseeing national agencies may need to rethink their roles and begin to interface with similar bodies of other nations. It may well be that global economic conglomerates will put pressure on governments to streamline regulation and licensing activities toward standard business practices and to offer approaches that are fairly uniform on a global scale. Indeed, recent policy changes at the White House regarding the export control of U.S. encryption products indicate that governments have already begun to think along those lines. These changes worry national agencies that deal with issues of defense and the protection of vital national infrastructures. We return to the dilemma of encryption policies in Section 1.5.

1.3   LEGISLATING ELECTRONIC AUTHENTICATION

More and more, the Internet and other electronic media provide a platform for ordering products, negotiating contracts, and paying for rendered or anticipated services. Thus consumers, government agencies, and commercial sectors wonder whether there is a need for new legislation that elaborates in which cases, and to what extent, electronic signatures are legally valid. Unfortunately, technical terminology is often misunderstood by legislative bodies, and technicians who consult in a legislative effort find it equally hard to appreciate the legal language. Needless to say, it is crucial that these communities work together in realizing a maximum of clarity in the legislative process. For example, there seems to be some confusion between the concepts of an *electronic signature* and a *digital signature.* The former can be thought of as any technical replacement of the usual handwritten signature functionality in an electronic system: digital pens, PIN numbers, and scanned hand-written signatures are a few examples. In some sense, digital signatures are a special case of electronic signatures in that they use public-key cryptosystems (the topic of Chapter 2) as a mechanism for ensuring the integrity and origin of digital messages; Section 4.1 discusses digital signatures in detail. In another sense, digital signatures are more appropriately thought of as *digital envelopes,* for the signer may not know, or endorse, the signed message. Upon closer inspection, digital signatures have a much broader range of applications than (electronic) signatures in the narrow sense. Digital signatures can be used to authenticate servers in a computing network, web pages, software, or any data that is stored digitally.

Legislators may take a *technical* approach – declaring, for example, a specific digital signature system as a (possibly required) standard for implementing certain electronic authentication functions. This view generally provides no insights into the legal consequences of using, or misusing, such systems. One of the first laws on digital signatures, the German Digital Signature Law, used a legal instrument to set a technical standard: specifically, for the required security of the public-key infrastructures. The law does not explicitly state any legal consequences that would result from using digital signature systems that are compliant with the standard prescribed by the law.

A *legal* approach, on the other hand, attempts to equate handwritten and electronic signatures and may not impose any restrictions as to which technology may realize electronic signature systems. The Utah Digital Signature Act of 1995 regulates digital signatures based on public-key cryptosystems and legally equates such digital signatures with handwritten ones, provided that the corresponding cryptosystem meets all the requirements described in the Act.[5] The State of Utah has a common law system that often allows a more liberal interpretation of the use of signatures; expressing one's intentions explicitly, for example, may be considered "signing". Unfortunately, the Utah Digital Signature Act does not adequately reflect the different functions of signatures. This kind of law could threaten the development and growth of electronic commerce in that it also identifies functions of handwritten signatures with novel digital functions, such as certifying a web server.

In practice, most (draft) law and directives present a mixture of these approaches, thereby creating both legal uncertainty and possible impediments to the evolution of electronic commerce. The United Nations Commission on International Trade Law (UNCITRAL) crafted Draft Uniform Rules on Electronic Signatures; these rules would be nonbinding and technologically nonspecific, but they would provide guidance to legislative authorities during their own process of designing legislation for electronic authentication. These rules distinguish between "electronic signatures" and "*enhanced* electronic signatures"; the latter must meet a higher standard of security with regard to the signing and signature verification process. It is assumed that data signed with enhanced electronic signatures are legally signed. The EU Directive of the European Parliament and of the Council on a Common Framework for Electronic Signatures gives similar open-ended definitions for an "electronic signature" and for what is now called an "*advanced* electronic signature"; however, the Directive focuses on digital signatures and does not provide legal recognition of electronic signatures pertaining to the validity of contracts requiring signatures. The CA Working Group of the Electronic Commerce Promotion Council of Japan issued guidelines for the operation and management of certification authorities (CAs), an infrastructure used to establish a notion of trust in the authenticity of public keys. This is an example of a *self-regulated* effort, where one hopes that industry will establish common practice in accord with such guidelines.

---

[5] At the time of this writing, nobody has come forward to register a public-key cryptosystem under this Act.

In the past, one could observe a preference for technology-specific legislation that most often dealt with digital signature systems. The Italian Digital Document Regulations of 10 November 1997 state that, under certain conditions, digital signatures can be legally equated with handwritten signatures. At the same time, these regulations are restricted to public-key cryptosystems with public-key infrastructures used for digital signature systems. The prevalence of a mixed approach is largely due to the fact that digital signature systems are the basis of important tools for electronic commerce: Pretty Good Privacy (PGP), Secure Electronic Transactions (SET), and Secure Socket Layer (SSL) all make crucial use of such technology.

Policymakers often think that the success of electronic commerce depends on having a well-specified technical signature system with well-understood legal consequences. This wishful thinking stands in direct opposition to new technological developments and the need for novel signature roles that electronic commerce is likely to bring about. A variety of alternative approaches to electronic signatures exist already. Virtual Credit Card (VCC), used by the Brazilian bank Unibanco, electronically authorizes credit-card purchases without using the public-key infrastructures (PKIs) upon which digital signature systems rely. Another example is iPIN, an Internet-based payment system for small amounts that can be managed by Internet service providers.

On 30 June 2000, President Clinton signed the Electronic Signatures in Global and National Commerce Act, a bill that recognizes and clarifies the legal status of electronic signatures. This bill requires consumers to agree to electronically signed contracts; they also must consent to receiving records over the Internet. Companies, on the other hand, must verify that customers have a viable e-mail address and the necessary equipment to receive electronic information.

There are a number of biometric approaches to electronic authentication. The idea is to authenticate individuals by means – it is hoped – of dependably unique biological data. For example, fingerprint readers on small chips can be integrated into keyboards, and one may scan a person's iris or palm at an automatic teller machine. It is unclear whether biometrics can replace, or even supplement, cheaper authentication mechanisms that don't rely on biological data. Because useful biometric data ought to remain fixed during a person's lifetime, such information may have to be considered as *personal property* in the legal sense. At any rate, the handling of such data requires reliable legal frameworks that protect the privacy and identity of individuals.

The examples just given show that regulatory efforts need to reflect the possibility of swift and dramatic technological changes. The downside of technology-neutral legislation is that courts may have to develop case law when such legislation cannot achieve a precise definition of legal concepts. Another source of tension is that one country's national law often conflicts with other national (or international) law. The UNCITRAL Model Law on Electronic Commerce was drafted within the larger context of achieving a more uniform and cohesive international trade law; it is technologically nonspecific, thus allowing and anticipating fast and dramatic technological changes. International legislation must also make room for flexible interpretations of legal requirements of form; for example, common law and civic law systems typically offer different interpretations of "legally binding signatures".

Since electronic commerce is, by its very nature, an international phenomenon, we need drafts and guidelines for digital law at an international level. The pressing need for legal clarity, however, requires national legislation, as this can be enacted much sooner. Additionally, nations may have an inherent cultural and historical outlook on legal concepts. Laws about handwritten signatures, for instance, may emphasize the signer's intention to be legally bound by his or her signature (often the case in common law, as in the United States), or it may stress the security of the actual signing process (often occurring in civic law, as in Germany). When nations draft new digital law, they may also have to "clean up" and streamline some of their existing law. At the time of this writing, a handwritten signature on a document transmitted via facsimile (fax) is legally binding in the Netherlands but not so in Germany. Nations and unions may also have a different view of privacy and civil rights and of their implementation in systems that support electronic commerce.

In the meantime, it appears that legislation should largely be nonspecific about technological details of electronic authentication. It should pay considerable attention to the various functions and features of handwritten and electronic signatures, making clear if and how such functional roles allow for a match between electronic and nonelectronic signatures. This legislative process needs to be internationally oriented but must also reflect the specific intent and nature of national law. Clearly, these objectives have inherent conflicts. It is hoped that a more mature electronic commerce will also see a slower technological change of authentication mechanisms in order for technology-specific legislation to be effective. Whether one believes that legislation (hard law) is necessary or that self-regulation (soft law) – or some combination of both – is needed to aid and oversee the development of electronic commerce, it is evident that these problems require an unprecedented degree of cooperation among technicians, government and nongovernment organizations, industry executives, and legislative bodies. This provides one of the many reasons why computer science professionals and students ought to be informed about the basic concepts, designs, modes of analysis, and implementations of cryptographic systems.

1.4 THE MATHEMATICAL JUDGE

Regardless of whether a security protocol or its cryptographic primitives are secure or not, they will typically be sold and used as a commercial product. So far, software vendors have generally not been liable for flawed software, provided that they could show that they followed established "software engineering practice". However, it is not clear whether such a line of argument will continue to be successful if software erroneously confirms or denies the authenticity of a contract signature, or if it exposes confidential information resulting in physical, monetary, or psychological harm to the sender or receiver. For example, what about cases in which agents sign data electronically and later claim that the signature has been forged? Even if the signature system had a built-in nonrepudiation mechanism, the agent could still claim that its implementation was somehow flawed. Using a digital signature scheme, the agent could also claim that somebody obtained her private signature key – say, by corrupting the public-key infrastructure or some certification authority. Even if the protocol adds more and more protective layers against such possibilities, the agent could always contest the functioning of the *lowest* or at least *some* level. This is in striking contrast to the traditional practice of using pens and handwritten signatures. We can hardly blame the company that manufactured a pen used by someone else to forge our signature! Likewise, we cannot sensibly assert that somebody acquired the knowledge and skill of reproducing our original signature perfectly. Consequently, the question of establishing the circumstances under which electronically signed documents will be recognized in court as legally binding is more delicate than one may initially suppose.

In the technical part of this text, we see that basically all practical cryptographic systems come with an inherent degree of unsecurity, even if we were to assume a flawless implementation process. Admittedly, the likelihood of a security violation occurring in a perfect implementation may be extremely small, but can we establish a definite threshold saying that a digital signature scheme is legally binding if the probability for the claimed signer *not* to have signed a document using this scheme is smaller than some $\varepsilon > 0$? Who will come up with such a value? Who will assess a given implementation of a cryptographic system to estimate that threshold? Who will certify that the concrete implementations of such abstract digital signature cryptosystems meet all the relevant security specifications? If, say, RSA were used for such a certified signature generation scheme, then how would a jury react to defense lawyers exposing jurors to popular-science and technical articles that describe the occasional success story of "breaking" a large RSA key? Would the jury not feel uneasy about resting their judgment on conflicting presentations on the security of key lengths? And would a substantial number of future court cases require a *mathematical judge*?

Although it may be somewhat of a stretch, electronic signatures could conceivably become key evidence in first-degree murder cases. One may recall that prosecutors have a hard time convincing juries when their only hard piece of evidence is a sample of nonmitochondrial DNA, found at a crime scene, with a "close" match to the DNA of a defendant. Jurors find it difficult to relate sophisticated scientific facts to the concept of "beyond reasonable doubt".

To play devil's advocate, suppose one has legislation that endorses a specific technology and a specific implementation for a digital signature scheme and also states explicitly the legal consequences of electronic signatures produced with the system it describes. Suppose further that, after some time, this implementation turns out to have serious flaws. Who would deal with the long case list of past system users who now contest having signed their mortgages and car loans? It seems that one might have to rely on higher implementation standards than those for software used on commercial aircraft – but meeting such standards is expensive and time-consuming. A more sensible approach may be to make the implementation and verification effort a function of the importance of the data that the tool is intended to sign. Clearly, a system that handles only small-scale transactions requires less effort than one that deals with major stock trading. Even so, the former could see class-action lawsuits by consumer groups and the like. Perhaps car loans and other big-ticket items will still rely, at least partially, on traditional signing methods and evidence provided by the particular (nonelectronic) business context. At the risk of repeating ourselves, only time can tell how people and other agents will sign what – and how successful courts will be in using electronic signatures as hard evidence.

1.5 ENCRYPTION POLICIES

The economic promises of global electronic commerce and its need for uniform interfaces suggest that support for reliable and secure cryptographic components should be available worldwide; nonetheless, some governments impose restrictions on the use, import, or export of such products. This largely occurs in the context of cryptographic systems used to render text unintelligible to everybody except the sender and receiver of the message. Obviously, such capabilities pose threats to national interests; they can make it hard or impossible for law-enforcement agencies to conduct investigations or to gain convictions; and they can affect national security if used to cover up terrorist activity. They also can facilitate extortion schemes: former or current employees of some company or agency may encrypt important data and then demand money from their employer for making the data legible again. But let us not forget that the same tools that aid terrorists are also instrumental in protecting the privacy and confidentiality of people's speech and their lawful participation in democracies – not to mention the protection this technology offers to pro-democracy activists in certain parts of the world. This is clearly a political point of friction that will not go away, but the interests of democratic movements and existing democracies must not be taken lightly.

The reference to the Crypto Law Survey (given in the bibliographical notes to this chapter, Section 1.7), provides an excellent resource for finding out what nations apply what sorts of encryption control at present. The current U.S. government went through an interesting learning process that caused it to change its encryption export policies. Interestingly enough, digital *signature* systems were never controlled in this manner in the United States. Encryption systems for functions other than signing, formerly classified as *ammunition,* can now be exported (after a technical review) to commercial firms and other nongovernment end users unless they reside in states named on the U.S. State Department's evolving list of supporters of terrorism. If the key-length of the cryptosystem is longer than 64 bits – which is true of the new AES Rijndael – then the vendor may be required to submit a post-export report that is facilitated by reflecting standard industrial practice. Foreign nationals no longer need a license if they want to work for U.S. firms on the development and maintenance of cryptosystems. Fortunately, the idea of mandatory recovery keys (which would have allowed the authorized decryption of text even if the keyholder refuses to hand over the key) seems to have been abandoned, much to the dismay of U.S. agencies concerned with national security. For details, see the press release of the U.S. Department of Commerce dated 12 January 2000.[6] Encryption policies have their own dilemmas. They must be strong enough to adequately protect law enforcement and national security but at the same time liberal enough to maintain or improve a nation's political structures and processes – as well as its competitiveness in the lucrative global market of electronic security products and resulting e-commerce. This may well be the principal reason why the U.S. government solicits public comments on these regulations for 120 days before final revised policy rules are implemented.

1.6 TRUST AND COMMUNITIES

Today, we witness a fierce global economy with large multinational conglomerates that encourage governments to provide incentives for setting up shop within their territory. For example, the German car manufacturer BMW let European states "bid" for hosting

---

[6] http://www.bxa.doc.gov/Encryption/regs.htm

their new production facility. AOL Europe asked the German government to enact policies that would lower the base access rate to the Internet within Germany, identifying current rates as a major obstacle to the growth of German e-commerce. Major companies nervously try to find strategic partners that complement and strengthen their competitiveness worldwide. The World Trade Organization (WTO) may see China as a future member, and worldwide free trade and mobility seem within reach. At the same time, however, international, national, and regional interest groups actively campaign against the possibly harmful sociological, environmental, and economic implications of increasingly global production and management structures. The riots at the WTO meeting in Seattle (United States) and the voices of protest at the last World Economic Forum in Davos (Switzerland) are indicative of such concerns. Through meetings such as the Davos forum, top executives are beginning to appreciate that the concerns of communities are a serious component of their managerial decision processes. The customer boycott of Shell in Europe, triggered by Shell's plan to dump a polluted oil rig in the North Sea, suggests that consumer values can affect company policies.[7] The Internet and other digital communication technologies give traditional and emerging communities a powerful tool for reaching their constituency and other affected groups they mean to impact; these technologies also enable the creation of novel interest groups and communities at a speed and to an extent that were previously impossible.

All these communities, even the ones based on business relationships, critically depend on working notions of *trust*. This may seem ironic, considering that the current economic climate conjures up images of Manchester Capitalism. However, even the most aggressive and hostile parties depend on some form of trust if they want to communicate at all. Vodaphone AirTouch placed considerable trust in the publicly available reports issued by Mannesmann regarding its financial performance and marketing goals. If you were to apply for admission into the graduate school at Tulane University and then received mail – on 100% cotton paper emblazoned with the crest of Tulane University of Louisiana – informing you of your acceptance or rejection, you would trust that this mail is coming from that university, *all things being equal*.

Such trust has practical advantages; it would simply be impossible to be "perfectly paranoid" and still maintain a productive and meaningful life. We tend to question trust when all things are *not* equal! – as when your bank inspects your signature more closely on a check for $10,000 than on one for $10. In the rapidly evolving realm of electronic commerce, we have seen attempts to provide business websites with stamps of approval given by some generally trusted certification or accreditation company. TRUSTe[8] is one such (nonprofit) service provider; its certification vouches for certain privacy policies that consumers can expect to be met. However, companies are often hesitant to attain such a certification; among other things, clearly stated privacy policies open the door to lawsuits if the company violates those policies. In July 2000, there were alleged cases of failed e-commerce businesses that – in order to appease creditors – sold private consumer data in violation of company policy.

The need for trust evidently poses a dilemma for implementing systems that hold any value at all, be they production facilities, information systems, or strategic centers such as

---

[7] www.ens.lycos.com/ens/nov98/1998L-11-27-03.html
[8] www.truste.org/

the NATO headquarters. The widespread use of mobile code (e.g., by accessing active web pages) also implies trusting that the evaluation of foreign code on a local system does not compromise the security or safety rules of that local system. Even if such code is authenticated prior to its execution, we still have to trust its execution behavior. *Proof-carrying code* – though for now a mere research topic – has the potential to provide a platform for the specification of local safety rules, the verification that programs meet these rules, a means of communicating this fact by attaching a certificate to code, and an efficient way of checking such certificates. One may then confine the need of trust to those aspects that are not expressed or implied by the formally specified safety policy.

The design and use of cryptographic systems does not dispense with such security-threatening needs. Digital signature systems were invented to eliminate the need to trust a third party with the job of delivering a secret key from one agent to another. Ironically, and not surprisingly, this solution created a new need for trust. Such systems have no mechanism for certifying that the public key, which an agent advertises as belonging to him, actually is associated with that agent. The protocol attack described on page 22 illustrates the need for third parties that vouch for such correct matchings of agents and their keys. Commercial products realize this through certification authorities, a "web of trust", or other public-key infrastructures. In that sense, cryptographic systems render the same dilemma of possibly extreme needs for protection and security and a concurrent need for trust. We believe that this dilemma cannot be entirely resolved qualitatively, but only to certain degrees. As D. Denning put it so aptly in her statement before the Subcommittee on Courts and Intellectual Property (Committee on the Judiciary, U.S. House of Representatives) regarding the Security and Freedom Through Encryption Act: "In short, encryption is no silver bullet." The reader of this text will be well advised to keep this in mind.

1.7 BIBLIOGRAPHIC NOTES

A good descriptive account of the shift from production-based to access-based economies has been given by Rifkin (2000). Denning (1999) discusses information systems in general, provides a systematic exposition of their threats, and competently presents possible strategies (and their tradeoffs) for countering a possible corruption of their security. Her website "The Cryptography Project",[9] contains well-organized and topical material on national and international encryption policies. Schneier (2000) gives an entertaining and revealing analysis of information security in the networked world. Also recommended is B.-J. Koops' Crypto Law Survey,[10] an up-to-date discussion of legislation pertaining to cryptographic systems that protect information against unauthorized access. The details on U.S. encryption policy given in Section 1.5 of this chapter reflect the Fact Sheet issued on 16 September 1999 by the Office of the Press Secretary of The White House and the press release of the U.S. Department of Commerce from 12 January 2000.[11] B. P. Aalberts and S. van der Hof have conducted an analysis of legislative approaches to electronic authentication, providing evidence that the emphasis on digital signature schemes

---

[9] www.cosc.georgetown.edu/~denning/crypto/index.html
[10] http://cwis.kub.nl/~frw/people/koops/lawsurvy.htm
[11] http://www.bxa.doc.gov/Encryption/regs.htm

may impede the growth and progress of electronic commerce and increase legal uncertainty;[12] Section 1.3 largely draws from that work. The books by Negroponte (1995) and Roszak (1994) represent two rather extreme – and opposing – positions regarding the role of information technology in modern societies. Denning and Lin (1994) present a compact but rich overview of the moral and legal challenges that come with the participation and management of (electronically) networked communities. For a discussion of the security features of the Java programming language, see McGraw and Felten (1997). Last, but not least, M. Curtin's website[13] contains a nice survey on "Snake oil warning sign: Encryption software to avoid".

---

[12] http://cwis.kub.nl/~frw/people/hof/ds-fr.htm
[13] http://www.interhack.net/people/cmcurtin/snake-oil-faq.html

CHAPTER 2

Public-Key Cryptography

The chief objective of cryptography is the design and analysis of systems that ensure secure communication along an otherwise untrusted channel of communication. Given a set $\mathcal{P}$ of *plain-texts* – ordinary text in a natural language, or any original and presumably sensitive or secret information – one seeks a set $\mathcal{C}$ of *cipher-texts* as well as encryption functions $E_K(\cdot)\colon \mathcal{P} \to \mathcal{C}$ that have a key $K \in \mathcal{K}$ (where $\mathcal{K}$ is a *key space*) as a parameter and that produce the *cipher-text* $E_K(M)$ of a plain-text M. In order to recover the plain-text, we require a key-dependent family of decryption functions $D_K(\cdot)\colon \mathcal{C} \to \mathcal{P}$ such that

$$D_K(E_K(M) = M \tag{2.1}$$

for all $M \in \mathcal{P}$ and all keys K from a key space $\mathcal{K}$. The objectives in securely realizing and efficiently implementing such a mathematical model are manifold and often conflicting.

Convention 2.1
We write E_K and D_K for the keys and possibly for all other implicit information needed in instantiating the encryption function $E_K(\cdot)$ and decryption function $D_K(\cdot)$, respectively.

Clearly, we require *key-dependent* algorithms that implement $E_K(\cdot)$ and $D_K(\cdot)$ efficiently. Such efficiency demands may constrain the security of the cryptographic system. The most relevant notions of security may be listed as follows.

1. *Unconditional security,* which requires that it be impossible to recover a key K even if attackers have plenty of matching plain-text/cipher-text pairs and unlimited computational resources.
2. *Semantic security,* meaning that we cannot make any inferences as to the nature of M given $E_K(M)$; thus, if M is a bit string then we cannot predict even a single bit of M.
3. *Proven security,* which provides a formal proof that breaking a cryptographic system is equivalent to solving a well-defined and presumably well-understood mathematical problem, such as factoring large integers.
4. *Computational security,* which refers to guarantees that a cryptographic system cannot be broken within certain specified computational limitations.

In practice, the concrete use of such systems may determine what notion of security is appropriate. For example, unconditional security of encryption on a smartcard may not be attainable owing to product constraints such as limited power consumption, ease of use, and so forth. In order to realize cryptographic systems in practice, one requires that:

- for each K in the key space $\mathcal{K}$, one can efficiently create a pair of keys $\langle E_K, D_K \rangle$ that satisfies (2.1); and
- for each key pair $\langle E_K, D_K \rangle$, it should be *easy* to derive the algorithms for decrypting and encryption with the keys E_K and D_K, respectively.[1]

Secret-key cryptography (SKC) schemes all rest on the principle that the key for the encryption and decryption of messages is, essentially, the same. This is why such schemes are also referred to as *symmetric* cryptography. An example of a symmetric scheme is the Data Encryption Standard (DES), developed by IBM in the 1970s for unclassified government applications and adopted by what is now the National Institute for Standards and Technology (NIST). Like most symmetric schemes, DES was designed to have very efficient hardware implementations; we discuss it in detail in Chapter 3. Because of their great efficiency, symmetric schemes are the method of preferred choice if the plain-text to be communicated is rather long, or if lots of data need to be communicated over a given time period. A fundamental problem with such schemes is that all "friendly" agents who want to use a secret symmetric key for successful communication need to share the same secret key; the problem then becomes the secure *distribution* of this key. This is particularly problematic when there is a need to generate such keys dynamically for each communication session. Another crucial obstacle for using such schemes in a communication network is that, for n network users, we require a total of

$$\binom{n}{2} = \frac{n \cdot (n-1)}{2} \tag{2.2}$$

many different keys to ensure that all users can communicate securely with each other. In practice, one may use a trusted third authority who acts as a *key server* and who shares a key with each network agent. If two agents want to communicate, the authority can assign a *session key* to the two agents in question. We study the use of trusted authorities in the context of identification protocols in Section 4.2. This approach is problematic, however, on large and dynamically evolving networks. Public-key cryptography (PKC) was invented by M. Hellman and W. Diffie specifically to avoid the intrinsic problems with key exchanges for symmetric schemes, bringing the number of required keys in (2.2) down to the linear $2 \cdot n$. It is an *asymmetric* scheme because the keys for decryption and encryption are different. Thus it becomes possible to place encryption keys into (certified) public directories, where all network users may retrieve them. In the first part of this chapter, we sketch the idea of public-key cryptography and demonstrate that it can fulfill functions that go beyond the mere encryption and decryption of messages – for example, it can provide digital signatures.

The basic design proposal of PKC systems can be seen as a specification of a cryptographic scheme, but its elegance and simplicity are no guarantee that it can be realized algorithmically. In the second part of this chapter, we describe the RSA public-key encryption scheme (named after its inventors R. Rivest, A. Shamir, and L. Adleman). Security products that make use of RSA – notably RSA SecurID® strong two-factor authentication solutions and RSA BSAFE® encryption technology – are widely used in U.S. government

---

[1] This is why we often identify such keys with the corresponding algorithms.

institutions (e.g., the Office of the President of the United States, all U.S. Cabinet departments, the U.S. Congress, and various federal courts). This technology is also used by financial institutions worldwide and the emerging networked electronic health-care infrastructure to ensure authentication and encryption of online transactions and privacy. These security components can be found in web servers and browsers, in electronic mailers, and in some log-in protocols and electronic payment systems. These products animate Hellman's and Diffie's ideas algorithmically by making heavy and ingenious use of nontrivial number theory. Therefore, parts of this chapter give an introduction to basic concepts of number theory and develop the insights necessary to prove that the RSA encryption can be realized and that its realization is a correct implementation of the public-key cryptography scheme; we will also see why this implementation has a feasible running time. We conclude with a general discussion on the degree of security that RSA public-key encryption may be able to offer.

2.1 SPECIFICATION OF RSA

The general idea behind public-key cryptosystems is that each participant A in a communication network with *unsecure* communication channels has two keys: one public key P_A and one private key S_A.[2] Agent A's public key P_A is freely available or may be obtained from a certifying and trusted authority on demand. The agent's private key S_A is meant to be secret: only A knows this key, and letting others know this key will allow them to assume A's identity as well as decrypt all messages (if intercepted) that were addressed to A. Thus it is of paramount importance that A keep this key secret. Needless to say, P_A and S_A are different keys, so this is an example of an *asymmetric scheme*. These keys transform messages, which we may think of as strings of characters over some alphabet (Unicode, ASCII, etc.), into cipher-text; hence they specify functions $P_A : \mathcal{P} \to \mathcal{C}$ and $S_A : \mathcal{C} \to \mathcal{P}$, representing the encryption and decryption tasks, respectively. Equation (2.1) now reads as

$$S_A(P_A(M)) = M \tag{2.3}$$

for all messages $M \in \mathcal{P}$. If any agent on the network would like to send a message M to agent A, he uses A's public key P_A to *encrypt* M – that is, to produce the cipher-text $P_A(M)$ – and sends this off to agent A, who can then *decrypt* $P_A(M)$ by applying her private key S_A to the received cipher-text to recover the original message M. Note that this equation also allows an intruder I to recover the original message if I manages to intercept $P_A(M)$ and if I knows the private key S_A. It goes without saying that the cipher-text $P_A(M)$ should provide little insight into the nature of the original message M or the private key S_A. Also, knowledge of the public key P_A should not allow an attacker to gain any conclusive knowledge about the nature of agent A's private key S_A. In principle, attacks based on such potential weaknesses of cryptographic systems are always possible, so one often needs to know how much effort must be put into such attacks in order to assess adequately the amount of protection provided by a given cryptography system.

---

[2] We won't make explicit the dependency of P_A and S_A on an actual key but emphasize instead the agent's name; it is understood that an agent could have different keys for different purposes or at different times.

Remark 2.2 (PKCs as Digital Signature Schemes)

If we mean to use PKCs for *digital signatures,* then we also may want $\mathcal{P}$ to equal $\mathcal{C}$ and

$$P_A(S_A(C)) = C \tag{2.4}$$

to hold for all messages $C \in \mathcal{C}$. The cipher-text $S_A(C)$ then can be seen as A's signature of C. Agent A can send $S_A(C)$ to some agent B, along with C, and B can make use of A's public key to verify that signature based on (2.4).

Since we mean to discuss public-key cryptography with both functionalities in mind (i.e., secure data exchange and digital signatures), we will insist on both equations (2.3) and (2.4). Cryptographic systems that use PKCs for both functional roles typically use different PKCs or keys for each of these tasks. To have any hope of legally enforcing digital signatures, they must allow time-stamps, enable the exposure of fraudulent signing, and be undeniable.

Remark 2.3 (Security Requirement for Public-Key Cryptography)

For public-key cryptographic systems we demand, for almost all choices of key pairs[3] $\langle P_A, S_A \rangle$, that it be computationally infeasible to derive (from the public knowledge of P_A) an algorithm that is equivalent to the decryption algorithm based on S_A.

Remark 2.4 (Chosen Plain-Text Attack)

Public-key cryptography is different from symmetric-key cryptography, discussed in Chapter 3, in two crucial ways.

1. If agent B encrypts a plain-text M with agent A's public key P_A and afterwards "loses" the original message M, then agent B has no means of recovering M other than asking agent A to decrypt $P_A(M)$ for him.
2. Since public keys are *public,* an attacker can freely choose a plain-text M and produce the resulting cipher-text $P_A(M)$. Thus, public-key cryptography systems are subject to a *chosen plain-text attack.*

Some possible security concerns with this basic encryption scheme remain:

- one may be able to attack the cipher-text $S_A(M)$ or $P_A(M)$ in order to obtain partial information about the private key S_A or M, respectively;
- an intruder I may gain access to A's private key S_A by other means (e.g. blackmail);
- there may be a design flaw in a communication protocol that regulates and arbitrates the secure exchange of messages on the network.

These concerns are actually shared by *all* cryptographic systems, not just the ones based on public keys. We won't say much about the first two here. The third concern we study in detail later on, for it is mostly an issue of *protocols* – and their proper design and analysis – and not of cryptographic schemes as such. The requirement that the secret key S_A cannot be computed from the public key P_A constitutes the principal challenge that is indigenous to a public-key cryptography system; if this challenge is not met, then system security will be undermined completely.

---

[3] The scheme may have some keys that are unsecure and, it is hoped, publicly known to be such.

Equation (2.3) prescribes that S_A be a left inverse of P_A. Thus the challenge lies in finding a concrete mathematical function f that (a) implements P_A, (b) can be computed efficiently, and (c) has a left inverse g that implements S_A but cannot be computed in any feasible amount of time, even if the function f and its implementation are fully known. However, g should be easy to compute provided one owns secret information: the secret key S_A. In the theory of computational complexity, researchers have collected strong evidence suggesting that such a computational asymmetry does indeed exist. In fact, the RSA encryption scheme that we will discuss incorporates such a "solution" grounded in insights that combine classical number theory with modern complexity theory.

EXERCISES 2.1

1. Let $E_K(\cdot)\colon \mathcal{P} \to \mathcal{C}$ and $D_K(\cdot)\colon \mathcal{C} \to \mathcal{P}$ satisfy (2.1).
   (a) Show that the function $E_K(\cdot)\colon \mathcal{P} \to \mathcal{C}$ is *injective*; that is, show for all $M, M' \in \mathcal{P}$ that the equation $E_K(M) = E_K(M')$ implies $M = M'$.
   (b) Explain why and under which circumstances an encryption function should be injective.
   (c) Assume that $\mathcal{P}$ equals $\mathcal{C}$ and is finite. Show that $E_K(D_K(C)) = C$ holds for all $C \in \mathcal{C}$. Thus, if $D_K(\cdot)$ cannot be computed from $E_K(\cdot)$, such a scheme could be used for digital signatures.
2. *Types of attacks*   Consider the following types of attacks on a key-dependent cryptosystem. The attacker attempts to recover the key. She
   • possesses a sample of cipher-text (cipher-text-only attack);
   • has (temporary) access to the decryption function and so can choose cipher-texts and compute matching plain-texts (chosen cipher-text attack);
   • somehow obtained a plain-text sample with a matching cipher-text (known plaintext attack);
   • has (temporary) access to the decryption function and so can choose plain-texts and compute matching cipher-texts (chosen plain-text attack).
   Which of these attacks are always possible for public-key cryptosystems? Which ones are conceivable?

2.1.0.1   Digital Signatures

Most of us have to sign checks, many sign leases, and some choose to sign prenuptial agreements. Signing a document attests at least that the signer agrees to the terms of the contract and that the signer is identical to the person that (usually) produces this signature. The latter is often corroborated by means of additional signatures by witnesses or a notary public. For the purpose of a contract, these additional signatures function as certificates issued by trusted authorities. With the advent of electronic commerce, electronic cash, electronic mail, and secure transfer of network routing information, there is a pressing need to implement procedures that allow one to sign a document digitally. This is quite easy to do with a PKC system satisfying (2.4). If agent A, let's call her Alice, wants to send a signed message M to agent B, let's call him Bob, then she may send the pair $\langle M, S_A(M) \rangle$, encrypted with Bob's public key, to Bob. How can Bob make sure that M could only have been signed by Alice? He first uses his secret key to recover the pair

$\langle M, S_A(M)\rangle$; then he applies Alice's public key P_A to the cipher-text $S_A(M)$, which he retrieves from the second component of the pair he just computed, and checks whether the result equals the first component M of that pair. Only in that case does he accept Alice's signature. Otherwise, the message M was corrupted, or some key other than Alice's private one was used to produce the signature. Of course, this scheme works only on the assumption that Alice's private key S_A is known only to Alice; it also assumes that Bob knows that Alice sent a pair and not just one atomic message. The latter can be modeled by thinking of messages as sequences of atomic messages with separators that are discernible by Alice, Bob, and anybody else who listens to the network traffic. In practice such aspects are taken care of by communication protocols, and one uses different schemes for the activities of signing and encryption.

EXERCISES 2.2

1. Describe how Bob can send a signed and *secure* message N to Alice.
2. Think of some possible scenarios in which Alice may successfully dispute that she actually signed a message according to the protocol just discussed. What changes to this protocol can you suggest that will make it more difficult for Alice to deny the authenticity of her digital signature?
3. The boolean function $\oplus$ computes the exclusive-or of two boolean values: for $v, w \in \{0, 1\}$, we have $v \oplus w \overset{\text{def}}{=} 1$ if and only if $v \neq w$; otherwise, $v \oplus w \overset{\text{def}}{=} 0$.
   (a) Show that $(x \oplus v) \oplus v = x$ for all $x, v \in \{0, 1\}$.
   (b) Let M be a string of length n over the alphabet $\{0, 1\}$, and let K be another string of the same length over the same alphabet. Let $M \oplus K$ be the string obtained by applying $\oplus$ one character or bit at a time to M and K.
      (i) Compute $M \oplus K$ where $M = 010001100011100$ and $K = 100110111101100$.
      (ii) Explain in what sense we may think of K as a key for encrypting messages.
      (iii) How can you decrypt encrypted messages?
      (iv) Could this idea be used for public-key encryption?
      (v) What is your intuition about the "quality" of such a cryptographic scheme?
   (c) (i) Discuss in what sense the public-key approach discussed here assumes that agents on a network *trust* each other. For example, think about the link between physical identities and their (alleged) public keys. Do your assumptions depend on the agent's being human?
      (ii) Can one eliminate entirely the need for trust in public-key cryptography schemes?
      (iii) What infrastructures can you imagine that would manage and support trust of public keys on the Internet?

2.1.0.2 A Protocol for Secure Communication

Hash functions are, after symmetric and asymmetric encryption schemes, a third technique used in commercial encryption tools. We will describe the secure hash standard in Chapter 3. Such functions should:

H1 *efficiently* map messages M to a "digital fingerprint" $h(M)$, typically much shorter than M and of some standard length;

H2 make it impossible to use the hash $h(M)$ to make valid inferences about the length or contents of the message M;

H3 make it computationally infeasible, given a hash value $h(M)$ but not knowing M, to produce a message M' with $h(M') = h(M)$; and

H4 make it computationally infeasible to construct two messages M and M' such that $h(M) = h(M')$.

Note the difference between H3 and H4. For the former, the attacker must match a value over which she has no control, whereas in the latter case she may freely choose messages to get the desired effect. The technique of using such functions h in applications is often referred to as *one-way encryption*, since it is basically impossible to recover any information about M from the hash value $h(M)$. Two main applications of such functions are digital fingerprints of a file's contents (to detect unauthorized modifications – e.g., those carried out by a malicious computer virus) and the encryption of passwords (e.g., the Unix operating system does not store actual passwords but rather their hash values as computed by the crypt$(\cdot)$ function). It is also common to hash documents prior to signing them, as most signing schemes require relatively short input for reasons of efficiency.

All three encryption techniques play an important role in setting up a secure communication network. One uses public-key encryption to communicate the keys for symmetric, secret-key encryption; hash functions are used as a more efficient way of signing that message digitally.

Protocol 2.5 (A Public-Key Communication Protocol)
Suppose that Alice wants to send a signed message m securely to Bob. If she wants to use a more efficient symmetric key for m's encryption, she may choose the following communication protocol.

1. Alice and Bob agree on which symmetric encryption algorithm(s) and hash function they want to use for the exchange of messages. They may also negotiate and specify circumstances and time frames for using particular such algorithms. These activities will be guided by additional protocols.

2. Alice generates a random symmetric key K to be used for an agreed-upon symmetric cryptographic algorithm (e.g. Rijndael); in Chapter 3, we discuss how such a random generation of keys can be done (you can already see such a generator in Exercise 2.7-6, p. 33).

3. Alice encrypts m using K. We write crypt$_K(m)$ to denote the message obtained by applying a cryptographic algorithm with the *symmetric* key K to message m.

4. Alice encrypts the symmetric key K using Bob's public key P_B to obtain $P_B(K)$.

5. As for the digital signature, Alice produces a hash $h(m)$ of her message m and then signs that hash value with her secret key[4] S_A to obtain $S_A(h(m))$.

6. Alice sends Bob the triple

   $$\langle S_A(h(m)), \text{crypt}_K(m), P_B(K) \rangle.$$

---

[4] In practice, agents would have a separate key pair for signing.

Alice's beliefs:	Bob's beliefs:
$P_M = P_B$	$P_M = P_A$
$(S_M = S_B)$	$S_M = S_A$

Figure 2.1. Beliefs of Alice and Bob during the attack.

7. Upon receipt, Bob recovers the secret session key K by applying his private key S_B to the third component of the received packet.

8. Using the key K' computed in the previous step and the agreed-upon symmetric cryptographic algorithm, Bob can decrypt the second component of the packet to recover the putative original message; let us denote this result by m'. If K' is different from K (there may have been a transmission error, or the packet may have come from an attacker who pretends to be Alice), m' will likely be gibberish and Bob may then want to abort the protocol. Otherwise, he goes to step 9.

9. Bob uses Alice's public key P_A to recover $h(m)$ from the first component of the packet. He uses the same hash function on m' and compares $h(m)$ with $h(m')$. If they coincide, then he can be sure that this packet has been signed by Alice, that she sent message m to him, and that the package has not been altered in transit. Otherwise, the packet was corrupted in some way.

This protocol is already pretty complicated, and more realistic protocols are much more complex. It is then important to analyze such protocols *formally* to gain a better understanding of the possible attacks an intruder may launch by exploiting potential weaknesses in a protocol's design.

Attack 2.6 (Man-in-the-Middle Attack)

For example, this protocol can be corrupted by the *man-in-the-middle* attack. Assume that:

1. Mallory is another agent who can intercept and temporarily halt all communication between Bob and Alice (we will model such capabilities formally in Section 4.5);

2. Mallory somehow manages to convince Bob that her public key, P_M, is Alice's public key P_A;

3. she also persuades Alice into thinking that P_M is really Bob's public key P_B; and

4. she knows for which symmetric encryption algorithm Alice and Bob are exchanging the symmetric key K, and she knows which hash function (h) Alice and Bob are using.[5]

See Figure 2.1 for the resulting beliefs of Alice and Bob. If Mallory succeeds in doing and knowing all of the above, then she can launch an attack as follows:

1. The protocol proceeds as before. Alice computes and sends the same package, but now with all occurrences of P_B replaced by P_M:

$$\langle S_A(h(m)), \text{crypt}_K(m), P_M(K)\rangle.$$

---

[5] *Kerckhoff's principle* states that one should assume that attackers know which cryptographic systems their targets use. It is generally wise to work under those assumptions.

2. Mallory intercepts that triple and uses her secret key S_M to recover the symmetric key K from $P_M(K)$. Since she knows which public-domain encryption algorithm Bob and Alice are using, she can enter the key K into this algorithm and recover the message m from $\text{crypt}_K(m)$.

3. Mallory now uses Alice's public key P_A to compute $h(m)$ from $S_A(h(m))$.

4. Since Mallory already knows m, K, and $h(m)$, she can use Bob's public key P_B to compute the triple

$$\langle S_M(h(m)), \text{crypt}_K(m), P_B(K) \rangle,$$

which she now sends to Bob.

5. Upon receipt, Bob proceeds with the protocol as before (after all, he is unaware of any changes of procedure). He dutifully uses his secret key S_B to recover K and then recovers $h(m)$ using what he thinks is Alice's public key P_M; after computing m' from K and $\text{crypt}_K(m)$, he computes $h(m')$ and compares it with $h(m)$. If they coincide, then he is sure that this packet has been signed by Alice and that Alice sent the package containing message m to him. Too bad that Bob is wrong about all this, but he has no way of realizing it!

We will return in Chapter 4 to the important topic of analyzing and verifying security protocols. By the way, it is generally not advisable to implement a digital signature scheme by (i) hashing the message and then (ii) signing the hash value with a secret key. The properties of hash functions H1–H4 are not sufficient to provide rigorous security of signing schemes designed in this way. We address this issue in detail in Chapter 5 in the context of the random oracle methodology.

EXERCISE 2.3

1. (a) Discuss how realistic or unrealistic the assumptions are concerning the attacker's capabilities and knowledge in Attack 2.6.
   (b) (i) Modify Attack 2.6 so that Mallory replaces Alice's message with one of her own choosing.
      (ii) Explain why Bob will be unaware of this replacement.
      (iii) Is Mallory capable of doing this even if Alice is offline?
      (iv) If Alice signs a document for Mallory and sends it to her, can Mallory then forward that document to Bob and say that this is a signed document from Alice to Bob?
   (c) Suppose that Alice does not sign $h(m)$ in Protocol 2.5, so that $h(m)$ is only used to check that the message m has not been altered in transit. Describe the revised protocol and sketch how Attack 2.6 changes.

2.2 A REALIZATION OF PKCs: RSA

In describing the RSA public-key encryption system, we present only how the public and private keys of agents A are generated and how encryption and decryption works for such keys. One may then use implementations of these tasks, along with implementations of random secret-key generation and their corresponding symmetric cryptographic algorithms, to implement the communication protocols sketched here. We refer to Chapter 5 for a practical realization of RSA. Before we present the RSA encryption scheme at a technical level, we need to discuss some elementary number-theoretic concepts.

Definition 2.7 (Divisor)
The collection of natural numbers

$$1, 2, 3, 4, \ldots$$

is denoted by $\mathbb{N}$. We write $\mathbb{Z}$ for the set of integers:

$$\mathbb{Z} \stackrel{\text{def}}{=} \{-n, n \mid n \in \mathbb{N}\} \cup \{0\}.$$

For $a, b \in \mathbb{Z}$, we call a a *divisor* of b if and only if there is some $k \in \mathbb{Z}$ such that $b = k \cdot a$; we write $a \mid b$ in that case.

For example, 7 is a divisor of 21 (choose k to be 3), and any a is a divisor of 0 (choose k to be 0). Clearly, 1 and b are always divisors of b.

Definition 2.8 (Primes and Factors)
A number $p \in \mathbb{N}$ is *prime* if and only if 1 and p are the only divisors of p in $\mathbb{N}$. If $a \in \mathbb{N}$ is a divisor of b other than 1 or b, then we call a a *factor* of b.

For example, the numbers 3, 17, and 1729 are prime, but 91 is not since it has 7 and 13 as factors ($91 = 7 \cdot 13$). Thus, prime numbers are those natural numbers that don't have factors.

Definition 2.9 (Dividend and Remainder)
Given $a \in \mathbb{Z}$ and $b \in \mathbb{N}$, let $a \bmod b$, pronounced "a modulo b", be the unique number r that satisfies

$$a = r + k \cdot b,$$
$$0 \leq r < b,$$

for some $k \in \mathbb{Z}$; we call $a \bmod b$ the *remainder* for the division of a by b. We write $a \operatorname{div} b$ for the unique number k satisfying $a = (a \bmod b) + k \cdot b$ and call it the *dividend* for the division of a by b.

In particular, we have

$$a = (a \bmod b) + (a \operatorname{div} b) \cdot b.$$

As examples, we deduce $157 \bmod 23 = 19$ since $157 = 19 + 6 \cdot 23$ and $0 \leq 19 < 23$. Therefore, $157 \operatorname{div} 23 = 6$ because $157 = (157 \bmod 23) + 6 \cdot 23$. The operator $\bmod n$ has lower binding priority than arithmetic operations, so $(a \bmod k) + b \bmod n$ means $((a \bmod k) + b) \bmod n$.

EXERCISES 2.4

1. Explain: A number $n \in \mathbb{N}$ is not prime if and only if it has a factor $a \in \mathbb{N}$ such that $2 \le a \le \sqrt{n+1}$.
2. Show that $a \bmod b$ and $a \operatorname{div} b$ are well-defined. That is, show that if r, r' are two numbers in $\{0, 1, 2, \ldots, b-1\}$ and $k, k' \in \mathbb{Z}$ such that $a = r + k \cdot b$ and $a = r' + k' \cdot b$, then $r = r'$ and $k = k'$ follow. (*Hint:* Use $0 = (r - r') + (k - k') \cdot b$.)
3. Describe and implement an algorithm that uses only addition and subtraction and takes integers a, b in decimal representation as input and computes $a \bmod b$. You may first address this for $a, b \ge 0$.
4. Repeat the previous exercise for computing $a \operatorname{div} b$.
5. Prove: If $m \mid x$ and $m \mid y$, then $m \mid (r \cdot x + s \cdot y)$ for all $r, s \in \mathbb{Z}$.
6. For integers k and l such that $k \mid l$ and $l \mid k$, what can you say about the relationship between k and l?

After this brief excursion into elementary number theory, we have established all the necessary terminology for specifying the RSA cryptographic public-key scheme. In that PKC, each agent A creates a public and a private key with the following protocol.

Protocol 2.10 (RSA Key Generation)

1. Agent A generates two "very large" prime numbers p and q; they may typically have 512 (or even more) binary digits each.
2. She computes the product $n \stackrel{\text{def}}{=} p \cdot q$ of these two primes.
3. She selects an (odd) integer e that has no common factor with $p - 1$ and $q - 1$.
4. She computes a number d such that $d \cdot e$ equals 1 plus an integral multiple of $(p - 1) \cdot (q - 1)$.
5. She computes the pair

$$P_A \stackrel{\text{def}}{=} \langle e, n \rangle, \tag{2.5}$$

$$S_A \stackrel{\text{def}}{=} \langle d, n \rangle \tag{2.6}$$

as her public and secret RSA keys, respectively.

The RSA scheme assumes that the domain of plain-texts $\mathcal{P}$ is finite and equals the domain of cipher-texts $\mathcal{C}$. From Exercise 2.1-1(c), we therefore know that all encryption and decryption functions are mathematical inverses in both directions. The domain of messages can be identified with a subset of $\{0, 1, 2, \ldots, n-1\}$. If k is in $\{0, 1, 2, \ldots, n-1\}$ and if $l \ge 0$, then we can compute the power k^l "modulo n" by first computing k^l and then repeatedly subtracting n from the result until we reach a number in $\{0, 1, 2, \ldots, n-1\}$. For example, if $n = 48$, $k = 3$, and $l = 7$, then k^l equals $3 \cdot 3 \cdot 3 \cdot 3 \cdot 3 \cdot 3 \cdot 3 = 2187$ and the repeated subtraction of 48 results in 27. Shortly, we will learn a much more efficient algorithm for computing $k^l \bmod n$.

Definition 2.11 (RSA Encryption and Decryption)

Because a message M is an element of $\{0, 1, 2, \ldots, n-1\}$, we may *encrypt* M by computing $P_A(M)$, the result of applying A's public key to M, as

$$P_A(M) \stackrel{\text{def}}{=} M^e \bmod n. \tag{2.7}$$

Similarly, agent A is able to *decrypt* any M, assuming that it has been encrypted with A's public key, through the application of A's secret key as

$$S_A(M) \stackrel{\text{def}}{=} M^d \bmod n. \tag{2.8}$$

This proposal may seem rather obscure. For example, it is not immediately clear whether it guarantees that P_A and S_A satisfy equations (2.3) and (2.4). Moreover, it is not at all clear whether large primes (and plenty of them) can be found on demand or whether the required arithmetic can be carried out in feasible time, given the constraints on power consumption and memory requirements (think smartcard) and noting the size of these prime numbers. Finally, there is the important question about potential weaknesses of this proposal – that is, whether one may launch an attack to decrypt messages, or even to retrieve a private key. Although most of these issues can be resolved with nontrivial results from number theory, it remains an open question whether powerful attacks on this scheme might work for *any* possible implementation.

Example 2.12 (RSA Encryption at Work)

Let us examine RSA encryption and decryption at work on an unrealistically small example. Suppose that p is 1367 and q is 1999. Then the modulus n equals 2732633 and $(p-1) \cdot (q-1)$ is 2729268. We choose the public key exponent e to be 1111 and compute 2206015 as the number d for which $d \cdot e$ equals 1 modulo $(p-1) \cdot (q-1)$. The secret-key exponent d is therefore 2206015. Let the message M be 2749352179431168947825. Since M is larger than the modulus n, we may encrypt this message but we are not guaranteed that decryption recovers the original. (Why?) Thus we divide M into blocks of numbers that are less than n and encrypt them individually. For example, we may write

$$M = 2749\,352179\,431168\,947825; \tag{2.9}$$

encrypting each block separately results in the cipher-text

$$C = 917617\,354949\,613690\,2318407. \tag{2.10}$$

For example, $431168^{1111} \bmod 2732633 = 613690$.

EXERCISES 2.5

1. **RSA example** Let $p = 7$ and $q = 17$.
   (a) Compute n.
   (b) Let $e = 5$. Compute d.
   (c) Encrypt 49 and 12. Verify that the decryption of those resulting numbers recovers the original ones.
   (d) Decrypt 49 and 12. Verify that the encryption of those resulting numbers recovers the original ones.
2. We said that the set of plain-texts equals the set of cipher-texts for the RSA cryptosystem. However, can you think of some values in the message space that are undesirable?

3. Consider the RSA cryptosystem, where

$$p \stackrel{\text{def}}{=} 2552563543590084273034974830392944117,$$

$$q \stackrel{\text{def}}{=} 2599652422845157888267321102402072509 49.$$

   (a) Compute the modulus n.
   (b) Compute $(p - 1) \cdot (q - 1)$.
   (c) Which of the two possible public-key exponents e is legitimate, 3 or 31?
   (d) Take the one legitimate e from the previous item and compute the secret-key exponent d. If need be, use the extended Euclid algorithm of Exercise 2.19-1.
   (e) Encrypt the message 19857367.
   (f) Decrypt the message 27.

4. Discuss the difference between attacks that are dependent on a specific implementation of a cryptosystem and attacks that would work for all implementations.

2.3 GENERATING LARGE PRIMES

We now develop concepts and insights into the theory of numbers step by step as they are needed for realizing and reasoning about the RSA public-key encryption scheme. First, we demonstrate that one can efficiently generate large prime numbers.

Definition 2.13 (Complexity Bounds)
Given a real number x, we write $\lfloor x \rfloor$ for the unique integer a satisfying $a \leq x < a + 1$. Let $\lceil x \rceil$ be the unique integer b satisfying $b - 1 < x \leq b$. For a function $f : \mathbb{N} \to \mathbb{N}$, we define $\Theta(f)$ to be a set of functions of type $\mathbb{N} \to \mathbb{N}$; we have $g \in \Theta(f)$ if and only if there exist positive real constants $0 < c_1 \leq c_2$ and some $n_0 \in \mathbb{N}$ such that $0 \leq c_1 \cdot f(n) \leq g(n) \leq c_2 \cdot f(n)$ holds for all $n \geq n_0$.

For example, we have $\lfloor \pi \rfloor = 3$ and $\lceil \pi \rceil = 4$. For the function $f : \mathbb{N} \to \mathbb{N}$ with $f(n) = n^3$ we have $g \in \Theta(f)$, where $g(n) = 3.75 \cdot n^3 + 0.56 \cdot n^2 - 134.23$.

   Given a natural number n, we can turn the definition of prime numbers into a straightforward algorithm that tests whether n is prime: the only possible factors of n are in the set $\{2, 3, 4, \ldots, \lfloor \sqrt{n} \rfloor\}$, so we "merely" have to see whether n has any of these numbers as a factor. A simple test for primality of n, therefore, computes

$$n \bmod 2, \ n \bmod 3, \ n \bmod 4, \ \ldots, \ n \bmod \lfloor \sqrt{n} \rfloor$$

until either (a) one of these numbers is 0, in which case n has a factor and so it is not a prime number, or (b) all numbers $n \bmod 2$ up to $n \bmod \lfloor \sqrt{n} \rfloor$ turn out to be different from 0, in which case we know that n has no factors and so n is prime. This test is simple and returns a definite factor of n if one exists, but its computational complexity does not scale up to the size of numbers that are required for secure cryptographic schemes.

EXERCISES 2.6

1. (a) Show: $n \in \mathbb{N}$ is prime if and only if all numbers

$$n \bmod 2, \ n \bmod 3, \ \ldots, \ n \bmod \lfloor \sqrt{n} \rfloor$$

are different from 0. Show that if the computation of $n \bmod k$ takes constant time, then this primality test is in $\Theta(\sqrt{n})$.

(b) Show: If n has a binary representation with β bits, then β equals $\lceil \ln(n+1) \rceil$.

(c) Show: For β and n as in (b), we have $\sqrt{n} \in \Theta(2^{\beta/2})$. Conclude that the primality test in (a) has an exponential running time in the number of bits of n.

(d) Implement the test of part (a) and run it on small inputs of n – say, fewer than 20 digits. If your programming language has a large integer type, make use of it and run the program with inputs of increasing numbers of digits; observe the dramatic increase of its running time.

In the exercises, we saw that our simple primality test is correct and works well for small numbers n, but its running time grows exponentially with the number of bits needed for representing n. This means that we can hardly make use of this test if n has more than, say, 60 decimal digits. Although this test is not applicable to very large numbers, it manages to find out whether n is prime for reasonably small values of n and it also computes a factor of n in case that n is not prime. The question of whether there exists an *efficient* algorithm of this kind that works for arbitrarily large values of n is an important open problem in computer science. There is evidence suggesting that such an algorithm is unlikely to exist. Thus, our desire to generate large prime numbers meets a first significant obstacle. Surprisingly, one can test for primality by (i) replacing the trial test

$$n \bmod k \overset{?}{=} 0,$$

which may render an actual factor k of n, with a deeper number-theoretic test that gives no insights into possible factors of n and then (ii) choosing a limited set of candidates $k \in \{2, 3, 4, \ldots, n-1\}$ *at random*. Such a randomized algorithm (due to Miller and Rabin), is developed next and presents a nice example of the computational power of randomization. In general, randomized algorithms have many applications, ranging from combinatorics to network algorithms for switchboards. Randomized algorithms are also an important tool in analyzing and attacking cryptographic systems.

The algorithm `Miller-Rabin(n,s)` has two parameters as input: n, the number to be tested for primality, and s, the number of tests we want to perform on n. In our simple primality test based on "$n \bmod k \overset{?}{=} 0$", this s is of the order $\lfloor \sqrt{n} \rfloor$, so it depends *exponentially* on the number of bits of n. This dependence is removed in the algorithm of Miller and Rabin. The pseudo-code for the algorithm is given in Figure 2.2. The algorithm depends on the following two additional programs.

- The procedure invocation `Random(a,b)` calls a pseudo-random generator that returns a random integer in the interval $[a, b]$. We assume the existence of a "good" random number generator and present criteria for evaluating the quality of such generators in Chapter 3.

- The program `Witness(a,n)` returns the boolean value `true` if a provides conclusive evidence that n is *not* prime; it replaces the test "$n \bmod a \overset{?}{=} 0$" of the naive "sieve" algorithm. If one of the calls `Witness(a,n)` returns `true`, then `Miller-Rabin(n,s)`

```
Miller-Rabin(BigInteger n, int s) { // returns ''true'' or ''false''
// tests whether n is prime;
// if it returns ''false'', then n is not prime;
// if it returns ''true'', then n is prime
// with probability at least 1 - 2 ** (-s).
 BigInteger a;
 for (int i = 1; i <= s; ++i) {
   a = Random(2,n-1);
   if Witness(a,n) return false;
 }
 return true;
}
```

Figure 2.2. Pseudo-code for the primality testing algorithm of Miller and Rabin.

terminates by replying with `false`, saying that n is definitely not prime. Otherwise, the for-statement performs all s tests and all these tests are negative. The call `Miller-Rabin(n,s)` then concludes with `true`, "guessing" that n is prime.

In designing the program `Witness(n,s)`, it will became apparent that its `true` replies are always correct. Thus, if the Miller–Rabin algorithm replies with `false`, then n is indeed not a prime number. Hence, the tricky question is whether this algorithm might return `true` even though n is *not* prime. This is indeed possible, but we will prove a reassuring upper bound on the probability of such a flawed reply.

The pseudo-code for the program `Witness(a,n)` is given in Figure 2.3. This code bears little resemblance to the code one would write based on the test "$n \bmod a \overset{?}{=} 0$", which decides whether a is a factor of n. The correctness of the program `Witness(a,n)` relies on nontrivial number theory. Our first goal is to show that n is not a prime number whenever a call `Witness(a,n)` returns `true`. Yet this will not imply that a is a factor of n. Such a positive reply puts us in the strange position of knowing for certain that n is not prime but not knowing any of its factors. Inspecting the control flow of the program `Witness(a,n)`, we see only two program points where a return with value `true` occurs.

l1: Within the for-statement: if $t = 1$, $x \neq 1$, and $x \neq n - 1$ hold, then this results in an immediate return to `Miller-Rabin(n,s)` with value `true`.

l2: The for-statement terminates without a premature internal return, reaches location l2, and t does then not equal 1, causing a return of the call `Miller-Rabin(n,s)` with value `true` as well.

Therefore, it suffices to show that n is not prime whenever the control flow of the program `Witness(a,n)` reaches one of these two locations and their respective conditions are true. The correctness proof of this claim can thus be given by:

(c1) noting that $t = x^2 \bmod n$ at location l1;
(c2) proving that if $x^2 \bmod n = 1$ for $x \neq 1$ and $x \neq n - 1$, then n cannot be prime;
(c3) showing that the value of `t` at location l2 is $a^{n-1} \bmod n$; and
(c4) demonstrating that n cannot be prime if $a^{n-1} \bmod n \neq 1$ for any $a \in \mathbb{N}$ with $2 \leq a \leq n - 1$.

```
Witness(BigInteger a, BigInteger n) {
// returns ''true'' if a is a witness for n not being prime;
// otherwise, it returns ''false'';
// the array b stores the binary representation of n - 1;
// and b[k] is the most significant bit,
// k being a global variable determined by n
  int[] b;
  BigInteger x;
  BigInteger t = 1; // test value
  for (int i = k; i >= 0; --i) {
    x = t;
    t = (t * t) mod n;
11: if (t == 1 && x != 1 && x != n - 1) return true;
    if (b[i] == 1) t = (t * a) mod n;
  }
12: if (t != 1) { return true; } else { return false; }
}
```

Figure 2.3. Pseudo-code for the witness function used in the Miller–Rabin algorithm. If `Witness(a,n)` returns `true`, then a is conclusive evidence that n is not prime.

This proof strategy mirrors the intent of the algorithm `Witness(a,n)`: its global concern is to compute a^{n-1} mod n and then check whether this equals 1, but on the fly it keeps track of potential nontrivial "square roots of 1" modulo n, which provide another means of proving the nonprimeness of n. We begin with showing (c1) and (c3), which are merely claims about the program's control flow. For (c1), note that the two statements immediately preceding location 11 are two assignment statements: first, x is assigned the current value of t, then t is assigned the value t^2 mod n. Since there are no other jumps to 11, $x = t^2$ mod n holds at location 11. As for (c3), this is a bit harder to realize.

2.3.1 Iterative Squaring

Our claim in (c3) is that $t = a^{n-1}$ mod n holds at location 12. Because we assume that we'll reach that location, we may ignore the if-statement at location 11. Similarly, we may ignore the assignment $x = t$; since a and n are never modified therein and since t does not depend on x. Thus for the purpose of reasoning about (c3), we may "slice" `Witness(a,n)` to obtain the more compact program given in Figure 2.4. To see that this sliced program works as expected, we need to understand the essence of its for-statement. This can be done by finding a suitable *invariant*, a property that (i) depends on the number of iterations, (ii) holds before and after each iteration, and (iii) implies the property we are interested in after (and if) the loop terminates. A candidate invariant is that the value of t is a^s mod n, where s is the natural number corresponding to the binary representation $b[k]b[k-1]\ldots b[i]$. If this is true, then the value of t at location 12 is a^{n-1} mod n, since then the value of i is 0 and so s is the number represented by $b[k]b[k-1]\ldots b[0]$, which is $n-1$. To study this claim, it is useful to enrich our code with computation over an ancillary variable s, although s does not contribute to

```
Witness(BigInteger a, BigInteger n) {       // sliced
int[] b;
BigInteger t = 1; // test value
  for (int i = k; i >= 0; --i) {
    t = (t * t) mod n;
    if (b[i] == 1) { t = (t * a) mod n; }
  }
}
```

Figure 2.4. Pseudo-code of the witness function, "sliced" with respect to the behavior of the variable t.

```
Witness(BigInteger a, BigInteger n) {  // sliced, plus ancillary variable s
  int[] b;
  int s = 0; // variable for invariant behavior
  BigInteger t = 1; // test value
  for (int i = k; i >= 0; --i) {
    s = 2 * s;
    t = (t * t) mod n;
    if (b[i] == 1) { s = s + 1;
                     t = (t * a) mod n;
    }
  }
}
```

Figure 2.5. The sliced version of the witness function with an ancillary variable that aids in illustrating an invariant.

computing the value of t at all. This pseudo-code is depicted in Figure 2.5. The candidate invariant can now be stated as: "The value of s equals the decimal value of the binary representation

$$b[k]b[k-1]\ldots b[i],$$

and the value of t equals a^s mod n after each iteration of the for-statement".

After careful inspection of the body of the for-statement, we conclude that each iteration of the for-statement transforms t according to the identities

$$t^{2s} \bmod n = (t^s)^2 \bmod n,$$
$$t^{2s+1} \bmod n = (t^s)^2 \cdot a \bmod n.$$

(2.11)

The program `Witness(a,n)` simply turns these equations into iterative computations. If `b[i]` has value 0 (i.e., if s is even), then there is only one assignment to t – namely, `t = (t * t) mod n;` – having the effect of the first equation. If s is odd then there is a subsequent assignment `t = (t * a) mod n;` – so its net effect reflects the second equation. In the exercises, you are asked to prove that our candidate invariant is indeed an invariant and that the equations in (2.11) are valid.

The technique employed in computing a^{n-1} mod n is called *iterative squaring*, motivated by the equations in (2.11), and is often used to make iterative computation over integers (or exponentiation in any mathematical group; see Definition 2.18, p. 36) more efficient.

Example 2.14

To compute $3^{22} \bmod 23$, note that the binary representation of 22 is 10110. Hence $3^{22} \bmod 23$ may be written as

$$(((((1^2 \cdot 3)^2)^2 \cdot 3)^2 \cdot 3)^2.$$

Observe that this expression suggests the manner in which the program execution of Witness(a,n) will compute this. From Exercise 2.7-2, we infer that

$$
\begin{aligned}
3^{22} &= (((((1^2 \cdot 3)^2)^2 \cdot 3)^2 \cdot 3)^2 \bmod 23 \\
&= (((3^2)^2 \cdot 3)^2 \cdot 3)^2 \bmod 23 \\
&= ((81 \cdot 3)^2 \cdot 3)^2 \bmod 23 \\
&= ((12 \cdot 3)^2 \cdot 3)^2 \bmod 23 \\
&= (36^2 \cdot 3)^2 \bmod 23 \\
&= (13^2 \cdot 3)^2 \bmod 23 \\
&= (169 \cdot 3)^2 \bmod 23 \\
&= (8 \cdot 3)^2 \bmod 23 \\
&= 24^2 \bmod 23 \\
&= 1^2 \bmod 23 \\
&= 1 \bmod 23.
\end{aligned}
\tag{2.12}
$$

This computation is an instance of $a^{p-1} \bmod p$, where p is prime and $a \neq 0 \bmod p$. Later on, we see that all such expressions evaluate to 1.

EXERCISES 2.7

1. Prove formally that our candidate invariant is an actual invariant for the for-statement in the sliced program Witness(a,n) in Figure 2.5. If you know about program logics, you may use one; otherwise, use a proof by mathematical induction on the value of i.

2. Let $n \in \mathbb{N}$ and $x, y \in \mathbb{Z}$. Prove:
   (a) $(x + y) \bmod n = (x \bmod n) + (y \bmod n) \bmod n$;
   (b) $(x \cdot y) \bmod n = (x \bmod n) \cdot (y \bmod n) \bmod n$; and
   (c) $x^t \bmod n = (x \bmod n)^t \bmod n$ for all $t \in \mathbb{N}$.

3. Prove the two equations in (2.11), using the facts of the previous exercise.

4. Implement the algorithm Miller-Rabin(n,s) in a programming language of your choice. Why did we not write a = Random(1,n-1) in Figure 2.2?

5. *Generating primes with specific properties* Often, one wants to generate primes with some specific properties. For example, you are asked to generate two large primes p and q such that:

(a) the primes p and q differ in length by only a few binary digits;

(b) the numbers $p - 1$ and $q - 1$ contain large prime factors; and

(c) the greatest common divisor (see Definition 2.22) of $p - 1$ and $q - 1$ is small.

Add another layer to your implementation of generating p and q that realizes these three conditions (the first and third conditions are easily checked). For the second condition, generate a large prime p' and then test the numbers $p' + 1$, $2 \cdot p' + 1$, $3 \cdot p' + 1$, ... in sequence for primality. Choose p as the first one that `Miller-Rabin` classifies as a prime number. Do the same for q.

6. **Pseudo-random numbers**   Use an implementation of the Miller–Rabin algorithm and the technique of iterative squaring to implement the pseudo-random number generator due to M. Blum and S. Micali. (Note that the Miller–Rabin algorithm already relies on some pseudo-random number generator.) The algorithm of Blum and Micali outputs a sequence $b_0 b_1 b_2 \ldots$ of pseudo-random bits. Let g be a prime number; it may be even, or small (e.g. 2). Use `Miller-Rabin(n,s)` to generate a large prime p, large and "secure" enough so that computing x_i from x_{i+1} in (2.13) is computationally hard; for example, p could be of the form $2 \cdot q + 1$, where q is prime as well. (How can you ensure that p has such a form?) The algorithm takes as further input a key $x_0 \in \mathbb{N}$ such that $1 < x_0 < p$. Compute

$$x_{i+1} \stackrel{\text{def}}{=} g^{x_i} \bmod p \tag{2.13}$$

for all $i = 0, 1, 2, \ldots$ up to some implementation-specific bound, or implement this program with a "button" such that each mouse click on that button produces the next pseudo-random bit in the sequence. Let b_i be 1 if $x_i < (p - 1)/2$; otherwise, set $b_i \stackrel{\text{def}}{=} 0$.

7. **Primality testing**   Consider the infinite list of natural numbers, where the first element of that list is 12 and the next list element, as a string, is the concatenation of the previous number-string with a digit d, where d is $e + 1 \bmod 10$ and e is the rightmost digit of the previous number. Thus the list begins as

[12, 123, 1234, 12345, 123456, 1234567, 12345678, 123456789,

1234567890, 12345678901, 123456789012, ...].

(a) How many probable primes can you find in this list?

(b) For which numbers in that list can you say, with absolute certainty, that they are not prime?

(c) For which numbers in that list can you find actual factors?

(d) What is the largest number in that list for which you can find all of its factors?[6]

8. **Pseudo-random numbers**   L. Blum, M. Blum, and M. Shub designed a more efficient pseudo-random number generator with the additional property that the ith bit b_i can be computed "directly" from i and the seed x_0. Use `Miller-Rabin(n,s)` to implement it as follows.

(a) Generate two large prime numbers, p and q, such that $p = 3 \bmod 4$ and $q = 3 \bmod 4$. (Which is more efficient to perform first: the test of whether p is prime, or the test of whether p and q both equal 3 mod 4?)

---

[6] You may want to make use of the fact that some of these numbers are defined "recursively" in terms of smaller numbers in that list.

(b) Compute $n \overset{\text{def}}{=} p \cdot q$; such an n, with p and q as in (a), is called a *Blum integer*.

(c) Choose a random integer $x \in \mathbb{Z}$ such that x has no common factor with n; note that this choice also depends on a pseudo-random generator – say, the one that `Miller-Rabin(n,s)` uses.

(d) Compute the seed $x_0 \overset{\text{def}}{=} x^2 \bmod n$ for the pseudo-random number generator to be constructed.

(e) The ith bit b_i of the new pseudo-random output sequence is the least significant bit of x_i, where

$$x_i \overset{\text{def}}{=} x_{i-1}^2 \bmod n \tag{2.14}$$

for all $i \in \mathbb{N}$.

(f) Assume that

$$x_i = x_0^{2^i \bmod (p-1) \cdot (q-1)} \bmod n \tag{2.15}$$

for all $i \in \mathbb{N}$. (The mathematics required for showing this will be addressed in Exercise 2.11-12, p. 42.) The user of your algorithm should be able to choose whether the sequence is generated based on definition (2.14) or (2.15). Compare the efficiency of these versions.

Not only is this generator useful – since it allows us to compute the ith bit without having computed the previous bits of the sequence – it also has the pleasant property that the generated sequence is *unpredictable* to the left and right: one cannot predict the bit to the left (or right) of a given bit in the sequence.

9. *Blum–Goldwasser PKC*   We refer to the notation and concepts of the previous exercise to implement a public-key cryptosystem (due to M. Blum and S. Goldwasser) which requires computational resources comparable to those of RSA[7] but which, unlike RSA, has the security feature that the encryption algorithm is *not deterministic*.[8] For two large Blum integers p and q (see the previous exercise), we let their product $n = p \cdot q$ be the public key. Messages are bit strings M of length $l \in \mathbb{N}$. Your implementation should allow for changing the parameters p, q, and l. Please reuse (or adapt) software that you have written for earlier exercises as you see fit.

(a) Implement the encryption of l-bit messages M, given a public key $n = p \cdot q$:

   (i) randomly select a nonzero $x \in \mathbb{Z}_n$;

   (ii) compute the x_i for $i = 0, 1, \ldots, l+1$ as in the previous exercise, where b_i is the least significant bit of x_i;

   (iii) let the encrypted text be the pair $\langle x_{l+1}, C \rangle$, where C is the bitwise exclusive-or of M and the string $b_1 b_2 \ldots b_l$.

(b) Implement the decryption component as follows.

   (i) Compute the "private" key

   $$d \overset{\text{def}}{=} 2^{-(l+1)} \bmod (p-1) \cdot (q-1).$$

   (ii) Given a cipher-text $\langle x', C \rangle$, where $x' \in \mathbb{Z}_n$ and C is a binary word of length l, we think of x' as the seed and compute the sequence

---

[7] However, it uses the RSA encryption function more than once for a single encryption operation.
[8] That is to say, if we encrypt the same message twice, the results will differ.

$$x_0' \stackrel{\text{def}}{=} (x')^d \bmod n,$$

$$x_{i+1}' \stackrel{\text{def}}{=} (x_i')^2 \bmod n$$

accordingly for $i = 0, 1, \ldots, l-1$. Letting b_i' be the least significant bit of x_i', the decrypted text is the bitwise exclusive-or of C and the string $b_1' b_2' \ldots b_l'$.

(c) Prove that this scheme is sound using equation (2.15), and explain why all its components have efficient implementations.

(d) Do you have to recompute d for handling a new message?

(e) Does the security of this public-key cryptosystem depend on the size of l or n?

(f) Experiment with various choices of l and study the performance of this cryptosystem as a function of l.

(g) What does or should your implementation do if $x' = 0 \bmod n$?

(h) Suppose that we change all preceding occurrences of $l + 1$ to l. Could you still prove soundness? Could you still guarantee the security of the cryptosystem?

(i) Can an attacker launch a chosen plain-text attack if she knows only the public key?

(j) How often does a single encryption or decryption operation require a call to the underlying RSA function for modular exponentiation? Thinking of this operation as the performance bottleneck, what do your findings say about the efficiency of this PKC?

2.3.2 Correctness of `Witness(a,n)`

2.3.2.1 Fermat's Theorem

In demonstrating the correctness of `Witness(a,n)`, it remains to prove (c2) and (c4) from page 29. We consider (c4) first. Since the value of a is chosen at random from $\{2, 3, \ldots, n - 1\}$, it could be any one of them, so we need to show that $a^{n-1} \bmod n = 1$ for all such a if n is prime. This is known as Fermat's theorem.

Theorem 2.15 (Fermat's Theorem)
Let $p \in \mathbb{N}$ be a prime number. Then $a^{p-1} \bmod p = 1$ for all $a \in \{1, 2, \ldots, p - 1\}$.

It is advantageous to couch this proof – sketched in Exercise 2.11-10 (p. 42) – in the general framework of basic group theory. That way we may also apply group-theoretic techniques for subsequent correctness arguments. Before we define groups in full generality, let us introduce an important example of a group.

Definition 2.16 (Congruence Modulo n)
For $n \in \mathbb{N}$, we define a binary relation $=_n$ over the domain of integers. For $x, y \in \mathbb{Z}$, the relation $x =_n y$ holds if and only if

$$x - y \bmod n = 0.$$

In that case, we say that x and y are *congruent modulo n*. Moreover, define $[x]_n$ to be the set of all $y \in \mathbb{Z}$ with $x =_n y$.

For example, $13 =_4 21$ and $5 =_3 2$ hold, but $7 =_5 16$ does not because $7 - 16 \bmod 5 = 4$. The class $[-2]_5$ equals $\{\ldots, -12, -7, -2, 3, 8, 13, \ldots\}$.

EXERCISES 2.8

1. Show that $=_n$ is an *equivalence relation* for each $n \in \mathbb{N}$. That is, show that $=_n$ is
   (a) *reflexive:* $x =_n x$ for all $x \in \mathbb{Z}$;
   (b) *symmetric:* $x =_n y$ implies $y =_n x$ for all $x, y \in \mathbb{Z}$; and
   (c) *transitive:* $x =_n y$ and $y =_n z$ imply $x =_n z$ for all $x, y, z \in \mathbb{Z}$.

2. (a) Show that $\mathbb{Z}$ is the disjoint union of sets $[x]_n$, where x ranges over $\mathbb{Z}$. Thus you need to show that $\mathbb{Z}$ is the union of such sets and that $[x]_n$ and $[x']_n$ are either the same or have empty intersection for any $x, x' \in \mathbb{Z}$.
   (b) Show that there are exactly n different such classes $[x]_n$.

Definition 2.17 $(\mathbb{Z}_n$ as a Group)
Let $\mathbb{Z}_n$ be the set $\{[x]_n \mid x \in \mathbb{Z}\}$. We define *addition* and *multiplication* on $\mathbb{Z}_n$ by

$$[x]_n +_n [y]_n \overset{\text{def}}{=} [x + y]_n, \tag{2.16}$$

$$[x]_n *_n [y]_n \overset{\text{def}}{=} [x * y]_n. \tag{2.17}$$

By the previous exercise, the set $\mathbb{Z}_n$ has n elements. For example, we have $[5]_7 +_7 [2]_7 = [5 + 2]_7 = [0]_7$ and $[5]_7 *_7 [2]_7 = [5 \cdot 2]_7 = [3]_7$, since $5 \cdot 2 = 3 \bmod 7$.

EXERCISES 2.9

1. Show that the operation $+_n \colon \mathbb{Z}_n \times \mathbb{Z}_n \to \mathbb{Z}_n$ is well-defined. That is, show that if $x' =_n x$ and $y' =_n y$ then the classes $[x + y]_n$ and $[x' + y']_n$ are the same.
2. Show that the operation $*_n \colon \mathbb{Z}_n \times \mathbb{Z}_n \to \mathbb{Z}_n$ is well-defined. That is, if $x' =_n x$ and $y' =_n y$, then the classes $[x \cdot y]_n$ and $[x' \cdot y']_n$ are the same.
3. Is 3 a member of $[12]_{13} +_{13} [17]_{13}$?
4. Is 5 a member of $[41]_7 *_7 [6]_7$?

The addition operation $+_n$ on $\mathbb{Z}_n$ makes this set a finite, commutative group.

Definition 2.18 (Groups)
A *group* is a triple $\langle G, \circ, e \rangle$, where G is a set, e is an element of G, and $\circ \colon G \times G \to G$ is a function that satisfies the following.

1. $\circ$ is *associative:* $x \circ (y \circ z) = (x \circ y) \circ z$ for all $x, y, z \in G$.[9]
2. e is a *two-sided identity* for $\circ$, so $x \circ e = e \circ x = x$ for all $x \in G$.

---

[9] As is customary, we write $\circ$ in infix notation: $x \circ y$ instead of $\circ(x, y)$.

3. Each element has an *inverse:* for any $x \in G$, there is a y such that $x \circ y = y \circ x = e$; we call such a y an *inverse* of x.

We call a group *finite* if and only if the set G is finite. We call a group *commutative* if and only if $x \circ y = y \circ x$ for all $x, y \in G$.

There is an abundance of groups that are used in mathematics, physics, and even computer science. Our main interest lies in two families of finite, commutative groups based on the operations $+_n$ and $*_n$ on $\mathbb{Z}_n$ (respectively) ranging over $n \in \mathbb{N}$. The proof of Fermat's theorem makes instrumental use of a group structure on those elements of $\mathbb{Z}_n$ that have a multiplicative inverse.

Definition 2.19 (Units)
Let $n \in \mathbb{N}$. An element $[a]_n \in \mathbb{Z}_n$ is called a *unit* if there exists some $x \in \mathbb{Z}$ such that

$$[a]_n *_n [x]_n = [1]_n.$$

Let $\mathbb{Z}_n^*$ be the set of all units in $\mathbb{Z}_n$.

Note that $[0]_n$ is not in $\mathbb{Z}_n^*$, but $[1]_n$ is in $\mathbb{Z}_n^*$ for any $n \in \mathbb{N}$. More concretely, $[3]_7$ is a unit because $[3]_7 *_7 [5]_7 = [3 \cdot 5]_7 = [1]_7$ since $3 \cdot 5 = 1 \bmod 7$. However, $[2]_6$ is *not* a unit, as $[2]_6 *_6 [x]_6 = [1]_6$ implies $2 \cdot x = 1 \bmod 6$, which is impossible for any $x \in \mathbb{Z}$.

Proposition 2.20
Let $n \in \mathbb{N}$. Then $\langle \mathbb{Z}_n, +_n, [0]_n \rangle$ and $\langle \mathbb{Z}_n^*, *_n, [1]_n \rangle$ are finite, commutative groups.

Proof We relegate the proof for $\langle \mathbb{Z}_n, +_n, [0]_n \rangle$ to Exercise 2.10-4(b). As for $\langle \mathbb{Z}_n^*, *_n, [1]_n \rangle$, the class $[1]_n$ is in $\mathbb{Z}_n^*$ and serves as a two-sided identity with respect to $*_n$. Also, $\mathbb{Z}_n^*$ is finite because it is contained in the finite set $\mathbb{Z}_n$. Observe that $*_n$ is an associative and commutative operation on the entire set $\mathbb{Z}_n$. Next we argue that $\mathbb{Z}_n^*$ is closed under the operation $*_n$ of type $\mathbb{Z}_n \times \mathbb{Z}_n \to \mathbb{Z}_n$. That is, if $[a]_n$ and $[b]_n$ are in $\mathbb{Z}_n^*$, we need to show that $[a]_n *_n [b]_n$ is in $\mathbb{Z}_n^*$ as well. By definition, there exist $x, y \in \mathbb{Z}$ such that $[a]_n *_n [x]_n = [x]_n *_n [a]_n = [1]_n$ and $[b]_n *_n [y]_n = [y]_n *_n [b]_n = [1]_n$, for $*_n$ is commutative. Using these equations, along with the fact that $*_n$ is associative and commutative on $\mathbb{Z}_n$, we conclude that $([a]_n *_n [b]_n) *_n ([y]_n *_n [x]_n) = [1]_n$ and $([y]_n *_n [x]_n) *_n ([a]_n *_n [b]_n) = [1]_n$. Thus, if we restrict the associative and commutative operation $*_n$ to the set $\mathbb{Z}_n^*$ of units, then that operation is certainly still associative and commutative, but all units also have an inverse with respect to the two-sided identity $[1]_n$. In summary, $\langle \mathbb{Z}_n^*, *_n, [1]_n \rangle$ is a finite, commutative group. $\qquad \square$

Proposition 2.21 (Unique Inverses)
In any group $\langle G, \circ, e \rangle$, the inverses of group elements $x \in G$ are unique, so we may denote the unique inverse of x as x^{-1}. Moreover, for all $x, y \in G$, we have

$$(x \circ y)^{-1} = y^{-1} \circ x^{-1}. \tag{2.18}$$

Proof   This is the content of Exercise 2.10-5.   □

Note in particular that the inverses of units in $\mathbb{Z}_n^*$ are unique, since this is the case in any group. For example, the inverse of $[3]_7$ in $\mathbb{Z}_7^*$ is $[5]_7$, as $3 \cdot 5 = 1 \bmod 7$.

EXERCISES 2.10

1. Explain *in detail* why $[2]_6$ is not a unit.
2. Recall the definition of $x \oplus y$, the exclusive-or of x and y, from Exercise 2.2-3 (p. 20). Show that

   $$x \oplus y = x + y \bmod 2$$

   for all $x, y \in \{0, 1\}$.
3. Show that $[160]_{841}$ is a unit in $\mathbb{Z}_{841}^*$ by computing an $x \in \mathbb{Z}$ with $160 \cdot x = 1 \bmod 841$. (*Hint:* Use the algorithm Extended_Euclid from Exercise 2.19-1, p. 60.)
4. Show that the following are groups.
   (a) $\langle S_n, \oplus, \hat{0} \rangle$, where S_n is the set of binary strings of length n, $\oplus$ is the exclusive-or operation applied bitwise on such words, and $\hat{0}$ is the string of 0s of length n. Can you use the fact of Exercise 2 for a quick argument that the operation $\oplus$ must be associative?
   (b) $\langle \mathbb{Z}_n, +_n, [0]_n \rangle$.
   (c) $\langle \mathbb{Z}, +, 0 \rangle$. For which value of n does this "follow" from the previous item?
   (d) $\langle G, \circ, e \rangle$, where
   - G is the set of functions $f : S \to S$, over some set S, that have a mathematical inverse $f^{-1} : S \to S$,
   - $f \circ g$ is the function that maps all $s \in S$ to $f(g(s))$, and
   - e is the function that leaves all $s \in S$ fixed.
   (e) Which of the groups in (a)–(d) are finite? Which ones are commutative?
5. (a) Show that inverses in groups are unique. That is, if $x \circ y = y \circ x = e$ and $x \circ y' = y' \circ x = e$, then $y = y'$. Make sure that you indicate clearly which properties of groups your argument uses and at which points.
   (b) Use the previous item to show (2.18).
6. Show that e is the only two-sided identity in a group $\langle G, \circ, e \rangle$.
7. Explain why the following data are not sufficient for obtaining a group and explain in which cases you may complete the given data to obtain a group; otherwise, explain why no group could result from the given data.
   (a) Consider the set of finite binary strings with the operation $x \circ y \stackrel{\text{def}}{=} x$.
   (b) Consider the set of *injective* functions $f : \mathbb{N} \to \mathbb{N}$, that is, functions satisfying

   $$f(x) = f(y) \text{ implies } x = y \text{ for all } x, y \in \mathbb{N}.$$

   Let e be the function $e(n) \stackrel{\text{def}}{=} n$ for all $n \in \mathbb{N}$. Define $f \circ g$ to be the function that maps n to $f(g(n))$ for all $n \in \mathbb{N}$.
   (c) Consider the set of finite binary strings, let e be the empty string of length 0, and define $x \circ y$ to be the bitwise merge of x and y. For example, $a_1a_2a_3a_4a_5 \circ b_1b_2b_3$ equals $a_1b_1a_2b_2a_3b_3a_4a_5$.

2.3.2.2 Greatest Common Divisor

In order to prove Fermat's theorem, we need to know the size of the group $\mathbb{Z}_p^*$ for prime numbers p. The greatest common divisor of two integers is a tool that allows us to determine that $\mathbb{Z}_p^*$ has $p - 1$ elements.

Definition 2.22 (Greatest Common Divisor)
Let $x, y \in \mathbb{Z}$. The *greatest common divisor* of x and y, written $\gcd(x, y)$, is the greatest integer that is a divisor of both x and y – unless x or y is 0, in which case $\gcd(x, y)$ is defined as the maximum of the absolute values of x and y.

It is intuitively clear that we have defined a function

$$\gcd: \mathbb{Z} \times \mathbb{Z} \to \mathbb{N} \cup \{0\}.$$

For example, $\gcd(770, -42) = 14$ and $\gcd(-3, 0) = 3$. The greatest common divisor has the following important characterization.

Proposition 2.23 (Linear Representation of the gcd)
Let $x, y \in \mathbb{Z} \setminus \{0\}$.[10] *Then $\gcd(x, y)$ is the smallest positive element of the set*

$$\{r \cdot x + s \cdot y \mid r, s \in \mathbb{Z}\}$$

of integral linear combinations of x and y.

Proof   It is clear that there exists a smallest positive element m of the form $r \cdot x + s \cdot y$ for some $r, s \in \mathbb{Z}$, since every nonempty subset of $\mathbb{N}$ has a smallest element. We compute

$$
\begin{aligned}
x \bmod m &= x - m \cdot (x \operatorname{div} m) \\
&= x - (r \cdot x + s \cdot y) \cdot (x \operatorname{div} m) \\
&= (1 - (x \operatorname{div} m) \cdot r) \cdot x + ((x \operatorname{div} m) \cdot (-s)) \cdot y
\end{aligned}
\tag{2.19}
$$

and so realize $x \bmod m$ as a linear combination of x and y. But then $0 \leq x \bmod m < m$, together with the fact that m is the minimal positive such linear combination, implies $x \bmod m = 0$. Therefore $m \mid x$, and we can argue similarly that $m \mid y$. Since $\gcd(x, y)$ is the greatest common divisor of x and y, we obtain $m \leq \gcd(x, y)$. For the reverse inequality note that $\gcd(x, y) \mid m$, since $\gcd(x, y)$ is a divisor of x and y and since m is an integral linear combination of these two natural numbers (see Exercise 2.4-5, p. 25). But then $\gcd(x, y) \leq m$ is clear, as $\gcd(x, y)$ and m are nonnegative. $\square$

For example, $\gcd(60, 21) = 3$ and $3 = (-1) \cdot 60 + 3 \cdot 21$. Any other such integral combination of 60 and 21 is either bigger than 3 or nonpositive.

Definition 2.24 (Euler's Totient Function)
Let $\phi(n)$ be the number of elements of the finite group $\langle \mathbb{Z}_n^*, *_n, [1]_n \rangle$.

---

[10] For sets S and T, we write $S \setminus T$ for the set that contains all elements of S that are *not* in T.

Example 2.25

For $n = 12$, we find that $[1]_{12}$, $[5]_{12}$, $[7]_{12}$, and $[11]_{12}$ are the only units. Therefore, $\phi(12) = 4$.

Proposition 2.26 (Characterization of Units)

Let $n \in \mathbb{N}$ and $a \in \mathbb{Z}$. Then $[a]_n \in \mathbb{Z}_n^*$ if and only if $\gcd(a, n) = 1$.

Proof

1. Let $[a]_p \in \mathbb{Z}_n^*$. Then there exists some $x \in \mathbb{Z}$ such that $[a]_n *_n [x]_n = [1]_n$, meaning that $a \cdot x = 1 \bmod n$. Hence there exists a $k \in \mathbb{Z}$ with $x \cdot a + (-k) \cdot n = 1$. By Proposition 2.23, we infer that $\gcd(a, n) = 1$, for 1 is the smallest positive integer.
2. Conversely, let $\gcd(a', n) = 1$. By Proposition 2.23, there exist integers $r, s \in \mathbb{Z}$ such that $r \cdot a' + s \cdot n = 1$. But then $[a']_n *_n [r]_n = [a' \cdot r + s \cdot n]_n = [1]_n$ implies that $[a']_p \in \mathbb{Z}_n^*$. □

With this result, we may list the elements of $\mathbb{Z}_n^*$ for "small" values of n. For example, if $n = 8$ then $\mathbb{Z}_8^*$ is $\{[1]_8, [3]_8, [5]_8, [7]_8\}$, since 1, 3, 5, and 7 are the only numbers a in $\{1, 2, \ldots, 7\}$ with $\gcd(a, 8) = 1$. Thus $\phi(8) = 4$. With some computational effort, we can conclude that

$$\phi(394856) = 153600.$$

Corollary 2.27

If n is prime, then $\phi(n) = n - 1$.

Proof   This follows from the previous proposition, because each a from the set $\{1, 2, \ldots, p - 1\}$ satisfies $\gcd(a, p) = 1$ since p is prime. □

Proposition 2.28

Let p and q be primes greater than 1. Then

$$\phi(p \cdot q) = (p - 1) \cdot (q - 1).$$

Proof   This is to be shown in Exercise 2.11-12(a) (p. 42). □

Note that the last proposition does not generalize in this manner to more than two prime factors, but one can still compute $\phi(n)$ if one knows all prime factors of n and how often they occur therein. See Exercise 2.21-5 (p. 68). Observe further that $\phi(p \cdot q)$ is used in the computation of the RSA secret key.

Subgroups of a group are essentially subsets that are closed under all group operations. The group structure puts severe limitations on the size of subgroups, for they must be divisors of the group's size.

Definition 2.29 (Subgroups)

A *subgroup* of a group $\langle G, \circ, e \rangle$ is a subset S of G such that:

1. $e \in S$;
2. $\{s \circ t \mid s, t \in S\} \subseteq S$; and
3. $\{s^{-1} \mid s \in S\} \subseteq S$.

Thus, subgroups are subsets of groups which contain the group's two-sided identity element and which are closed under group multiplication and the computation of inverses. This allows us to refer to subgroups as mere sets, provided that they actually *are* subgroups! For example, the nonzero rational numbers form a subgroup of the nonzero real numbers, where group multiplication is the usual multiplication of real numbers and where the two-sided identity is 1. The set of even integers forms a subgroup of the group of integers, where group multiplication is the usual addition of numbers and where the two-sided identity is 0.

Theorem 2.30 (Lagrange's Theorem)
Let H be a subgroup of G. Then $|H|$, the size of H, is a divisor of $|G|$, the size of G.

Proof See Exercise 2.11-4. □

We prove Fermat's theorem by applying Lagrange's theorem to the group $\langle \mathbb{Z}_p^*, *_p, [1]_n \rangle$, noting that subsets of groups generate subgroups in a unique manner.

Definition 2.31 (Generated Subgroup)
Let T be a subset of a group $\langle G, \circ, e \rangle$. We write $\langle T \rangle$ for the smallest subgroup of G that contains T. If $T = \{g\}$ for some $g \in G$, we write $\langle g \rangle$ instead of $\langle \{g\} \rangle$.

For example, $\{2\}$ generates the subgroup of even numbers in $\langle \mathbb{Z}, +, 0 \rangle$, and $[3]_7$ generates the entire group $\mathbb{Z}_7^*$ in $\langle \mathbb{Z}_7^*, *_7, [1]_7 \rangle$; please verify this.

EXERCISES 2.11

1. Write a program that uses Proposition 2.26 to compute $\phi(n)$ for "small" values of n.

2. Prove:

(a) If A is a subset of S, then $|A| \le |S|$.

(b) For any subset A of S, we have $|S| = |A| + |S \setminus A|$, where $S \setminus A$ is the set of all elements of S that are not in A.

(c) For any subsets A and B of S, let $A \cap B$ be their intersection and $A \cup B$ their union; then

$$|A| + |B| = |A \cap B| + |A \cup B|. \tag{2.20}$$

3. Let $\langle G, \circ, e \rangle$ be a group and let H be a nonempty subset of G. Show that H is a subgroup of G if and only if $a \circ b^{-1} \in H$ for all $a, b \in H$.

4. *Lagrange's theorem* Prove Lagrange's theorem. For each $a \in G$, define the set

$$aH \stackrel{\text{def}}{=} \{a \circ h \mid h \in H\}.$$

Show the following.

(a) The set G is the union of all sets aH, where a ranges over G.

(b) For $a, b \in G$, if the sets aH and bH have a nonempty intersection then they are equal.

(c) For $a, b \in G$, the sets aH and bH are of the same size. (*Hint:* Consider the function $f : aH \to bH$ with $f(a \circ h) \stackrel{\text{def}}{=} b \circ h$ and argue that f has an inverse.)

(d) Use (a)–(c) to prove Lagrange's theorem.

(e) What is the equivalence relation R that corresponds to this partition? That is, can you define when $aH = bH$ holds based on an equation in the group in terms of a and b?

5. **Prime factorization**   Prove that every $n \in \mathbb{N}$ has a unique factorization

$$n = p_1^{\alpha_1} \cdot p_2^{\alpha_2} \cdots p_k^{\alpha_k}, \tag{2.21}$$

where the p_i are prime numbers in increasing order and $\alpha_i \in \mathbb{N}$. (*Hint:* Use mathematical induction on n. In the inductive step, argue by cases: what if $n + 1$ is prime; what if it isn't?)

6. **Infinitely many prime numbers**   Prove: There are infinitely many prime numbers. (*Hint:* Show that, for any $n \in \mathbb{N}$, there is a prime number p such that $n < p \leq 1 \cdot 2 \cdot 3 \cdots (n - 1) \cdot n + 1$.)

7. Let H_i be a subgroup of G for all $i \in I$. Show that the intersection of all these subgroups, $\bigcap_{i \in I} H_i$, is also a subgroup of G.

8. Show: For $g \in G$, the subgroup $\langle g \rangle$ of a group $\langle G, \circ, e \rangle$ is commutative. (Is it always finite?)

9. Let T be a subset of a group $\langle G, \circ, e \rangle$. Show that $\langle T \rangle$ equals the intersection of all subgroups of G that contain T. Thus, $\langle T \rangle$ in Definition 2.31 is indeed well-defined.

10. **Fermat's theorem**   Prove Fermat's theorem (Theorem 2.15). Consider the group $\langle \mathbb{Z}_n^*, *_n, [1]_n \rangle$.

(a) Show that

$$\langle [a]_n \rangle = \{[1]_n\} \cup \{[a^m]_n \mid m \in \mathbb{N}\}$$

for any $[a]_n \in \mathbb{Z}_n^*$.

(b) For $a \in \mathbb{Z}$ with $\gcd(a, n) = 1$, argue that there must exist a smallest number l in $\{0\} \cup \mathbb{N}$ such that $[a^l]_n = [1]_n$.

(c) Use Lagrange's theorem to conclude that there exists some $k \in \mathbb{N}$ such that

$$k \cdot l = \phi(n)$$

for the minimal l of part (b).

(d) Use Corollary 2.27 and the equation $k \cdot l = \phi(p)$ to show that $[a^{p-1}]_p = [1]_p$. Explain why this proves Fermat's theorem.

11. **Euler's theorem**   Generalize the proof of Fermat's theorem appropriately to prove Euler's theorem: For any $n > 1$, the number $a^{\phi(n)} \bmod n$ equals 1 for all a such that $[a]_n \in \mathbb{Z}_n^*$.

12. Let p and q be prime numbers.

(a) Prove that $\phi(p \cdot q) = (p - 1) \cdot (q - 1)$.

(b) Let $n \stackrel{\text{def}}{=} p \cdot q$ and $x \in \mathbb{Z}$. Define $x_0 \stackrel{\text{def}}{=} x^2 \bmod n$ and $x_{i+1} = x_i^2 \bmod n$ for all $i \geq 0$.

(i) Use mathematical induction on i to show that $x_i = x_0^{2^i} \bmod n$.

(ii) Use the facts from Exercises 11 and 12(a) to show that $x_0^{2^i} \bmod n = x_0^{\alpha_i} \bmod n$, where

$$\alpha_i = 2^i \bmod (p-1) \cdot (q-1).$$

(iii) Conclude that $x_i = x_0^{\alpha_i} \bmod n$ for all $i \geq 0$.

2.3.2.3 Square Roots of 1

In Exercise 2.11-10 we were able to prove Fermat's theorem, which addresses the correctness criterion (c4) for `Witness(a,n)` to our complete satisfaction. Thus we have only to deal with (c2) to guarantee that all `true` replies of `Witness(a,n)` are correct. Recall what (c2) claims: "If $x^2 \bmod n = 1$ for x different from 1 and $n-1$ modulo n, then n cannot be prime." This is what we now prove. Again, we prove the contrapositive of this claim.

Theorem 2.32 (Square Roots of 1)
Let $p > 1$ be a prime number and let $x \in \{1, 2, \ldots, p-1\}$ be such that $x^2 \bmod p = 1$. Then x equals 1 or $p - 1$.

Evidently, a proof of this theorem requires that we be able to compute "square roots modulo n". This can be done quite easily when the group $\langle \mathbb{Z}_p^*, *_p, [1]_p \rangle$ is generated by a single element.

Definition 2.33 (Primitive Roots)
Let $n \in \mathbb{N}$. An element $g \in \mathbb{Z}$ is a *primitive root* for $\mathbb{Z}_n^*$ if and only if

- $[g]_n \in \mathbb{Z}_n^*$ and
- the subgroup generated by $[g]_n$ in $\mathbb{Z}_n^*$ equals $\mathbb{Z}_n^*$.

In that case, given any $[x]_n$ in $\mathbb{Z}_n^*$, we know that there exists a minimal number t in $\mathbb{N} \cup \{0\}$ such that $[x]_n = [g^t]_n$, by the definition of $*_n$. We call t the *logarithm* of x in $\mathbb{Z}_n^*$ with respect to the primitive root g as a base, and we denote t as $\log_{\langle n,g \rangle}(x)$.

For example, 2 is a primitive root for $\mathbb{Z}_{11}^*$. To compute the logarithm of $[3]_{11}$, you may verify that $[3]_{11} = [2^8]_{11}$ and $[3]_{11} \neq [2^d]_{11}$ for any $0 \leq d < 8$. Therefore, $\log_{\langle 11,2 \rangle}(3) = 8$. The presence of a primitive root in $\mathbb{Z}_n^*$ allows us to "take logarithms". More precisely, we may switch from reasoning within the multiplicative group $\langle \mathbb{Z}_n^*, *_n, [1]_n \rangle$ to reasoning within the additive group $\langle \mathbb{Z}_{\phi(n)}, *_{\phi(n)}, [0]_{\phi(n)} \rangle$.

EXERCISES 2.12

1. Verify that 2 is a primitive root for $\mathbb{Z}_{11}^*$.
2. Compute all primitive roots g for $\mathbb{Z}_{11}^*$ with $0 < g < 11$.
3. Determine the smallest positive primitive root g for $\mathbb{Z}_{13}^*$ and compute $\log_{\langle 13,g \rangle}(x)$ for all $x \in \{1, 2, 3, \ldots, 12\}$.

4. Find the smallest value of $n > 2$ such that $\mathbb{Z}_n^*$ has no primitive root.

5. *Computing primitive roots*　In this problem you may use two mathematical facts that are demonstrated in the Appendix of this text. First, the proof of Theorem A.20 (p. 268) reveals that if g is a primitive root for $\mathbb{Z}_{p^2}^*$ then it is also a primitive root for $\mathbb{Z}_{p^k}^*$, where k is any natural number greater than 2. Second, Theorem A.16 (p. 267) says that if g is a primitive root for $\mathbb{Z}_p^*$ then g or $g + p$ is a primitive root for $\mathbb{Z}_{p^2}^*$.[11] Use these facts to compute a primitive root for $\mathbb{Z}_n^*$, where n equals 31920079960009999.

6. (a) Give an upper bound on how many operations $i \mapsto g^i \bmod n$ one must perform in order to verify (or refute) that an invertible element g is a primitive root for $\mathbb{Z}_n^*$.

   (b) Assume that you have a complete prime factorization of $\phi(n)$. Using Lagrange's theorem, how many operations $g^i \bmod n$ do you now require, and for which values of i?

7. *Nontrivial square roots of 1*

   (a) Count the number of n between 1 and 1000 such that there are exactly 14 non-trivial square roots of 1 modulo n (the trivial ones are 1 and $n - 1$).

   (b) Repeat part (a) with 4 in place of 14. How many n do you count now?

Definition 2.34 (Isomorphic Groups)

We say that two groups $\langle G, \circ_G, e_G \rangle$ and $\langle H, \circ_H, e_H \rangle$ are *isomorphic* if and only if there exist functions $\eta\colon G \to H$ and $\psi\colon H \to G$ such that

$$\eta(\psi(h_1)) = h_1,$$
$$\psi(\eta(g_2)) = g_2,$$
$$\eta(e_G) = e_H,$$
$$\psi(e_H) = e_G,$$
$$\eta(g_1 \circ_G g_2) = \eta(g_1) \circ_H \eta(g_2),$$
$$\psi(h_1 \circ_H h_2) = \psi(h_1) \circ_G \psi(h_2)$$

for all $g_1, g_2 \in G$ and $h_1, h_2 \in H$.

Thus isomorphic groups are *structurally identical*, since the mediating maps η and ψ respect the size of the underlying set as well as all the group structure: two-sided identities and multiplication. In Exercise 2.13-3, we see that such maps must also preserve inverses.

For example, consider the commutative group $\langle\{\text{odd}, \text{even}\}, +, \text{even}\rangle$ given by odd + odd = even, odd + even = odd, and even + even = even. This group is isomorphic to the group $\langle \mathbb{Z}_2, +_2, [0]_2 \rangle$. Please specify the maps η and ψ.

Theorem 2.35 (Discrete Logarithm Theorem)

Let g be a primitive root for $\mathbb{Z}_n^*$ ($n \in \mathbb{N}$). Then the groups $\langle \mathbb{Z}_n^*, *_n, [1]_n \rangle$ and $\langle \mathbb{Z}_{\phi(n)}, *_{\phi(n)}, [0]_{\phi(n)} \rangle$ are isomorphic. The isomorphism is given by the maps

---

[11] That is to say, at least one of these two numbers is a primitive root.

$$\eta: \mathbb{Z}_n^* \to \mathbb{Z}_{\phi(n)}, \qquad \eta[x]_n \overset{\text{def}}{=} [\log_{\langle n, g \rangle}(x)]_{\phi(n)};$$

$$\psi: \mathbb{Z}_{\phi(n)} \to \mathbb{Z}_n^*, \qquad \psi[t]_{\phi(n)} \overset{\text{def}}{=} [g^t]_n.$$

The proof of this proposition is relegated to the exercises. It is important to stress that, although we have an explicit isomorphism between these groups in the mathematical sense, there is no known efficient way of *computing* this isomorphism. One the one hand, there is the problem of knowing $\phi(n)$; on the other hand, even with the knowledge of $\phi(n)$ it can be computationally difficult to find $\eta[x]_n$. This problem is so important that it has its own name.

Definition 2.36 (Discrete Logarithm Problem)
Let p be prime, g a primitive root for $\mathbb{Z}_p^*$, and β any element of $\mathbb{Z}_p^*$. Compute $\log_{\langle p, g \rangle}(\beta)$.

EXERCISES 2.13

1. Show that $\langle \mathbb{Z}_0, +_0, [0]_0 \rangle$ is isomorphic to $\langle \mathbb{Z}, +, 0 \rangle$.
2. Find a simply described group that is isomorphic to $\langle \mathbb{Z}_1, +_1, [0]_1 \rangle$.
3. Show that, if $\eta: G \to H$ and $\psi: H \to G$ are isomorphisms between two groups, then they preserve inverses: $\eta(g^{-1}) = \eta(g)^{-1}$ and $\psi(h^{-1}) = \psi(h)^{-1}$ for all $g \in G$ and $h \in H$.
4. Prove Theorem 2.35 as follows.
   (a) Show that η and ψ are well-defined.
   (b) Show that η preserves two-sided identities, that is, $\eta[1]_n = [0]_{\phi(n)}$.
   (c) Show that ψ preserves two-sided identities, that is, $\psi[0]_{\phi(n)} = [1]_n$.
   (d) Show that η preserves group multiplication, that is,

   $$\eta([x]_n *_n [y]_n) = \eta[x]_n +_{\phi(n)} \eta[y]_n.$$

   What equation must you show for the logarithm?
   (e) Show that ψ preserves group multiplication, that is,

   $$\psi([t_1]_{\phi(n)} +_{\phi(n)} [t_2]_{\phi(n)}) = \psi[t_1]_{\phi(n)} *_n \psi[t_2]_{\phi(n)}.$$

   (f) Show that $\eta(\psi[t]_{\phi(n)}) = [t]_{\phi(n)}$ for all $[t]_{\phi(n)} \in \mathbb{Z}_{\phi(n)}$.
   (g) Show that $\psi(\eta[x]_n) = [x]_n$ for all $[x]_n \in \mathbb{Z}_n$.

Before we can show Theorem 2.32, we need to understand how many solutions linear equations in $\mathbb{Z}_n$ have. Concretely, we are interested in the equation $x^2 \bmod p = 1$, which isn't linear at all. Yet if $\mathbb{Z}_p^*$ has a primitive root, then we may apply Theorem 2.35 and translate this equation into a linear one in $\mathbb{Z}_{\phi(p)}$. Thus we obtain $\log_{\langle p, g \rangle}(x) + \log_{\langle p, g \rangle}(x) = 0 \bmod \phi(p)$, which is equivalent to

$$2 \cdot \log_{\langle p, g \rangle}(x) = 0 \bmod \phi(p). \tag{2.22}$$

Thinking of $\log_{\langle p, g \rangle}(x)$ as an unknown x' and of $\phi(p)$ as some natural number n', we need to know how many solutions to equations of the form

$$a \cdot x' = b \bmod n' \tag{2.23}$$

we have in x', where $n' \in \mathbb{N}$ and $a, b \in \mathbb{Z}$. We may rewrite this equation in $\mathbb{Z}_{n'}^*$ as

$$[a]_{n'} *_{n'} [x']_{n'} = [b]_{n'}. \tag{2.24}$$

Definition 2.37 (Order of Group Element)
Let $\langle G, \circ, e \rangle$ be a finite group and let $g \in G$. We define

$$g^0 \overset{\text{def}}{=} e,$$
$$g^1 \overset{\text{def}}{=} g,$$
$$g^{k+1} \overset{\text{def}}{=} g \circ g^k$$

for all $k \in \mathbb{N}$. The *order* of g in G, denoted by $\text{ord}^G(g)$, is the least number $t \in \mathbb{N}$ such that $g^t = e$. We write $\text{ord}(g)$ if the group G is determined by the context.

Note that the order is well-defined, as the set $\{m \in \mathbb{N} \mid g^m = e\}$ is nonempty. For example, we always have $g^m = e$, where m is the size of G; why? More concretely: in the group $\mathbb{Z}_7^*$, the element $[3]_7$ has order 6 since $[3]_7^6 = [1]_7$ and $[3]_7^d \neq [1]_7$ for all $1 \leq d < 6$. The next two lemmas are proven in the exercises.

Lemma 2.38
Let g be an element in a finite group $\langle G, \circ, e \rangle$. Then $\text{ord}^G(g)$ equals the size of the subgroup that g generates in G.

Lemma 2.39
Let $n \in \mathbb{N}$ and $[a]_n \neq [0]_n$. Then $\text{ord}^{\mathbb{Z}_n}([a]_n)$ is equal to $n/\gcd(a, n)$.

EXERCISES 2.14

1. Determine the order of the element $[2]_7$ in the group $\langle \mathbb{Z}_7^*, *_7, [1]_7 \rangle$.
2. Prove Lemma 2.38.
   (a) Let t be $\text{ord}^G(g)$. Show that $\langle g \rangle$ equals $\{g^1, g^2, \dots, g^t\}$.
   (b) Conclude that the size of $\langle g \rangle$ is less than or equal to t.
   (c) Show that the set $\{g^1, g^2, \dots, g^t\}$ has exactly t many elements.
3. Prove Lemma 2.39.

Lemma 2.40
Let $[a]_n \neq [0]_n$. The equation $[a]_n *_n [x]_n = [b]_n$ has either exactly $\gcd(a, n)$ many distinct solutions in $\{0, 1, \dots, n - 1\}$ or none at all.

Proof Let us assume that this equation has a solution. We need only argue that there are exactly $\gcd(a, n)$ many distinct solutions to this equation in $\mathbb{Z}_n$. By Lemma 2.39, we have that $\text{ord}^{\mathbb{Z}_n}([a]_n)$ equals $n/\gcd(a, n)$. The sequence $([a]_n *_n [x]_n)_{x=0}^{n-1}$ repeatedly lists all elements of $\langle [a]_n \rangle$ in $\gcd(a, n)$ many blocks. If the equation in Lemma 2.40 has a solution, then $[b]_n \in \langle [a]_n \rangle$ must hold. In that case, $[b]_n$ shows up exactly once in each of the $\gcd(a, n)$ blocks of the sequence $([a]_n *_n [x]_n)_{x=0}^{n-1}$. $\square$

For example, $\gcd(16, 8) = 8$, but $16 \cdot x = -3 \mod 8$ has no solutions since $16 \cdot x = 0 \neq -3 \mod 8$. However, the equation $16 \cdot x = 0 \mod 8$ has exactly eight solutions in $\{0, 1, \ldots, 7\}$.

2.3.2.4 Proof of Theorem 2.32

We are now in a position to prove Theorem 2.32. Recall that we need to solve $2 \cdot x' = 0 \mod \phi(p)$, where $x' \stackrel{\text{def}}{=} \log_{\langle p, g \rangle}(x)$ and $p > 1$ is prime. Since $x' = 0$ is obviously a solution to this equation, we invoke Lemma 2.40 and conclude that the equation $2 \cdot x' = 0 \mod \phi(p)$ has exactly $\gcd(2, \phi(p))$ many solutions. If $p = 2$, then $\gcd(2, \phi(p)) = \gcd(2, 1) = 1$, so $x' = 0$ is the only solution. If $p > 2$ then we have that $\phi(p) = p - 1$ is even, so $\gcd(2, \phi(p)) = 2$ follows. If $\mathbb{Z}_p^*$ has a primitive root, then Theorem 2.35 ensures that the groups $\langle \mathbb{Z}_p^*, *_p, [1]_p \rangle$ and $\langle \mathbb{Z}_{\phi(p)}, *_{\phi(p)}, [0]_{\phi(p)} \rangle$ are isomorphic. Moreover, the isomorphisms translate the equation $2 \cdot x' = 0 \mod \phi(p)$ into $x^2 = 1 \mod p$, so the latter has exactly as many solutions as the former, but 1 and $p - 1$ are two such solutions (well, one if $p = 2$) for the latter. Note that this argument depends on the existence of a primitive root for $\mathbb{Z}_p^*$.

Theorem 2.41
If a call Witness(a,n) *returns* true, *then n is not prime.*

Proof We have only to prove that $\mathbb{Z}_p^*$ has a primitive root, where $p > 2$ is prime. This is done in Section A.1 of the Appendix. □

EXERCISES 2.15

1. *gcd recursion theorem*   Prove the gcd recursion theorem: For any $a \in \mathbb{N} \cup \{0\}$ and $b \in \mathbb{N}$, we have

$$\gcd(a, b) = \gcd(b, a \bmod b). \tag{2.25}$$

   (*Hint:* Show that both expressions are divisors of each other. Why does this guarantee their equality?)

2. *Euclid's algorithm*   Use the gcd recursion theorem to prove that Euclid's algorithm, written as a recursive program in pseudo-code below, computes $\gcd(a, b)$:

   ```
   Euclid(BigInteger a, BigInteger b) {
        if (b == 0) return a;
             else  return Euclid(b,a mod b);
   }
   ```

3. The Fibonacci numbers F_n ($n \in \mathbb{N}$) are defined by

$$F_1 \stackrel{\text{def}}{=} 1,$$

$$F_2 \stackrel{\text{def}}{=} 1,$$

$$F_{n+2} \stackrel{\text{def}}{=} F_{n+1} + F_n$$

   for all $n \in \mathbb{N}$.

(a) Compute F_7.

(b) Prove: If $a > b \geq 0$ are integers such that the program Euclid(a,b) makes $k \in \mathbb{N}$ recursive calls, then $a \geq F_{k+2}$ and $b \geq F_{k+1}$ hold. (*Hint:* Use mathematical induction on k.)

(c) Prove: The program Euclid(F[k+1],F[k]) makes exactly $k - 1$ recursive calls for all $k \in \mathbb{N}$. (*Hint:* Use mathematical induction on k and the recursive definition of the Fibonacci numbers F[k].) Use part (b) to conclude that consecutive Fibonacci numbers are a worst-case input for Euclid's algorithm with respect to the number of recursive calls.

4. Specify a computation trace for execution of the function call Euclid(653,134).

5. Compute gcd(2354, 456).

6. Implement Euclid's algorithm in a programming language of your choice.

2.3.3 When Witness(a,n) Fails

We have established that Witness(a,n) correctly identifies that n is not prime if it returns with value true. But what can we say about its returns of type false? Within the context of Miller–Rabin(n,s), such replies stand for: "According to a, the number n is prime". The program Miller–Rabin(n,s) then decides that n is prime if it so happens that s random choices of a result in such a reply. Unfortunately, there are numbers n which are not prime but which Miller–Rabin(n,s) classifies as being prime for some value of s and some random program execution. Therefore, this algorithm is not correct for all its inputs in the strict, *qualitative,* sense of the word. However, it is still *extremely useful* in practice for several reasons.

- It can only make one kind of error: all its negative decisions, "n is not a prime number", have been proved to be correct. Probabilistic algorithms with this property are called *no-biased Monte Carlo* algorithms.
- We shortly prove that a failure of this algorithm is very unlikely by giving an upper bound on the probability of such failures that depends only on s, not on n. Thus we arrive at a proved *quantitative* notion of program correctness.
- Even if the algorithm fails in that it incorrectly advertises p or q to be prime, we can implement a little test encryption–decryption for the RSA encryption scheme based on p and q to see if the scheme works for the message we mean to send securely. (This is for the truly paranoid among us.)

Definition 2.42

A *yes-biased Monte Carlo algorithm* is a randomized algorithm that returns an answer of type boolean such that all true replies are correct. A randomized algorithm of the same output type is *no-biased* if all false replies are correct.

A no-biased Monte Carlo algorithm may compute incorrect true replies, so one is interested in upper bounds on the probability of this happening. We established such an upper bound for the no-biased Monte Carlo algorithm of Miller and Rabin. The call Miller–Rabin(n,s) would certainly fail if $n \in \mathbb{N}$ had the peculiar properties that n was not prime, $a^{n-1} = 1 \bmod n$ for all $1 \leq a \leq n - 1$, and n had only 1 and $n - 1$ as square roots of 1 modulo n. For such an n the algorithm would reply "n is prime" no matter what value of s we choose. Fortunately, we see shortly that such numbers cannot exist.

Definition 2.43 (Carmichael Numbers and Witness Set)
A number $n \in \mathbb{N}$ is a *Carmichael number* if it is not prime and satisfies $a^{n-1} = 1 \bmod n$ for all $[a]_n \in \mathbb{Z}_n^*$. For any odd number $n \in \mathbb{N}$ that is not prime, we define

$$W(n) \stackrel{\text{def}}{=} \{a \in \mathbb{N} \mid 2 \le a \le n - 1, \texttt{Witness(a,n)=true}\}, \qquad (2.26)$$

the set of test numbers a that make the witness program realize that n is not prime.

For example, 561, 1105, and 1729 are the three smallest Carmichael numbers. Amazingly, one can show that there are infinitely many Carmichael numbers. Clearly, $W(n)$ is nonempty if n is not a Carmichael number. Since `Miller-Rabin(n,s)` makes s random choices of a to find some element of $W(n)$, we require that a random pick of $a \in \{2, 3, \ldots, n - 1\}$ have a probability of at least $1/2$ that $a \in W(n)$, whether or not n is a Carmichael number. Assuming that the s choices are made independently, we then have an upper bound of 2^{-s} for the probability of not finding a witness during the execution of `Miller-Rabin(n,s)`. Therefore, it suffices to show that

$$|W(n)| \ge (n - 1)/2 \qquad (2.27)$$

for all numbers n that are odd and not prime. Since `Witness(a,n)` has two criteria for detecting a witness a, our analysis splits into two corresponding cases. Its second (more difficult) case makes vital use of the existence of a primitive root in $\mathbb{Z}_{p^k}^*$, where p is an odd prime and $k > 1$, a fact that we secure in Theorem A.20. Further, we must be able to solve simultaneously linear equations modulo different values n_i, where the n_i have no factors in common. This technique rests on the Chinese remainder theorem, whose proof we relegate to the exercises.

Definition 2.44 (Product Group)
For each $i = 1, 2, \ldots, k$, let $\langle G_i, \circ_i, e_i \rangle$ be a group. We define the *product* $\langle \prod_{i=1}^k G_i, \prod_{i=1}^k \circ_i, \prod_{i=1}^k e_i \rangle$ of these groups as follows:

1. $\prod_{i=1}^k G_i$ is the set of all k-tuples $\langle g_1, \ldots, g_k \rangle$ with $g_i \in G_i$ for $i = 1, 2, \ldots, k$;
2. $\prod_{i=1}^k \circ_i$ is a map of type $\prod_{i=1}^k G_i \times \prod_{i=1}^k G_i \to \prod_{i=1}^k G_i$ and defined by coordinate-wise multiplication,

$$\langle g_1, \ldots, g_k \rangle \prod_{i=1}^k \circ_i \langle h_1, \ldots, h_k \rangle \stackrel{\text{def}}{=} \langle g_1 \circ_1 h_1, \ldots, g_k \circ_k h_k \rangle; \qquad (2.28)$$

3. the element $\prod_{i=1}^k e_i$ is $\langle e_1, \ldots, e_k \rangle$.

For example, $\langle [1]_2, [2]_3 \rangle$ and $\langle [3]_2, [5]_3 \rangle$ are elements of $\mathbb{Z}_2 \times \mathbb{Z}_3$, and their addition renders the pair $\langle [1 + 3]_3, [2 + 5]_3 \rangle = \langle [0]_2, [1]_3 \rangle$.

Lemma 2.45
The triple $\langle \prod_{i=1}^k G_i, \prod_{i=1}^k \circ_i, \prod_{i=1}^k e_i \rangle$ is a finite commutative group if all the groups $\langle G_i, \circ_i, e_i \rangle$, $i = 1, 2, \ldots, k$, are finite and commutative.

Proof   This is to be shown in Exercise 2.16-7 (p. 52).   □

Theorem 2.46 (Chinese Remainder Theorem)

Let $n = n_1 \cdot n_2 \cdots n_k$ *in* $\mathbb{N}$ *with* $k \geq 2$ *such that* $\gcd(n_i, n_j) = 1$ *for* $i \neq j$. *Then the group* $\langle \mathbb{Z}_n, +_n, [0]_n \rangle$ *is isomorphic to*

$$\left\langle \prod_{i=1}^{k} \mathbb{Z}_{n_i}, \prod_{i=1}^{k} +_{n_i}, \prod_{i=1}^{k} [0]_{n_i} \right\rangle. \tag{2.29}$$

The pair of isomorphisms is given by

$$\eta: \mathbb{Z}_n \to \prod_{i=1}^{k} \mathbb{Z}_{n_i}, \qquad\qquad \eta[a]_n \stackrel{\text{def}}{=} \langle [a]_{n_1}, \ldots, [a]_{n_k} \rangle;$$

$$\psi: \prod_{i=1}^{k} \mathbb{Z}_{n_i} \to \mathbb{Z}_n, \quad \psi\langle [a_1]_{n_1}, \ldots, [a_k]_{n_k} \rangle \stackrel{\text{def}}{=} [a_1 \cdot c_1 + a_2 \cdot c_2 + \cdots + a_k \cdot c_k]_n,$$

where $c_i \stackrel{\text{def}}{=} m_i \cdot (m_i^{-1} \bmod n_i)$ *and* $m_i \stackrel{\text{def}}{=} n/n_i$.

Proof   This proof is relegated to Exercise 2.16-8 (p. 52).   □

Corollary 2.47

Let $n = n_1 \cdot n_2 \cdots n_k$ *in* $\mathbb{N}$ *with* $k \geq 2$ *such that* $\gcd(n_i, n_j) = 1$ *for* $i \neq j$. *Then, for any* $\langle a_1, \ldots, a_k \rangle \in \prod_{i=1}^{k} \mathbb{Z}$, *the equations*

$$x = a_i \bmod n_i \quad (i = 1, 2, \ldots, k) \tag{2.30}$$

have a unique solution $x \bmod n$.

Proof   This proof is relegated to Exercise 2.16-9 (p. 52).   □

Corollary 2.48

Let $n = n_1 \cdot n_2 \cdots n_k$ *in* $\mathbb{N}$ *with* $k \geq 2$ *such that* $\gcd(n_i, n_j) = 1$ *for* $i \neq j$. *Then, for any* $a \in \mathbb{Z}$, *we have*

$$x = a \bmod n_i \quad (i = 1, 2, \ldots, k) \tag{2.31}$$

if and only if $x = a \bmod n$.

Proof   See Exercise 2.16-10 (p. 52).   □

Example 2.49

Let us solve the system of equations

$$\begin{aligned} x &= 3 \bmod 13, \\ x &= 7 \bmod 9. \end{aligned} \tag{2.32}$$

In this case, $n_1 = 13$, $n_2 = 9$, $a_1 = 3$, and $a_2 = 7$. Note that $k = 2$ and $\gcd(n_1, n_2) = 1$, as 13 is prime. Since $n = n_1 \cdot n_2 = 117$, we compute $n/n_1 = 117/13 = 9$ and $n/n_2 = 117/9 = 13$. The required inverses are $(n/n_1)^{-1} \bmod n_1 = 9^{-1} \bmod 13 = 3$ and

$(n/n_2)^{-1} \bmod n_2 = 13^{-1} \bmod 9 = 7$. Now $c_1 = (n/n_1) \cdot ((n/n_1)^{-1} \bmod n_1) = 9 \cdot 3 = 27$ and $c_2 = (n/n_2) \cdot ((n/n_2)^{-1} \bmod n_2) = 13 \cdot 7 = 91$. Thus $x = a_1 \cdot c_1 + a_2 \cdot c_2 \bmod n = 3 \cdot 27 + 7 \cdot 91 \bmod 117$ implies that $x = 16$. Please verify that 16 is indeed a solution to the equations in (2.32).

The Chinese remainder theorem is a vital reasoning tool in number theory. For example, we use it for proving probabilistic lower bounds on the correctness of the Miller–Rabin algorithm. However, it also has practical impact because it often allows one to conduct computation with respect to each factor n_i as opposed to the entire product thereof. This may gain efficiency in that the n_i may have significantly fewer bits than n itself and may well allow an effective use of parallel processing. Such implementation changes typically require a reevaluation of a cryptographic system's security.

EXERCISES 2.16

1. Use the Chinese remainder theorem to compute the unique solution of

$$x = 2 \bmod 3,$$
$$x = 3 \bmod 5, \tag{2.33}$$
$$x = 2 \bmod 7,$$

where $0 \leq x < 105$.

2. Consider the Carmichael number 561.
   (a) Compute the set $W(561)$. Is $|W(561)| < (561 - 1)/2$?
   (b) How many nontrivial square roots of 1 modulo 561 are there?

3. Carmichael numbers n are defined via conditions on units modulo n. This makes sense. Show: If a is not a unit modulo n, then $a^{n-1} \bmod n \neq 1$.

4. Compute all the Carmichael numbers that are less than one million. The three smallest Carmichael numbers are listed immediately after Definition 2.43 (p. 49); there are few such numbers below one million. The crucial part of this exercise is the program you write.

5. Let $n = p_1^{k_1} \cdot p_2^{k_2} \cdots p_m^{k_m}$ be the unique prime factorization of n. Define $\lambda(n)$ as the least common multiple (see p. 259) of all $\phi(p_i^{k_i})$, where $i = 1, 2, \ldots, m$. Prove:
   (a) $\lambda(n) \mid \phi(n)$;
   (b) $a^{\lambda(n)} = 1 \bmod n$ for all $[a]_n \in \mathbb{Z}_n^*$;
   (c) if n is a Carmichael number, then $k_i = 1$ for all $i = 1, 2, \ldots, m$;
   (d) if n is a Carmichael number, then n is the product of at least three different primes.
   (e) Is 27935017 a Carmichael number?

6. (a) Write a program that takes a "small" integer n as input and returns the smallest Carmichael number that is greater or equal to n.[12]
   (b) Test your program with the inputs 323, 645, 1521, and 1999; compare your first three outputs to the three Carmichael numbers listed after Definition 2.43.

---

[12] Since there are infinitely many Carmichael numbers, this output is always well-defined, but your program will take too long for integers that are not "small".

7. Prove Lemma 2.45.
8. Prove Theorem 2.46 as follows.

    (a) Show that the map $\eta \colon \mathbb{Z}_n \to \prod_{i=1}^k \mathbb{Z}_{n_i}$ with

    $$\eta[a]_n \overset{\text{def}}{=} \langle [a]_{n_1}, \dots, [a]_{n_k} \rangle \tag{2.34}$$

    is well-defined.

    (b) For $m_i \overset{\text{def}}{=} n/n_i$, show that there exists some $m_i^{-1} \in \mathbb{Z}$ such that $[m_i^{-1}]_{n_i}$ is an inverse of $[m_i]_{n_i}$ in $\mathbb{Z}_{n_i}^*$.

    (c) For $c_i \overset{\text{def}}{=} m_i \cdot (m_i^{-1} \bmod n_i) \in \mathbb{Z}$, consider the map ψ of type $\prod_{i=1}^k \mathbb{Z}_{n_i} \to \mathbb{Z}_n$ with

    $$\psi \langle [a_1]_{n_1}, \dots, [a_k]_{n_k} \rangle \overset{\text{def}}{=} [a_1 \cdot c_1 + a_2 \cdot c_2 + \cdots + a_k \cdot c_k]_n. \tag{2.35}$$

    Show that ψ is well-defined.

    (d) Prove that η preserves the two-sided identity and group multiplication.

    (e) Prove that ψ preserves the two-sided identity and group multiplication.

    (f) Prove that η and ψ are mutually inverse functions.

9. Prove Corollary 2.47.
10. Prove Corollary 2.48.
11. Can you apply the Chinese remainder theorem to obtain a more efficient algorithm for the decryption in (2.8) of the RSA PKC system? Could this be done for the encryption operation in (2.7)?

Theorem 2.50

Let $n \in \mathbb{N}$ be an odd number that is not prime. Then the size of $W(n)$ is at least $(n-1)/2$.

Proof Let $W(n)^c$ be the set $\mathbb{Z}_n \setminus W(n)$, that is, the set of *nonwitnesses*. Thus $[a]_n \in W(n)^c$ if and only if the program call `Witness(a,n)` returns with `false`. Therefore, any $[a]_n \in W(n)^c$ satisfies $a^{n-1} = 1 \bmod n$, so $W(n)^c$ is contained in the set $\mathbb{Z}_n^*$. Our strategy is to show that $W(n)^c$ is contained in G, some proper subgroup of the group $\mathbb{Z}_n^*$ (i.e., $G \neq \mathbb{Z}_n^*$). In that case, Lagrange's theorem implies that $|G|$ is a divisor of $\phi(n)$, but since $G \neq \mathbb{Z}_n^*$ we have

$$|W(n)^c| \leq |G| \leq \phi(n)/2 \leq (n-1)/2.$$

Thus

$$|W(n)| = |\mathbb{Z}_n \setminus W(n)^c| \geq n - (n-1)/2 = (n+1)/2 \geq (n-1)/2$$

finishes the proof. The construction of the subgroup G and the argument that it is smaller than $\mathbb{Z}_n^*$ are split into two cases, depending on whether n is a Carmichael number.

Case 1: Assume that n is not a Carmichael number. By definition of that concept, there exists some $[x]_n \in \mathbb{Z}_n^*$ such that $x^{n-1} \neq 1 \bmod n$. Define

$$G \overset{\text{def}}{=} \{[a]_n \in \mathbb{Z}_n^* \mid a^{n-1} = 1 \bmod n\}. \tag{2.36}$$

As discussed before, $W(n)^c$ is a subset of G. Since $1^{n-1} = 1 \bmod n$, G contains the two-sided identity, $[1]_n$, of $\mathbb{Z}_n^*$. Given $[a]_n$ and $[b]_n$ in G, we easily see that $(a \cdot b)^{n-1} = 1 \bmod n$, so $[a]_n *_n [b]_n = [a \cdot b]_n \in G$. As for inverses, let $[a]_n \in G \subseteq \mathbb{Z}_n^*$. Then there exists some $[y]_n$ with $[a]_n *_n [y]_n = [1]_n$. But then

$$
\begin{aligned}
[1]_n &= [1]_n^{n-1} \\
&= ([a]_n *_n [y]_n)^{n-1} \\
&= [a]_n^{n-1} *_n [y]_n^{n-1} \\
&= [y]_n^{n-1},
\end{aligned}
\tag{2.37}
$$

as $[a]_n \in G$. Thus the inverse $[y]_n$ of $[a]_n$ is in G as well and so G is a subgroup of $\langle \mathbb{Z}_n^*, *_n, [1]_n \rangle$. By assumption, $[x]_n \in \mathbb{Z}_n^* \setminus G$, so G is proper.

Case 2: Assume that n is a Carmichael number: $a^{n-1} = 1 \bmod n$ for all $a \in \mathbb{Z}_n^*$. Then let $n - 1 = 2^\alpha \cdot u$ with u odd. For any $a \in \{1, 2, \ldots, n-1\}$, consider

$$
\tilde{a} \stackrel{\text{def}}{=} \langle a^u \bmod n, a^{2 \cdot u} \bmod n, \ldots, a^{2^\alpha \cdot u} \bmod n \rangle.
\tag{2.38}
$$

Since $n - 1 = 2^\alpha \cdot u$ with u being odd, the binary representation of $n - 1$ has exactly α many 0-bits on its least significant end. Thus the values in $\tilde{a}$ are the last $\alpha + 1$ values of t in the computation of `Witness(a,n)`: all last α operations are squarings. Define

$$
J \stackrel{\text{def}}{=} \{j \in \mathbb{Z} \mid 0 \leq j \leq \alpha, \ v^{2^j \cdot u} = -1 \bmod n \text{ for some } [v]_n \in \mathbb{Z}_n^* \}.
\tag{2.39}
$$

Since u is odd, it follows that J is nonempty; for example, for $j = 0$ we have $v = -1$, ensuring that $(-1)^{2^0 \cdot u} = -1 \bmod n$ and so $0 \in J$. Let j_m be the largest element in J and let $[v_m]_n \in \mathbb{Z}_n^*$ be such that $v_m^{2^{j_m} \cdot u} = -1 \bmod n$. Our candidate for a subgroup is

$$
G \stackrel{\text{def}}{=} \{[a]_n \in \mathbb{Z}_n^* \mid a^{2^{j_m} \cdot u} \bmod n \text{ equals 1 or } -1 \}.
\tag{2.40}
$$

Since $1^{2^{j_m} \cdot u} \bmod n$ equals 1, we have $[1]_n \in G$. Since $\{x, y\} \subseteq \{1, -1\}$ implies $x \cdot y \in \{1, -1\}$, it is easily seen that $[a]_n, [b]_n \in G$ imply $[a]_n *_n [b]_n \in G$. For the same reason, one can see that $[a]_n \in G$ implies that its inverse is also in G (indeed, this is similar to how we reasoned in Case 1). Thus G is a subgroup of $\mathbb{Z}_n^*$. It remains to show that G is a proper subgroup of $\mathbb{Z}_n^*$ and that $W(n)^c$ is contained in G.

We begin by constructing some $[x]_n \in \mathbb{Z}_n^* \setminus G$. This is where the division of n into relatively prime factors n_1 and n_2 is instrumental. For that we need to argue that n cannot be the power of an odd prime number. Otherwise, $n = p^k$ for $p > 2$ prime and $k > 1$. In that case, $\mathbb{Z}_n^*$ has a primitive root g by Theorem A.20. But then Theorem 2.35 implies that the equation $x^{n-1} = 1 \bmod n$ is equivalent to $n - 1 = 0 \bmod \phi(n)$. By Lemma A.15,

$$
\phi(n) = p^{k-1} \cdot (p-1)
$$

and so $n - 1 = 0 \bmod \phi(n)$ entails

$$
p^{k-1} \cdot (p-1) \mid p^k - 1.
$$

Since $k > 1$, we have

$$p \mid p^{k-1} \cdot (p - 1);$$

but then $p \nmid p^k - 1$ (by Exercise 2.17-1, p. 55) contradicts $p^{k-1} \cdot (p-1) \mid p^k - 1$. Therefore, n is not such a prime power. Since n is an odd integer that is not a prime power, its prime factorization

$$n = p_1^{k_1} \cdot p_2^{k_2} \cdots p_m^{k_m}$$

must satisfy $m > 1$, since the case $m = 1$ has already been ruled out. Thus we may split n into two factors $n_1 > 2$ and $n_2 > 2$ that are relatively prime:

$$n = n_1 \cdot n_2, \quad \gcd(n_1, n_2) = 1. \tag{2.41}$$

Because

$$v^{2^{jm} \cdot u} = -1 \bmod n,$$

the Chinese remainder theorem implies that

$$v^{2^{jm} \cdot u} = -1 \bmod n_1.$$

Moreover, it guarantees the existence of a unique solution x, modulo n, of the equations

$$\begin{aligned} x &= v \bmod n_1, \\ x &= 1 \bmod n_2. \end{aligned} \tag{2.42}$$

But then

$$\begin{aligned} x^{2^{jm} \cdot u} \bmod n_1 &= v^{2^{jm} \cdot u} \bmod n_1 = -1 \bmod n_1, \\ x^{2^{jm} \cdot u} \bmod n_2 &= 1^{2^{jm} \cdot u} \bmod n_2 = 1 \bmod n_2 \end{aligned} \tag{2.43}$$

follow. Thus, $x^{2^{jm} \cdot u} \bmod n$ cannot be 1 or -1. Hence $[x]_n \notin G$. By the Chinese remainder theorem, $[v]_n \in \mathbb{Z}_n^*$ implies $[v]_{n_1} \in \mathbb{Z}_{n_1}^*$, so $[x]_{n_1} \in \mathbb{Z}_{n_1}^*$ follows. But $x = 1 \bmod n_2$ renders $[x]_{n_2} \in \mathbb{Z}_{n_2}^*$. Thus $[x]_{n_1} \in \mathbb{Z}_{n_1}^*$ and $[x]_{n_2} \in \mathbb{Z}_{n_2}^*$ imply $[x]_n \in \mathbb{Z}_n^*$, again by the Chinese remainder theorem. Thus $[x]_n \in \mathbb{Z}_n^* \setminus G$ as desired.

Finally, let $[a]_n \in W(n)^c$. We are done if $[a]_n \in G$. We show the process of this argument in Figure 2.6.   □

Corollary 2.51 (Probabilistic Correctness of Miller–Rabin)

Let $n \in \mathbb{N}$ be any odd number, and let s be any natural number.

1. *If the execution of program* `Miller-Rabin(n,s)` *returns with* `false`, *this answer is always correct.*
2. *If n is not prime, then the probability that this execution replies (correctly) with* `false` *is at least $1 - 2^{-s}$.*

One can show that if a prime candidate n is chosen randomly, then `Rabin-Miller(n,s)` is unlikely to fail for small values of s, even smaller than 10. A more sophisticated

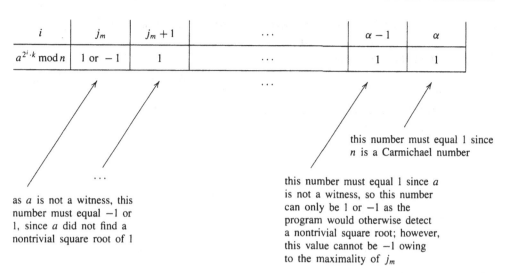

i	j_m	$j_m + 1$		$\cdots$		$\alpha - 1$	α
$a^{2^i \cdot k} \bmod n$	1 or -1	1		$\cdots$		1	1

this number must equal 1 since
n is a Carmichael number

this number must equal 1 since a
is not a witness, so this number
can only be 1 or -1 as the
program would otherwise detect
a nontrivial square root; however,
this value cannot be -1 owing
to the maximality of j_m

as a is not a witness, this
number must equal -1 or
1, since a did not find a
nontrivial square root of 1

Figure 2.6. A schematic showing the argument that $[a]_n \in G$, finishing the proof of Theorem 2.50. Please read this from the right to the left.

analysis can improve the bound in Theorem 2.50 so that $|W(n)^c| \leq (n-1)/4$; however, this bound is tight, for there are $n \in \mathbb{N}$ where $|W(n)^c|$ equals $(n-1)/4$.

EXERCISES 2.17

1. Let $p > 1$ be prime. Prove: $p \nmid p^k - 1$ for all $k \in \mathbb{N}$.
2. Prove Corollary 2.51.
3. Compute an $n \in \mathbb{N}$ such that $|W(n)^c| = (n-1)/4$.
4. *Factoring with square roots* Let $x \in \{2, 3, \ldots, n - 2\}$ be a nontrivial square root of 1 modulo n. Show that $\gcd(x - 1, n)$ is a factor of n. Can you even show

   $$n = \gcd(x - 1, n) \cdot \gcd(x + 1, n)\,?$$

   Explain how knowledge of such an x allows one to factor n efficiently.
5. Design a randomized algorithm that takes as input a Carmichael number or a prime, n, and whose output is either a factorization of n or a message saying that n is a probable prime. What obstacles are there if you want to extend this algorithm to apply to all natural numbers?
6. Prove or disprove: If $W(n)$ is empty for an odd number $n \in \mathbb{N}$, then n is prime.
7. *Quadratic nonresidues modulo n* The set Q_n of *quadratic residues modulo n* consists of those $[a]_n \in \mathbb{Z}_n^*$ for which we can solve $x^2 = a \bmod n$ for some x with $[x]_n \in \mathbb{Z}_n^*$.
   (a) Let p be an odd prime and g a primitive root for $\mathbb{Z}_p^*$.
       (i) Show that $[a]_p$ is a quadratic residue modulo p if and only if
       $$a = g^{2 \cdot i} \bmod p$$
       for some $i \in \mathbb{N}$.
       (ii) Conclude that Q_p has exactly $(p-1)/2$ many elements.

(iii) Show: If $a \in Q_p$, then there are exactly two elements in $\{0, 1, \ldots, p - 1\}$ that solve $x^2 = a \bmod p$.

(b) Compute the set Q_{31}.

(c) Let $n = p \cdot q$ for odd prime numbers p and q. Show that $[a]_n \in Q_n$ if and only if $[a]_p \in Q_p$ and $[a]_q \in Q_q$.

8. *Primality test based on quadratic residues* Assume that there is an efficient algorithm Jacobi(a,n) that outputs

- 0 if $\gcd(a, n) > 1$,
- 1 if $a \in Q_n$, and
- −1 otherwise

(such an algorithm does exist). Assume further that the output of Jacobi(a,n) is equal to $a^{(n-1)/2} \bmod n$ whenever $\gcd(a, n) = 1$ and n is an odd prime (this is indeed the case and is known as *Euler's criterion*).

(a) Design a probabilistic algorithm for primality testing based on the test function Jacobi(a,n).

(b) Use the fact from Exercise 7(a)(ii) to specify a lower bound for false positives (i.e., program executions that falsely classify n as being prime).

2.3.4 Efficiency of Finding Large Primes

A second obstacle to generating large prime numbers is that the algorithm of Miller and Rabin decides correctly (with high probability) that a given number n is prime, yet it does not *generate* such a number. If its reply is negative, which we then know to be correct, we must look for some other number n', roughly the same size as n, and repeat Miller and Rabin's algorithm with n'. The question, therefore, is how often we may need to repeat this algorithm; that is, how "dense" are prime numbers in $\mathbb{N}$?

Definition 2.52 (Number of Primes below $n + 1$)
Let $n \in \mathbb{N}$. We set

$$\pi(n) \stackrel{\text{def}}{=} |\{p \in \mathbb{N} \mid p \leq n \text{ and } p \text{ is prime}\}|. \tag{2.44}$$

Thus $\pi(n)$ is the number of primes that are strictly below $n + 1$. The function $\pi : \mathbb{N} \to \mathbb{N}$ serves as a measure of how often prime numbers occur in $\mathbb{N}$. This function has been studied for quite some time. In 1896, J. Hadamard and Ch. de la Vallée-Poussin proved the first approximation of $n \mapsto \pi(n)$.

Theorem 2.53

$$\lim_{n \to \infty} (\pi(n) \cdot \ln n)/n = 1. \tag{2.45}$$

Equation (2.45) tells us that, for large values of n, we may approximate $\pi(n)$ with $n/\ln n$. For example, $\pi(10^6)$ equals 78498 and $10^6/\ln 10^6 \approx 72382$ (a difference of less than 8%); $\pi(10^9)$ equals 50847478 and $10^6/\ln 10^6 \approx 48254942$ (about 6%). Assuming that the prime numbers in $\{1, 2, \ldots, n\}$ are distributed with a Laplace distribution (all have equal

Number of Bits	Trials	
10	77	
20	17	
30	915	
40	268	
50	294	
60	86	
70	67	
80	1355	
90	254	
100	569	
110	543	
120	886	
130	405	
140	80	
150	51	
160	776	
170	1292	
180	752	
190	377	
200	1	(how about that?;-)
⋮	⋮	
512	1329	
⋮	⋮	
1024	1804	

Figure 2.7. Sample execution of prime generation: number of trials running the method `isProbablePrime` of Java 2 on a Sun UltraSparc 1.

probability of being prime), this gives us a probability of $1/\ln n$ that n is prime. We may also use this approximation to estimate the region of the nth prime number. One can prove that (2.45) implies that the nth prime number is approximately $\lceil n \cdot \ln n \rceil$. In this fashion we may obtain probabilistic estimates that are practical enough to be implemented. For example, if n is a number with 200 decimal digits, then it is prime with probability $1/\ln 10^{200} \approx 1/461$. The probability of not finding a prime is therefore about $460/461$. The probability of not finding a prime in ten trials is then estimated as

$$\left(\frac{460}{461}\right)^{10}. \tag{2.46}$$

Thus we can expect to find such primes rather sooner than later. If n has 400 decimal digits, the probability of failure in k trials is $\left(\frac{921}{922}\right)^k$, and so on. In Figure 2.7, we list the number of trials and the size of primes generated for one execution of the program listed in Figure 2.8.[13]

---

[13] Since reading input from the keyboard is surprisingly difficult in Java, this program is not self-contained and relies on a class KeyboardReader.java, which you may find at the book's website.

```
import java.math.*;
import java.util.*;
public class Prime_Count {
 private static KeyboardReader keyboard = new KeyboardReader();
 public static void main(String[] args) {
   Random seed;
   BigInteger p;
   int l = keyboard.readInt("number of bits of prime:  ");
   int counter = 0;
   do {
     seed = new Random();
     p = new BigInteger(l, seed);
     counter++;
   } while (!p.isProbablePrime(50));
   System.out.println(counter + " trials to find prime " + p);
 }
}
```

Figure 2.8. A Java program that generates a prime and counts the number of
trials.

EXERCISES 2.18

1. Use your implementation of `Miller-Rabin(n,s)` to build a user interface that takes
   as input two natural numbers d_l and d_u with $d_l \leq d_u$ and produces as very likely output a prime number n whose number d of *decimal* digits satisfies $d_l \leq d \leq d_u$.

2. Show that $2^{32} + 1$ is not a prime number. (*Hint:* Since the algorithm `Miller-`
   `Rabin(n,s)` is correct for negative replies, you could use that algorithm for such a
   "proof".)

3. Run `Miller-Rabin(2**16+1,s)` for a number of different s. Although it is known
   that $2^{16} + 1$ is prime, what is the best probabilistic bound you have for that fact based
   on your program executions?

4. For a sequence $(x_n)_{n \in \mathbb{N}}$ of real numbers, $\lim_{n \to \infty} x_n$ exists and equals the real number x if and only if, for all real positive numbers ε, there exists some $n(\varepsilon) \in \mathbb{N}$ such
   that the absolute value of $x - x_n$ is less than ε for all $n \geq n(\varepsilon)$.

   (a) Prove that $\lim_{n \to \infty} 1/n = 0$.

   (b) Prove that limits are unique, provided that they exist.

5. (a) Use Theorem 2.53 to approximate the number of primes whose binary represen-
       tation has between 512 and 1024 bits.

   (b) Assume that there are about 10^{77} atoms in our universe and that this universe is
       about 10^{10} years old. Assume also that, from the beginning of time, every atom
       in the universe requires, each second, 10^9 many primes with b bits (where $512 \leq$
       $b \leq 1024$) for its own mysterious cryptographic purposes. Assuming that these
       atoms never use a prime that they (or some other atom) have used before, would
       there still be such primes available today? If so, for how long?

6. *Sophie Germaine primes* A prime number $p > 2$ is called a *Sophie Germaine*
   prime if $2 \cdot p + 1$ is also prime. A 32-bit Sophie Germaine prime is $p = 2008465313$
   with prime $2 \cdot p + 1 = 4016930627$ (found after 644 trials). It took 2253 trials to

generate a 64-bit Sophie Germaine prime $p = 10155921358726090901$ with prime $2 \cdot p + 1 = 20311842717452181803$.

(a) Compute another 32-bit Sophie Germaine prime p.

(b) Compute another 64-bit Sophie Germaine prime p.

(c) What is the largest Sophie Germaine prime you can generate (without upsetting your systems administrator)?

(d) A natural number is a *palindrome in decimal representation* if its string of decimal digits is symmetric with respect to reading it from the left or the right. For example, 131 and 314413 are each palindromes. Find a Sophie Germaine prime that is a palindrome in decimal representation.

2.4 CORRECTNESS OF RSA

We have already established an efficient framework for generating very large prime numbers. The algorithm that generates such primes has a very small probability of failing: with a sufficiently large choice of s, you are much more likely to win all state lotteries of the next year than to ever observe a failure of this algorithm. Paranoid people may even implement a double check that spots such a rare cosmic fluke; see Exercise 2.19-3 (p. 60).

Protocol 2.54 (RSA Key Generation)
Let us revisit Protocol 2.10 (p. 25) for producing an RSA public and private key for Alice.

1. Alice now knows how to generate two very large prime numbers p and q; for added security, they should be about the same size.
2. Alice already has efficient algorithms for computing the product $n \stackrel{\text{def}}{=} p \cdot q$ of two large integers.
3. Alice needs to compute an odd integer e such that

$$\gcd(e, (p-1) \cdot (q-1)) = 1. \tag{2.47}$$

A naive algorithm would try $e = 3, 5, 7, \ldots$, using Euclid's algorithm to compute $\gcd(e, (p-1) \cdot (q-1))$, and then stop the iteration with the current e as output if that gcd equals 1.[14] In Exercise 2.15-3 (p. 48), we saw that there exists a reassuring upper bound on the number of iterations of Euclid's algorithm. That same analysis applies to the extended Euclid algorithm that we need for computing the inverse of e modulo $\phi(n)$. Hence these tasks have efficient computational solutions.[15] A more sophisticated version would generate e at random until a solution is found. For example, one could randomly generate numbers e with $\max(p, q) \leq e$ and test them for primality. If such an e is prime, then it is clearly relatively prime to $p - 1$ and $q - 1$.

4. Alice solves the equation $e \cdot x = 1 \bmod (p-1) \cdot (q-1)$ for x. By Proposition 2.26 (p. 40), there exists a unique solution, d, with $1 \leq d < \phi(n)$. In the exercises, we extend Euclid's algorithm to provide an efficient procedure for computing such a d.

---

[14] This is potentially problematic, as attacks for small values of e are conceivable; see Exercise 2.21-13 (p. 72).

[15] If n has k bits, then modular multiplication is in $\mathcal{O}(k^2)$ and modular exponentiation with iterative squaring is in $\mathcal{O}(k^3)$.

5. Alice computes

$$P_A \stackrel{\text{def}}{=} \langle e, n \rangle, \qquad S_A \stackrel{\text{def}}{=} \langle d, e \rangle$$

as her RSA public and private keys, respectively.

EXERCISES 2.19

1. *Extended Euclid algorithm*   Consider the following pseudo-code for the extended algorithm of Euclid.

```
Extended_Euclid(BigInteger x, BigInteger y) {
   BigInteger d, d', r, r', s, s';
   if (y == 0) return (x,1,0);
      else {
      (d',r',s') = Extended_Euclid(y,x mod y);
      (d,r,s)    = (d',s',r' - floorint(x/y) * s');
      return (d,r,s);
   }
}
```

The function floorint(x) computes $\lfloor x \rfloor$ from Definition 2.13 (p. 27). Prove: For all $x, y \in \mathbb{Z}$, the program call Extended_Euclid(x,y) terminates and its result (d,r,s) satisfies

$$\gcd(x, y) = d = r \cdot x + s \cdot y. \tag{2.48}$$

2. Consider the following pseudo-code for a program Linear(a,b,n):

```
Linear(BigInteger a, BigInteger b, BigInteger n) {
   BigInteger d, x', y', x0;
   (d,x',y') = Extended_Euclid(a,n)
   if (b mod d == 0) {
      x0 = x' * (b / d) mod n;
      for (int i = 0; i <= d-1; ++i) {
         printout x0 + i * (n / d) mod n;
      } else
      printout ''no solutions'';
   }
}
```

For any $a, b \in \mathbb{Z}$ and $n \in \mathbb{N} \setminus \{1\}$, show that this program terminates and prints out all solutions to

$$a \cdot x = b \bmod n, \tag{2.49}$$

assuming this equation has any solutions. Show also that the program behaves correctly if no solutions exist.

3. After Alice has generated two large "prime numbers" – according to the algorithm based on Miller-Rabin(n,s) – what precaution could she take to ensure that the numbers p and q work as expected, at the very least for a specific message (e.g., a secret key she wants to share with Bob)?

4. For the RSA encryption system:
   (a) What is the smallest possible value you could choose for e?
   (b) If $e \stackrel{\text{def}}{=} 2^{16} + 1$, how many multiplications modulo n does the computation of a cipher-text $P_A(M)$ require?

5. The RSA cryptosystem is based on the fact that n is the product of two very large prime numbers. Discuss to what extent you could redefine such systems if n were to be the product of *more* than two very large prime numbers – say, $n = p \cdot q \cdot r$. Your discussion should include aspects of definition, correctness, efficiency, and possible attacks.

6. Consider the RSA keys $P_A = \langle e, n \rangle$ and $S_A = \langle d, n \rangle$, where $n = p \cdot q$ for primes p and q. It is possible that the encryption of the plain-text fragment $M \in \mathbb{Z}_n$ results in M again. For example, for $p = 11$, $q = 5$, and $e = 3$, we have $P_A(M) = M^3 \mod 55 = M$ for nine numbers between 0 and 54, namely 0, 1, 10, 11, 21, 34, 44, 45, 54.
   (a) Can you find an expression in terms of e, p, and q that computes the number of $M \in \mathbb{Z}_n$ for which $M^e \mod n = M$?
   (b) Can you say why, for realistic sizes of the parameters p and q, the answer to (a) is not more of a security concern to RSA than, say, the assumption that a random number $r \in \mathbb{Z}$ is a unit modulo n?

7. Complete your implementation of the RSA public-key encryption such that your program allows a user to re-generate a pair of RSA public and private keys on demand.

8. Suppose that Alice uses the prime numbers $p = 1699$ and $q = 1999$ for generating RSA private and public keys.
   (a) Compute an RSA public key $\langle e, n \rangle$ for Alice such that $e \geq 3$.
   (b) For your choice of e, compute the resulting private key $\langle d, n \rangle$.
   (c) Encrypt the message $M = 3297415$ and verify that $S_A(P_A(M))$ equals M.
   (d) What suggestion do you have for handling messages that are bigger than n?

9. *RSA-based pseudo-random number generator*   One may design (slow) pseudo-random number generators whose security is based on that of the RSA encryption scheme. Assume that Alice has already generated two large primes p, q and that her corresponding RSA public key is $P_A \stackrel{\text{def}}{=} \langle e, n \rangle$. If a trusting Bob wants to generate a pseudo-random sequence of bits $b_0, b_1, b_2, \ldots$ from Alice's public key, he chooses a *random seed* $x_0 \in \mathbb{N}$ with $1 < x_0 < n$. He computes b_i as the least significant bit of the binary representation of

$$x_{i+1} \stackrel{\text{def}}{=} P_A(x_i). \tag{2.50}$$

   (a) Use your implementation of RSA encryption along with the technique of iterative squaring to implement a pseudo-random number generator based on (2.50).
   (b) What is the longest possible initial sequence of the bit sequence $b_0, b_1, b_2, \ldots$ that does not show any periodic output, and why is this number of interest?

10. *RSA-based hash function*   One may use RSA public-key encryption to build a (slow) one-way hash function. Alice generates a pair of RSA keys as before: Let p and q be large primes and $P_A \stackrel{\text{def}}{=} \langle e, n \rangle$, where $n \stackrel{\text{def}}{=} p \cdot q$ and $\gcd(e, (p-1) \cdot (q-1)) = 1$. If M is a message, then the hash of M is defined as

$$h(M) \stackrel{\text{def}}{=} M^e \mod n; \tag{2.51}$$

that is, $h(M)$ is simply the cipher-text $P_A(M)$. If Alice "throws away" p, q, and her private key $S_A \overset{\text{def}}{=} \langle d, n \rangle$, or if she never computes S_A in the first place, then breaking the hash means breaking the RSA encryption system. Unfortunately, this method is rather slow compared to others.

(a) Nonetheless, you are asked to implement it. The algorithm should have a message M as its only input and the hash value, $h(M)$, as its only output.

(b) Hash functions have important characteristics, listed as H1–H4 in Section 2.1.0.2 (p. 21). Discuss to what extent your implementation satisfies these criteria.

11. Suppose that an operating system stores passwords PW as hashed values h(PW). During log-in, the user enters a message M as the password, which should verify his identity and authority of access. The system then computes $h(M)$ and allows access if and only if $h(M)$ equals h(PW).

(a) Assume that the user has access to the hashed values of user passwords as well as knowledge of (and access to) the hash function being used. Which properties of H1–H4 (p. 21) are required to ensure that a user could not launch a log-in attack?

(b) Discuss what security measures are required for handling the storage of hashed passwords.

12. **Knapsack problems and PKCs**   A *knapsack problem* is a pair $\langle s, \langle i_1, \ldots, i_n \rangle \rangle$, where s and i_j are in $\mathbb{N}$. We call s the *sum* of the problem. A *solution* to this problem is a bit vector $b_1 b_2 \ldots b_n$ such that

$$s = b_1 \cdot i_1 + b_2 \cdot i_2 + \cdots + b_n \cdot i_n. \tag{2.52}$$

We call such a problem *super-increasing* if $i_1 + \cdots + i_k < i_{k+1}$ for all $k = 1, 2, \ldots, n - 1$, that is, if each item i_j is greater than the sum of all previous items.

(a) Verify or refute that 1011001011 is a solution to the knapsack problem

$$\langle 1864, \langle 21, 56, 7, 1234, 345, 3, 456, 935, 35, 111 \rangle \rangle.$$

(b) Show that the super-increasing knapsack problem

$$\langle 341864, \langle 2, 11, 23, 65, 123, 4567, 65432 \rangle \rangle$$

has a solution.

(c) Does the super-increasing knapsack problem

$$\langle 341864, \langle 3, 11, 23, 65, 123, 4567, 65432 \rangle \rangle$$

have a solution?

(d) Design and implement an algorithm that (i) decides whether a super-increasing knapsack problem has a solution and (ii) returns a solution if there is one.

(e) One can use knapsack problems for an implementation of the public-key cryptographic scheme. (This proposal to PKC has been broken, though, and is completely unsecure, but it's educational to see that the idea of PKC has other mathematical realizations.) Let $\langle i_1, \ldots, i_m \rangle$ be a super-increasing sequence that functions as the private key S_A. Choose n at random but bigger than the sum of all i_j, and choose a random k such that $\gcd(k, n) = 1$. The public key P_A is then the sequence $\langle i'_1, \ldots, i'_m \rangle$, where

$$i'_j \overset{\text{def}}{=} i_j \cdot k \bmod n. \tag{2.53}$$

Given a message M as a bit vector, partition M into blocks of m bits, padding the final block with random bits if necessary. Each block determines a sum s according to the sequence $\langle i'_1, \ldots, i'_m \rangle$. The encrypted message $P_A(M)$ is defined as the concatenation of all these sums. For decryption, Alice computes k^{-1}, the multiplicative inverse of k modulo n, and multiplies each segment of the encrypted message with $k^{-1} \bmod n$.

(i) Consider the super-increasing sequence

$$\langle 2, 11, 34, 37, 43, 56, 61, 67, 78, 123 \rangle,$$

where n equals 1999 and k is 239. Encrypt the message 1011011011011000\\ 11110100111001 and verify that its decryption recovers the original message.

(ii) Explain why this scheme works correctly. Explain which parts of this scheme are secret. What implicit assumptions do we make if we deem this scheme to be secure?

Our discussion of the RSA encryption scheme leaves two concerns open. We still need to show that RSA encryption and decryption are mutually inverse, and we must address possible security concerns about this scheme.

Proposition 2.55 (Correctness of RSA)
The encryption and decryption algorithms determined by the RSA keys $P_A \stackrel{\text{def}}{=} \langle e, n \rangle$ and $S_A \stackrel{\text{def}}{=} \langle d, n \rangle$ result in mutually inverse transformations of the finite set $\{0, 1, 2, \ldots, n-1\}$, the domain of messages.

Proof Given a message $M \in \{0, 1, 2, \ldots, n-1\}$, recall that

$$
\begin{aligned}
P_A(S_A(M)) &= P_A(M^d \bmod n) \\
&= (M^d \bmod n)^e \bmod n \\
&= M^{d \cdot e} \bmod n.
\end{aligned}
\tag{2.54}
$$

Similarly,

$$S_A(P_A(M)) = M^{d \cdot e} \bmod n.$$

Thus it suffices to show that $M^{d \cdot e} = M \bmod n$, which is clearly the case if $M = 0$. Otherwise, since $d \cdot e = 1 \bmod (p-1) \cdot (q-1)$, we have some $k \in \mathbb{Z}$ with

$$M^{d \cdot e} = M^{1+k \cdot (p-1)} = M^1 \cdot (M^k)^{p-1} = M^1 \cdot 1 = M \bmod p$$

by Fermat's theorem. Similarly, we have

$$M^{d \cdot e} = M \bmod q.$$

By the Chinese remainder theorem, we obtain $M^{d \cdot e} = M \bmod n$ as $n = p \cdot q$ and $\gcd(p, q) = 1$. $\qquad\square$

EXERCISES 2.20

1. Consider the parameters from Example 2.12 (p. 26).
   (a) Verify that the decryption of each block of C in (2.10) recovers the corresponding block in (2.9).
   (b) Encrypt the entire message M, viewed as an integer, and check whether you recover M after decrypting the resulting number.
2. Prove that the RSA encryption scheme is still correct if the private key d is computed such that

$$d \cdot e = 1 \bmod \mathrm{lcm}(p - 1, q - 1),$$

using the generalized version of Euler's theorem that was proved in Exercise 2.16-5(b) (p. 51).[16]

2.5 SECURITY OF RSA

The question of how secure is the RSA public-key encryption scheme presumes that we already have a clear concept of what we mean by "RSA" and "security". Are we considering an entire RSA cryptosystem (with a network of agents and keys to be managed), or an implementation of the RSA decryption and encryption tasks, or are we merely studying the security of the mathematical RSA encryption function based on an agent's public key? Clearly, what we mean by "RSA" affects – but does not completely determine – what we mean by "security". For example, if we study the RSA encryption function

$$f : \{2, 3, \ldots, n-1\} \to \{2, 3, \ldots, n-1\}, \quad f(x) = x^e \bmod n, \tag{2.55}$$

associated with a public key, we could call this function secure if M cannot be recovered from the resulting cipher-text $f(M)$ alone, even if one could produce and study a large collection of cipher-texts. Note that this property implies that the secret key cannot be recovered from the repeated use of f, for we have an efficient way of computing the left inverse of f given the secret key d. *Semantic security,* on the other hand, is much more demanding in that it should be impossible to compute *any* information about M. In particular, one should not even be able to compute a single bit of M. We hasten to point out that RSA encryption as such is not semantically secure. Given $f(M)$, one may compute *some* information about M – namely, Jacobi(M,n) (see Exercise 2.17-8, p. 56). Random padding of messages can often achieve semantic security, but such padding must be done with care. Randomized PKCs, such as the one in Exercise 2.7-9 (p. 34), are much closer to realizing semantic security. For a realistic and efficient implementation, see Chapter 5. The security of RSA may also depend on whether it is used for encryption or as a digital signature scheme, and we will see attacks for each of these tasks.

In summary, a sensible security analysis and its quantitative and qualitative assessments ought to be relative to our understanding of "RSA" and "security". In this section, we mainly study RSA as the RSA encryption function (2.55) without knowledge of the

---

[16] The definition of $\mathrm{lcm}(a, b)$ can be found in the appendix (Definition A.1, p. 259).

corresponding private key. To this day, none of the publicly known attacks present a fatal blow to RSA in that sense; rather, they suggest proper use of the RSA scheme and provide strong evidence that achieving its secure implementation is far from trivial, as demonstrated in Chapter 5.

One popular way of assessing security is to say that something is at least as secure as something else. This can be done for RSA encryption and relates it to other, well-studied computational problems.

Proposition 2.56 (Factoring Attack)
If there is an efficient algorithm that factors all nonprime numbers, then there is an efficient algorithm that invariably breaks the RSA public-key encryption scheme.

Proof Let Factor(n) be an efficient program that returns a factor k of n in case n is not prime. We sketch informally how to use Factor(n) to design an efficient program Breaking_RSA(e,n) that takes as input an agent's RSA public key pair $\langle e, n \rangle$ and computes her private key pair $\langle d, n \rangle$; of course, the program only needs to return the value of d. The algorithm initially calls Factor(n) to get a factor k of n. But then

$$(p - 1) \cdot (q - 1) = (k - 1) \cdot ((n/k) - 1) \tag{2.56}$$

and we can compute the right-hand side. Since the agent's public key $\langle e, n \rangle$ is known, we may compute the unique solution of $e \cdot d = 1 \bmod (p - 1) \cdot (q - 1)$, for we know e and $(p - 1) \cdot (q - 1)$, the latter from (2.56). Thus we know the private key $\langle d, n \rangle$. □

This result – saying that breaking the RSA encryption cannot be harder than factoring very large integers – is useful because it provides some insight into the difficulty of the problem, but it is hardly the sort of thing that reassures CEOs of financial institutions whose sensitive transactions depend on RSA public-key cryptography. "If one can break X, then one can also break Y" is a far cry from the desired "nobody can break Y", especially if it is open whether X can be broken at all. The problem of factoring large integers has been studied intensely. The recent and steady improvement of computing power, combined with the refinement of existing factorization techniques and the invention of novel ones, has resulted in tremendous progress. At the time of this writing, it seems possible to factor an RSA modulus of about 400 to 600 binary digits, although with quite some computational effort.[17] But at present, it is also not known to what extent the difficulty of factoring implies security of the RSA cryptosystem. The particular challenge of factoring large integers was addressed in March 1991 by RSA Data Security, Inc.[18] to monitor the state of the art in factoring large integers. There are variations of the RSA PKC that are *proven secure,* meaning that one can show the converse of Proposition 2.56; if such a system is broken, then one can factor its modulus. Although this allows us to measure the mathematical security of such systems against the factoring problem, if leaves aside security concerns of concrete implementations and compares a system's security to that of an open problem.

---

[17] See Attack 2.60 in Section 2.6 (p. 73).
[18] www.rsa.com/rsalabs/html/factoring.html

Even though p and q may be large enough to suggest security, care must be taken. For example, if $p - 1$ has no prime factor larger than r, then n can be factored in time less than r^3. The good news, as far as integer factorization is concerned, is that we seem to be able to manage the improvement of factorization methods and computing power by increasing the key size appropriately (e.g., by letting $p \cdot q$ have about 1024 binary digits). For general RSA PKCs, the converse of Proposition 2.56 is an open question: Assuming that one can efficiently break the RSA function f in (2.55), can one derive from this an efficient algorithm for factoring its parameter n? What *is* known is that the computation of the private key and the factoring of n are equivalent problems. This is significant because it means the exposure of a secret key necessitates the re-instantiation of the entire RSA system with new parameters.

However, the success of an attack may come not from solving hard computational problems but rather from exploiting a poor choice of RSA parameters or by allowing a certain behavior when implementing the RSA cryptosystem. Blinding is an example of the latter.

Attack 2.57 (Blinding)
Consider an RSA digital signature key pair $S_A = \langle n, d \rangle$ and $P_A = \langle n, e \rangle$ for Alice, and assume that Marvin wants to make Alice sign an unfavorable prenuptial contract $M \in \mathbb{Z}_n$. Marvin is wise enough not to present the plain contract M to Alice, so he cunningly picks a random $r \in \mathbb{Z}_n$ and computes

$$M' \overset{\text{def}}{=} r^e \cdot M \bmod n$$

using Alice's public signature key. He then asks Alice to sign the random-looking M'. If Alice is naive enough to do so, then Marvin obtains

$$S' \overset{\text{def}}{=} (M')^d \bmod n$$

and can compute

$$S \overset{\text{def}}{=} S' \cdot r^{-1} \bmod n.$$

He may then claim that S is Alice's digital signature of M, for

$$S^e = (S')^e \cdot (r^e)^{-1} = (M')^{de} \cdot (r^e)^{-1} = (r^e \cdot M) \cdot (r^e)^{-1} = M \bmod n. \tag{2.57}$$

Is is somewhat misleading to describe blinding as an attack. If agents don't sign random messages, this attack can be avoided. Signing random messages actually turns into a useful technique – for example, to ensure *anonymity of signatures* that are used for electronic cash transactions.

Another attack, due to M. Wiener, can be mounted if the private-key exponent d is small rather than randomly large. This is unfortunate because decryption based on iterative squaring takes time linear in $\log d$, so the smaller the d, the faster we can decrypt a message. In smartcards with power constraints, this creates a genuine tradeoff between security and realizability.

Attack 2.58 (Low Private-Key Exponent)
Let $n = p \cdot q$ with $q < p < 2q$ and $d < \frac{1}{3} \cdot n^{1/4}$. Given the key pair $S_A = \langle n, d \rangle$ and $P_A = \langle n, e \rangle$, one can recover d efficiently from the public key $P_A = \langle n, e \rangle$.

Proof We sketch the argument and leave some of the details to Exercise 2.21-14. An attacker knows n and e but does not know $\phi(n)$, which equals $(p-1) \cdot (q-1)$. The sought-after secret key d is known to satisfy $e \cdot d = 1 \bmod \phi(n)$. Therefore, there exists some $k \in \mathbb{Z}$ with $e \cdot d - k \cdot \phi(n) = 1$. Using division over the reals, we obtain

$$\left| \frac{e}{\phi(n)} - \frac{k}{d} \right| = \frac{1}{d \cdot \phi(n)}, \tag{2.58}$$

with k, d, and $\phi(n)$ as unknowns. The idea is now to approximate $\phi(n)$ with n and to turn (2.58) into a continued fraction expansion of the approximation e/n. Clearly,

$$\phi(n) = n - (p + q - 1).$$

By our previous assumptions, we can show

$$p + q - 1 < 3 \cdot \sqrt{n}. \tag{2.59}$$

Combining these two facts yields $|n - \phi(n)| < 3 \cdot \sqrt{n}$. Approximating $\phi(n)$ with n in (2.58), we obtain

$$\left| \frac{e}{n} - \frac{k}{d} \right| = \left| \frac{e \cdot d - k \cdot \phi(n) - k \cdot n + k \cdot \phi(n)}{n \cdot d} \right| \leq \frac{3 \cdot k}{d \cdot \sqrt{n}}. \tag{2.60}$$

Since $k \cdot \phi(n) = e \cdot d - 1 < e \cdot d$ and $e < \phi(n)$, we infer $k < d$, but d is assumed to be less than $\frac{1}{3} \cdot n^{1/4}$. Thus

$$\left| \frac{e}{n} - \frac{k}{d} \right| \leq \frac{1}{2 \cdot d^2}. \tag{2.61}$$

The number of fractions k/d satisfying (2.61) with $d < \frac{1}{3} \cdot n^{1/4}$ is bounded by $\log n$. Indeed, one need only compute that number of expansions of the continued fraction for e/n until k/d, and therefore d, is recovered. $\qquad \square$

One may avert this attack by replacing e with $e + l \cdot \phi(n)$ for some large integer l. This does not alter encryption as such but does, unfortunately, increase encryption time. In Exercise 2.21-14 (p. 72), we indicate how one may circumvent such an attack without giving up small values of d. In Exercise 2.21-7 (p. 70), you are asked to demonstrate the following.

Attack 2.59 (Nontrivial Square-Root Attack)
If one can find a nontrivial square root of a modulus n that is used for a pair of RSA keys $P_A = \langle e_A, n \rangle$ and $S_A = \langle d_A, n \rangle$, then one can efficiently compute the secret key S_A.

The most serious (and successful) attacks are those that exploit implementation aspects of the RSA encryption scheme. For example, one may use the Chinese remainder theorem to reduce the generation of an RSA digital signature by a factor of 4. Given the private-key exponent d, let

$$d_p \overset{\text{def}}{=} d \bmod p - 1,$$

$$d_q \overset{\text{def}}{=} d \bmod q - 1.$$

To sign a message $M \in \mathbb{Z}_n$, compute

$$C_p \stackrel{\text{def}}{=} M^{d_p} \bmod p,$$
$$C_q \stackrel{\text{def}}{=} M^{d_q} \bmod q.$$

By the Chinese remainder theorem, the signature $C = M^d \bmod n$ equals

$$t_p \cdot C_p + t_q \cdot C_q \bmod n, \tag{2.62}$$

where

$$t_p = 1 \bmod p, \quad t_p = 0 \bmod q,$$
$$t_q = 0 \bmod p, \quad t_q = 1 \bmod q.$$

Given a single random fault – caused, for instance, by a hardware flaw or some electromagnetic interference – one of the two "signatures", say C_p, will be incorrectly computed as C_p'. An attacker who knows M may realize that $(C')^e \neq M \bmod n$, where C' is computed according to (2.62) but with the flawed signature C_p' instead of C_p. Using (2.62), we see that $(C')^e \neq M \bmod p$ and $(C')^e = M \bmod q$. Thus the computation of $\gcd((C')^e - M, n)$ reveals a factor of n. Note that this attack can be averted by randomly padding the message prior to signing it.

A class of very disturbing attacks are those that measure physical quantities of an encryption device and manage to observe statistical correlations (or their absence) that reveal information about the parameters of the underlying cryptosystem. P. Kocher used such an approach to expose the private key of a smartcard used for RSA signatures, exploiting the knowledge that the card used iterative squaring. Thus the program flow at the ith iteration depends on the value of the ith bit of d. He managed to find two families of timing variables, each ranging over the same family of random messages that were supplied to the card to be signed. These attacks are so disturbing because they can hardly be ruled out, or predicted, by mathematical models or even by a flow analysis of their implementation programs. We return to this important topic in Chapter 6.

EXERCISES 2.21

1. Justify all equations in (2.57).
2. Discuss to what extent the RSA cryptosystem satisfies the criteria of the two bullets on page 16 and the requirement expressed in Remark 2.3.
3. In Attack 2.57:
   (a) Explain why Marvin must compute $r^{-1} \bmod n$.
   (b) How could Marvin compute Alice's secret key if r were not a unit in $\mathbb{Z}_n^*$?
4. Devise an algorithm that can compute an RSA private key from its public key, assuming that there exists an efficient program `Euler(n)` that computes Euler's totient function $n \mapsto \phi(n) \colon \mathbb{N} \to \mathbb{N}$.
5. *Totient of prime factorization*   Exercise 4 is a direct consequence of a more general fact and Proposition 2.56. Follow the outline presented next as (a)–(e) to show that one can construct an efficient algorithm for computing $n \mapsto \phi(n) \colon \mathbb{N} \to \mathbb{N}$ if there

exists an efficient algorithm `PrimeFactorization(n)` that computes the unique prime factorization of all natural numbers n. Let $n \in \mathbb{N}$. Recall that $\phi(n)$ equals the size of the set $\{a \in \mathbb{Z} \mid 1 \leq a \leq n - 1,\ \gcd(a, n) = 1\}$. Lemma A.15 (p. 266) shows that

$$\phi(p^k) = p^{k-1} \cdot (p - 1) \tag{2.63}$$

for all prime numbers p and $k \in \mathbb{N}$.

(a) Let $n = p_1^{\alpha_1} \cdot p_2^{\alpha_2} \cdots p_n^{\alpha_m}$ be the unique prime factorization of n. Use the Chinese remainder theorem to prove that

$$\phi(n) = \phi(p_1^{\alpha_1}) \cdot \phi(p_2^{\alpha_2}) \cdots \phi(p_m^{\alpha_m}). \tag{2.64}$$

(b) Explain how you could obtain an efficient algorithm for complete prime factorization, `PrimeFactorization(n)`, given an efficient algorithm `Factor(n)` for factoring n.

(c) Use equations (2.64) and (2.63) to show that

$$\phi(n) = n \cdot \prod_{p \mid n} (1 - 1/p). \tag{2.65}$$

(d) Explain how you can use an efficient algorithm for complete prime factorization, `PrimeFactorization(n)`, to derive an efficient program `Euler(n)` that computes $\phi(n)$.

(e) Use equation (2.65) to compute $\phi(2176893)$.

6. For an RSA system, anybody who knows n and $\phi(n)$ can factor n and thus expose the system.

(a) Show: Since $n = p \cdot q$ and $\phi(n) = (p - 1) \cdot (q - 1)$, we can replace q with n/p and obtain

$$p^2 - (n - \phi(n) + 1) \cdot p + n = 0, \tag{2.66}$$

a quadratic equation in p.

(b) Use a programming language with a BigInteger package to compute p when (i) n equals[19]

> 5255425353815092596650492913013091564491702892920909473368684\\
> 4176662999095494612248327785952405308208386587687522225396375\\
> 3648396734494273388351787005927348314990289956823437646104\\
> 0384815770010822649673917676492572451544539584844478305 9075\\
> 2296704690252947102767509252200518689319666511460 99712686764\\
> 6392121651,

concatenated from top to bottom, and (ii) $\phi(n)$ equals

> 5255425353815092596650492913013091564491702892920909473368684\\
> 4176662999095494612248327785952405308208386587687522225396375\\
> 3648396734494273388351787005927346640740130942126279149 79100\\
> 8988583431707756995135673244256468745878653938077830288 13781\\
> 2069182686333078392553787505188003963276505319015948118 74527\\
> 67331400.

---

[19] You may copy these numbers from the book's website.

7. Prove the statement in Attack 2.59. (*Hint:* Look at Exercise 2.17-4, p. 55.)

8. *Using $\phi(n)$ to compute inverses in $\mathbb{Z}_n^*$*
   (a) Show that $a^{\phi(n)-1} \bmod n$ is a solution to $a \cdot x = 1 \bmod n$ whenever $[a]_n \in \mathbb{Z}_n^*$.
   (b) Compute $\phi(73562181)$.
   (c) Design and implement an efficient algorithm that takes as input $n \in \mathbb{N}$, $\phi(n)$, and $a \in \mathbb{Z}$. First, the program checks whether $[a]_n \in \mathbb{Z}_n^*$. In that case, it computes an inverse of $[a]_n$ in $\mathbb{Z}_n^*$, based on the insight of Exercise 8(a). Otherwise, it reports that no such inverse exists. Compare the running time of your program to that of the algorithm `Extended_Euclid`.
   (d) Run your algorithm for $n = 73562181$ and $a = 1939$.
   (e) Run your algorithm for $n = 73562181$ and $a = 1999$.

9. Let the RSA modulus be 333603832036. The public key is 2345. The cipher-text, 93423448013, represents a 4-digit plain-text, the PIN number for the author's British bank account.[20] Compute that PIN number by (i) factoring n, (ii) computing $\phi(n)$, (iii) computing the secret key d, and (iv) decrypting 93423448013.

10. *Common modulus attack*   One may attack the RSA encryption scheme if all agents A on a network share the same value n (i.e., they share p and q) but each has different key values e_A and d_A. The attacker, Mallory, knows the public exponents e_A and e_B of agents A and B and somehow intercepted two encryptions $P_A(M)$ and $P_B(M)$ for a message M; Mallory is aware of their actual format and the fact that the two original messages are identical.
   (a) Prove: If $\gcd(e_A, e_B) = 1$, then Mallory has an efficient attack that recovers M. (*Hint:* The call `Extended_Euclid(e_A,e_B)` computes numbers $r, s \in \mathbb{Z}$ such that $r \cdot e_A + s \cdot e_B = 1$. Argue that either r or s must be negative. Assume without loss of generality that r is negative. Show that

   $$(P_A(M)^{-1})^{-r} \cdot P_B(M)^s = M \bmod n$$

   and explain why Mallory may compute $(P_A(M)^{-1})^{-r} \cdot P_B(M)^s \bmod n$ efficiently.)
   (b) Regardless of the value of $\gcd(e_A, e_B)$, can agent A compute agent B's secret key?
   (c) Apply this attack when
   • the common modulus is

       7665448606666073317684148965146276834900571307109519352921\\
       6182848689439299823;

   • the public-key exponent of Alice, e_A, is 5;
   • the public-key exponent of Bob, e_B, is 17;
   • the cipher-text $P_A(M)$ equals 323604428863968; and
   • the cipher-text $P_B(M)$ equals

       2157988634065272485199948695134643624322 6204438528.

   Compute M.

---

[20] Relax – the most you will ever get out of this exercise is credit for your homework!

11. **Signing unknown messages**   Blinding already suggests that one should be careful about signing random messages. Blinding, and a slight variation of this attack, rest on the fact that RSA encryption and decryption are *multiplicative*.

    (a) Let $P_A \stackrel{\text{def}}{=} \langle e, n \rangle$ and $S_A \stackrel{\text{def}}{=} \langle d, n \rangle$. Prove: For all $m_1, m_2 \in \{0, 1, \dots, n-1\}$ we have
    $$
    \begin{aligned}
    (m_1 \cdot m_2)^e &= m_1^e \cdot m_2^e \bmod n, \\
    (m_1 \cdot m_2)^d &= m_1^d \cdot m_2^d \bmod n.
    \end{aligned}
    \tag{2.67}
    $$

    (b) Use the fact that RSA encryption is multiplicative to prove the possibility of an attack – provided that Alice is willing to sign, using her private key $S_A = \langle d, n \rangle$, a message that she has never seen before. The attacker, Mallory, listens to the network traffic and manages to hear $C \stackrel{\text{def}}{=} S_A(M)$. She would like to recover M. (This is different from blinding, where M is known to Mallory and she seeks to obtain C.) Because Alice's modulus n is public, as part of Alice's public key $P_A = \langle e, n \rangle$, Mallory may then choose a random number r such that $r < n$ and $\gcd(r, n) = 1$.

        (i) Explain why Mallory may compute
        $$
        \begin{aligned}
        X &\stackrel{\text{def}}{=} r^e \bmod n, \\
        Y &\stackrel{\text{def}}{=} X \cdot C \bmod n, \\
        T &\stackrel{\text{def}}{=} r^{-1} \bmod n
        \end{aligned}
        \tag{2.68}
        $$
        efficiently.

        (ii) Assume that Alice is somehow willing to sign a random-looking message from Mallory with her private key and return it to Mallory. Then Mallory sends Alice the message Y, and so Alice dutifully returns
        $$
        U \stackrel{\text{def}}{=} Y^d \bmod n
        $$
        to Mallory. Use the fact that RSA encryption is multiplicative to prove that Mallory may now quickly recover M.

12. **Forgery by change of public key**   Let p and q be two large and different primes. Let M be some integer; think of M as being a legitimate message.

    (a) Prove: If Mallory knows M, p, and q, then she can choose any forged message $M' \in \mathbb{Z}$ and will be able to compute some $x \in \mathbb{N}$ such that $(M')^x = M \bmod p \cdot q$. (*Hint:* Use the Chinese remainder theorem to rewrite this equation in x as a system of two equations. Use Theorem 2.35 to rewrite these two equations as linear ones.)

    (b) Protocols based on RSA encryption may need to regulate when (and how often) agents may choose, or change, their RSA keys. For example, assume that Bob initially has the RSA keys $P_B \stackrel{\text{def}}{=} \langle e_B, n_B \rangle$ and $S_B \stackrel{\text{def}}{=} \langle d_B, n_B \rangle$ and that he is able to publish a new public key $\langle e_B', n_B \rangle$ later on. Assume further that Alice encrypts a message M using Bob's initial public key and that she then signs the result with her private key and sends the result to Bob. Using part (a), explain in detail how Bob can, for a fixed message M', compute a new public key e_B' with respect to which he can prove that Alice sent and signed message M' and not M. Would the use of hash functions prevent such an attack? Would Bob still be able to launch this attack if Alice first signed and then encrypted the message?

13. **Broadcast attack**   Using a low public-key exponent can also be a cause for concern. Consider a network with $k + 1$ agents, one of whom is Alice and with the other k agents having public keys

$$P_i = \langle 3, n_i \rangle$$

for $i = 1, 2, \ldots, k$, respectively. Alice would like to broadcast a message M, assumed to be less than any of the n_i, to all network participants. According to the RSA scheme, Alice may encrypt M as

$$C_i \stackrel{\text{def}}{=} M^3 \bmod n_i$$

for each agent i and broadcast these k cipher-texts across the network. Mallory then manages to intercept all these cipher-texts; her goal is to recover M. (These attacks remain valid if messages are padded with a fixed polynomial transformation; only randomized pads can shield against this threat.)

(a) How can Mallory achieve her goal if $\gcd(n_i, n_j) \neq 1$ for some $i \neq j$?

(b) By part (a), we may assume that n_i and n_j have no common factor whenever $i \neq j$.

   (i) Explain how Mallory can compute some $C' \in \mathbb{Z}_{n_1 \cdot n_2 \cdots n_k}$ such that

$$C' = M^3 \bmod n_1 \cdot n_2 \cdots n_k.$$

   (ii) Explain why C' equals M^3 as an integer and why this allows Mallory to recover M.

   (iii) Could Mallory recover M if she intercepted only three different cipher-texts?

(c) If the public keys are generally e_i for each agent i, how many cipher-texts would Mallory have to intercept for this attack? Would this attack still be feasible for some large e_i?

14. **Low private-key exponent**

(a) For the proof of Attack 2.58, explain in detail why (2.59), (2.60), and (2.61) hold.

(b) If n is 1024 bits long, what is the minimum number of bits that d must have in order to avoid Attack 2.58?

(c) One may avert this attack by replacing e with $e + l \cdot \phi(n)$ for some large integer l. This does not alter encryption, but alas it increases encryption time. Show: If $e + l \cdot \phi(n)$ is larger than $n^{3/4}$ then the attack cannot be carried out.

(d) Could one use the Chinese remainder theorem to allow for a large d yet still guarantee fast decryption based on small private exponents?

15. **Partial key-exposure attack**   Let $n = p \cdot q$ have $l \in \mathbb{N}$ bits with $l = 0 \bmod 4$, where $\langle e, n \rangle$ and $\langle d, n \rangle$ are the public and private RSA key, respectively. Show: If Mallory knows the least $l/4$ bits of the private-key exponent d, then she can efficiently factor n. Use a theorem (due to D. Coppersmith) stating that one can factor n efficiently given the $l/4$ least significant bits of p.

(a) Conclude that there exists some $k \in \mathbb{Z}$ with

$$e \cdot d - k \cdot (n - p - q + 1) = 1. \tag{2.69}$$

(b) Argue that k must satisfy $0 < k \leq e$, noting that $d < \phi(n)$.

(c) Show that

$$(e \cdot d) \cdot p - k \cdot p \cdot (n - p + 1) + k \cdot n = p. \tag{2.70}$$

(d) Explain why Mallory knows the value of $e \cdot d$ mod $2^{l/4}$ and why this transforms (2.70) into a quadratic equation in p for "fixed" k modulo $2^{l/4}$. (One can now solve for p mod $2^{l/4}$ for each $k \leq e$ and test whether Coppersmith's procedure returns a factor of n.)

(e) Can you give an upper bound on the number of possible candidates for p mod $2^{l/4}$?

2.6 INTEGER FACTORIZATION

We saw that RSA encryption is breakable if large integers can be factored efficiently. The converse – whether RSA public-key encryption is unbreakable if there is no efficient algorithm for factoring all large integers – is an open problem in computer science. This is one reason why security managers of financial institutions may be nervous about using the RSA scheme. The second reason is that it remains an open problem whether there is an efficient algorithm for factoring all integers. If security managers had their way, it is clear how they would like to see these problems resolved (if they ever will be!): there "ought" not exist an efficient algorithm for factoring all integers, and RSA encryption "ought" only be breakable if integers can be factored. A careful implementation of RSA encryption would then be unbreakable in principle. However, the nonexistence of an algorithm that efficiently factors *all* integers by no means rules out the existence of efficient algorithms that fail to factor many numbers but manage to "get lucky" with some others (e.g., the ones used during a particular RSA encryption session). Such algorithms exist, and we present one approach as a representative example. The power of these algorithms is illustrated by the following attack.

Attack 2.60 (Factorization of RSA-155)
There exist factorization algorithms that allow formidable attacks carried out by networks of PCs and workstations. Individual machines access a central database that stores test relations used for determining a factor of an RSA modulus. If any machine tests a relation that reveals a factor, then the attack succeeds. Tests that don't succeed will never again be processed by another machine. The fact that these tests can be done *concurrently* poses a serious threat to the secure use of RSA. Such an attack broke the RSA modulus of the 155-digit RSA Challenge in August 1999.[21] This number has 512 bits, suggesting that implementors of RSA choose a significantly larger modulus. The factoring algorithm used in the attack was the general number field sieve. The sieving took 35.7 CPU-years in total on:

- one hundred sixty 175–400-MHz SGI and Sun workstations,
- eight 250-MHz SGI Origin 2000 processors,
- one hundred twenty 300–450-MHz Pentium II PCs, and
- four 500-MHz Digital/Compaq boxes.[22]

The entire effort of breaking this number required 3.7 months (of regular calendar time).

[21] http://www.rsasecurity.com/rsalabs/challenges/factoring/rsa155.html
[22] http://www.rsasecurity.com/rsalabs/challenges/factoring/rsa155.html

The development of factorization algorithms that allow networked attacks needs to be watched and taken into account when assessing the security of cryptographic systems that depend on factorization being a hard problem.

2.6.1 Pollard's Rho Heuristic

Recall that the Miller–Rabin algorithm is provably correct if it classifies a number n as being composite. In that case, n has a nontrivial factor k; that is, $n = k \cdot l$ for $k, l \in \mathbb{N}$ and $1 < k < n$. This algorithm is of little use, however, if we need to *know* such a nontrivial factor – for example, if we mean to compute Alice's secret RSA key S_A from her public key P_A by trying to factor the modulus n. Pollard's rho heuristic is an algorithm that takes n as input and either replies with a (small) factor k of n or does not terminate; it is because of this latter possibility that we speak of a heuristic. Since this algorithm works only for small factors, it cannot be used for attacking realistic instances of RSA.

The algorithm uses randomization in that, given n, it will create a "random seed" which in turn creates a deterministic run of the algorithm with n as input. Even if the algorithm terminates, it may run too long to be practical, but experience has shown that it can be used quite successfully to find "small" prime factors and to completely factor "small" values of n. Whereas the naive sieve algorithm discussed earlier can factor numbers only up to m^2 (provided that the sieve values range up to m), Pollard's rho heuristic can improve this bound to m^4. The existence of algorithms like Pollard's is the reason why many cryptographic methods prescribe that certain prime numbers used in a scheme not be permitted to feature "small" prime factors. For example, it may be desirable to generate very large primes p and q such that $p - 1$ and $q - 1$ contain at least one prime factor larger than some specified threshold $B > 0$. To make matters worse (from the standpoint of cryptosystem security), one can use elliptic curve methods to improve the performance of Pollard's rho heuristic.

We won't discuss these more sophisticated algorithms; we focus instead on the specification of Pollard's algorithm (see Figure 2.9) and describe it informally. For a more technical discussion, see the references listed at the end of this chapter. The pseudo-code in Figure 2.9 seems somewhat enigmatic but is really not that difficult to understand. The integer variable i serves as a counter of the number of iterations (minus 1) that the while-statement has already performed. Note that the boolean guard to this while-statement is true, so this program can terminate only if it reaches stop – that is, if the computed value of d differs from 1 and n. But since the value of d is always of the form gcd(y-x,n), where gcd computes the greatest common divisor of its input, the program terminates only if the value of d is a factor of n. The remaining variables of the algorithm are x and k.

- The variable x plays the role of a random seed, randomly assigned in its initialization; during each iteration of the while-statement, the value of x is updated to $x^2 - 1$ mod n. It is helpful to think of

$$x \mapsto x^2 - 1 \bmod n$$

as a pseudo-random number generator.

```
Pollard-Rho(BigInteger n) {
// tries to compute a non-trivial factor of n
// by placing a random seed x with 2 <= x <= n - 1
// and then running a deterministic algorithm with
// x and n as parameters
int i = 1;
BigInteger d;
BigInteger x = Random(2, n - 1);
BigInteger y = x;
int k = 2;
while true {
  ++i;
  x = (x * x - 1) mod n;
  d = gcd(y - x, n);
  if (d != 1 && d != n) { printout ''one factor is:  ''  d;
          stop;
       }
    else {
       if (k = i) { y = x;
                    k = 2 * k;}
       }
    }
}
```

Figure 2.9. Pseudo-code for Pollard's rho heuristic, which may find a "small" prime factor of n or may fail to terminate.

- The variable k only takes on values that are powers of 2; if this value is 2^j and if $2^j - 1$ iterations of the while-statement have been performed (that is to say, if i and k hold the same value), then the current value of x is saved in y as the new basis for computing gcd(y-x,n).

Pollard's algorithm has a special-purpose version, the "$n - 1$" variant, that computes a prime factor p of a composite number n provided that $n - 1$ is "smooth". For details we refer to the bibliographic notes at the end of this chapter. We give a simplified introduction to elliptic curves and their associated commutative group structure in Section 4.1.2; one can use such curves to improve Pollard's rho heuristic. In this text, we use them only for a variant of the Digital Signature Standard of Section 4.1.1.

EXERCISES 2.22

1. Implement Pollard's rho heuristic in a programming language of your choice.
2. Is it safe to terminate the Pollard algorithm and report "failure" if the gcd expression computes to n? That is to say, can we then rule out that the program run ever reaches stop?
3. Implement an improved Pollard heuristic that asks the user which constant $a \in \mathbb{Z}$ to use for the "pseudo-random" function $x \mapsto x^2 + a \mod n$. Run some inputs with this version and verify that, in general, the success of the algorithm – as well as the computed factor – depend on the choice of a.

4. Run Pollard's heuristic on some "small" integers (between 20 and 60 digits; use only numbers for which the Miller–Rabin algorithm has replied that they are definitely not prime). Here are some possible numbers to try (from a certain number onward, Pollard's method may take a *long* time, or fail):[23]

(a) 7928360769247;

(b) 229458832697429029;

(c) 133466331868482001;

(d) 152657547690783791;

(e) 2064298239197436113;

(f) 7880980433793621001145753;

(g) 4458768158210990847362498729;

(h) 287611983724618008231029395911280447;

(i) 1117737631180939833405271756103468685041851489741;

(j) the number

3921128526850394342784613447682081729654402134853385338997210750\\
8298663541659589829967

(this number has 82 digits).

2.7 OTHER KEY-EXCHANGE REALIZATIONS BASED ON DISCRETE LOGARITHMS

The key-exchange mechanisms described in this section are the basis for methods used in several commercial products, such as Pretty Good Privacy (PGP) for electronic mail, the AT&T 3600 Telephone Security Device, and certain cryptographic cards. In Definition 2.33 we called t a *logarithm* of x in $\mathbb{Z}_n^*$, with respect to a primitive root g as a base, if t is the minimal value in $\mathbb{N} \cup \{0\}$ that satisfies $x = g^t \bmod n$; we denoted t as $\log_{(n,g)}(x)$.

2.7.1 Diffie–Hellman Key-Exchange System

We now describe the original Diffie–Hellman key-exchange system.

Protocol 2.61 (Diffie–Hellman Key Exchange)

Let q be a big and somehow "secure"[24] prime. Alice and Bob want to agree on a shared key; for example, they may plan to use this key for initializing a symmetric encryption algorithm for the secure exchange of large amounts of data along an unsecure channel. The key they generate is a "random" element of $\mathbb{Z}_q^*$:

1. Alice generates a random number a with $2 < a < q - 1$, which she keeps secret;
2. Alice computes $g^a \bmod q$ and publishes this result, where g is a known primitive root of $\mathbb{Z}_q^*$;
3. Bob generates a random number b with $2 < b < q - 1$, which he keeps secret;

---

[23] You may copy these numbers from the book's website.

[24] In all these protocols, such a prime number should make it difficult for existing heuristic algorithms that attempt to compute discrete logarithms to be successful in $\mathbb{Z}_q^*$.

4. Bob computes $g^b \bmod q$ and publishes that result;
5. Bob and Alice agree on sharing the key $g^{a \cdot b} \bmod q$.

It should be intuitively clear that the security of schemes based on discrete logarithms in finite groups rests on the choice of system parameters. In this case, we have to choose "good" g and q. Minimal requirements for such choices are that $[g]_q$ generate a "large" subgroup of $\mathbb{Z}_q^*$, ideally the entire group. This can be achieved if we are somehow able to compute a primitive root for $\mathbb{Z}_q^*$. In any event, these choices must be informed by the state-of-the-art algorithms that attempt to compute discrete logarithms over finite groups. This protocol is also subject to a man-in-the-middle attack, whose description is relegated to the next exercise.

EXERCISE 2.23

1. If Mallory succeeds in convincing Bob that Alice published $g^{a'} \bmod q$ and also persuades Alice to believe that Bob published $g^{b'} \bmod q$, then Mallory could end up establishing the key $g^{a \cdot b'} \bmod p$ with Alice and the key $g^{a' \cdot b}$ with Bob. Mallory is thus positioned for a man-in-the-middle attack. Explain how that attack works and what it can accomplish for Mallory.

2.7.2 Station-to-Station Protocol

We can avert the attack of Exercise 2.23-1 by assuming that Alice and Bob have digital signing schemes and certificates $\mathtt{Cert}(A)$ and $\mathtt{Cert}(B)$ from a trusted authority.

Protocol 2.62 (Station-to-Station Protocol)

1. Alice generates a random number a with $2 < a < q - 1$, computes $g^a \bmod q$, and sends the result to Bob.
2. Bob chooses a random number b with $2 < b < q - 1$, signs $\langle b, g^a \bmod q \rangle$ with S_B, and uses his certificate $\mathtt{Cert}(B)$ to send the triple

   $$\langle \mathtt{Cert}(B), g^b \bmod q, \mathsf{S}_B(\langle b, g^a \bmod q \rangle) \rangle$$

   to Alice.
3. Alice verifies Bob's signature using Bob's public key P_B and then verifies his certificate through the trusted authority. In turn, she signs $\langle g^a \bmod q, g^b \bmod q \rangle$ with her secret key S_A and uses her certificate to send the pair $\langle \mathtt{Cert}(A), \mathsf{S}_A(\langle g^a \bmod q, g^b \bmod q \rangle) \rangle$ to Bob.
4. Bob can now verify Alice's certificate and her signature in a similar way.

2.7.3 Massey–Omura Cryptosystem

Protocol 2.63 (Massey–Omura Cryptosystem)
This protocol presumes that all users of a network have previously agreed on using a very large "secure" prime number q. Each agent A secretly selects a random integer e_A with $1 < e_A < q - 1$ such that

$$\gcd(e_A, q - 1) = 1$$

and then uses the algorithm `Extended_Euclid` to compute a multiplicative inverse d_A of $e_A \bmod q - 1$. Messages are viewed as elements of $\mathbb{Z}_q$. If Alice wants to send a message M to Bob, then:

1. she computes $M^{e_A} \bmod q$ and sends this to Bob;
2. since Bob knows neither d_A nor e_A, he cannot recover M, but he takes $M^{e_A} \bmod q$ and raises it to the e_Bth power and passes the resulting $M^{e_A \cdot e_B} \bmod q$ on to Alice;
3. Alice takes $M^{e_A \cdot e_B} \bmod q$, raises it to the d_Ath power, and returns the resulting number to Bob;
4. Bob receives this number and raises it to the d_Bth power to retrieve M.

In Exercise 2.24-3 (p. 79), you are asked to discuss why this protocol works as advertised.

2.7.4 ElGamal Cryptosystem

Protocol 2.64 (ElGamal Cryptosystem)
The setup for this cryptosystem is similar to the one of Massey–Omura. Each agent on the network shares a large, "secure" prime number q and an element $g \bmod q$ that generates a large and "secure" subgroup in $\mathbb{Z}_q^*$. Messages are again simply elements of $\mathbb{Z}_q$. Each agent A generates a key pair by (i) picking

$$S_A \stackrel{\text{def}}{=} a_A,$$

where a_A is a random number between 2 and $q - 1$ that A keeps secret, and (ii) setting

$$P_A \stackrel{\text{def}}{=} g^{a_A} \bmod q$$

as the public key. If Bob wants to send Alice a message M, then:

1. he chooses an integer k at random, and
2. he sends Alice the pair $\langle g^k \bmod q, \ M \cdot g^{a_A \cdot k} \bmod q \rangle$;
3. since Alice knows a_A, she can efficiently raise the first component, $g^k \bmod q$, of that message to the a_Ath power. Then she can take the resulting number d and divide the second component, $M \cdot g^{a_A \cdot k} \bmod q$, of Bob's message by d to recover M.

At the time of this writing, there are no known efficient algorithms for computing x from a constant fraction of its bits and the value $g^x \bmod n$. Thus – unlike the RSA cryptosystem – these schemes are not (yet) subject to partial-key exposure attacks; see Exercise 2.21-15 (p. 72) for details.

EXERCISES 2.24

1. In the Diffie–Hellman key-exchange protocol:
   (a) Explain how Alice and Bob manage to compute the shared key in step 5 of the protocol, based on their knowledge after completion of step 4.

(b) Explain how an eavesdropper (Mallory) can compute the key that Bob and Alice share in the end, provided that Mallory (i) can listen to the communication traffic between Alice and Bob and (ii) has a feasible algorithm for computing discrete logarithms in $\mathbb{Z}_q^*$. In particular, Mallory knows which g and q Bob and Alice have agreed to use.

2. Make changes to the station-to-station protocol so that it includes *key confirmation*. This means not only that Alice and Bob securely exchanged some key but also that they know for certain that both obtained the same key.

3. In the Massey–Omura cryptosystem:

(a) Explain the mathematics behind this protocol. That is, what mathematical properties guarantee that Bob actually recovers M in the end?

(b) In step 2, why do you think it's important that Bob does not know e_A or d_A, given that Bob and Alice communicate all this information over a public and unsecure channel?

(c) Explain how Mallory, who has the same capabilities as in Exercise 1, can defeat this protocol. (*Hint:* You may need to rely on Theorem 2.35, p. 44.)

4. In the ElGamal cryptosystem:

(a) Keeping in mind that Bob does not know Alice's secret key e_A, explain why he can nonetheless generate the message pair $\langle g^k \bmod q, M \cdot g^{a_A \cdot k} \bmod q \rangle$.

(b) Explain how an eagerly listening Mallory with the same capabilities as in Exercise 1 can defeat this protocol and compute Alice's and Bob's shared secret key.

2.8 BIBLIOGRAPHIC NOTES

Diffie and Hellman (1976) put forward the idea of public-key cryptography; in response to that work, Rivest, Shamir and Adleman (1978) proposed the RSA encryption scheme as an actual and feasible realization of these ideas. At the time, it was not publicly known that J. Ellis from the Communications-Electronic Security Group (a British government agency) had already described very similar ideas in internal reports in 1974 and 1976, because these documents were classified until December 1997. Shortly after the work of Ellis, C. Cocks and M. Williamson found practical implementations. For details on that story, we highly recommend Singh (2000). The public-key system of ElGamal, along with a scheme for digital signatures, is described in ElGamal (1985). A more detailed account of the Miller–Rabin algorithm and other randomized algorithms for primality testing can be found in Motvani and Raghavan (1995). A good general source for computational number theory is Bach and Shallit (1996). An online source of basic explanations of integer factorization algorithms (e.g., quadratic sieve algorithms) and additional scientific references is Eric's Treasure Troves of Science.[25] The textbook of Cormen, Leiserson, and Rivest (1990) also serves as a reference for a host of important algorithms and their analysis. For a comprehensive textbook on modern computational methods in algebra, see von zur Gathen and Gerhard (1999). The section in this chapter on the security of RSA is largely inspired by the survey paper of Boneh (1999). The original paper on the random

---

[25] http://www.treasure-troves.com/

number generator described in Exercise 2.7-8 is Blum, Blum, and Shub (1986). A survey article on discrete logarithms in finite fields and their significance in cryptography is Oldyzko (1994). The World Wide Web site[26] maintained by R. Hofer discusses encryption systems based on elliptic curves. E. W. Weisstein has collected a nice tutorial on such issues.[27] For a thorough mathematical presentation of elliptic curves in cryptography, see Blake, Seroussi, and Smart (1999).

[26] www.sbox.tu-graz.ac.at/home/j/jonny/projects/crypto/asymmetr/ecdlp/ecdlp.htm
[27] www.treasure-troves.com/math/LenstraEllipticCurveMethod.html

CHAPTER 3

Symmetric-Key Cryptography

3.1 STREAM CIPHERS

Symmetric cryptographic algorithms are often classified and divided into *stream ciphers* and *block ciphers*. In a stream cipher, the atomic computation step is the encryption of a single symbol. For example, if the input is a plain-text bit stream

$$m_0, m_1, m_2, \ldots,$$

then a stream cipher will first encrypt m_0, then m_1, and so forth. That way, one obtains a cipher-text bit stream

$$c_0, c_1, c_2, \ldots.$$

Note that the encryption of m_j may depend on any of the symbols m_i ($0 \leq i \leq j$), for the computational state of the algorithm may be a function of the symbols it has "seen" so far. The encryption of m_i is most often achieved by

$$c_i \stackrel{\text{def}}{=} s_i \oplus m_i,$$

where $s_0, s_1, \ldots$ is the *key stream*, typically generated by a deterministic algorithm run with a *random seed*; see Figure 3.1. The stream ciphers of that figure are *synchronous*, since their key bit stream is completely determined by the random seed (the key). (More general designs could make s_{i+1} a function of the message stream and the entire cipher-text computed so far.) In a block cipher, one encrypts an entire block of input symbols (say, 64 bits) at a time, and the "key stream" is constant. Later on, we see that this division is not as crisp and dramatic as it may sound here. For example, one can run a block cipher algorithm in a "stream mode", and this division further depends on what we mean by an "atomic" symbol.

Stream ciphers are still the workhorse of many cryptographic applications, and they possess features that sometimes make them the preferred method of choice. Stream ciphers can often be analyzed mathematically, allowing for a formal assessment of system security parameters. Block ciphers, on the other hand, rarely offer such an analysis – apart from showing that they are immune to known attacks and meet certain desirable design criteria. Stream ciphers also offer an advantage in that their encryption speed is typically higher than that of block ciphers. In our discussion of feedback shift registers, it becomes apparent that stream ciphers are not *self-synchronizing*. If an attacker manipulates (or deletes) at least one symbol of the encrypted stream before it reaches its intended destination, then the decryption operation will not recover from the point of the alteration

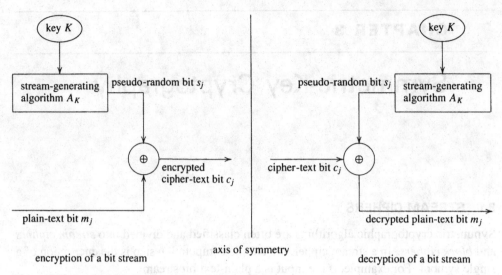

Figure 3.1. A schematic for the design of stream ciphers. Encryption and decryption are achieved by forming the bitwise exclusive-or of the input sequence with a pseudo-random sequence that is the stream output of a key-dependent generating algorithm A_K.

onward, thereby detecting a fraudulent intrusion or a hardware failure, as the case may be. Block ciphers usually have much better error propagation properties, and it depends on the system's overall objectives and concerns to determine which of these properties, and to what degree, are actually desirable.

Stream ciphers can also be used as generators of random bit strings needed for other cryptographic purposes. The majority of cryptographic systems requires random bit strings of fixed length. For example, in the key-exchange protocols of Section 2.7, Alice and Bob must be able to generate "good" random keys a and b, respectively. Public-key and digital signature schemes often generate random strings to mask the plain-text before encryption. We see this at work in Chapter 5.

3.1.1 Some History

The history of cryptography dates back at least a few thousand years. The human need for ensuring the secure communication of sensitive information (e.g., the positions of troops for an upcoming battle, or the location of a fraternity's beer keg) across a public communication channel (e.g., a messenger who is subject to capture by its enemies) is presumably as old as the ability to communicate, whether in oral or written form. In this section, we only take a peek at some of the cryptographic systems that people have used before the advent of the digital computer age. We engage in this discussion not merely out of historical interest: these examples help us identify basic principles on which modern symmetric encryption algorithms rest, as modern designs are improvements and complex combinations of earlier, unsecure, approaches.

In Chapter 2 we saw that it is convenient to view our domain of messages to be $\mathbb{Z}_n$ for a suitable value of n. We identify $[i]_n$ with i whenever $0 \le i < n$. For example, to represent the characters of the English alphabet in $\mathbb{Z}_n$, we may take $n = 26$ and identify 0 with the letter a, 6 with the letter g, and so on.

Definition 3.1 (Symmetric Cryptographic System)

A cryptographic algorithm dependent on a key K is *symmetric* if $D_K(\cdot)$ and $E_K(\cdot)$ from (2.1) (p. 15) are essentially the same operations or algorithms.

This definition is deliberately somewhat vague. Symmetric cryptographic algorithms allow us to derive $D_K(\cdot)$ from $E_K(\cdot)$ in a clearly defined and quickly computed manner. For example, DES generates 16 subkeys from a key K. The corresponding encryption and decryption operations are almost identical, expect that $D_K(\cdot)$ processes these 16 keys in *reverse* order from the one used in $E_K(\cdot)$. The new advanced encryption standard Rijndael also possesses a high degree of similarity between its encryption and decryption functions, as demonstrated in Section 3.2.2.[1] Notice also the distinction between a specification of a cryptographic algorithm and its actual realization or implementation. Apart from Chapter 6, this text (like most others) predominantly concentrates on reasoning about the security of the algorithm's specification, its "computational essence". It is hoped that such analyses will prevent us from using algorithms whose very design makes them inherently unsecure. Unfortunately, the vast majority of successful attacks of cryptographic algorithms exploit weaknesses in their *implementation*. For example, even the strongest possible algorithm is of little use if its run-time encryption key K and its source code are stored on a medium – such as a regular hard drive – that can easily be read by competent users. Believe it or not, this is more or less what happened with the digital encryption standard commissioned by the music industry for DVD! Incidentally, the history of cryptography has shown overwhelming empirical evidence that only publicly available cryptographic algorithms have a chance of being strong and reliable. Naturally, the security of public, key-dependent algorithms depends upon the secrecy and protection of their keys.

There are two important techniques for designing cryptographic algorithms over $\mathbb{Z}_n$. In ancient Rome, Caesar used a cipher in which he and his generals shifted each letter of the alphabet a fixed number of positions to the right. To achieve this for the English alphabet, we think of the character a as being the right-hand neighbor of the letter z, and of a key as being a number between 0 and 25. This view results in the following cryptosystem for $n = 26$.

Definition 3.2 (Caesar Cipher)

The *Caesar cipher* $\mathtt{Caesar}_n$ over $\mathbb{Z}_n$ is defined by the key space

$$\mathrm{Keys}(\mathtt{Caesar}_n) \stackrel{\mathrm{def}}{=} \{0, 1, \ldots, n-1\}$$

and the encryption operation

$$E_K(M) \stackrel{\mathrm{def}}{=} M + K \bmod n. \tag{3.1}$$

For example, a Roman diplomat who wanted to send Caesar the highly classified message "cleopatradesirestosteeyousoon" may have used the key "C", corresponding to 2, encrypting this message as "engqrcvtcfguktgvtquggaqwuqqp".

---

[1] Incidentally, don't trust any algorithm that is supposed to be secure without keys simply because its code is "secret". However, the mere fact that an algorithm depends on some key does not make it a secure cryptographic component. See the discussion that follows for some examples.

Obviously, this cryptosystem is completely unsecure, assuming Kerckhoff's principle that an opponent knows that Caesar's cipher is being used. For example, note the high frequency of occurrences of g in the cipher-text, suggesting that this letter represents e.

EXERCISES 3.1

1. (a) Write a simple program that inputs a plain-text string s and a key $K \in$ Keys(Caesar$_{26}$) and outputs the cipher-text string s' obtained by applying $E_K(\cdot)$, as specified in (3.1), to s at each character, identifying the English alphabet with $\mathbb{Z}_{26}$.

   (b) Modify the program in part (a) so that you can specify whether it should encrypt or *decrypt* a message. For that, you need to specify $D_K(\cdot)$.

   (c) Use your program to write a simple interface that takes as input a cipher-text s computed by a Caesar cipher and outputs all 26 possible plain-texts. Test it with several previously generated cipher-texts.

2. Repeat the previous exercise, but now with the 256-letter alphabet of the ASCII code.

3. *Affine ciphers*   Affine ciphers are generalizations of Caesar's cipher. Over $\mathbb{Z}_{26}$, the key space is given by all pairs $\langle a, b \rangle$ of numbers in $\{0, 1, \ldots, 25\}$ such that $\gcd(a, 26) = 1$. Encryption works as

   $$E_{\langle a,b \rangle}(M) \stackrel{\text{def}}{=} a \cdot M + b \bmod 26.$$

   (a) Describe the decryption operation.

   (b) Can you specify how many different affine ciphers there are over $\mathbb{Z}_{26}$?

Caesar's cipher is easily broken because of its very small key space. But even for large values of n, this cipher is totally unsecure if all letters of the alphabet are mapped to elements of $\mathbb{Z}_n$ (no matter what the order) and if the plain-text is intelligible English. This is because each letter in any given natural language, such as English, has a well-understood frequency of occurring in *any* text. To make matters worse, we even know well the transition probabilities between two, three,... letters in any given natural language. For example, if you observe an a in an English text, then your best predictions for the next letter (without any further "inside" knowledge of the plain-text) are l, n, r, or t. Such linguistic insight, combined with a probabilistic analysis, makes substitution ciphers totally unsecure.

Definition 3.3 (Substitution Cipher)
The *substitution cipher* Subst$_n$ is defined by the key space Keys(Subst$_n$) of all permutations $\sigma : \mathbb{Z}_n \to \mathbb{Z}_n$, which are functions of type $\mathbb{Z}_n \to \mathbb{Z}_n$ that have an inverse σ^{-1} of the same type. The encryption and decryption operations are given by

$$
\begin{aligned}
E_\sigma(M) &\stackrel{\text{def}}{=} \sigma(M), \\
D_\sigma(M) &\stackrel{\text{def}}{=} \sigma^{-1}(M),
\end{aligned}
\tag{3.2}
$$

respectively.

Example 3.4

1. Let $n = 2$. There are only two functions of type $\mathbb{Z}_2 \rightarrowtail \mathbb{Z}_2$ that have an inverse:

$$\text{id}(0) = 0, \qquad \text{id}(1) = 1;$$
$$\text{swap}(0) = 1, \quad \text{swap}(1) = 0.$$

The first one is the identity function id, and the second swaps the values 0 and 1.

2. Let $n = 8$. Then there are $8! = 40320$ many keys in $\text{Keys}(\text{Subst}_8)$. Let σ be given by

$$(4, 7, 2, 3, 0, 1, 5, 6),$$

meaning that $\sigma(0) = 4$, $\sigma(1) = 7$, and so on. The message 074635261 is encrypted via σ into 460531257. Note that this key always leaves two symbols unchanged. Identifying 0..7 with a..g, the word "aged" would be mapped to "dfac".

Observe that the Caesar cipher is just a subset of the substitution cipher: the key space for Caesar_n is contained in the key space for Subst_n, and the encryption and decryption operations in (3.1) and (3.2) are the same for that subset.

EXERCISE 3.2

1. Consider the following string.

> zjlnpre hozqnoylnzjlnhra lyleeonqzuygnranzjlnbr plqzfnvunhozqk

This is a cipher-text produced with a key from Subst_{29}; the numbers 0 to 25 represent the letters a to z, respectively. The number 26 represents the "space" character, 27 encodes the exclamation mark !, and 28 stands for the period.[2] The plain-text is about the astonishing improvement of a certain American College football team; the plain-text is known to contain the fragments "Cinderella" and "cats", the latter occurring twice in the text. Assume further that the plain text does not distinguish between lowercase and uppercase characters. Note that you can hardly solve this problem by an exhaustive key search, since Subst_{29} has 29! elements. (How big is 29!, anyway?)[3]

The substitution cipher demonstrates that a very big key space does not in itself guarantee a secure cryptographic algorithm. One can strengthen this cipher by building a cryptosystem that encrypts a stream $m_0, m_1, m_2, \ldots$ of elements in $\mathbb{Z}_n$ by means of p substitutions σ_j ($1 \leq j \leq p$), each of them applied in that order periodically.

Definition 3.5 (Polyalphabetic Substitution Cipher)

Let n and p be natural numbers. The *polyalphabetic substitution cipher* $\text{Polysubst}\langle p, n\rangle$ has as key space $\text{Keys}(\text{Polysubst}\langle p, n\rangle)$, the set of ordered p-tuples

---

[2] It may be good advice to delete all special symbols from a text before encrypting it. Of course, this can result in undesired ambiguity.

[3] Recall that $0! \stackrel{\text{def}}{=} 1$ and $(n + 1)! \stackrel{\text{def}}{=} (n + 1) \cdot (n!)$ for all $n \geq 0$.

$\langle \sigma_1, \ldots, \sigma_p \rangle$

of elements in $\text{Keys}(\text{Subst}_n)$. Any sequence $m_0, m_1, m_2, \ldots$ of plain-text elements over $\mathbb{Z}_n$ is encrypted into the sequence $c_0, c_1, c_2, \ldots$, where

$$c_j \overset{\text{def}}{=} \sigma_{j \bmod p}(m_j). \tag{3.3}$$

Note that $\sigma_{j \bmod p}$ denotes the substitution with index $j \bmod p$.

Example 3.6

Let $n = 29$ as in Exercise 3.2-1 and let $p = 7$. The seven chosen substitutions are all in $\text{Keys}(\text{Caesar}_{29})$. We represent each of these as the letter that represents the key. Thus, the key is completely determined by a word of length seven – say, "junkets". If we encrypt the string

  hillary clinton

with that key under the polyalphabetic substitution cipher, we obtain

  q.yvehnhwysrjdw

This example may look impressive, but such encryptions are totally unsecure. Also observe that this cryptographic algorithm is simply the substitution cipher where the period p equals 1. More generally, if we fix any k with $0 \leq k < p$ and focus on the subsequence

$$m_k, m_{p+k}, m_{2p+k}, \ldots,$$

then this cryptosystem is a substitution cipher with key σ_{k+1}. Since substitution ciphers are unsecure, the security of this system resides only in the secrecy – and possibly the size – of the period p. A probabilistic method called the *index of coincidences,* in conjunction with a test proposed by the Prussian officer F. Kasiski, make it possible to compute that very period.

The *Vigenère cryptographic algorithm* is the special case of a polyalphabetic substitution cipher where the substitutions are all Caesar ciphers (as in the previous example). This system is even easier to break. However, if the period p is as long as the message itself, and if the key is chosen truly at random, then we obtain the *one-time pad* (due to an AT&T employee named G. Vernam). C. E. Shannon later proved that this cryptographic algorithm has perfect security from the mathematical point of view. The hotline between Moscow and Washington makes use of this system. Unfortunately, most practical situations make it hard (or impossible) to use a key that is as long as the message itself. Much research has therefore gone into the design and analysis of cryptographic systems that can encrypt a stream of values $m_0, m_1, m_2, \ldots$ over $\mathbb{Z}_n$ with a key of fixed and manageable length. This research has established some results and methods for building and reasoning about such systems, but to this day the topic lacks an embracing foundational and unifying theory. Our discussion of stream ciphers focuses on the (unsecure) linear feedback shift registers for two principal reasons. First, we have tools for designing linear systems and assessing their relative cryptographic strengths. Second, linear components form the main building blocks of many nonlinear encryption algorithms – such as the data encryption standard (DES) and the Rijndael standard studied later on in this chapter – and we can sometimes perform an analysis of the nonlinear composition of these linear components.

3.1.2 Notions of Randomness

"Random" events are often puzzling, as they seem to conflict with "ordinary" experiences and our desire to predict and compartmentalize the world we live in. At the same time, we cannot manage to describe fundamental processes without the language of probabilities. Quantum physics, risk management in a company's expansion policy, the management of retirement funds, and the assessment of safety-critical systems such as a commercial aircraft all necessarily use notions that reason about random events. Although the established probability theory, based on Kolmogorov's axioms, has a long-standing history (European nobility needed decision models for their casino trips) and a very impressive track record, it also comes with its inherent paradoxes and offers only one way of modeling "true" randomness. Given a finite set

$$X = \{x_0, x_1, \ldots, x_{n-1}\}$$

of elementary events, a *probability distribution over X* is a function

$$\pi : X \rightarrow [0, 1]$$

such that

$$\sum_{i=0}^{n-1} \pi(x_i) = 1. \tag{3.4}$$

Example 3.7 (Probability Distribution)
Consider the set $\{x_0, x_1, x_2\}$ with $\pi(x_0) = 0.25$, $\pi(x_1) = 0.5$, and $\pi(x_2) = 0.25$, where $i \in \mathbb{N}$ is the number of heads seen after having tossed a fair coin twice.

C. E. Shannon studied probability distributions that aren't perfectly random by developing an *information theory* in which a message is perfectly random if its information content has no *redundancy* at all. He proposed the following measure of information content, a kind of information-theoretic entropy:

$$H(X) \stackrel{\text{def}}{=} -\sum_{i=0}^{n-1} \pi(x_i) \cdot \ln \pi(x_i). \tag{3.5}$$

Example 3.8 (Entropy)
For the distribution of Example 3.7, we have

$$\begin{aligned}
H(X) &= -(0.25 \cdot \ln 0.25 + 0.5 \cdot \ln 0.5 + 0.25 \cdot \ln 0.25) \\
&= -(0.25 \cdot (-2) + 0.5 \cdot (-1) + 0.25 \cdot (-2)) \\
&= 1.5,
\end{aligned}$$

suggesting that we require 1.5 bits on average to encode X. Let x_1 be encoded by 0, x_0 by 10, and x_2 by 11. Then we may compute the expected value of the bit length of the encoding for $x \in X$:

$$0.5 \cdot 1 + 0.25 \cdot 2 + 0.25 \cdot 2 = 1.5.$$

This framework allowed Shannon to prove that the one-time pad is unconditionally secure. However, the main drawback of this theory is that it cannot generate perfectly random strings from *shorter* perfectly random strings, for redundancy would contradict perfect randomness. In practice, this means that the one-time pad needs a key that is as long as the message itself. Clearly, this can only work for a very limited number of applications.

   Another approach to defining perfect randomness is due to Kolmogorov. His *descriptive complexity theory* measures the complexity of objects by the shortest program that can generate a complete description of that object. Such a program can successfully say why the string 100101001001011 is more complex or random than the string 101010101010101. Note that this is a *computational* approach to randomness, based on a fixed notion of computability – say, Java programs. Perfect randomness is again defined as an extreme case but now applies to single objects, not to collections thereof. Unfortunately, one cannot in general decide (i.e. compute) the Kolmogorov complexity of objects, so there is no hope of generating perfect random strings from shorter perfect random strings in this framework either.

   A promising and fruitful approach to randomness in the context of crytographic systems is due to M. Blum, S. Goldwasser, S. Micali, and A. Yao. Their work is rooted in conventional complexity theory, which groups computational problems into complexity classes that measure how many resources are needed for their solutions in terms of time or memory. Their point is rather philosophical in nature but potentially has far-reaching practical consequences. To these authors, randomness is not an *intrinsic property* of a computational object but instead depends upon the computational power of an observer. To put it simply, it is possible to generate random strings from much shorter random strings efficiently such that the longer string *appears* perfectly random to an observer whose computational powers are insufficient for observing the nonrandom features of that string. This is no modest goal, but it is essentially what practitioners are looking for as well: a short random seed that efficiently generates a long random string, accompanied with well-understood quantitative or qualitative security guarantees, such that an attacker could not observe any nonrandom features of the longer sequence.

Definition 3.9
For $l \in \mathbb{N}$, we write $\mathbb{Z}_2^l$ for the set of bit strings of length l. A (k, l)-*pseudo-random bit generator* is an algorithm, efficient as a function of k, that computes a function $f : \mathbb{Z}_2^k \to \mathbb{Z}_2^l$.

From our discussion so far, it should be apparent that pseudo-random bit generators should make it computationally hard to distinguish the output sequence $f(s_0 s_1 \ldots s_k)$, a bit string of length l, from a perfectly random one of the same length. At the same time, the algorithm should be efficient, l should be a "large" polynomial function of k, and the algorithm should have easy implementations in hardware. We now discuss linear feedback shift registers in light of these criteria.

3.1.3 Linear Feedback Shift Registers

Our discussion of modern stream ciphers focuses on the alphabet $\mathbb{Z}_2$, although the presented designs and analyses can (for the most part) be extended to any finite field. Our systems will take a (possibly infinite) sequence $m_0, m_1, m_2, \ldots$ of plain-text bits as input and produce a sequence $c_0, c_1, c_2, \ldots$ of cipher-text bits such that c_j is the encryption of the plain-text bit m_j. We assume that this encryption is achieved by means of

$$c_j \stackrel{\text{def}}{=} m_j + s_j \bmod 2, \tag{3.6}$$

where

$$s_0, s_1, s_2, \ldots \tag{3.7}$$

is a sequence of bits as long as the plain-text sequence. If this sequence were truly random, equation (3.6) would render a totally secure one-time pad. Owing to practical considerations, however, we construct this possibly infinite sequence of s_j bits from a finite key K and an algorithm A, taking K as its input such that $A_K(\cdot)$ is a (k, l)-pseudo-random bit generator for some suitable value of l. Recall that $a + b \bmod 2$ is just another way of writing $a \oplus b$ (see Exercise 2.2-3, p. 20). Since $(m \oplus s) \oplus s = m$, it is apparent that the decryption of the cipher-text sequence $c_0, c_1, c_2, \ldots$ is carried out in the very same manner as the encryption of the input sequence. Such stream ciphers are absolutely symmetric in their encryption and decryption mode. See Figure 3.1 for a schematic of such stream ciphers.

For a finite key K and an algorithm A with only finitely many states, any infinite execution trace of $A_K(\cdot)$ must enter a cycle that repeats the same sequence of states periodically from a certain point onward. Naturally, this means that its output sequence in (3.7) reaches a point s_k with $k \geq 0$ such that there exists a period $p \in \mathbb{N}$ with

$$s_{k+j} = s_{k+j+n \cdot p} \quad (n \geq 1) \tag{3.8}$$

for all $j, n \in \mathbb{N}$. In this text, we assume that the initial nonperiodic segment $s_0, s_1, \ldots, s_{k-1}$ is of length zero, in which case the entire sequence in (3.8) is an infinite concatenation of the initial block $s_0, s_1, \ldots, s_{p-1}$ with itself, for k then equals 0.

3.1.3.1 Feedback Shift Registers

A commonly used and studied architecture that realizes the stream ciphers of Figure 3.1 very efficiently in hardware is the *feedback register system*; see Figure 3.2. Such systems are built from n registers

$$R_0, R_1, \ldots, R_{n-1}$$

that can store binary values. The contents of these registers serve as the input to a boolean function f in n variables, as indicated in Figure 3.2. A state σ of such a system is determined by the contents of all registers. A state therefore determines a unique value

$$v \stackrel{\text{def}}{=} f(@R_0, @R_1, \ldots, @R_{n-1}),$$

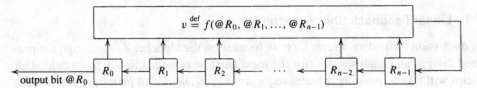

Figure 3.2. Architecture of a feedback shift register with n registers and a boolean function f in n variables. The current register values determine the next value of register R_{n-1}; the current value of R_0 is the new output bit, and the next values of R_i are those of R_{i+1} for each $0 \leq i \leq n-2$.

where $@R$ is the value currently stored in register R. The successor state of σ is then obtained by shifting the register contents one to the left, loading register R_{n-1} with v, and making $@R_0$ the output bit of this iteration. See Figure 3.2 for a pictorial representation of this process.

It is intuitively clear that the strength and security of stream ciphers rest on the quality of the pseudo-random sequence (3.7) generated by $A_K(\cdot)$. If the latter is realized by a feedback register system, then the choice of the number of registers and the choice of the boolean function f may well be motivated by implementation constraints. Such a stream cipher design therefore strives for a maximal security within a given parameter space for n and f.

There are inherent tradeoffs between the analysis and the design of feedback shift registers. The less secure the boolean function, the easier one can analyze the resulting cipher. However, an extremely complicated boolean function may be impossible to analyze, yet its complexity alone is no guarantee of cryptographic security. A currently dominant approach in the design of stream ciphers thus aims at systems whose components are easily analyzed and unsecure in isolation but whose composition (a) provides sufficient cryptographic security and (b) enables an analysis of the entire system based on the analysis of its components. We illustrate this approach with linear feedback shift registers, simple building blocks whose theory is well understood.

3.1.3.2 Linear Boolean Functions

Definition 3.10 (Linear Function and Linear Feedback Shift Register)
Let f be a boolean function in n variables $x_0, x_1, \ldots, x_{n-1}$. We call f *linear* if and only if there exist values $c_0, c_1, \ldots, c_{n-1}$ in $\{0, 1\}$ such that

$$f(x_0, x_1, \ldots, x_{n-1}) = c_0 \cdot x_0 + c_1 \cdot x_1 + \cdots + c_{n-1} \cdot x_{n-1} \bmod 2 \qquad (3.9)$$

holds for all argument values of f. A *linear feedback shift register* (LFSR) is a feedback shift register (as in Figure 3.2) such that the boolean function f is linear. If $c_0 = 1$, then f and its LFSR have *degree n*.

Example 3.11
The boolean function

$$f_1(x_0, x_1, x_2) \stackrel{\text{def}}{=} x_1 + x_2 \bmod 2$$

is linear, and so is

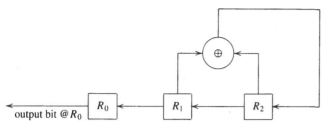

Figure 3.3. Example of a linear feedback shift register, based on the architecture in Figure 3.2, for the boolean function $f_1(x_0, x_1, x_2) \overset{\text{def}}{=} x_1 + x_2 \bmod 2$.

$$f_2(x_0, x_1, x_2, x_3, x_4, x_5) \overset{\text{def}}{=} x_1 + x_3 + x_5 \bmod 2.$$

However, the function

$$f_3(x_0, x_1, x_2) \overset{\text{def}}{=} x_0 \cdot x_1 + x_2$$

is not linear. The linear feedback shift register for f_1 is depicted in Figure 3.3. If it has initial state 010 – meaning that $@R_0 = 0$, $@R_1 = 1$, and $@R_2 = 0$ – then this LFSR goes through the following sequence of computational states:

010, 101, 011, 110, 101,

at which point it will repeat the last three states periodically.

Remark 3.12 (LFSR as Boolean Function)
Any linear feedback shift register is completely determined by its number of registers n and its boolean function f. Since this function has n variables, the entire LFSR is determined by its function f, although an execution trace also depends on the respective initial state. Thus we identify an LFSR with its boolean function whenever this is appropriate.

Example 3.13
Given an LFSR of degree 4 with boolean function

$$f(x_0, x_1, x_2, x_3) \overset{\text{def}}{=} x_0 + x_1 \bmod 2,$$

we consider the key stream seed $s_0 s_1 s_2 s_3$ to be 1000. The first 45 bits of the resulting key stream are

100110101111000 100110101111000 100110101111000.   (3.10)

Note that this key stream has period 16. The same period will result for any other 4-bit key seed different from 0000.

EXERCISES 3.3

1. Is the boolean function

$$f(x_0, x_1, \ldots, x_{n-1}) \overset{\text{def}}{=} 1$$

linear? What about

$$g(x_0, x_1, \ldots, x_{n-1}) \stackrel{\text{def}}{=} 0 ?$$

(Explain your answer.)

2. In Example 3.11, we claimed that the boolean function f_3 is not linear. Although its "formula" does not have the form required of a linear function, it is still possible that this form is equivalent to one, as in (3.9). Show that f_3 cannot satisfy (3.9) for any choices of c_0, c_1, or c_2.

3. Consider the LFSR given by the linear function

$$f(x_0, x_1, x_2, x_3) \stackrel{\text{def}}{=} x_0 + x_2 \bmod 2.$$

Let 1011 be the initial state of this LFSR. Compute the execution trace of this LFSR beginning in this initial state and determine the period of the resulting trace.

4. What can you say about the behavior of an LFSR in the initial state where all registers are loaded with 0?

5. *One-time pad*   Let C be a 128-bit string that resulted from forming the bitwise exclusive-or of a 128-bit plain-text M and a 128-bit, randomly generated key K. If the leftmost bit of K is 0 then what can you conclude about the plain-text M? (Assume that you know the cipher-text C in its entirety.) Is there anything else you can infer about M?

The pseudo-random bit stream produced by an LFSR is determined not only by the boolean function f of that LFSR (which we may identify with a bit string $c_0 c_1 \ldots c_{n-1}$)[4] but also by the initial state of that entire system – that is, the initial contents of its registers. Again, we may think of that state as a bit string $r_0 r_1 \ldots r_{n-1}$. Note that this string should contain at least one 1-bit, for otherwise the LFSR outputs only 0-bits forever. (Why?) Observe that we would get into the same kind of trouble if the zero vector occurred as a register state at a later point in our key stream.

Linear feedback shift registers always produce key streams that are periodic (this applies to *all* synchronous stream ciphers whose key stream is generated by some finite-state program). There are only 2^n different states possible, and we have already seen why we need to rule out the one in which each register is loaded with "0". Thus $2^n - 1$ is an upper bound on the period of the key stream. There is a beautiful algebraic theory that relates certain properties of LFSRs to properties of polynomials. In particular, one can construct many(!) LFSRs in n variables such that each initial state other than $00 \ldots 0$ generates a key stream of period $2^n - 1$. Moreover, no such execution will ever generate the zero vector. The example in Exercise 3.3-3 featured this pleasant property.

Unfortunately, even LFSRs with period $2^n - 1$ can be easily broken with a chosen plain-text attack. If an attacker has access to the stream cipher that uses an LFSR to generate its key stream $s_0, s_1, \ldots$, then he can choose any message stream $m_0, m_1, \ldots$ to generate the corresponding cipher-stream $c_0, c_1, \ldots$. Since

$$c_i = s_i \oplus m_i,$$

---

[4]   Note that we assume $c_0 = 1$, for otherwise f has degree less than n.

he can compute the stream $s_0, s_1, \ldots$ via

$$s_i = c_i \oplus m_i,$$

for he knows c_i and m_i. Given this key stream and knowing that the system used an LFSR, we also assume that he knows the degree n of the LFSR. Otherwise, he could launch the same attack for smaller values of n and increase n until the attack turns out to be successful. The attack is based on a simple recurrence law on the computation of the next bit in the key stream. Let us assume that the initial state of the LFSR is the vector $s_0 s_1 \ldots s_{n-1}$. By definition, we have

$$
\begin{aligned}
s_n &\stackrel{\text{def}}{=} f(s_0, s_1, \ldots, s_{n-1}), \\
s_{n+1} &\stackrel{\text{def}}{=} f(s_1, s_2, \ldots, s_n), \\
&\vdots \\
s_{n+n-1} &\stackrel{\text{def}}{=} f(s_{n-1}, s_n, \ldots, s_{n+n-2}),
\end{aligned}
\tag{3.11}
$$

which is a system of n linear equations in n unknowns $c_0, c_1, \ldots, c_{n-1}$, the coefficients of f. One can show that this system has a unique solution; in fact, this remains true even if we replace the fragment of the key stream $s_0 s_1 \ldots s_n s_{n+1} \ldots s_{n+n-1}$ used in (3.11) with any consecutive fragment $s_k s_{k+1} \ldots s_{k+2n-1}$ of length $2 \cdot n$. Such systems can be efficiently solved with standard software packages, so an attacker need only:

- have access to the cipher system;
- know that the stream cipher is generated by an LFSR of degree n;
- generate a piece of cipher-text corresponding to a chosen plain-text of length $2n$, thereby obtaining a consecutive piece of the key stream with the same length in the manner just described; and
- solve the resulting system of linear equations to expose the LFSR completely.

EXERCISES 3.4

1. Implement a program that – given

   ```
   n
   c[0]c[1]...c[n-1]
   s[0]s[1]...s[n-1]
   ```

   as input – generates a key stream of an LFSR whose boolean function is represented by `c[0]c[1]...c[n-1]` and whose seed is given by the bit string `s[0]s[1]...s[n-1]`.
2. You are asked to break an LFSR of degree 10, given 20 consecutive bits of plain-text 10101110101010011110 and their corresponding cipher-text 11011010100111000010.
3. Repeat Exercise 2 with an LFSR of degree 20, 40 consecutive bits of plain-text

   0100111111010110001100011011100001001000,

and cipher-text[5]

001110111101100100110111010101010101111100.

3.1.4 Nonlinearity

We saw that LFSRs are amenable to a rigid analysis. Unfortunately, we also realized that they are completely unsecure in isolation. Strong cryptographic systems therefore require *nonlinear* features, although most of their components may themselves be linear. Yet nonlinearity in itself is no guarantee of strong cryptographic properties. The S-boxes in the block cipher DES (see Section 3.2.1) are nonlinear. Presumably, a lot of insider expertise and experience went into their design; the National Security Agency helped out on some details. However, it would be poor advice – to anyone "re-inventing" these boxes – to emphasize solely their nonlinearity. The S-boxes seem to be optimal against attempts to approximate S-boxes with linear functions, an attack known as *linear cryptanalysis,* but they are not optimal against *differential cryptanalysis.* For DES, this attack systematically looks at plain-text with minor differences and investigates how those differences propagate through the execution of DES. This can be used as a means of adjusting the uniform probability distribution on the unknown encryption key. Because DES uses 16 encryption rounds, it is immune against both attacks, given *past* hardware constraints. Today, triple DES is believed to be secure for the foreseeable future; see Section 3.2.1.3 for details.

Various methods for the construction of nonlinear stream ciphers from LFSRs have been proposed.

- *Nonlinear filtering* combines the stages of these LFSRs in a nonlinear manner. Often, one can predict certain parameters – for example, the *linear complexity* – of the resulting system from the corresponding parameters of the LFSRs.
- *Nonlinear composition* may take the output streams of several LFSRs as input streams to a nonlinear function. Such systems can gain strength through the judicious use of a bit of memory in the composition process.
- *Control LFSRs* use one or several LFSRs to control the "clock" of another LFSR. Again, one can sometimes predict some crucial system parameters from those of the system's components.

We refer to the bibliographic notes for references on these advanced topics.

Our discussion of nonlinear pseudo-random bit generators concludes with that devised by L. Blum, M. Blum, and M. Shub (see Exercise 2.7-8, p. 33). If we randomly choose 512-bit primes p and q as[6]

9047969817806701008966807304777433934882108801417570278584864166110 5\\
311352223941103858654884250667490711208745422062359254797315471579706\\
414516095544069107

and

---

[5] These bit strings can be found on the book's website.
[6] These numbers can be found on the book's web site.

60297251135965569675412888171220733861849935458016017819954087059931\\
79647698993426616155053225765483582954507138414522740456609641044529\\
4306053550234921131

(respectively) and the random seed x_0 as

98233751931974189387322934194955048396662398840395344134380476388995\\
56633299074466735842402852390134813499130048518378804338036394842211\\
18734256385564675800388168283781916239020668803685287981370814465757\\
54712111430353908253262020863869851074245612770784334395442352442065\\
19597122427936807574843684582396310224,

then the first 490 bits of the pseudo-random sequence are given by

00000011010001011111110101111001111010000000101100010011010000011100010111\\
10000001101001111000100110011100010100100000000101101000011011011011001011\\
00110010010001011111111111001011101100001001101011011010001010001001110001\\
11101000001101001010010001101101011100010001110000111100010011101110000000\\
10011001011010110000100101011110010011010101000000010010011001000111101001\\
01001000101111001110101010111010010000100010010101001000101101001011110000\\
100101001011000111101110000110011111010011100110010.

As pointed out earlier, one way to assess the strength of a pseudo-random bit generator f is to distinguish the uniform probability distribution over $\mathbb{Z}_2^l$ from the one induced by f using a small threshold value $\varepsilon > 0$. A theoretical result (due to A. Yao) states that if such a distinguishing algorithm exists then there is also a *next-bit predictor* for f with a threshold of ε/l; that is, such a predictor correctly guesses the next bit of the output sequence with probability $0.5 + \varepsilon/l$. What makes this insight interesting in the context of the Blum–Blum–Shub generator is that one can prove its relative security in the following sense. If there is an ε/l-next-bit predictor for this generator then one can derive, for any positive error probability, a Monte Carlo algorithm that computes quadratic residues over $p \cdot q$; see Exercise 2.17-7 (p. 55) for a definition of this concept. Since nobody can say at present how to construct such an algorithm without knowing the factorization of n, this generator is believed to be secure.

3.2 BLOCK CIPHERS

3.2.1 Data Encryption Standard: DES

In the early 1970s, the Data Encryption Standard (DES) emerged as the first standardized symmetric encryption algorithm, approved by what is now the American National Institute of Standards and Technology (NIST). The development of the DES algorithm was largely carried out by a team at IBM. The U.S. National Security Agency (NSA) was actively involved in reviewing and assessing the IBM design. Interestingly enough, the NSA proposed some changes to the design, causing public concern about an "NSA trapdoor" in the modified version of DES. In the end, the suggestions of the NSA were incorporated into the standard. Although DES is no longer recommended for U.S. government agencies for encrypting sensitive (but unclassified) data, we feature it as our first example of a block-cipher algorithm for a number of reasons:

- it has successfully withstood attacks for more than 20 years, and the only known way of breaking the algorithm is by a more or less brute-force, exhaustive search of the key;
- the design principles of its components are typical of many block-cipher algorithms;
- the same algorithm can be used both to encrypt and decrypt messages;
- new standards for block-cipher algorithms – such as the new advanced encryption standard Rijndael – will be evaluated in terms of comparisons with the security and speed of DES;
- DES can be used, or is prescribed, in various standards (e.g., for passwords, random seeds for digital fingerprints or signatures, and message authentication codes);
- DES gives rise to a more powerful standard, called triple DES, since its key space is not a group; triple DES currently provides adequate protection while being backwards-compatible with DES for a given key option.

3.2.1.1 The Electronic Codebook Mode

In its simplest mode of operation, the *electronic codebook (ECB) mode,* the DES algorithm takes a block B of 64 bits as input and encrypts it into another block of 64 bits by means of a 64-bit key K. Actually, eight bits of the key K are reserved for parity checks, so the key is effectively only $56 = 64 - 8$ bits long. Thus the entire key space has only size 2^{56} instead of 2^{64}. More precisely, bits $8, 16, \ldots, 64$ of K are used to guarantee that each byte of K has odd parity. In the sequel, we write any 64-bit block B as a concatenation LR of its left half L and right half R, where each half is 32 bits long. Conceptually, the DES algorithm operates in three phases; see Figure 3.4. First, the input block B is permuted with a fixed and key-independent permutation, the initial permutation $\texttt{IP}$ given in Figure 3.5; for example, the permuted block $\texttt{IP}(B)$ has the 58th bit of B as its first bit, the 52nd bit of B as its 10th bit, and so forth. The resulting permuted block $\texttt{IP}(B)$ is divided into the leftmost 32-bit block L_0 and the rightmost 32-bit block R_0:

$$L_0 R_0 \stackrel{\text{def}}{=} \texttt{IP}(B). \tag{3.12}$$

In the second phase, DES conducts 16 rounds of computing subsequent blocks L_i and R_i with $1 \leq i \leq 16$, each 32 bits long. These blocks are defined as

$$L_{i+1} \stackrel{\text{def}}{=} R_i, \tag{3.13}$$

$$R_{i+1} \stackrel{\text{def}}{=} L_i \oplus f(R_i, K_{i+1}) \tag{3.14}$$

for all $0 \leq i \leq 15$. However, L_{16} and R_{16} – once computed as in (3.13) and (3.14) – are *swapped,* as indicated in Figure 3.4. We will see in the exercises that this allows us to use the same algorithm for decrypting a block. In (3.14), we still need to explain the nature of the function f and the entities K_i with $1 \leq i \leq 16$. Each K_i is a 48-bit block computed from the original 64-bit key K by the *key scheduler,* depicted in Figure 3.6. The input to this key scheduler is the original 64-bit key K, which undergoes a first permuted choice PC1 resulting in two blocks C_0 and D_0 of 28 bits each. See Figure 3.7 for

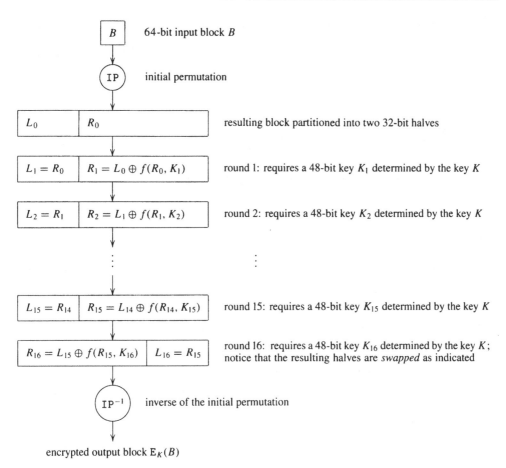

resulting block partitioned into two 32-bit halves

round 1: requires a 48-bit key K_1 determined by the key K

round 2: requires a 48-bit key K_2 determined by the key K

round 15: requires a 48-bit key K_{15} determined by the key K

round 16: requires a 48-bit key K_{16} determined by the key K; notice that the resulting halves are *swapped* as indicated

inverse of the initial permutation

encrypted output block $\mathrm{E}_K(B)$

Figure 3.4. Coarse structure of the DES algorithm in its encryption state, operating on a 64-bit input block B in the electronic codebook (ECB) mode.

58	50	42	34	26	18	10	2
60	52	44	36	28	20	12	4
62	54	46	38	30	22	14	6
64	56	48	40	32	24	16	8
57	49	41	33	25	17	9	1
59	51	43	35	27	19	11	3
61	53	45	37	29	21	13	5
63	55	47	39	31	23	15	7

Figure 3.5. The initial permutation IP of the 64-bit input block B. The 50th bit of B renders the second bit of IP(B), the 52nd bit of B will be the 10th bit of IP(B), etc.

the details of constructing C_0 and D_0. The first table lists C_0: the 57th bit of K is the first bit of C_0, the 58th bit of K is the 9th bit of C_0, ...; the second table specifies D_0 in the same manner. Notice that the numbers $8, 16, \ldots, 64$ are all absent from these tables, since they are merely parity bits and not part of the actual 56-bit key. Before computing K_i, we compute blocks C_i and D_i as circular left shifts of their previous version C_{i-1}

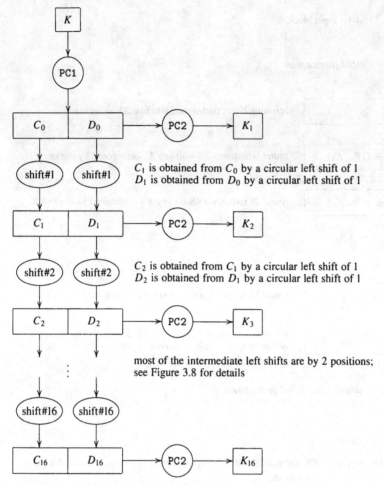

Figure 3.6. Schematic for computation of the 16 48-bit subkeys K_i, $1 \leq i \leq$ 16, from the original 64-bit key K. The shifts are circular left shifts and are performed on C_i and D_i *separately.*

and D_{i-1}, respectively. The number of left shifts is round-dependent, as specified in Figure 3.8; it is the same for the C-blocks and D-blocks. For example, C_1 is obtained from C_0 by one left shift, whereas D_3 is obtained from D_2 by two left shifts, and so on. We then define

$$K_i \stackrel{\text{def}}{=} \text{PC2}(C_i D_i) \tag{3.15}$$

for each i with $1 \leq i \leq 16$, where PC2 maps the 56-bit block $C_i D_i$ to a 48-bit block K_i, as specified in Figure 3.9. For example, the 14th bit of $C_i D_i$ is the first bit of K_i, whereas the 28th bit of $C_i D_i$ is the 8th bit of K_i, et cetera.

It remains to describe the *cipher function f*, which must provide all the strength of the algorithm, for all other components are linear in the sense of Definition 3.10 and can be analyzed easily. In general, the cipher function

C_0

57	49	41	33	25	17	9
1	58	50	42	34	26	18
10	2	59	51	43	35	27
19	11	3	60	52	44	36

D_0

63	55	47	39	31	23	15
7	62	54	46	38	30	22
14	6	61	53	45	37	29
21	13	5	28	20	12	4

Figure 3.7. The permuted choice PC1, which maps the 56 actual key bits of K onto two 28-bit blocks C_0 and D_0. The first table constructs C_0; the second, D_0.

round number	1	2	3	4	5	6	7	8	9	10	11	12	13	14	15	16
number of left shifts	1	1	2	2	2	2	2	2	1	2	2	2	2	2	2	1

Figure 3.8. Number of left shifts required to compute C_k and D_k from C_{k-1} and D_{k-1}, respectively, where k is the round number.

14	17	11	24	1	5
3	28	15	6	21	10
23	19	12	4	26	8
16	7	27	20	13	2
41	52	31	37	47	55
30	40	51	45	33	48
44	49	39	56	34	53
46	42	50	36	29	32

Figure 3.9. Table for the permuted choice PC2, which maps a 56-bit block onto a 48-bit block.

$$(R, K) \mapsto f(R, K)$$

takes two arguments, a 32-bit block R and a 48-bit block K, to produce a 32-bit block $f(R, K)$ as output. This output is computed in four phases, as depicted in Figure 3.11. *First,* the block R is expanded into a 48-bit block $E(R)$, where the mapping E is given by the table shown in Figure 3.10. For example, the 32nd bit of R renders the first bit of $E(R)$, the 5th bit of R yields the 8th bit of $E(R)$, and so forth. Note that this is not an invertible process, since some bits are copied more than once – for example, the 32nd bit of R also renders the 47th bit of $E(R)$. *Second,* we compute the 48-bit block $E(R) \oplus K$, which we write as a concatenation of eight 6-bit blocks as in

$$M_1 M_2 M_3 M_4 M_5 M_6 M_7 M_8 \stackrel{\text{def}}{=} E(R) \oplus K. \tag{3.16}$$

32	1	2	3	4	5
4	5	6	7	8	9
8	9	10	11	12	13
12	13	14	15	16	17
16	17	18	19	20	21
20	21	22	23	24	25
24	25	26	27	28	29
28	29	30	31	32	1

Figure 3.10. The expansion mapping E, which turns a 32-bit block into a 48-bit block.

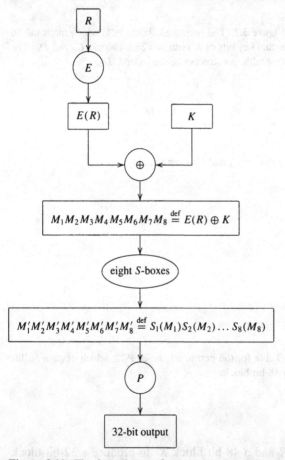

Figure 3.11. The four phases of computing the cipher function $f(R, K)$ needed in (3.14).

Third, for each i with $1 \leq i \leq 8$, we feed M_i into an *S-box* S_i to produce a 4-bit output M_i'. The outputs of the eight *S*-boxes are then concatenated, as shown in Figure 3.11, resulting in the 32-bit output $M_1'M_2'M_3'M_4'M_5'M_6'M_7'M_8'$. *Fourth,* this output is subjected to a permutation P, as specified in Figure 3.12, to compute the final result of $f(R, K)$:

$$f(R, K) \stackrel{\text{def}}{=} P(M_1'M_2'M_3'M_4'M_5'M_6'M_7'M_8'). \tag{3.17}$$

16	7	20	21
29	12	28	17
1	15	23	26
5	18	31	10
2	8	24	14
32	27	3	9
19	13	30	6
22	11	4	25

Figure 3.12. The final permutation P performed during the last phase of computing $f(R, K)$.

x/y	0	1	2	3	4	5	6	7	8	9	10	11	12	13	14	15
0	14	4	13	1	2	15	11	8	3	10	6	12	5	9	0	7
1	0	15	7	4	14	2	13	1	10	6	12	11	9	5	3	8
2	4	1	14	8	13	6	2	11	15	12	9	7	3	10	5	0
3	15	12	8	2	4	9	1	7	5	11	3	14	10	0	6	13

Figure 3.13. Specification of the S-box S_1.

In order to complete the description of how to compute $f(R, K)$, we must specify the S-boxes S_i, where $1 \leq i \leq 8$. These boxes are the only nonlinear components of the DES algorithm, and this is where the NSA suggested some changes. We specify S_1 in the table of Figure 3.13, which is interpreted as follows. Any 6-bit input block M_i determines a pair of coordinates $\langle x, y \rangle$ with $0 \leq x \leq 3$ and $0 \leq y \leq 15$; we let x be the number whose binary representation equals $b_1 b_6$, where M_i equals $b_1 b_2 b_3 b_4 b_5 b_6$ (i.e., b_1 and b_6 are the first and last bit, respectively, of M_i). Similarly, y is the number whose binary representation equals $b_2 b_3 b_4 b_5$. For any input pair $\langle x, y \rangle$, the output $S_1(M_i)$ is defined to be the number in row x and column y of the table in Figure 3.13. It should be apparent that this table completely specifies the function

$$M_i \mapsto S_1(M_i).$$

For example: If M_1 equals 010011, then x equals 1 and y equals 9, so the output is 0110 – the binary representation of 6, the entry in row 1 and column 9. In Figure 3.14, we list in this manner all seven remaining S-boxes and their behavior.

Returning to the DES algorithm itself, the overall encryption of the DES input block B concludes with applying the inverse permutation of the one in Figure 3.5 to the 64-bit block $R_{16} L_{16}$, as indicated in Figure 3.4.

EXERCISES 3.5

1. Draw a table for the inverse permutation of the initial permutation in Figure 3.5.

2. *Inverse of DES* Prove that the same DES algorithm can be applied to decrypt the encrypted block with the only change being that the subkeys K_i are supplied to the

S_2	0	1	2	3	4	5	6	7	8	9	10	11	12	13	14	15
0	15	1	8	14	6	11	3	4	9	7	2	13	12	0	5	10
1	3	13	4	7	15	2	8	14	12	0	1	10	6	9	11	5
2	0	14	7	11	10	4	13	1	5	8	12	6	9	3	2	15
3	13	8	10	1	3	15	4	2	11	6	7	12	0	5	14	9

S_3	0	1	2	3	4	5	6	7	8	9	10	11	12	13	14	15
0	10	0	9	14	6	3	15	5	1	13	12	7	11	4	2	8
1	13	7	0	9	3	4	6	10	2	8	5	14	12	11	15	1
2	13	6	4	9	8	15	3	0	11	1	2	12	5	10	14	7
3	1	10	13	0	6	9	8	7	4	15	14	3	11	5	2	12

S_4	0	1	2	3	4	5	6	7	8	9	10	11	12	13	14	15
0	7	13	14	3	0	6	9	10	1	2	8	5	11	12	4	15
1	13	8	11	5	6	15	0	3	4	7	2	12	1	10	14	9
2	10	6	9	0	12	11	7	13	15	1	3	14	5	2	8	4
3	3	15	0	6	10	1	13	8	9	4	5	11	12	7	2	14

S_5	0	1	2	3	4	5	6	7	8	9	10	11	12	13	14	15
0	2	12	4	1	7	10	11	6	8	5	3	15	13	0	14	9
1	14	11	2	12	4	7	13	1	5	0	15	10	3	9	8	6
2	4	2	1	11	10	13	7	8	15	9	12	5	6	3	0	14
3	11	8	12	7	1	14	2	13	6	15	0	9	10	4	5	3

S_6	0	1	2	3	4	5	6	7	8	9	10	11	12	13	14	15
0	12	1	10	15	9	2	6	8	0	13	3	4	14	7	5	11
1	10	15	4	2	7	12	9	5	6	1	13	14	0	11	3	8
2	9	14	15	5	2	8	12	3	7	0	4	10	1	13	11	6
3	4	3	2	12	9	5	15	10	11	14	1	7	6	0	8	13

S_7	0	1	2	3	4	5	6	7	8	9	10	11	12	13	14	15
0	4	11	2	14	15	0	8	13	3	12	9	7	5	10	6	1
1	13	0	11	7	4	9	1	10	14	3	5	12	2	15	8	6
2	1	4	11	13	12	3	7	14	10	15	6	8	0	5	9	2
3	6	11	13	8	1	4	10	7	9	5	0	15	14	2	3	12

S_8	0	1	2	3	4	5	6	7	8	9	10	11	12	13	14	15
0	13	2	8	4	6	15	11	1	10	9	3	14	5	0	12	7
1	1	15	13	8	10	3	7	4	12	5	6	11	0	14	9	2
2	7	11	4	1	9	12	14	2	0	6	10	13	15	3	5	8
3	2	1	14	7	4	10	8	13	15	12	9	0	3	5	6	11

Figure 3.14. Specification of the remaining S-boxes S_2 to S_8.

cipher function f in reverse order; that is, we replace K_{i+1} in equation (3.14) with K_{16-i}. Does your argument depend on the nature of the cipher function f?

3. We noted that the cipher function f is the only nonlinear component of the DES algorithm. Recalling the definition of a linear function (Definition 3.10, p. 90), explain why permutations, permuted choices, and expansion mappings (such as IP, PC1, and E) are linear.

4. *Implementing DES* Implement the DES algorithm as described here in a programming language of your choice. Your program's interface should expect a 64-bit block B, a 64-bit key K, and a boolean b as input. If b is false then the algorithm will encrypt B; otherwise, it will decrypt B. Although this is not really necessary for implementing DES, can you think of a way of computing the K_i *directly* in reverse order in case b is true?

5. *Design criteria for S-boxes*

   (a) Prove that the S-box S_1 is *nonlinear*. That is, prove there is no linear function

   $$f(x_1, x_2, x_3, x_4, x_5, x_6) = c_1 \cdot x_1 + c_2 \cdot x_2 + \cdots + c_6 \cdot x_6 \bmod 2$$

   with fixed values $c_i \in \{0, 1\}$ for $1 \le i \le 6$ that exactly captures the input–output behavior of this S-box.

   (b) Can you find some linear function that "models" the S-box S_1 for a reasonably high percentage of input–output pairs? (Such an approach leads to a technique called *linear cryptanalysis*.)

   (c) Verify: Each row of S_1's specification lists a permutation.

   (d) For S_1: Show that, for all 6-bit inputs, the change of exactly one input bit results in the change of at least two output bits of the 4-bit output. (This property guarantees that small changes in the original text make the two resulting cipher-texts appear to be "unrelated".)

   (e) Verify: For all 6-bit inputs x, the outputs $S_1(x)$ and $S_1(x \oplus 001100)$ differ in at least two bit positions.

6. *DES: complementation property* Consider the encryption of a block B with respect to a key K in the ECB mode of DES. Prove that the resulting cipher-block is the bitwise complement of the cipher-block computed by encrypting the bitwise complement of B with the bitwise complement of the key K. How do you structure your argument? Does your argument extend to some other modes of executing DES (discussed in the next section)?

7. *Security of software implementations* Discuss general security concerns of software implementations of the DES algorithm. Are these issues dependent on your choice of programming language? Are they dependent on your choice of hardware or operating system?

3.2.1.2 DES Modes of Operations

The DES algorithm in the ECB encryption mode transforms a 64-bit plain-text B into a 64-bit cipher-text $E_K(B)$, depending on a 56-bit key K. Therefore, we can apply this algorithm to an arbitrary message M by dividing M into 64-bit blocks – padding the final block if need be – and then processing each block in isolation. This mode of operation is called the *electronic codebook* (ECB) mode, since each plain-text produces the same cipher-text, given a fixed key K. In principle, one could thus compile a big codebook that lists pairs of plain-texts and cipher-texts for each possible key. This is a security concern. One can use the ECB mode of DES as an interface to build more secure modes of operation. Here we outline only the *cipher-block chaining* (CBC) mode and refer to the bibliographic notes and exercises for references on other modes of operation. In the CBC mode, we:

- operate on a sequence $B_0 B_1 \ldots B_n$ of n 64-bit blocks B_i;
- require a key K; and
- use a 64-bit initialization vector IV generated by a pseudo-random source.

To compute the cipher-blocks C_i of B_i, we define the first cipher-block as the result of (a) forming the bitwise exclusive-or of B_1 and the initialization vector IV and (b) encrypting the resulting block with the key K:

$$C_1 \stackrel{\text{def}}{=} E_K(B_1 \oplus IV). \tag{3.18}$$

For all i with $2 \leq i \leq n$, we set

$$C_i \stackrel{\text{def}}{=} E_K(B_i \oplus C_{i-1}) \tag{3.19}$$

and obtain the encryption $C_1 C_2 \ldots C_n$ of $B_1 B_2 \ldots B_n$. Notice how, in (3.19), the previously computed cipher block plays the role of the random initialization vector in (3.18).

EXERCISES 3.6

1. *Multiple encryption of identical messages*   Suppose that you plan to encrypt the same message repeatedly in the CBC mode with the same key. What guarantees that the resulting cipher-text will always be different from the previously computed ones?

2. *Inverse of DES in CBC mode*   Writing $D_K(C)$ for decrypting C with key K, explain in detail how one can decrypt the message $C_1 C_2 \ldots C_n$ obtained from $B_1 B_2 \ldots B_n$ in CBC mode. Prove that this indeed recovers the original message.

3. *Error propagation of CBC mode*   Suppose that the transmission of the cipher-text $C_1 C_2 \ldots C_n$ contains an error in block C_i but is otherwise error-free. Argue that decryption of the flawed cipher-text will recover all original blocks except B_i and B_{i+1}. Can you say something about the (expected) number of bits that will have changed in B_i and B_{i+1}?

4. Use your implementation of the DES algorithm to write a program that can encrypt and decrypt messages of bit length $64 \cdot n$ ($n \geq 1$) in the CBC mode.

5. *CFB mode*   Read about the DES *cipher-feedback* (CFB) mode in the FIPS 81 document;[7] then explain why both decryption and encryption in this mode use the basic DES algorithm in its *encryption* state.

6. *Message authentication code*   A *message authentication code* (MAC) is a sequence of bits appended to a message in order to ensure the *integrity* of the message, not its

---

[7] http://www.itl.nist.gov/fipspubs/fip81.htm

secrecy. Any alteration of the original message should result in a different MAC. Discuss how and why DES in the CBC and CFB modes can be used to generate MACs for messages.

7. **OFB mode** Telephone communications are often encrypted by using DES to build a stream cipher; recall the design idea of Figure 3.1 (p. 82). In DES *output-feedback mode,* one encrypts the first 64-bit block of a message and takes the resulting output as the first 64 bits of the key stream. This output block is then re-encrypted to produce the next 64 bits of the key stream and so forth, until the key stream is as long as the original message.

(a) Implement a key-stream generator that has a 64-bit input block and outputs the resulting key stream as just described.

(b) Implement DES in OFB mode for messages of bit length $64 \cdot n$ ($n \geq 1$). (How does decryption work?)

(c) Suppose you know that a cipher-text was encrypted in the manner described in part (b). Why and how can this cipher-text be attacked when the message is known to have a fixed header?

3.2.1.3 Triple DES

The key space for DES in the ECB mode is 2^{56}, minus a handful of *weak keys* that should not be used in practice. A randomly generated key has a very small probability of being weak, and a cautious implementation would check for such keys (since they are known explicitly); see the FIPS 46-2 document[8] for details. Recent advances in hardware and reductions in memory and processor costs have made it possible to launch brute-force attacks – slight variations of an exhaustive key search – against DES. A possible way to defend against such exhaustive key searches is to encrypt a message multiple times with different keys. Since each $E_K(\cdot)$ has $D_K(\cdot)$ as its inverse function over the set of 64-bit blocks, multiple encryptions would not result in any additional power if the key space were closed, meaning that for all keys K_1 and K_2 there would be some key K_3 such that

$$E_{K_1}(E_{K_2}(B)) = E_{K_3}(B) \tag{3.20}$$

for all 64-bit blocks B. Fortunately, it is known that the key space for DES is *not* closed. The standard FIPS 43[9] specifies *triple DES* to operate on a 64-bit input block B to produce a 64-bit output block C using three DES keys K_1, K_2, K_3. Encryption and decryption are given (respectively) by

$$B \mapsto E_{K_3}(D_{K_2}(E_{K_1}(B))), \tag{3.21}$$
$$B \mapsto D_{K_3}(E_{K_2}(D_{K_1}(B))). \tag{3.22}$$

The standard specifies three alternative key options. In the first option, all three keys K_1, K_2, K_3 are independently chosen. In the second option, K_1 equals K_3 but is independent of K_2. Finally, all three keys are equal in the third option.

---

[8] http://www.itl.nist.gov/fipspubs/fip46-2.htm
[9] http://csrc.nist.gov/cryptval/des/fr990115.htm

EXERCISES 3.7

1. *Backwards compatibility of triple DES*   Which key option of triple DES produces backwards compatibility with the (single) DES algorithm? Is this option also compatible with the CBC mode of operation?
2. *Key space as a group*   Let K range over some key space $\mathcal{K}$, and let $E_K(\cdot)$ and $D_K(\cdot)$ be defined as mutually inverse functions of type $\mathcal{D} \rightarrow \mathcal{D}$, where $\mathcal{D}$ is some domain of messages. Suppose that equation (3.20) holds for all keys in the key space.
    (a) We define $K \approx K'$ for $K, K' \in \mathcal{K}$ if and only if $E_K(\cdot)$ equals the function $E_{K'}(\cdot)$. Show that $\approx$ is an equivalence relation on $\mathcal{K}$.
    (b) Let $[K]_\approx$ be the equivalence class of K with respect to $\approx$ in $\mathcal{K}$. We define $[K_1]_\approx \circ [K_2]_\approx$ to be $[K_3]_\approx$, where K_3 is as in (3.20). We let e be a two-sided identity for $\circ$. Show that the operation $\circ$ is well-defined and gives rise to a group structure on the key space.
3. How many possible invertible functions are there of type $\mathcal{D} \rightarrow \mathcal{D}$ if the message space is the one of all possible 64-bit blocks?
4. *Implementing triple DES*   Program an interface that asks for one of the three key options of triple DES, generates three random keys based on the specified option, and runs triple DES with those keys. Verify that one of these options produces the same results as single DES.
5. *Compression and encryption*   Discuss how the use of compression algorithms can potentially strengthen the security of a given cryptosystem.

3.2.2   Advanced Encryption Standard: Rijndael

One can show that the group for single DES, generated as in Exercise 3.7-2 via (3.20), has at least 10^{2499} many elements. This is a reassuring lower bound that indicates triple DES may be secure for some time to come.[10] Although NIST delegates DES to legacy systems and will continue to approve triple DES, the agency solicited proposals for a new *Advanced Encryption Standard* (AES). Fifteen initial submissions were narrowed down to five finalists after a demanding worldwide review by leading experts in the field. The submitted designs varied in:

- their high-level structure (similar to DES versus a novel structure);
- the instructions used (S-boxes, shifts, exclusive-or, etc.);
- specific techniques (e.g., using other algorithms as components); and
- the choice of platform for which to optimize the design (smartcards, popular processors for PCs, etc.).

The candidate algorithms differed in terms of performance, although the five finalists all provided for a high level of security.

On 2 October 2000, NIST announced the winner of this global competition: the AES proposal *Rijndael,* designed by J. Daemen and V. Rijmen from Belgium. Their design is quite simple and elegant, and it is not based on the architecture of DES. In the end, Rijndael

---

[10] Note that DES and triple DES are widely used in the financial service industries.

was chosen since it had the best combination of security, performance, efficiency, flexibility, and implementability. The proposed AES standard is currently subject to a period of public comment. Sometime between April and June 2001, it is expected that Rijndael will be approved as the official AES Standard by the U.S. Department of Commerce. The selection process was unique in encouraging the international cryptology community to advance the state of the art in cipher design. Commercial products based on the new standard will be available by the time this book is in print. It is believed that this algorithm may be secure for well beyond twenty years. This belief is based on Rijndael's very large key space and its shields against "all known" attacks. Only time will tell!

In November 1999, NIST issued a "white paper" for the second round of the AES competition, posing to the general public issues pertaining to a prospective standard. A key point of debate was whether one should choose a single or rather several algorithms as a standard. The latter would have provided:

(a) *resilience* – in case one algorithm were broken, there would still be secure algorithms available in an implementation;
(b) more "protection" against claims on *intellectual property rights* – were some party to claim such rights on a chosen single standard after its adoption;
(c) *flexibility* – in that several algorithms offer a combination of features (e.g., high security and high efficiency) to a degree that may be unattainable in a single algorithm;
(d) *interoperability problems* and inflated costs due to multiple implementations; and
(e) an *increased target* – attackers would be happy just to break one of the algorithms in the standard, and a successful attack would critically decrease public confidence in the remaining algorithms.

The stakeholders in this standard faced a dilemma: there was evidently no optimal solution. The decision was made in favor of a single design. No matter which way the decision went, there would have been a problem of perception management. When is an algorithm considered to be broken? A purely theoretical attack may create devastating damage through incompetently written press releases, causing a dramatic decline of companies' stock value. How important are software implementation characteristics compared with the performance of hardware implementations of AES candidates? Rijndael was impressive in both areas. How important is the realizability of implementations on low-end smartcards and future low-end environments? Rijndael's *encryption* mode performs well on 8-bit processors – its decryption mode, less so. How can one defend against well-known attacks that are specific to smartcards (see Chapter 6)? Rijndael can address this. What modes of operation are appropriate for the new AES standard? This is currently under investigation. We now describe the specification of Rijndael.

3.2.2.1 Bytes as Polynomials

The symmetric cryptographic algorithm Rijndael operates on *bytes,* strings of eight bits

$$b_7 b_6 b_5 \dots b_1 b_0,$$

as well as on *words,* 32-bit strings that can be thought of as strings of four bytes. The set $\mathcal{B}$ of all bytes contains 2^8 elements. Before we can explain the algorithm, we need to give $\mathcal{B}$ the structure of a finite field. For that, we need an addition on $\mathcal{B}$ that gives it the structure of a commutative group with a two-sided identity 00000000. Then we require a commutative multiplication such that all elements of B other than 00000000 have a multiplicative inverse. It is a mathematical fact that there is exactly one finite field for each prime power, up to isomorphism.[11] Thus there is essentially only one such field for B! However, in terms of implementation efficiency, the *representation* of the elements and operations makes all the difference. We already encountered this phenomenon, in terms of security, in the discussion of a mathematical isomorphism between $\mathbb{Z}_n^*$ and $\mathbb{Z}_{\phi(n)}$ when n has a primitive root (see Theorem 2.35, p. 44) – we had no effective means of *computing* this isomorphism.

Definition 3.14 (Representations of Bytes)
Given a byte $b_7 b_6 \dots b_0$, we will represent it in three ways and switch freely between those representations:

- a byte is a bit string of length eight, such as 10111011;
- a byte can be written as two hex digits,[12] such as BB;
- a byte can be written as a polynomial modulo 2 of degree ≤ 7, such as $x^7 + x^5 + x^4 + x^3 + x + 1$ (also representing the bit string 10111011).[13]

Note that the examples in these three versions represent the same byte.

Definition 3.15
We use **a** to denote a byte that is independent of its representation. Addition of two bytes, **a** $\oplus$ **b**, is achieved by adding their polynomials modulo 2.

Example 3.16
The byte 01000101 can be represented as the hexadecimal 45 and as the polynomial $x^6 + x^2 + 1$. The byte 01111000 has the representations 78 and $x^6 + x^5 + x^4 + x^3$. The element 45 $\oplus$ 78 is therefore

$$(x^6 + x^2 + 1) + (x^6 + x^5 + x^4 + x^3) = x^5 + x^4 + x^3 + x^2 + 1 \bmod 2,$$

resulting in the hexadecimal 3D.

Remark 3.17
The operation $\oplus$ makes B into a commutative finite group with two-sided identity 00. This operation corresponds to the bitwise exclusive-or on bit strings and constitutes its own inverse operation.

The nonlinear element of the Rijndael cipher originates from the multiplication on B. This is where the representation of bytes as polynomials is instrumental, as there will be no obvious way of defining this operation in the other two representations.

---

[11] Note that this fact conveys two things: (i) that finite fields of such a size indeed exist, and (ii) that all such fields, for a fixed size, are basically the same one.

[12] It is standard practice to think of 4-bit strings as hexadecimal digits 0, 1, …, 9, A, B, C, D, E, F; where A corresponds to 1010 (decimal 10), B corresponds to 1011 (decimal 11), etc.

[13] The *degree* of a polynomial $a_n x^n + a_{n-1} x^{n-1} + \cdots + a_1 x + a_0 \bmod k$ is the largest $l \in \{0, 1, \dots, n\}$ such that $a_l \neq 0 \bmod k$.

Definition 3.18

Given two bytes **a** and **b**, we define their *product,* **a** • **b**, as the multiplication of their polynomial representations modulo the polynomial

$$m(x) \stackrel{\text{def}}{=} x^8 + x^4 + x^3 + x + 1. \tag{3.23}$$

Example 3.19

If **a** and **b** are $x^6 + x^2 + 1$ and $x^3 + x$ (respectively), then their product is

$$(x^9 + x^5 + x^3) + (x^7 + x^3 + x) = x^9 + x^7 + x^5 + x \bmod 2,$$

since $a + a = 0 \bmod 2$. We can now divide this polynomial by $m(x)$ – using an algorithm you probably remember from your high-school days – to obtain

$$x^9 + x^7 + x^5 + x = (x^7 + x^4 + x^2) + x \cdot m(x).$$

Because we consider this expression modulo $m(x)$, our result is $x^7 + x^4 + x^2$; in hexadecimal, this reads

$$45 \bullet 0A = 94.$$

The operation

$$(\mathbf{a}, \mathbf{b}) \mapsto \mathbf{a} \bullet \mathbf{b} \colon \mathcal{B} \times \mathcal{B} \to \mathcal{B} \tag{3.24}$$

has no intuitive interpretation on bytes represented as bit strings.

Proposition 3.20

The set $\mathcal{B}$ is a finite field, where $\oplus$ is addition with 00 *as its two-sided identity and where* • *is multiplication with* 01 *as its two-sided identity.*

Proof

1. We already saw that $(\mathcal{B}, \oplus, 00)$ is a finite commutative group.
2. Note that 01 represents the polynomial 1, which is clearly a two-sided identity for multiplication of polynomials modulo $m(x)$. The operation in (3.24) is clearly associative and commutative, as the multiplication of polynomials modulo a fixed polynomial is.
3. We also need to show that every byte **a** (other than 00) has a multiplicative inverse. Let $p(x)$ be the polynomial corresponding to **a**; although we have not explicitly presented all the necessary background, we have implicitly enabled this assignment as follows. One can (a) generalize the definition of the greatest common divisor (Definition 2.22, p. 39) to polynomials modulo a fixed polynomial, (b) prove that this is a linear combination of its two arguments (cf. Proposition 2.23, p. 39), and (c) adapt the extended Euclid algorithm (see Exercise 2.19-1, p. 60) to polynomials. One can then effectively compute polynomials $r(x)$ and $s(x)$, which again represent bytes,[14] such that

$$r(x) \cdot p(x) + s(x) \cdot m(x) = 1 \bmod 2. \tag{3.25}$$

---

[14] Since their degree is ≤ 7.

The right-hand side of (3.25) equals 1 because $m(x)$ is irreducible. Reading (3.25) modulo $m(x)$, we infer that $r(x)$ is an inverse of $p(x)$ modulo $m(x)$. Thus

$$\mathbf{a} \bullet \mathbf{b} = \mathbf{b} \bullet \mathbf{a} = 01,$$

where $\mathbf{b}$ is the representation of $r(x)$.

4. Finally, multiplication and addition obey the required distributivity law:

$$\mathbf{a} \oplus (\mathbf{b} \bullet \mathbf{c}) = (\mathbf{a} \bullet \mathbf{b}) \oplus (\mathbf{a} \bullet \mathbf{c}), \tag{3.26}$$

which follows readily from the corresponding distributivity law of the operations $\cdot$ and $+$ on polynomials. $\square$

Fortunately, an implementation of (3.24) can be achieved, and very efficiently so, without relying on the pedestrian algorithm from high school. If we can implement (3.24), where $\mathbf{b}$ is the polynomial x (written 02 in hexadecimal), then we can use the operation

$$\texttt{xtime}: \mathcal{B} \to \mathcal{B},$$
$$\texttt{xtime}(\mathbf{a}) \overset{\text{def}}{=} \mathbf{a} \bullet 02 \tag{3.27}$$

to realize (3.24): first for any powers x^n ($n \le 7$) by the repeated application of $\texttt{xtime}$; second for general polynomials, making use of the distributivity law (3.26).

Definition 3.21 (The Operation $\texttt{xtime}$)
Given a general polynomial

$$b_7 x^7 + b_6 x^6 + \cdots + b_1 x + b_0$$

representing the byte $\mathbf{b} \overset{\text{def}}{=} b_7 b_6 \ldots b_1 b_0$, multiplication by x results in

$$b_7 x^8 + b_6 x^7 + \cdots + b_1 x^2 + b_0 x.$$

This is understood to be modulo $m(x)$, so there are two cases.

(i) If b_7 equals 0, then

$$b_7 x^8 + b_6 x^7 + \cdots + b_1 x^2 + b_0 x = b_6 x^7 + b_5 x^6 + \cdots + b_2 x + b_0 x$$

is already the result of computing $\texttt{xtime}(\mathbf{b})$.

(ii) Otherwise, b_7 equals 1, so we must subtract $m(x)$ from $b_7 x^8 + b_6 x^7 + \cdots + b_1 x^2 + b_0 x$. But since $m(x)$ is 1B in hexadecimal, this amounts to computing $\mathbf{b} \oplus 1B$, recalling that subtraction in $\mathcal{B}$ is the same as addition.

We see that $\texttt{xtime}$ can be implemented as a *left shift* followed by a *conditional bitwise exclusive-or* with 1B.

Example 3.22
Here we rework the previous example. The byte $\mathbf{a}$ is $x^6 + x^2 + 1$ or 45 in hexadecimal. The byte $\mathbf{b}$ is $x^3 + x$ or 0A in hexadecimal. We compute

$$\texttt{xtime}(\mathbf{a}) = 8A \qquad \text{(no exclusive-or)},$$
$$\texttt{xtime}(\texttt{xtime}(\mathbf{a})) = 8A \bullet 02 = 0D \quad \text{(exclusive-or)},$$
$$\texttt{xtime}(\texttt{xtime}(\texttt{xtime}(\mathbf{a}))) = 0D \bullet 02 = 96 \quad \text{(no exclusive-or)}.$$

EXERCISES 3.8

1. Verify that 1B is a representation of $m(x)$.
2. Compute the following bytes in hexadecimal:
   (a) $1B \oplus 01$;
   (b) `xtime(9C)`;
   (c) `xtime(7F)`;
   (d) $CD \bullet 10$;
   (e) $AD \oplus (02 \bullet 01)$.
3. For CD, find the unique byte **b** such that $\mathbf{b} \bullet CD = 01$.
4. What is the multiplicative inverse of 02?

The cipher Rijndael arranges plain-text and round keys in two-dimensional arrays of bytes (see Figure 3.15). While these arrays vary in their number of columns, *they always have four rows*. Thus, each column represents a 32-bit word. The cipher also performs operations on columns, so we need to record some operations on such words. Since a 32-bit word can be represented as a string of four bytes

$$\mathbf{a_3 a_2 a_1 a_0},$$

we may think of such words as polynomials of degree < 4:

$$p(x) = \mathbf{a_3}x^3 + \mathbf{a_2}x^2 + \mathbf{a_1}x + \mathbf{a_0},$$
$$q(x) = \mathbf{b_3}x^3 + \mathbf{b_2}x^2 + \mathbf{b_1}x + \mathbf{b_0}; \tag{3.28}$$

here the coefficients $\mathbf{a_i}$ and $\mathbf{b_i}$ are elements of $\mathcal{B}$. Since $\oplus$ operates on such coefficients, we can lift this operation to polynomials as follows:

$$p(x) \oplus q(x) \stackrel{\text{def}}{=} (\mathbf{a_3} \oplus \mathbf{b_3})x^3 + (\mathbf{a_2} \oplus \mathbf{b_2})x^2 + (\mathbf{a_1} \oplus \mathbf{b_1})x + (\mathbf{a_0} \oplus \mathbf{b_0}). \tag{3.29}$$

Similarly, we may lift the operation $\bullet$ of $\mathcal{B}$ to polynomials, as in (3.28). Using (3.26), we have

$$p(x) \bullet q(x) = \mathbf{c_6}x^6 + \mathbf{c_5}x^5 + \mathbf{c_4}x^4 + \mathbf{c_3}x^3 + \mathbf{c_2}x^2 + \mathbf{c_1}x + \mathbf{c_0}, \tag{3.30}$$

where

$$\mathbf{c_0} = \mathbf{a_0} \bullet \mathbf{b_0},$$
$$\mathbf{c_1} = \mathbf{a_1} \bullet \mathbf{b_0} \oplus \mathbf{a_0} \bullet \mathbf{b_1},$$
$$\mathbf{c_2} = \mathbf{a_2} \bullet \mathbf{b_0} \oplus \mathbf{a_1} \bullet \mathbf{b_1} \oplus \mathbf{a_0} \bullet \mathbf{b_2},$$
$$\mathbf{c_3} = \mathbf{a_3} \bullet \mathbf{b_0} \oplus \mathbf{a_2} \bullet \mathbf{b_1} \oplus \mathbf{a_0} \bullet \mathbf{b_3},$$
$$\mathbf{c_4} = \mathbf{a_3} \bullet \mathbf{b_1} \oplus \mathbf{a_2} \bullet \mathbf{b_2} \oplus \mathbf{a_1} \bullet \mathbf{b_3},$$
$$\mathbf{c_5} = \mathbf{a_3} \bullet \mathbf{b_2} \oplus \mathbf{a_2} \bullet \mathbf{b_3},$$
$$\mathbf{c_6} = \mathbf{a_3} \bullet \mathbf{b_3}.$$

If we reduce the polynomial in (3.30) by a polynomial of degree 4, then we arrive at a polynomial of degree 3 that therefore represents a 32-bit word.

Definition 3.23
Let

$$p(q) \otimes q(x) \stackrel{\text{def}}{=} p(x) \bullet q(x) \bmod M(x), \qquad (3.31)$$

where $M(x) \stackrel{\text{def}}{=} x^4 + 1$.

In the exercises, we find that

$$x^i \bmod x^4 + 1 = x^{i \bmod 4} \qquad (3.32)$$

for all $i \in \mathbb{N}$. Therefore, setting

$$p(q) \otimes q(x) = \mathbf{d}_3 x^3 + \mathbf{d}_2 x^2 + \mathbf{d}_1 x + \mathbf{d}_0,$$

we may compute the $\mathbf{d}_i$ from the $\mathbf{c}_i$ listed previously as:

$$\begin{aligned}
\mathbf{d}_0 &= \mathbf{a}_0 \bullet \mathbf{b}_0 \oplus \mathbf{a}_3 \bullet \mathbf{b}_1 \oplus \mathbf{a}_2 \bullet \mathbf{b}_2 \oplus \mathbf{a}_1 \bullet \mathbf{b}_3, \\
\mathbf{d}_1 &= \mathbf{a}_1 \bullet \mathbf{b}_0 \oplus \mathbf{a}_0 \bullet \mathbf{b}_1 \oplus \mathbf{a}_3 \bullet \mathbf{b}_2 \oplus \mathbf{a}_2 \bullet \mathbf{b}_3, \\
\mathbf{d}_2 &= \mathbf{a}_2 \bullet \mathbf{b}_0 \oplus \mathbf{a}_1 \bullet \mathbf{b}_1 \oplus \mathbf{a}_0 \bullet \mathbf{b}_2 \oplus \mathbf{a}_3 \bullet \mathbf{b}_3, \\
\mathbf{d}_3 &= \mathbf{a}_3 \bullet \mathbf{b}_0 \oplus \mathbf{a}_2 \bullet \mathbf{b}_1 \oplus \mathbf{a}_1 \bullet \mathbf{b}_2 \oplus \mathbf{a}_0 \bullet \mathbf{b}_3.
\end{aligned} \qquad (3.33)$$

Thus, for a given $q(x)$, the function

$$p(x) \mapsto p(x) \otimes q(x)$$

is linear and is given by the matrix multiplication in (3.33). As in the case of $\bullet$, we can reduce the general operation $\otimes$ to additions and applications of $x \otimes q(x)$. We merely have
to specialize (3.33) to $p(x) = x$ and so obtain

$$\begin{aligned}
\mathbf{d}_0 &= 00 \bullet \mathbf{b}_0 \oplus 00 \bullet \mathbf{b}_1 \oplus 00 \bullet \mathbf{b}_2 \oplus 01 \bullet \mathbf{b}_3, \\
\mathbf{d}_1 &= 01 \bullet \mathbf{b}_0 \oplus 00 \bullet \mathbf{b}_1 \oplus 00 \bullet \mathbf{b}_2 \oplus 00 \bullet \mathbf{b}_3, \\
\mathbf{d}_2 &= 00 \bullet \mathbf{b}_0 \oplus 01 \bullet \mathbf{b}_1 \oplus 00 \bullet \mathbf{b}_2 \oplus 00 \bullet \mathbf{b}_3, \\
\mathbf{d}_3 &= 00 \bullet \mathbf{b}_0 \oplus 00 \bullet \mathbf{b}_1 \oplus 01 \bullet \mathbf{b}_2 \oplus 00 \bullet \mathbf{b}_3.
\end{aligned} \qquad (3.34)$$

This linear operation is obviously a cyclic shift of the bytes of the input word.

EXERCISES 3.9

1. Prove equation (3.32).
2. The polynomial $M(x) = x^4 + 1$ is *not* irreducible; it has a polynomial other than 1
   or itself as a factor.
   (a) Prove this claim; that is, find such a nontrivial factor.
   (b) Use part (a) to argue that $p(x) \mapsto p(x) \otimes q(x)$ does not have an inverse for all
       choices of $q(x)$.
3. Compute $x \otimes p(x)$, where $p(x)$ equals $2Bx^3 + 94x^2 + FFx + 8D$.

$a_{0,0}$	$a_{0,1}$	$a_{0,2}$	$a_{0,3}$
$a_{1,0}$	$a_{1,1}$	$a_{1,2}$	$a_{1,3}$
$a_{2,0}$	$a_{2,1}$	$a_{2,2}$	$a_{2,3}$
$a_{3,0}$	$a_{3,1}$	$a_{3,2}$	$a_{3,3}$

$k_{0,0}$	$k_{0,1}$	$k_{0,2}$	$k_{0,3}$	$k_{0,4}$	$k_{0,5}$
$k_{1,0}$	$k_{1,1}$	$k_{1,2}$	$k_{1,3}$	$k_{1,4}$	$k_{1,5}$
$k_{2,0}$	$k_{2,1}$	$k_{2,2}$	$k_{2,3}$	$k_{2,4}$	$k_{2,5}$
$k_{3,0}$	$k_{3,1}$	$k_{3,2}$	$k_{3,3}$	$k_{3,4}$	$k_{3,5}$

Figure 3.15. The State and the cipher key for $Nb = 4$ and $Nk = 6$.

3.2.2.2 Rijndael's Encryption Mode

Rijndael is a block cipher, encrypting and decrypting one block of bits at a time. The length of a block and the length of the initial key may be 128, 192, or 256 bits. This cipher allows you to choose different numbers for the length of the block and the key. For example, you could use Rijndael on 128-bit blocks with a 256-bit key. The design allows even more flexibility in choosing these numbers, but the three listed values were part of the AES design requirements.

Definition 3.24

We write Nb for the block length divided by 32 and Nk for the key length divided by 32. The plain-text and (intermediate) cipher-text are called *the State* and are represented by a two-dimensional array of bytes with four rows and Nb columns. Similarly, the key is represented as a two-dimensional array of bytes with four rows and Nk columns.

From this definition we may infer that

$$(Nb, Nk) \in \{4, 6, 8\} \times \{4, 6, 8\},$$

giving us nine possible parameter scenarios.

Example 3.25

For $Nb = 4$ and $Nk = 6$, we obtain the representations shown in Figure 3.15.

Definition 3.26

1. The input and output blocks for Rijndael are *one-dimensional* arrays of 8-bit bytes, indexed from 0 to $4Nb - 1$. Similarly, the cipher key is a one-dimensional array of 8-bit bytes, indexed from 0 to $4Nk - 1$.
2. The bytes of the input block are mapped onto the State in the order $a_{0,0}$, $a_{1,0}$, $a_{2,0}$, $a_{3,0}$, $a_{0,1}$, $a_{1,1}$, ... Thus we fill the columns of the State from the top to the bottom, filling columns from the left to the right. Thus the byte with input index 0 is placed within $a_{0,0}$, the one with index 9 is placed in $a_{1,2}$, ... The two-dimensional key array in Figure 3.15 is filled in the same manner. For example, the key byte with index 2 is placed in $k_{2,0}$, the one with index 5 is placed in $k_{1,1}$, and so on.

Since Nb and Nk are in $\{4, 6, 8\}$, the index range of these arrays is

    0..15, 0..23, or 0..31,

Nr ⬎	Nb = 4	Nb = 6	Nb = 8
Nk = 4	10	12	14
Nk = 6	12	12	14
Nk = 8	14	14	14

Figure 3.16. The number of rounds, Nr, as a function of Nb and Nk.

respectively. (The top-level architecture of Rijndael's encryption mode is given in Figure 3.17.) Ignoring the indices in the array ExtendedKey for now, encryption consists of:

- an initial step in which we add the key to the State;
- Nr − 1 rounds with a round key, ExtendedKey[Nb*i], for round i derived from the CipherKey; and
- a final round.

Thus Nr *is the number of total rounds* and is a function of Nb and Nk; see Figure 3.16.

Compare this design to the top-level structure of DES. For DES, there is an initial permutation, which is useless in terms of security. As we will see, this is now strengthened to a bitwise exclusive-or operation. For DES, there are fifteen identical rounds, with a round-dependent key derived from the 56-bit cipher key. In Rijndael this is replaced by Nr − 1 identical rounds that – although having a round-dependent key derived from the cipher key – do not use the Feistel architecture of Figure 3.4. In DES, the last round does not permute the left and right halves, making decryption with the same algorithm possible. The last round in Rijndael serves a similar role, but it is less trivial to show that the same design may be used for successful decryption. We shall return to our discussion of the top-level view of Rijndael's decryption mode, but for now we describe how the Nr − 1 encryption rounds work.

Each round has the current State and a RoundKey as parameters. The call Round(State,RoundKey) updates the State according to the supplied RoundKey. The pseudo code for these rounds is given in Figure 3.17. We see that each round, except the final one, applies four transformations to the State in sequence. Only the last transformation makes use of the RoundKey.

1. The call

   ByteSub(State)

   performs a byte substitution such that each byte of the State is transformed deterministically and independently of any other bytes in the State. This allows for parallel computations, and this independence is also instrumental in realizing decryption with the same design. Specifically, each byte of the State is transformed, in place, via two operations:

   (a) first, the byte $a_{i,j}$ is transformed into its inverse with respect to the operation • of (3.24) – the byte 00 is left unchanged;

```
RijndaelEncryption(State,CipherKey) {
  KeyExpansion(CipherKey,ExpandedKey);
  AddRoundKey(State,ExpandedKey);
  for ( i = 1; i < Nr; i++ ) { Round(State,ExpandedKey[Nb*i-1]); }
  FinalRound(State,ExpandedKey[Nb*Nr-1]);
}
Round(State,Roundkey) {
  ByteSub(State);
  ShiftRow(State);
  MixColumn(State);
  AddRoundKey(State,RoundKey);
}
FinalRound(State,RoundKey) {
  ByteSub(State);
  ShiftRow(State);
  AddRoundKey(State,RoundKey);
}
```

Figure 3.17. Pseudo-code for the top-level structure of encryption with Rijndael.

(b) second, the resulting byte is transformed by means of the affine map

$$
\begin{bmatrix} b'_0 \\ b'_1 \\ b'_2 \\ b'_3 \\ b'_4 \\ b'_5 \\ b'_6 \\ b'_7 \end{bmatrix} \stackrel{\text{def}}{=} \begin{bmatrix} 1 & 0 & 0 & 0 & 1 & 1 & 1 & 1 \\ 1 & 1 & 0 & 0 & 0 & 1 & 1 & 1 \\ 1 & 1 & 1 & 0 & 0 & 0 & 1 & 1 \\ 1 & 1 & 1 & 1 & 0 & 0 & 0 & 1 \\ 1 & 1 & 1 & 1 & 1 & 0 & 0 & 0 \\ 0 & 1 & 1 & 1 & 1 & 1 & 0 & 0 \\ 0 & 0 & 1 & 1 & 1 & 1 & 1 & 0 \\ 0 & 0 & 0 & 1 & 1 & 1 & 1 & 1 \end{bmatrix} \cdot \begin{bmatrix} b_0 \\ b_1 \\ b_2 \\ b_3 \\ b_4 \\ b_5 \\ b_6 \\ b_7 \end{bmatrix} + \begin{bmatrix} 1 \\ 1 \\ 0 \\ 0 \\ 0 \\ 1 \\ 1 \\ 0 \end{bmatrix}, \tag{3.35}
$$

which is invertible. The resulting byte is the new value of location $a_{i,j}$ in State. The inverse operation InvByteSub(State) first applies the inverse of the affine mapping in (3.35) and then computes the inverse of the resulting byte with respect to • of (3.24) – again mapping 00 onto itself. Thus the second phase of InvByteSub(State) is identical to the first phase of ByteSub(State).

2. The call

ShiftRow(State)

performs transformations on the rows of State. The first row $(a_{0,0}, a_{0,1}, \ldots)$ is left unchanged. All other rows are subject to a cyclic left shift of bytes. The second row $(a_{1,0}, a_{1,1}, \ldots)$ is shifted C1 bytes, the third row C2 bytes, and the fourth row C3 bytes. The shift parameters C1, C2, C3 are a function of Nb, the block length in bytes divided by 32. In Figure 3.18, this dependency is listed in tabular form. Notice that C2 refers to row *three*, not two. The call InvShiftRow(State) operates in the same way as ShiftRow(State) except that C1, C2, and C3 are replaced by Nb − C1, Nb − C2, and Nb − C3, respectively. Obviously, row shifts may be carried out in parallel.

Nb	C1	C2	C3
4	1	2	3
6	1	2	3
8	1	3	4

Figure 3.18. The number of bytes shifted as a function of the row and Nb.

$a_{0,0}$	$a_{0,1}$	$a_{0,2}$	$a_{0,3}$
$a_{1,0}$	$a_{1,1}$	$a_{1,2}$	$a_{1,3}$
$a_{2,0}$	$a_{2,1}$	$a_{2,2}$	$a_{2,3}$
$a_{3,0}$	$a_{3,1}$	$a_{3,2}$	$a_{3,3}$

$k_{0,0}$	$k_{0,1}$	$k_{0,2}$	$k_{0,3}$
$k_{1,0}$	$k_{1,1}$	$k_{1,2}$	$k_{1,3}$
$k_{2,0}$	$k_{2,1}$	$k_{2,2}$	$k_{2,3}$
$k_{3,0}$	$k_{3,1}$	$k_{3,2}$	$k_{3,3}$

$$a_{i,j} \oplus k_{i,j}$$

Figure 3.19. Adding the RoundKey to the State for Nb = 4.

3. The call

   MixColumn(State)

   transforms each column of State independently of any other column. The $(i+1)$th column determines a polynomial $p_i(x) \stackrel{\text{def}}{=} a_{3,i}x^3 + a_{2,i}x^2 + a_{1,i}x + a_{0,i}$.[15] We update that $(i+1)$th column with the coefficients of $p_i(x) \otimes c(x)$ in the same order as defined by $p_i(x)$, where

   $$c(x) \stackrel{\text{def}}{=} 03x^3 + 01x^2 + 01x + 02. \tag{3.36}$$

   The latter polynomial is invertible modulo $x^4 + 1$; the inverse is

   $$d(x) = 0Bx^3 + 0Dx^2 + 09x + 0E. \tag{3.37}$$

   Thus the program InvMixColumn(State) operates in the same manner as the program MixColumn(State) – only with $d(x)$ instead of $c(x)$.

4. Finally, the call

   AddRoundKey(State,RoundKey)

   has an array RoundKey of the same dimensions as State (see Figure 3.19), and the State is updated according to

   $$a'_{i,j} \stackrel{\text{def}}{=} a_{i,j} \oplus k_{i,j}, \tag{3.38}$$

   where $k_{i,j}$ is the matching byte of the RoundKey. Since $\oplus$ is its own inverse operation, we conclude that AddRoundKey(State,Roundkey) may be used "as is" the inverse transformation InvAddRoundKey(State,RoundKey).

   The code for the final round (as depicted in Figure 3.17) looks similar to the one written for Round(State,RoundKey), except that it drops the operation MixColumn(State)

---

[15] Note that we number columns as $0 \ldots 3$ from left to right.

```
KeyExpansion(byte[] Key, word[] Exp) {
// input:  an 8-bit byte array Key with index range 0..4*Nk-1
// output: a 32-bit word array Exp with index range 0..Nb*(Nr+1)-1
// precondition:  Nk <= 6
 for ( i = 0; i < Nk; i++ ) {
   Exp[i] = (Key[4*i], Key[4*i+1], Key[4*i+2], Key[4*i+3]);
 }
 for ( i = Nk; i < Nb*(Nr+1); i++ ) {
   temp = Exp[i-1];
   if (i % Nk == 0) { temp = SubByte(RotByte(temp)) XOR Rcon[i/Nk]; }
   Exp[i] = Exp[i-Nk] XOR temp;
 }
}
```

Figure 3.20. Pseudo-code for key expansion of the cipher key Key into the expanded key Exp, where Nk $\leq$ 6.

and performs the remaining three operations in the same relative order as for the previous rounds.

EXERCISES 3.10

1. Show that the affine map in (3.35) is invertible. Since we can always undo the effect of adding a constant vector, it suffices to show that the matrix in that equation has an inverse.

2. Given $c(x) = 03x^3 + 01x^2 + 01x + 02$ and $d(x) = 0Bx^3 + 0Dx^2 + 09x + 0E$, show that

   $$c(x) \otimes d(x) = 01;$$

   that is, show that $d(x)$ is the multiplicative inverse of $c(x)$ modulo $x^4 + 1$.

It remains to explain the nature of the code for

$$\text{KeyExpansion(CipherKey,ExpandedKey)} \tag{3.39}$$

and the key scheduling for each round. As for DES, the round keys for Rijndael are deterministically derived from the CipherKey. From Figure 3.19, we infer that each round key consists of Nb words. These round keys are computed and stored in a one-dimensional array of 32-bit words, ExtendedKey, such that ExtendedKey[0..Nb-1] contains the key for the first round, ExtendedKey[Nb..2*Nb-1] holds the key for the second round, and so forth. The pseudo-code in Figure 3.17 lists such round keys *through their first index in the expanded key array*. Note that the index for the final round points to the rightmost location of that array. The reasons for that will become apparent when we describe the Rijndael cipher in its decryption mode.

The pseudo-code for the key expansion phase depends on the value of Nk. For Nk $\leq$ 6, it is given in Figure 3.20. The operation XOR is the bitwise exclusive-or. We write (a, c, b, d) for the ordered bytes within a word. Then RotByte transforms (a, b, c, d)

```
KeyExpansion(byte[] Key, word[] Exp) {
// input:  an 8-bit byte array Key with index range 0..4*Nk-1
// output:  a 32-bit word array Exp with index range 0..Nb*(Nr+1)-1
// precondition:  Nk = 8
 for ( i = 0; i < Nk; i++ ) {
   Exp[i] = (Key[4*i], Key[4*i+1], Key[4*i+2], Key[4*i+3]);
 }
 for ( i = Nk; i < Nb*(Nr+1); i++ ) {
   temp = Exp[i-1];
   if (i % Nk == 0) { temp = SubByte(RotByte(temp)) XOR Rcon[i/Nk];
   } else { if (i % Nk = 4) { temp = SubByte(temp); }
   }
   Exp[i] = Exp[i-Nk] XOR temp;
 }
}
```

Figure 3.21. Pseudo-code for key expansion of the cipher key Key into the expanded key Exp, where $Nk = 8$.

into the word (b, c, d, a). The operation SubByte(W) transforms a word W by applying the SubByte transformation to all its four bytes in place. For the remaining value of $Nk = 8$, the pseudo-code for the key expansion is depicted in Figure 3.21. It remains to define the constants Rcon[i], which are independent of Nk.

Definition 3.27 (Round Keys and Constants)

- We set Rcon[1] to be 01. All remaining constants are defined recursively:

$$Rcon[i] \stackrel{\text{def}}{=} 02 \bullet Rcon[i-1] \quad (i \geq 2). \tag{3.40}$$

  Note that 02 is the representation of x.
- After the call in (3.39), the *key for round i* is given by the words

    ExpandedKey[Nb*(i-1)..Nb*i-1],

  in that order.

This completes our description of the *encryption* mode of Rijndael.

EXERCISES 3.11

1. Inspecting the code for the key expansion, what is the required range of the array Rcon?
2. Each Rcon[i] stores a byte corresponding to a polynomial modulo 2. Find out which polynomial that is.

3.2.2.3 Rijndael's Decryption Mode

For the DES cipher, decryption is achieved with the same algorithm; the only difference resides in the order in which the round keys are supplied. Encryption works with round

```
InvRound(State,RoundKey) {
 AddRoundKey(State,RoundKey); // is its own inverse
 InvMixColumn(State);  // like MixColumn but based on d(x)
 InvShiftRow(State);   // like ShiftRow but with Nb-Ci
 InvByteSub(State);    // 1st:  undo affine map; 2nd:  inverse
}
InvFinalRound(State,Roundkey) {
 AddRoundKey(State,RoundKey);
 InvShiftRow(State);
 InvByteSub(State);
}
```

Figure 3.22. Final and nonfinal inverse (decryption) rounds.

keys $K_1, K_2, \ldots, K_{16}$ in that order, whereas decryption requires K_{16} as key for round one, K_{15} as key for round two, et cetera. With Rijndael, it takes more work to realize decryption with essentially the same design. Although the actual *components* of the decryption design may turn out not to be identical to the respective components of the encryption design, they are quite similar and often share *common functionality* – an important consideration in hardware implementations.

The order of the four basic operations within an encryption round may seem somewhat arbitrary. However, a table-lookup implementation (which we won't describe here) requires that the first operation be the nonlinear SubByte(State) and that rows be shifted with ShiftRow(State) before MixColumn(State) is applied. If we want to undo the effect of such a round then clearly we must process these operations in the reverse order. The inverses of the final and nonfinal rounds are listed in Figure 3.22.

Notice that the final decryption round looks like a regular decryption round except that the operation InvMixColumn(State) has been omitted. Since encryption began with a call AddRoundKey(State,ExpandedKey[0]) (see Figure 3.17), we can describe the sequence of basic calls for the decryption of a two-round[16] Rijndael as follows:

```
AddRoundKey(State,ExpandedKey[2*Nb-1]);
InvShiftRow(State);
InvByteSub(State);
AddRoundKey(State,ExpandedKey[1*Nb-1]);
InvMixColumn(State);
InvShiftRow(State);
InvByteSub(State);
AddRoundKey(State,ExpandedKey[0]);
```

The corresponding two-round encryption activity is:

```
AddRoundKey(State,ExpandedKey[0]);
ByteSub(State);
ShiftRow(State);
MixColumn(State);
```

---

[16] The AES requires more than two rounds, but this simplification makes our presentation more transparent.

```
AddRoundKey(State,ExpandedKey[1*Nb-1]);
ByteSub(State);
ShiftRow(State);
AddRoundKey(State,ExpandedKey[2*Nb-1]);
```

We now transform the former code into a sequence of activities that looks like the latter code except for some different parameters. For example, the order in which we process InvShiftRow(State) and InvByteSub(State) does not matter as far as the net effect on the State is concerned; this is so because InvByteSub operates on individual bytes independent of their position within the two-dimensional array of bytes. Thus we can reverse this order in two locations of our code and obtain:

```
AddRoundKey(State,ExpandedKey[2*Nb-1]);
InvByteSub(State);
InvShiftRow(State);
AddRoundKey(State,ExpandedKey[1*Nb-1]);
InvMixColumn(State);
InvByteSub(State);
InvShiftRow(State);
AddRoundKey(State,ExpandedKey[0]);
```

Next, we transform the segment

```
AddRoundKey(State,ExpandedKey[1*Nb-1]);
InvMixColumn(State);
```

into

```
InvMixColumn(State);
AddRoundKey(State,InvExpandedKey[1*Nb-1]);
```

where InvExpandedKey[1*Nb-1] is understood to mean:

- represent the key for round one as in Figure 3.19; and then
- perform MixColumns on the array of that round key to obtain the "inverse" round key InvExpandedKey[1*Nb-1].

This transformation is justified because the effect of MixColumns is described by a linear map A, the effect of AddRoundKey is addition $\oplus$, and linear maps A satisfy

$$A(v \oplus w) = A(v) \oplus A(w).$$

Our two-round decryption code now reads as:

```
AddRoundKey(State,ExpandedKey[2*Nb-1]);
InvByteSub(State);
InvShiftRow(State);
InvMixColumn(State);
AddRoundKey(State,InvExpandedKey[1*Nb-1]);
```

```
RijndaelDecryption(State,CipherKey) {
 InvKeyExpansion(CipherKey,InvExpandedKey);
 AddRoundKey(State,InvExpandedKey[Nb*Nr]);
 for ( i = Nr - 1; i > 0; i-- ) {
   Round(State,InvExpandedKey[Nb*i]);
 }
 FinalRound(State,InvExpandedKey[0]);
}
InvRound(State,InvRoundKey) {
 InvByteSub(State);
 InvShiftRow(State);
 InvMixColumn(State);
 AddRoundKey(State,InvRoundKey);
}
InvFinalRound(State,InvRoundKey) {
 InvByteSub(State);
 InvShiftRow(State);
 AddRoundKey(State,InvRoundKey);
}
```

Figure 3.23. Pseudo-code for the top-level structure of decryption with Rijndael.

```
   InvByteSub(State);
   InvShiftRow(State);
   AddRoundKey(State,ExpandedKey[0]);
```

The two-round decryption just described recovers the structure of the encryption activity for two rounds! The only differences are that:

- ByteSub, ShiftRow, and MixColumns run in their "inverse mode", possibly sharing functional components of their original counterparts;
- the array ExpandedKey is processed from right to left (i.e., in reverse order); and
- some of these round keys have to be transformed with InvMixColumns before use.

The code for rounds and final rounds is therefore as given in Figure 3.23. The top-level structure of Rijndael's decryption mode is also listed in Figure 3.23. Finally, we need to make precise how InvExpandedKey is computed:

```
InvKeyExpansion(CipherKey,InvExpandedKey) {
  KeyExpansion(CipherKey,InvExpandedKey);
  for ( i = 1; i < Nr; i++ ) {
    InvMixColumn(InvExpandedKey[Nb*i]);
  }
}
```

We see that all but the first and last round key are transformed by means of MixColumns.

EXERCISES 3.12

1. Write a program that, given a representation of a byte **a**, returns 00 if **a** equals 00 and otherwise computes the multiplicative inverse of **a** with respect to • of (3.24).

2. Use the data obtained from the program of Exercise 1 to create a software implementation of Rijndael in the electronic codebook mode. Your implementation should allow for all combinations of block and key lengths as required by the AES. Your program should simply ask for an input block and a cipher key and then check that their lengths meet the standard. If so, your program should ask whether you want to run the decryption or encryption mode and should then execute the specified mode, providing the resulting final State as output.

3.2.2.4   Rijndael's Design Criteria

The design criteria of Rijndael, listed in its AES proposal, are:

- resistance against all known attacks;
- speed and code compactness on a wide range of platforms; and
- design simplicity.

Each round contains three uniform layers of transformations. The linear mixing layer (the transformations MixRows and MixColumns) provides high diffusion over multiple rounds, shielding against attempts of linear and differential cryptanalysis. The nonlinear layer (the transformation ByteSub) consists of a parallel application of "S-boxes" that are designed to have optimal worst-case nonlinear behavior. The key-addition layer performs a simple exclusive-or of the round key and the present State. Since this operation is also applied before the first and after the last round, it guarantees that the layers of the last round cannot be "peeled off". In contrast, with DES we could easily peel off the initial and final permutation.

Speed and code compactness of Rijndael are quite impressive, but the cipher does not perform equally well for all platforms. The choice of the coefficients of $c(x)$ for MixColumns was based on optimal performance of multiplication with $c(x)$ on 8-bit processors. Its inverse $d(x)$ has coefficients 09, 0E, 0B, and 0D. In an 8-bit implementation, the multiplication with $d(x)$ therefore takes considerably more time. That degradation in performance was anticipated in the design. Many applications of a block cipher either do not use its decryption mode or make encryption the bottleneck operation.

The key expansion can also begin with the last Nk words of the round key information and "roll back" to the original CipherKey. That way, we may compute round keys for the decryption phase "on the fly". However, the key expansion for the decryption mode is slower, since all but two of the round keys require an application of InvMixColumns.

We hope that our presentation has convinced the reader of Rijndael's simplicity and elegance. More motivation for its design choices can be found in the Rijndael AES proposal, available at NIST's AES home page; see the bibliographic notes for a reference.

EXERCISES 3.13

1. Recall the various applications of block ciphers: MACs and the CFB, OFB, ECB, and CBC modes of operation. Which of these applications do not require the block cipher in its *decryption* mode? (In those cases, the performance degradation of Rijndael is irrelevant.)

2. Use Rijndael operating on a 256-bit block and a 256-bit key to implement a hash function: the first message block is the "cipher key", and a chaining variable is the "input" block. The new chaining variable is the exclusive-or of the previous chaining variable and the cipher output. The new message block is the next block of the message to be hashed. (See Section 3.2.3 for an example of such a design that does not use Rijndael.)

3. Inspecting the coefficients of $c(x)$ and $d(x)$, explain why multiplication with $d(x)$ is more expensive than multiplication with $c(x)$, given an 8-bit processor.

4. Implement a self-synchronizing stream cipher based on Rijndael in the CFB mode of operation.

3.2.3 Secure Hash Standard: SHA

We have already encountered hash functions as a component of a communication protocol based on public-key encryption (see Protocol 2.5, p. 21). Using RSA secret keys, we were able to define a (slow) hash function in Exercise 2.19-10 (p. 61). In this section, we discuss the *secure hash standard* (SHS), a hashing algorithm specifically designed with security, speed, and memory constraints in mind. The algorithm is published in the FIPS 180-1 document[17] and is based on the design principles for MD4, a hash algorithm due to R. L. Rivest; SHS improves on an older standard published in FIPS 180. For sake of brevity, we write

hash(M)

for the result of applying the secure hash algorithm to a message M (in FIPS 180-1, this is written as SHA-1(M)). Hash algorithms have plenty of applications.

- They are commonly used to encrypt passwords for log-in protocols (see Section 4.2).
- One can use hash functions for *cryptographic check-sums* of files and application programs to ensure that they have not been infested with (or altered by) a computer virus.
- Hash functions also play a prominent role in protocols for digital signatures. Indeed, the secure hash algorithm is a crucial component of the digital signature standard (DSS), featured in Section 4.1.1.

We discussed the properties H1 to H4 of hash functions in Section 2.1.0.2 (p. 21). For example, in the context of digital signatures, we need to ensure that the change of even a single bit in a message M results in a different hash value; otherwise, one could launch attacks by altering (say) details of a contract while maintaining the original digital signature.

3.2.3.1 Useful Terminology

In computer science, one often uses the alphabet of *hexadecimal digits* 0, 1, …, 9, A, B, C, D, E, F to represent any 4-bit string. (We write *hex digit* subsequently as an abbreviation.) For example, 1001 is represented by 9 and 1100 is represented by C, denoting the decimal "12". We already encountered this notation in the specification of Rijndael. Unlike the

---

[17] http://www.itl.nist.gov/fipspubs/fip180-1.htm

case for natural languages, a *word* in computer science is a 32-bit string that we may thus
represent as a sequence of eight hex digits. For example, the word

0011 0111 1010 1001 1100 1100 0111 1100

can be represented as

37A9CC7C.

We may think of any word, a 32-bit string X, as the unique number x with $0 \leq x < 2^{32}$
whose binary representation equals X. Similarly, given any number z with $0 \leq z < 2^{64}$,
we may uniquely identify it with a *pair* of words $\langle X, Y \rangle$ such that

$$z = x \cdot 2^{32} + y,$$

where X and Y are the binary representations of x and y, respectively. Finally, a 512-*bit*
block is a 512-bit string that we may represent as a sequence of sixteen words, since $512 =
16 \cdot 32$.

Definition 3.28 (Operations on 32-Bit Words)
We define a number of operations on words $X, Y, Z, \ldots$ as follows:

X AND Y – the bitwise logical "and" of X and Y;
X OR Y – the bitwise logical "or" of X and Y;
X XOR Y – the bitwise "exclusive-or" of X and Y;
NOT X – the bitwise logical "negation" of X;
$X + Y$ – the binary representation of $x + y$ mod 2^{32}, where X and Y are the binary
            representations of x and y, respectively;
Shift(n, X) – the circular shift of X by n positions to the left.

EXERCISES 3.14

1. Consider the 32-bit words

$$X \stackrel{\text{def}}{=} 0011\ 0111\ 1010\ 1001\ 1100\ 1100\ 0111\ 1100,$$

$$Y \stackrel{\text{def}}{=} 1001\ 0001\ 0010\ 1101\ 0010\ 1011\ 1101\ 0100.$$

Compute:
   (a) X AND Y;
   (b) X OR Y;
   (c) X XOR Y;
   (d) (NOT Y) XOR X;
   (e) $X + Y$;
   (f) Shift$(2, X)$;
   (g) Shift$(32, Y)$.

2. What bit string is represented by the hex-digit sequence A5C82B05 ?

3. Consider the words X and Y represented as hex-digit sequences A5C82B05 and
   37A9CC7C, respectively. Compute $X + Y$ and represent it as a sequence of hex
   digits.

3.2.3.2 The Algorithm

The algorithm for computing $\texttt{hash}(M)$ has as a precondition that M be a message of bit length $512 \cdot n$ for some $1 \leq n$ such that

$$512 \cdot n < 2^{64}.$$

We next describe the padding provided by the standard for messages that are shorter than 2^{64} bits – in case this precondition is not met. Thus we may assume that

$$M = M_1 M_2 \ldots M_n \quad (n \geq 1), \tag{3.41}$$

where each M_i is a 512-bit block. The output of $\texttt{hash}(M)$ is a 160-bit string, a sequence of five *words*

$$\texttt{hash}(M) \overset{\text{def}}{=} \text{the final value of the word sequence } H_0 H_1 H_2 H_3 H_4. \tag{3.42}$$

After initializing these words H_0 to H_4, the algorithm processes each block M_i in sequence to alter the words H_i. As indicated in (3.42), the final value of the sequence $H_0 H_1 H_2 H_3 H_4$ is the hash value of the message M. Each block M_i is processed in 80 rounds, and each round t requires a function f_t and a constant word K_t for its computations. Fortunately, these parameters can be divided into four phases such that the constants and functions are the same in each phase.

Definition 3.29 (Functions and Constants for SHS)

$$f_t(X, Y, Z) \overset{\text{def}}{=} \begin{cases} (X \text{ AND } Y) \text{ OR } ((\text{NOT } X) \text{ AND } Z) & (0 \leq t \leq 19), \\ X \text{ XOR } Y \text{ XOR } Z & (20 \leq t \leq 39), \\ (X \text{ AND } Y) \text{ OR } (X \text{ AND } Z) \text{ OR } (Y \text{ AND } Z) & (40 \leq t \leq 59), \\ X \text{ XOR } Y \text{ XOR } Z & (60 \leq t \leq 79); \end{cases}$$

$$\tag{3.43}$$

$$K_t \overset{\text{def}}{=} \begin{cases} \texttt{5A827999} & (0 \leq t \leq 19), \\ \texttt{6ED9EBA1} & (20 \leq t \leq 39), \\ \texttt{8F1BBCDC} & (40 \leq t \leq 59), \\ \texttt{CA62C1D6} & (60 \leq t \leq 79). \end{cases}$$

The functions f_t take three words as input and produce one word as output. Notice that the second and fourth phase use the same function f_t and that t is the round number for processing each block M_i. The constants K_t are 32-bit words represented as hex-digit sequences. The pseudo-code for computing $\texttt{hash}(M)$ is given in Figure 3.24. An implementation of this pseudo-code requires:

- an implementation of words and the operations on words from Definition 3.28;
- an implementation of the functions f[t] and constants K[t] as defined in (3.43);
- eleven buffers for words H1 to H4, A to E, and TEMP;
- a buffer for 80 words W[0] to W[79].

```
Secure_Hash_Standard(Block[] M, int n) {
// input:  a nonempty array of 512-bit blocks
//  M[0], M[1], ..., M[n-1] such that 512 * n < 2**64
// output:  a 160-bit hash value represented by the concatenation
// H0H1H2H3H4 of the final values of the five 32-bit words H0 to H4
// the pseudo-code assumes the functions f[t] and constants K[t] for
// 0 <= t <= 79 as defined in the text
// initialization of each Hi as a sequence of eight hex digits
  Word H0 = 67452301;
  Word H1 = EFCDAB89;
  Word H2 = 98BADCFE;
  Word H3 = 10325476;
  Word H4 = C3D2E1F0;
  Word A,B,C,D,E;
  Word TEMP;
// an array that holds 80 words W[0], ..., W[79]
  Word[]  = W;
  for (int i = 0; i < n; ++i) {
    assign to W[0] the left-most 32 bits of M[i];
    assign to W[1] the next 32 left-most bits of M[i];
    ...
    assign to W[15] the 32 right-most bits of M[i];
// at this point, the concatenation W[0]W[1]...W[15] equals M[i]
    for (int j = 16; j < 80; ++j) {
// Shift(n,W) computes a circular shift of W by n positions to the left
      W[j] = Shift(1,W[j-3] XOR W[j-8] XOR W[j-14] XOR W[j-16]);
    }
    A = H0; B = H1; C = H2; D = H3; E = H4;
    for (int t = 0; t < 80; ++t) {
// + is the operation on words as defined in the text
      TEMP = Shift(5,A) + f[t](B,C,D) + E + W[t] + K[t];
      E = D; D = C; C = Shift(30,B); B = A; A = TEMP;
    }
    H0 = H0 + A;
    H1 = H1 + B;
    H2 = H2 + C;
    H3 = H3 + D;
    H4 = H4 + E;
  }
  return the concatenation H0H1H2H3H4;
}
```

Figure 3.24. Pseudo-code for the secure hash standard: computing a 160-bit string, hash(M), for any message M of bit length $512 \cdot n$, where $512 \leq 512 \cdot n < 2^{64}$.

Observe that the program Secure_Hash_Standard(M,n) in Figure 3.24 iterates over all blocks from the leftmost block M[0] to the rightmost block M[n-1] in the outermost for-statement. For each block M[i], we first load M[i] into the words W[0] to W[15], thinking of a block as a sequence of sixteen words. The for-statement with increment variable j then computes the remaining buffer values W[16] to W[79] as a deterministic function of previous buffer values. Then, the word group A to E gets the current value of the word group H0 to H4. Next, the 80 rounds for this block M[i] are performed. Each round modifies the word group A to E deterministically, using the functions f[t]

```
Alternate_Secure_Hash_Standard(Block[] M, int n) {
// requires only W[0] to W[15] and a mask Mask
// instead of the entire array W[0] to W[79]
  ...
// the initial part up to the for-statement below is as before
 Word Mask = 0000000F; // implements ''W[0] == W[16]''
 for (int i = 0; i < n; ++i) {
   compute W[0] to W[15] as before;
   A = H0; B = H1; C = H2; D = H3; E = H4; // as before
   int s;
   for (int t = 0; t < 80; ++t) {
// in the next two statements, we identify integers with 32-bit words
     s = t AND MASK;
     if (t >= 16) {
       W[s] = Shift(1,W[(s+13) AND Mask] XOR W[(s+8) AND Mask] XOR
                    W[(s+2) AND Mask] XOR W[s]);
     }
     TEMP = Shift(5,A) + f[t](B,C,D) + E + W[s] + K[t];
// W[t] from previous version changes to W[s]
     E = D; D = C; C = Shift(30,B); B = A; A = TEMP; // as before
   }
... // as before
 }
 ...
}
```

Figure 3.25. Pseudo-code for the alternate method of computing the secure hash of a message; it requires 63 fewer words for storage but more computation time and computes the same hash value as the program `Secure_Hash_Standard(M,n)`.

and constants K[t] as defined in (3.43). After these 80 rounds, each block determines new values of the word group H0 to H4 by "adding" the current values of word A to E to the current value of the word H0 to H4, respectively.

The pseudo-code in Figure 3.25 was written with a minimization of execution time in mind. It may well be the case that physical specifications of a system put much higher demands on memory constraints. In this case, one may implement the sequence W[0] to W[15] in a circular way, using a masking variable Mask of type Word with the immutable value 0000000F. The only changes in the code are done in the for-statement with the increment variable t and in the computation of the group H0 to H4 immediately after that for-statement. These changes are indicated in Figure 3.25.

3.2.3.3 Message Padding

In applications, messages might not be exact sequences of 512-bit blocks. In general, we may think of a message M as in (3.41), where M_1 to M_{n-1} all are 512 bits long but where now the length of M_n is between 1 and 511 bits. So all we have to do is *pad* the final block M_n to a 512-bit block M_n'; then we can call the secure hash standard with $M_1 M_2 \ldots M_{n-1} M_n'$ and n as arguments. The FIPS 180-1 document does indeed outline the way in which such padding should be performed, although it is somewhat vague about a certain case that we now attempt to make more precise.

Definition 3.30 (Representation of Message Length)

Let l be the bit length of the original message $M_1 M_2 \ldots M_{n-1} M_n$ and let $\langle X, Y \rangle$ be the pair of words such that XY, as a binary string, is the binary representation of l (possibly with leading zeros). For example, if $l < 2^{32}$ then X contains only 0-bits.

Note that the pair $\langle X, Y \rangle$ is well-defined, as the original message has a bit length that is strictly less than 2^{64}. Before processing M_n we change it to M_n'; their formats are shown in (3.44) and (3.45), respectively. The leftmost bit of Z is always a 1 and the remaining bits of Z are all 0. Thus, Z is determined by its bit length m. The computation of m involves two cases.[18]

1. If the bit length of M_n is not more than 447, then we compute the 512-bit block M_n' as

$$M_n' \overset{\text{def}}{=} M_n ZXY; \tag{3.44}$$

that is, we append the word Z and the 32-bit words X and Y to M_n as indicated. As pointed out earlier, XY is just the binary representation of the bit length l of the original message. The word Z has length

$$m \overset{\text{def}}{=} 512 - 64 - l',$$

where l' is the bit length of the block M_n; Z always has a leading 1-bit followed by $m - 1$ 0-bits. Since $1 \le l' \le 447$, we conclude that Z has at least one bit.

2. If the bit length of M_n exceeds 447, then we don't have sufficient space for appending 65 bits (one 1-bit and 64 bits for l) within the same block. Thus the length of Z must be

$$m \overset{\text{def}}{=} 1024 - 64 - l'$$

instead of the $512 - 64 - l'$ of the first case. Hence, the resulting message is of the form $M_1 M_2 \ldots M_{n-1} M_n' M_{n+1}'$, where

$$M_n' M_{n+1}' \overset{\text{def}}{=} M_n ZXY \tag{3.45}$$

and with X, Y, Z as in (3.44).

Example 3.31

In the FIPS 180-1 document, padding is illustrated by this example. Suppose that the message M is

$$01100001\ 01100010\ 01100011\ 01100100\ 01100101. \tag{3.46}$$

First, we append a 1-bit to this message and obtain

$$01100001\ 01100010\ 01100011\ 01100100\ 01100101\ 1. \tag{3.47}$$

Since the original message has length $l' = 40$, we have

$$m = 512 - 64 - 40 = 408$$

---

[18] Oddly enough, this case analysis is absent from the standard.

and so Z is a 1-bit followed by 407 0-bits. The string MZ, in hex digits, is then

61626364 65800000 00000000 00000000 00000000 00000000 00000000\\
00000000 00000000 00000000 00000000 00000000 00000000 00000000.

Finally, we append to MZ the pair of words XY such that XY is the two-word representation of the length l of the original message M. Since $l' = 40$, we have that XY equals 00000000 00000028 in hex digits. Thus the complete padded message $MZXY$, in hex digits, equals

61626364 65800000 00000000 00000000 00000000 00000000 00000000\\
00000000 00000000 00000000 00000000 00000000 00000000 00000028.

The security of the secure hash standard is not based on the difficulty of well-understood computational problems, such as the discrete logarithm problem (Definition 2.36, p. 45). Its security can therefore be adequately assessed only over time. At least, it seems for now to be immune to the *birthday attack,* which attempts to find *collisions* – messages M and M' whose hash values coincide. A probabilistic analysis arrives at the estimate

$$k \approx 1.17 \cdot \sqrt{n}, \tag{3.48}$$

where n is the number of possible hash values and k is the number of random hashed messages needed in order to have a 50% chance of such a collision. For $n = 365$, a guide at a Club Med Resort requires a group of only $k \approx 23$ people to have a 50% chance that two of them would share a birthday. For a 160-bit hash value, an attacker would require more than 2^{80} random hashes for a 50% probability of a collision pair.

EXERCISES 3.15

1. *Maximal length of message to be hashed*   Considering that the secure hash standard works only on messages of bit length $l = 512 \cdot n$ such that $1 \le l < 2^{64}$, what is the maximal number of 512-bit blocks you can hash as a single message?
2. *Equivalence of two hash methods*   Consider the pseudo-code for computing hash(M) in Figure 3.24 and Figure 3.25.
   (a) Prove that the alternate method of computing hash(M) actually yields the same results.
   (b) For both versions, explain why the value of the word group H0 to H4 after the processing of block M[i] is a function of *all blocks* M[i'] with $i' < i$.
3. *Implementing SHS*   Implement the secure hash standard in a programming language of your choice. Note that the interface requires that the bit length of the input message be an integral multiple of 512. Consult the appendix of the FIPS 180-1 document for example messages and message digests, and run your implementation with these examples to "validate" it.
4. Suppose that your message is less than 512 bits long and is given in hex digits as 3A8C251B. Perform message padding to this block and write the resulting block(s) as sequences of hex digits, grouped in sixteen words.

5. Suppose that your message is less than 512 bits long and is given in hex digits as

> 3A8CD51B 01A4C7B2 378C251B 01A8C7C2 3ABC251B 01A4C7B2\\
> 3A8CE51B 01C4C7F2 3A8C171B 0194C5B2 3A8C241B 01A4C762\\
> 0A8C251B 01A4C7B2.

Perform message padding to this block and write the resulting block(s) as sequences of hex digits, grouped in sixteen words.

6. Write a program that computes the value $hash(M)$, where M is the contents of a file of bit length between 1 and $2^{64} - 1$. Note that you must check whether you need to do message padding before processing the final block. You may want to adapt the given pseudo-code so that you can read such files blockwise.

3.3 BIBLIOGRAPHIC NOTES

The book by Kahn (1967) is still a worthwhile read on the history of cryptographic systems and their (mostly successful) attacks. A more recent and compelling read on this fascinating history is Singh (2000). The monograph by Rueppel (1986) provides a much more advanced discussion of the design and analysis of stream ciphers. Section 3.1.2 is drawn from an article by Goldreich (1997). Information is available on the Internet regarding the current U.S. standards in data encryption,[19] secure hash functions,[20] and digital signature standards.[21] Also available is a publication[22] describing in detail the modes of operation of DES, as well as information on how to break DES with an exhaustive key search.[23] For information on error propagation and synchronization issues of the DES modes of operations, consult the document FIPS 81. A document[24] announcing FIPS 46-3 outlines triple DES and its key options; it also requests comments on candidate algorithms for the AES. There is a site[25] for current information on the AES adoption process; we also recommend the NIST White Paper.[26] E. Biham offers a succinct survey[27] on the AES finalists and their tradeoffs. The NIST maintains a website[28] with information about the new advanced encryption standard. Rijndael, too, has a home page.[29] Another NIST site[30] contains links to the AES winner Rijndael, its specifications, a workshop on its modes of operations, an AES fact sheet, and recent news and developments.

[19] www.itl.nist.gov/fipspubs/fip46-2.html
[20] www.itl.nist.gov/fipspubs/fip180-1.html
[21] www.csrc.nist.gov/fipspubs/fips186l.pdf
[22] www.itl.nist.gov/fipspubs/fip81.html
[23] http://www.eff.org/descracker/
[24] http://csrc.nist.gov/cryptval/des/fr990115.html
[25] http://csrc.nist.gov/encryption/aes
[26] http://csrc.nist.gov/encryption/aes/round2/Round2WhitePaper.htm
[27] http://www.cs.technion.ac.il/~biham/Reports/aes-comparing.ps.gz
[28] www.nist.gov/aes
[29] http://www.esat.kuleuven.ac.be/~rijmen/rijndael/
[30] http://csrc.nist.gov/encryption/aes/

CHAPTER 4

Security Protocol Design and Analysis

4.1 DIGITAL SIGNATURES

In Protocol 2.5 (p. 21) we saw the twofold use of public-key cryptography (PKC) as a means for

- making messages unintelligible before they are transmitted on an untrusted communication line; and
- ensuring the *authenticity* of messages, or digital documents in general, by digitally signing them.

Protocol 2.5 exemplifies the *dual role of private keys*. They may be used to *decipher* a message that was encrypted with an agent's public key; on the other hand, they may be used to *sign* messages, and the signature can then be verified with the corresponding public key. Implementations usually employ different PKCs, or at least different parameters, for each of these functional roles of private keys. (See the exercises that follow for possible reasons.) It is beyond the scope of this text to discuss more advanced types of realizable digital signature systems, but we mention them in passing.

Protocol 4.1 (Fail-Stop Digital Signature)
A digital signature system has this property if a signer can prove that a message that was signed with her key, based on a fraudulent attack, is a fake.

Protocol 4.2 (Proxy Digital Signature)
A digital signature system has this property if a signer can give his authority to sign a message to someone else *without* revealing his secret signature key.

Protocol 4.3 (Designated-Confirmer Digital Signatures)
These are protocols that allow a signer to designate a confirmer, possibly herself, whose cooperation is necessary for the verification of digital signatures. This prevents the exact copying of digital signatures.

Public-key cryptosystems are by no means the only systems that can realize digital signature schemes.

Definition 4.4 (Digital Signature Scheme)
A *digital signature scheme* consists of a finite set $\mathcal{P}$ of plain-texts, a finite set $\mathcal{S}$ of signatures, and a finite key-space $\mathcal{K}$ such that, for each $K \in \mathcal{K}$, we have a signing algorithm

$\text{Sign}_K(\cdot): \mathcal{P} \to \mathcal{S}$

and a verification algorithm

$\text{Verify}_K(\cdot, \cdot): \mathcal{P} \times \mathcal{S} \to \text{boolean}$

such that, for all $M \in \mathcal{P}$ and all $S \in \mathcal{S}$, we have $\text{Verify}_K(M, S) = \text{true}$ if and only if $S = \text{Sign}_K(M)$.

The algorithms $\text{Sign}_K(\cdot)$ and $\text{Verify}_K(\cdot, \cdot)$ should be efficiently derivable, given K, and should have reasonable performance. Needless to say, given M and $\text{Verify}_K(\cdot, \cdot)$, an opponent should have no chance of producing some S with $S = \text{Sign}_K(M)$ unless the opponent knows the key K.

EXERCISES 4.1

1. Discuss why PKCs can be seen as digital signature schemes in the sense of Definition 4.4.
2. *Functions of signatures*   Handwritten signatures on paper documents fulfill formal requirements to serve specific functions, or roles. Some of these requirements and functions may have an explicit and precise legal meaning in a given legal system. Please discuss the suitability of digital signatures (e.g., as used in Protocol 2.5 or embedded in web browsers) with respect to the following functions of (handwritten) signatures.
   (a) *Identification* – the receiver of the signed document can verify the signer's identity.
   (b) *Authentication* – the signature authenticates the content of the signed document, unless contrary evidence is produced.
   (c) *Declaration of will* – the signer declares, through his signing, his will and his agreement to be legally bound to the possible intentions stated in the signed document.
   (d) *Authorization* – the signer authorizes the receiver to perform a legal act (e.g., power of attorney).
   (e) *Safeguard against undue haste* – before signing the document, the signer is notified of possible legal consequences; in case of a sales contract, certain countries may require sufficient time for deliberating the purchase.
   (f) *Notice of contents* – the signer implicitly indicates that she knows the contents of the signed document.
   (g) *Originality* – signing the document allows one to distinguish the original from a copy.
3. *Features of signatures*   Discuss to what extent the following features of handwritten signatures transfer to the realm of digital signatures: Handwritten signatures are
   (a) easy to use and generate,
   (b) durable,
   (c) directly discernible, and
   (d) individual.

4. *Key recovery*   Study the consequences of a lost private key:
   (a) if it is used for decryption of messages;
   (b) if it is used for the generation of digital signatures.
   What does this entail for the requirements of, and constraints on, key-recovery infrastructures?

4.1.1   Digital Signature Standard: DSS

The U.S. Digital Signature Standard is a government technical standard used by federal departments and agencies in the design and implementation of public-key–based digital signature systems; its adoption by the private and commercial sector is encouraged but not legally prescribed. In the digital signature standard (DSS), a prover (see Definition 4.5) takes a message M, produces a digital fingerprint $\texttt{hash}(M)$ of M using the secure hash function described in Section 3.2.3, and signs the hash value $\texttt{hash}(M)$ with her secret digital signature key x; this produces two large integer values r and s:

$$\texttt{Sign}_x(M) \stackrel{\text{def}}{=} \langle r, s \rangle. \tag{4.1}$$

A verifier will receive the putative original message M' and the putative signature pair $\langle r', s' \rangle$. The verifier then can compute a value v, using the signer's public key y, where v equals r' if $M' = M$, $r = r'$, and $s = s'$:

$$\texttt{Verify}_y(M', \langle r, s \rangle) \stackrel{\text{def}}{=} (v = r'). \tag{4.2}$$

Let us now examine this procedure in more detail.

4.1.1.1   Protocol Parameters

The digital signature algorithm (DSA) requires:

- a prime number p with L significant bits, where L is any multiple of 64 in the range

  $512 \leq L \leq 1024;$

- a prime number q with 160 significant bits such that q divides $p - 1$;
- numbers g and h such that

  $g \stackrel{\text{def}}{=} h^{(p-1)/q} \bmod p,$

  where $2 \leq h \leq p - 2$ and $g \geq 2$;
- randomly generated numbers x and k satisfying $1 \leq x \leq q - 1$ and $1 \leq k \leq q - 1$; and
- a public key

  $y \stackrel{\text{def}}{=} g^x \bmod p.$

We will return to the issue of how to compute such parameters in Section 4.1.1.5 (p. 136).

4.1.1.2   Generating a Digital Signature

Definition 4.5 (Provers and Verifiers)
An agent that claims he or she signed a certain message digitally is called a *prover*. A *verifier* is an agent that checks whether such a claim is valid.

Both prover and verifier must follow precise protocols for these activities, as we shall outline. The parameters p, q, g, h should be considered public and may be used by several users. The prover's *secret signature key* is x; her *public signature key* is y. The prover uses this key pair for a period of time that is determined by a security analysis of the implemented DSS system and other factors. The random parameter k is used only *once,* so it has to be regenerated (or precomputed) for each signature. See Exercise 4.2-7 (p. 138) for what may happen otherwise.

Protocol 4.6 (Generation of Digital Signature)
Given a message M and a random k, the prover computes the pair of numbers $\langle r, s \rangle$ as a digital signature of M:

$$r \stackrel{\text{def}}{=} (g^k \bmod p) \bmod q, \tag{4.3}$$

$$s \stackrel{\text{def}}{=} (k^{-1} \cdot (\text{hash}(M) + x \cdot r)) \bmod q. \tag{4.4}$$

Recall that $\text{hash}(M)$ produces a 160-bit string, so in our present context $\text{hash}(M)$ denotes the integer whose binary representation equals that 160-bit string. Note that an implementation may need to conduct such a conversion before computing s.

4.1.1.3   Digital Signature Verification

A verifier is well advised to obtain all the public information – the two primes p and q, the base g, and the prover's public signature key y – in an *authenticated* manner. Thereafter, assume that the verifier received M' and the pair $\langle r', s' \rangle$, the putative signature of the original M. If r' and s' are positive and less than q, the verification algorithm is invoked. Otherwise, the signature is rejected immediately.

Protocol 4.7 (Digital Signature Verification)
For the actual verification, the verifier computes

$$w \stackrel{\text{def}}{=} (s')^{-1} \bmod q, \tag{4.5}$$

$$u_1 \stackrel{\text{def}}{=} \text{hash}(M') \cdot w \bmod q, \tag{4.6}$$

$$u_2 \stackrel{\text{def}}{=} r' \cdot w \bmod q, \tag{4.7}$$

$$v \stackrel{\text{def}}{=} (g^{u_1} \cdot y^{u_2} \bmod p) \bmod q. \tag{4.8}$$

If $v = r'$, then the verifier accepts that message M was signed by the prover. Otherwise, the signature is rejected.

4.1.1.4 Correctness of Protocol

At the very least, we need to guarantee that the verifier accepts a signature if it was generated in the prescribed manner by the prover, using the secret information k and x. For that, we need a little lemma whose proof is delegated to Exercise 4.2-1 (p. 138).

Lemma 4.8
Let p, q, g, and h be as in the digital signature standard. Then:

1. $g^q = 1 \bmod p$; *and*
2. *for all $a, b \in \mathbb{Z}$, $a = b \bmod q$ implies $g^a = g^b \bmod p$.*

To prove that the verifier accepts a properly signed digital signature, it suffices to show that $v = r'$ if the verifier receives the original message as well as the proper signature.

Theorem 4.9 (Correctness of Digital Signature Verification)
If $M' = M$, $r' = r$, and $s' = s$, then $v = r'$ holds for the value v computed in (4.8).

Proof We repeatedly use Lemma 4.8 to compute

$$
\begin{aligned}
v &= (g^{u_1} \cdot y^{u_2} \bmod p) \bmod q && \text{(by (4.8))}\\
&= (g^{\mathrm{hash}(M') \cdot w} \cdot y^{u_2} \bmod p) \bmod q && \text{(by (4.6))}\\
&= (g^{\mathrm{hash}(M) \cdot w} \cdot y^{u_2} \bmod p) \bmod q && \text{(since } M = M')\\
&= (g^{\mathrm{hash}(M) \cdot w} \cdot g^{x \cdot u_2} \bmod p) \bmod q && \text{(since } y = g^x \bmod p)\\
&= (g^{\mathrm{hash}(M) \cdot w} \cdot g^{x \cdot r' \cdot w} \bmod p) \bmod q && \text{(by (4.7))}\\
&= (g^{\mathrm{hash}(M) \cdot w} \cdot g^{x \cdot r \cdot w} \bmod p) \bmod q && \text{(since } r' = r)\\
&= (g^{(\mathrm{hash}(M) + x \cdot r) \cdot w} \bmod p) \bmod q. && (4.9)
\end{aligned}
$$

By (4.5) and (4.4), we have

$$
w = (k^{-1} \cdot (\mathrm{hash}(M) + x \cdot r))^{-1} \bmod q.
$$

Recalling that $(g \circ h)^{-1} = h^{-1} \circ g^{-1}$ and $(g^{-1})^{-1} = g$ hold in any group $\langle G, \circ, e \rangle$, we infer that

$$
\begin{aligned}
(\mathrm{hash}(M) + x \cdot r) \cdot w &= (\mathrm{hash}(M) + x \cdot r) \cdot (\mathrm{hash}(M) + x \cdot r)^{-1} \cdot (k^{-1})^{-1}\\
&= k \bmod q.
\end{aligned}
$$

Using Lemma 4.8 and (4.9), we obtain

$$
v = (g^k \bmod p) \bmod q;
$$

the right-hand side is the value defined to be r, which equals r' by assumption. □

4.1.1.5 Verifiable Generation of Public Protocol Parameters

The digital signature standard insists on using established algorithms for generating the secret x and k and the public p, q, and g. The generation of x, k, and g rely on random or pseudo-random number generators; for g, one generates a random h until $g > 1$. As for the prime numbers p and q, the standard proposes a deterministic algorithm for their computation that takes the number of bits of p and the number of bits of a random seed as input; it then uses the secure hash algorithm from Section 3.2.3 to compute p and q. Along with p and q, the successful seed `seed` becomes public information as well. Hence this algorithm provides a means for verifying that the parameters p and q *were generated in the prescribed manner*: take the seed to simulate the generation algorithm; check whether p and q are being generated. This also makes it next to impossible to set up a DSS system with "unsafe" primes p and q, for it is hard to conceive of how an attacker could program any computation that would yield "weak" numbers that would nonetheless pass that check.

See Figure 4.1 for the pseudo-code of the prescribed generation of p and q, and note how the algorithm operates. After some preprocessing, it enters a while-statement whose sole purpose is to generate a 160-bit prime number q. Each iteration of the while-statement corresponds to an attempt of finding a q based on a randomly generated seed value `seed`. This code uses `Miller-Rabin` as a primality test with 80 calls to the function `Witness`. The call to `Miller-Rabin` gives us a probability of at most 2^{-80} of generating a q that is not prime. The DSS standard requires this threshold. Note that the assignment-statement for q forces q to be odd and to have 160 significant bits.

As soon as a suitable q has been found, the algorithm executes a second while-statement whose task it is to find an L-bit prime p such that q divides $p - 1$. The variable `counter` keeps track of how many attempts of generating p have failed so far. If this value exceeds 4096, the program goes back to the first while-statement and generates a new q from which it hopes to compute a suitable p. The value `offset` also changes with each attempt of computing p. The value for x is computed based on the seed and a number of applications of the hash function, using an array `v[]` of length $n + 1$. Observe that $p = 1 \bmod 2 \cdot q$ holds.[1]

The DSS is based on the ElGamal digital signature scheme, but it is designed so that it signs a 160-bit message fingerprint (sometimes called a message digest) to produce a 320-bit signature (although all computations are done with a modulus, p, that is at least 512 bits long). This is achieved by generating a subgroup of size 2^{160} in $\mathbb{Z}_p^*$. Note also that DSS is nondeterministic: the same message can have many valid signatures, owing to the random k. As for implementations, DSS is rather fast in its signature generation but rather slow in signature verification – the reverse of a typical digital signature scheme based on RSA. This creates tradeoffs, and often there are no optimal solutions. For example, smartcards may have to perform both decryption and encryption.

---

[1] In practice, the same robustness of `Miller-Rabin` can be achieved for testing q and p if we reduce the number of tests from 80 to 18 and 5, respectively; but we won't discuss the mathematics that establishes this.

```
DSS_Prime_Generation(int l,int lseed) {
// generates two prime numbers p and q for the DSS
// input:    * an integer l between 0 and 8
//           * an integer lseed, the length of the seed
// output:   * a 160-bit prime q and a prime p with 512 + 64*l bits
//             such that q divides p - 1
//           * the value of an internal counter
//           * the value of the successful seed
 int L = 512 + 64 * l;
 int n = L - 1 div 160;
 int b = L - 1 mod 160;
 bool q_not_prime = true;
 loc:  while q_not_Prime {
        BigInteger seed = Random(1,2**lseed - 1) XOR 2**(lseed - 1);
        BigInteger u = hash(seed) XOR hash(seed + 1 mod 2**lseed);
        BigInteger q = u OR 2**159 OR 1;
        q_not_prime = Miller-Rabin(q,80);
        }
 int counter = 0;
 int offset =  2;
 while counter <= 4096 {
   for (int k = 0; k <= n; ++k) {
     v[k] = hash(seed + offset + k mod 2**lseed);
   }
     BigInteger w = v[0];
     for (int k = 1; k < n; ++k) { w = w + v[k] * 2**(k*160); }
     w = w + (v[n] mod 2**b) * 2**(2*160);
     BigInteger x = w + 2**(L - 1);
     BigInteger c = x mod 2*q;
     BigInteger p = x - (c - 1);
     if (p >= 2**(L-1) && Miller-Rabin(p,80)) {
       return (q,p,counter,seed);
     }
     counter = counter + 1;
     offset = offset + n + 1;
 }
 goto loc;
}
```

Figure 4.1. Pseudo-code for the generation of two primes p and q as required by the digital signature standard.

4.1.1.6 Security of DSS

Implementation constraints aside, it seems wise to choose 1024 bits for p. If one can deviate from the standard without compromising acceptable performance, one may choose an even larger number of bits for p. There are two principal security concerns: the logarithm in $\mathbb{Z}_p$, where powerful techniques (index-calculus methods) exist; and the computation of logarithms in the subgroup of order q, generated by g. For the latter, methods that run in the order of $\sqrt{q}$ are known. The Digital Signature Standard is also subject to implementation flaws that corrupt its security. For example, one may attack this system if k is the same random number for each issued signature. See the following exercises for more on that.

EXERCISES 4.2

1. Prove Lemma 4.8. (*Hint:* Use Fermat's theorem for p.)
2. Let p, q, g, h be parameters of the DSS protocol. Show that $[g]_p$ generates a subgroup of order q in $\mathbb{Z}_p^*$.
3. Let $n, m \in \mathbb{N}$ and $x \in \mathbb{Z}$. What can you say, in general, about how the values $(x \bmod n) \bmod m$ and $(x \bmod m) \bmod n$ compare? Specify under which circumstances they compute the same results.
4. *Implementing DSS prime generation* Implement, in a programming language of your choice, the algorithm DSS_Prime_Generation(1,lseed).
5. *Implementing DSS signature verification* Write and implement an algorithm DSS_Proper_Primes?(q,p,counter,seed) which returns a boolean. This simulates the computation that occurs in the call DSS_Prime_Generation(1,lseed) but here for the length lseed of the *given* value of the seed seed; it returns true if and only if the simulation computes the same values as the input values for counter, p, and seed.
6. Why would it be difficult to compute "weak" prime numbers p and q that would pass the test call DSS_Proper_Primes?(q,p,counter,seed) of Exercise 5? Give an intuitive explanation.
7. *Attack on repeated use of signature* Explain how you could compute the secret digital signature key x if you could observe the communication of two runs of the DSS protocol, provided that the prover used the *same* random number k for signing two *different* messages M_1 and M_2. Let r_1, r_2, s_1, and s_2 be defined as in (4.3) and (4.4) for messages M_1 and M_2, respectively.
   (a) Argue that r_1 equals r_2.
   (b) Show: If $s_1 - s_2 \neq 0 \bmod q$, then

$$k = (s_1 - s_2)^{-1} \cdot (\text{hash}(M_1) - \text{hash}(M_2)) \bmod q. \tag{4.10}$$

   (c) Prove that, in the DSS protocol, we have

$$x = (s \cdot k - \text{hash}(M)) \cdot r^{-1} \bmod q \tag{4.11}$$

   in general.
   (d) Use parts (a)–(c) to explain your attack. Detail what you know and compute and in which order such knowledge arises.
   (e) What property of hash functions makes it unlikely that $s_1 - s_2 = 0 \bmod q$?
   (f) Does this attack work if the two messages are identical?
8. Consider the program DSS_Prime_Generation(1,lseed) from Figure 4.1. Explain why:
   (a) $2^{L-1} \leq x < 2^L$ holds right after the assignment-statement for x;
   (b) $p = 1 \bmod 2 \cdot q$ holds right after the assignment-statement for p; and
   (c) p has L significant bits upon program termination.

9. *Time-stamping digital signatures*   Suppose that Alice wants to sign a message M with her secret digital signature key $\text{Sign}_A(\cdot)$. At the same time, she wants to be able to prove that she signed M on a specific day. She is allowed to use publicly available (but not predictable) information from that day and to publish her signature in a national newspaper the following day. Propose how she should proceed.

10. (a) Generalize the definition of a digital signature scheme by including a third parameter $\mathcal{A}$, an efficient probabilistic algorithm such that a call $\mathcal{A}(n)$ generates a digital signature scheme

$$\text{Sign}_K(\cdot)\colon \mathcal{P} \to \mathcal{S},$$

$$\text{Verify}_K(\cdot, \cdot)\colon \mathcal{P} \times \mathcal{S} \to \texttt{boolean},$$

where the length of elements in $\mathcal{P}$ and $\mathcal{S}$ is a function of $n \in \mathbb{N}$.

   (b) Express the Digital Signature Standard as such a system. In particular, what are the lengths of elements in $\mathcal{P}$ and $\mathcal{S}$?

4.1.2 Elliptic Curve Digital Signature Algorithm

The digital signature in the DSS consists of the pair $\langle r, s \rangle$, which requires 320 bits for its representation. As discussed already, the security of DSS rests on the fact that the computation of logarithms in $\mathbb{Z}_p^*$ is hard and that it is likewise hard to compute the logarithm in the subgroup of order q generated by g. However, one may read the DSS protocol at a more abstract level, taking note that most of its basic steps still make sense when interpreted to apply in any finite field $(F, +, 0, \cdot, 1)$. In a field, all nonzero elements have a multiplicative inverse and the operations $+$ and $\cdot$ satisfy laws that we intuitively apply in the field $\mathbb{Z}_p$, where p is prime. Recall that the AES cipher Rijndael made use of a finite field whose elements are all 8-bit bytes.

4.1.2.1 Elliptic Curves

Often one can build a group from geometric data. This is done in cryptographic techniques that rely on the quite difficult but most intriguing mathematics of *elliptic curves*. Although such curves can be defined in great generality, we simplify our presentation to a special class of elliptic curves that illustrate well their application to cryptology.

Definition 4.10 (Elliptic Curve)
Let $p > 3$ be a prime and let $a, b \in \{1, 2, \dots, p-1\}$ be such that

$$4 \cdot a^3 + 27 \cdot b^2 \neq 0 \bmod p. \tag{4.12}$$

An *elliptic curve* $\mathrm{E}(\mathbb{Z}_p)$ *over* $\mathbb{Z}_p$ has the numbers a and b as implicit parameters; the set $\mathrm{E}(\mathbb{Z}_p)$ consists of all pairs $\langle x, y \rangle$ that satisfy

$$y^2 = x^3 + a \cdot x + b \bmod p \quad (0 \leq x, y \leq p-1) \tag{4.13}$$

together with an additional element $\mathcal{O}$, the "point at infinity".

Example 4.11

Let $p = 13$, $a = 4$, and $b = 12$. Then equation (4.12) is satisfied, and the set $\mathrm{E}(\mathbb{Z}_{13})$ (without $\mathcal{O}$) consists of the pairs

$(0, 5)$, $(0, 8)$, $(1, 2)$, $(1, 11)$, $(3, 5)$, $(3, 8)$, $(4, 1)$, $(4, 12)$, $(5, 1)$,

$(5, 12)$, $(8, 6)$, $(8, 7)$, $(9, 6)$, $(9, 7)$, $(10, 5)$, $(10, 8)$, $(11, 3)$, $(11, 10)$.

Note that the set $\mathrm{E}(\mathbb{Z}_{13})$ has 19 elements in all.

From (4.13) it follows that

$$\langle x, y \rangle \in \mathrm{E}(\mathbb{Z}_p) \implies \langle x, -y \rangle \in \mathrm{E}(\mathbb{Z}_p).$$

If such curves are defined over the real numbers instead of $\mathbb{Z}_p$, then two points on that curve determine a third one: the "addition" of the former two. This geometric operation can be transferred to the case $\mathbb{Z}_p$, in which case the operation can be expressed in a completely algebraic fashion. It then forms the basis for the derivation of a group operation.

Definition 4.12 (Group Structure on Elliptic Curve)

1. Let $\mathrm{E}(\mathbb{Z}_p)$ be an elliptic curve. We define an operation

$$+ : \mathrm{E}(\mathbb{Z}_p) \times \mathrm{E}(\mathbb{Z}_p) \to \mathrm{E}(\mathbb{Z}_p) \tag{4.14}$$

   as follows:
   - $\mathcal{O} + \mathcal{O} \stackrel{\text{def}}{=} \mathcal{O}$;
   - $\langle x, y \rangle + \mathcal{O} \stackrel{\text{def}}{=} \mathcal{O} + \langle x, y \rangle \stackrel{\text{def}}{=} \langle x, y \rangle$;
   - $\langle x, y \rangle + \langle x, -y \rangle \stackrel{\text{def}}{=} \mathcal{O}$;
   - if $\langle x_1, y_1 \rangle$ and $\langle x_2, y_2 \rangle$ are in $\mathrm{E}(\mathbb{Z}_p)$ with $y_1 \neq y_2 \bmod p$, then define $\langle x_1, y_1 \rangle + \langle x_2, y_2 \rangle$ to be $\langle x_3, y_3 \rangle$, where

$$\lambda \stackrel{\text{def}}{=} \begin{cases} (y_2 - y_1) \cdot (x_2 - x_1)^{-1} \bmod p & \text{if } \langle x_1, x_2 \rangle \neq \langle y_1, y_2 \rangle, \\ (3 \cdot x_1^2 + a) \cdot (2 \cdot y_1)^{-1} \bmod p & \text{if } \langle x_1, x_2 \rangle = \langle y_1, y_2 \rangle; \end{cases} \tag{4.15}$$

$$x_3 \stackrel{\text{def}}{=} \lambda^2 - x_1 - x_2 \bmod p,$$
$$y_3 \stackrel{\text{def}}{=} \lambda \cdot (x_1 - x_3) - y_1 \bmod p. \tag{4.16}$$

2. If $P = \langle x, y \rangle \in \mathrm{E}(\mathbb{Z}_p)$, then we write $-P$ for the pair $\langle x, -y \rangle \in \mathrm{E}(\mathbb{Z}_p)$.

3. Generally, for $r \in \mathbb{N}$ we define

$$r \cdot \langle x, y \rangle \stackrel{\text{def}}{=} \sum_{i=1}^{r} \langle x, y \rangle. \tag{4.17}$$

Example 4.13

For $p = 23$, $a = 1$, and $b = 1$, we have points $P \stackrel{\text{def}}{=} \langle 3, 10 \rangle$ and $Q \stackrel{\text{def}}{=} \langle 9, 7 \rangle$. We compute $P + Q$ as follows:

$$\lambda = (7 - 10) \cdot (9 - 3)^{-1} = -3 \cdot 6^{-1} = 11 \bmod 23;$$
$$x_3 = 11^2 - 3 - 9 = 6 - 3 - 9 = -6 = 13 \bmod 23;$$
$$y_3 = 11 \cdot (3 - (-6)) - 10 = 11 \cdot 9 - 10 = 89 = 20 \bmod 23.$$

Thus

$$P + Q = \langle 17, 20 \rangle.$$

As for scalar multiplication, let $R \stackrel{\text{def}}{=} \langle 3, 10 \rangle$. Then $2 \cdot R \stackrel{\text{def}}{=} R + R$. The latter computes to:

$$\lambda = (3 \cdot 3^2 + 1) \cdot 20^{-1} = 5 \cdot 20 = 6 \bmod 23;$$

$$x_3 = 6^2 - 6 = 7 \bmod 23;$$

$$y_3 = 6 \cdot (3 - 7) - 10 = -24 - 10 = 12 \bmod 23.$$

Hence,

$$2 \cdot R = \langle 7, 12 \rangle.$$

EXERCISES 4.3

1. (a) Let $p > 3$ be prime. Show that $\langle x, y \rangle \in E(\mathbb{Z}_p)$ implies $\langle x, -y \rangle \in E(\mathbb{Z}_p)$.
   (b) Explain why the definition of (4.14) is *complete* in the sense that we did not forget to add some combination of elements in $E(\mathbb{Z}_p)$.
   (c) Explain what implicit assumption was made in the definition of λ in (4.15).
   (d) Prove that $+$ is commutative.
   (e) Prove that $+$ is associative. (This may be harder than you think!)
   (f) Conclude that $\langle E(\mathbb{Z}_p), +, \mathcal{O} \rangle$ is a finite commutative group.
2. Consider the elliptic curve where $a = b = 1$ and $p = 11$.
   (a) Compute the set $E(\mathbb{Z}_{11})$. (*Hint:* Without $\mathcal{O}$, it has 13 elements.)
   (b) Use the definition in (4.16) to compute $\langle 1, 5 \rangle + \langle 8, 2 \rangle$ in $E(\mathbb{Z}_{11})$.
   (c) Use the definition in (4.17) to compute $2 \cdot \langle 1, 5 \rangle$, $3 \cdot \langle 1, 5 \rangle$, and $4 \cdot \langle 1, 5 \rangle$.
3. Let $p = 1999$ and $a = b = 1$. How many elements does $E(\mathbb{Z}_{1999})$ have? (More than 2000, so you may want to write a program for this.)

Definition 4.14 (ECDSA)

In the *elliptic curve digital signature algorithm* (ECDSA), we modify the DSS at some key places.

1. We replace $\mathbb{Z}_p$ with some elliptic curve $E(\mathbb{Z}_p)$ over $\mathbb{Z}_p$ such that the order of the group $E(\mathbb{Z}_p)$ has a "large" prime factor q (say, 160 bits long).
2. We find a point $G \in E(\mathbb{Z}_p)$ whose order is q (G was called g in the DSS).
3. The public signature x is computed (as in DSS) as a random value between 1 and $q - 1$, but now the secret signature Y, called y in the DSS, is defined as the scalar multiplication of the point G with the scalar x:

   $$Y \stackrel{\text{def}}{=} x \cdot G.$$

4. The computation of r is entirely different now, for r was computed in $\mathbb{Z}_p$ before.
   (a) Compute the random k in the same manner as for the DSS.
   (b) Let $\langle x_1, y_1 \rangle$ be the point on $E(\mathbb{Z}_p)$ obtained by computing $k \cdot G$. If $x_1 \bmod q = 0$, use part (a) to re-compute k. Otherwise,

   $$r \stackrel{\text{def}}{=} x_1 \bmod q.$$

5. The computation of s now proceeds exactly as for the DSS.
6. To verify a digital signature, the computations of w, u_1, and u_2 are as in (4.5)–(4.7), but we replace the exponentials in (4.8) with scalar multiplications in the elliptic curve $E(\mathbb{Z}_p)$:

$$\langle x_0, y_0 \rangle \stackrel{\text{def}}{=} u_1 \cdot G + u_2 \cdot Y, \tag{4.18}$$

$$v \stackrel{\text{def}}{=} x_0 \bmod q. \tag{4.19}$$

Note that $+$ in this equation refers to the addition of points in the elliptic curve.

The "scalar multiplication"

$$\langle k, G \rangle \mapsto k \cdot G \colon \mathbb{N} \times E(\mathbb{Z}_p) \to E(\mathbb{Z}_p)$$

is, of course, simply the exponentiation operation in the group $E(\mathbb{Z}_p)$. The security of the ECDSA thus relies, at the very least, on the fact that it is hard to compute logarithms in this group. With a 160-bit q, this algorithm may provide similar security as the DSS. The apparent advantage is that one can often choose a much smaller p than with the DSS when generating a subgroup of order q. Also, scalar multiplication may be easier to implement than exponentiation in $\mathbb{Z}_p^*$ if p is chosen appropriately. Note, however, that the first two items of the ECDSA require efficient algorithms for generating p and G with these requirements. Such algorithms exist, but we will not discuss them in this text. Finally, it is not clear whether the elliptic curve PKC has an inherent advantage over PKCs that are based on $\mathbb{Z}_p^*$. Although elliptic curves have been studied by many excellent mathematicians for about 150 years, their security analysis in PKCs is a fairly recent endeavor; it is simply too early to make a conclusive judgment in this matter. In particular, one can show that certain kinds of curves are always "weak", so algorithms that generate elliptic curves for cryptographic applications must detect (and weed out) such undesirable curves.

EXERCISES 4.4

1. Prove the correctness of the ECDSA: If $M' = M$, $r' = r$, and $s' = s$, then $v = r'$ holds for the value v computed in (4.19).
2. What nice aspect about the generation of the DSS parameters is absent from the ECDSA, at least as far as we have described it?

4.2 SECURE LOG-IN PROTOCOLS

We have seen in this chapter how hash functions, together with public-key cryptography, can be used to obtain protocols for the secure exchange of digitally signed messages. In this section, we demonstrate another useful application of hash functions in the domain of authentication. In particular, we describe a protocol that can realize one-time – or token-based – password management and verification for log-in procedures. Citibank already uses such tools to protect certain accounts, and this approach is increasingly pursued by industry.

Users of computer networks must typically prove their identity before using a computer terminal or gaining access to other network services.

Protocol 4.15 (Traditional Log-Ins)

On Unix and Windows operating systems, one usually obtains access to the system by a simple password protocol:

- you enter your log-in name;
- if the network knows a user with that name, you are asked to provide a "password" associated with that name;
- the system then compares this password with the actual password that is stored on the system;
- if the entered and stored passwords match, network access is granted.

This approach to controlling network access comes with a host of security problems. For example, passwords may be sent "in the clear" across communication lines in order to verify whether they match their stored versions. This is why Unix, for example, uses a hash function to encrypt passwords. Passwords are stored in their encrypted form; entered passwords are encrypted and then compared to the stored hash value. But even this usage of hash functions does not address all major security concerns. The system must store the hash values of all user passwords in some file; in Unix this may be found in /etc/password. Thus the system needs to ensure that this file can be neither copied by legitimate users nor modified by intruding ones. Anyone who manages to read this file can engage in a chosen plain-text attack. Since the hash function used by the system is publicly known, one can guess passwords, encrypt them with the hash function, and compare them for a match in the file. For a complete password file, such attacks are quite practical and can easily expose a significant portion of all passwords.

The problem is simply that the system must store a *secret* that identifies a user, and so the system must also properly *protect* this secret from others. The user, too, must store this secret. The way our brains work, we prefer to invent passwords that we can memorize easily (actual English words, or words in other languages reflecting the user's cultural background or interest – e.g., Chinese words written in alphanumeric characters). This is what makes chosen plain-text attacks so successful: they need only go through a user-customized dictionary of plausible passwords. To shield against such attacks, the system may analyze any new password proposed by a legitimate user and reject passwords that are deemed to be "too obvious". Clearly, such measures mitigate the threat of dictionary attacks, but they also make it more likely for people to forget their passwords or to write them down on the inside of their desk drawer.

Definition 4.16 (Provers and Verifiers)

A network user who wishes to log-in to a network is called a *prover*. The part of the system that runs the log-in protocol and decides whether to grant access to provers is called the *verifier*. More generally, any program or system resource that can be requested by a client (a user, some other program, etc.) is seen as a verifier; all clients are called provers.

We present a suite of protocols for log-in, or general server access, that meet the following set of criteria:

- no secret information is transmitted across the network;
- no secret has to be stored by the verifier;
- ideally, the verifier should not know the user's secret (to avoid impersonation);
- upon demand, a server should have a means of proving that a client used that server;
- mutual authentication should be possible;
- the protocols should not put severe constraints on computational resources.

Criteria H1 and H3 (p. 21) state that a hash function $x \mapsto h(x)$ should have an efficient way of computing $h(x)$ but that it should be computationally infeasible to find any x such that $h(x)$ equals a given y. Our log-in protocols assume the existence of such a hash function. Our draft scheme requires a trusted authority that initializes the system:

- it equips a prover with a pair $\langle x_0, k \rangle$, where x_0 is a secret value (in essence, a random value that the prover needs to remember) and $k \in \mathbb{N}$ specifies an implementation-specific number determining how often that prover can present the password to the verifier;
- the authority also provides the verifier with a pair $\langle x_k, k \rangle$, where $x_k = h^k(x_0)$, as the identity information of the prover.

Note that x_k is obtained by k many applications of h to x_0:

$$x_{n+1} \stackrel{\text{def}}{=} h(x_n) \quad (n \geq 0). \tag{4.20}$$

Protocol 4.17 (Verification of Prover's Identity)
The (successful) verification of a prover's identity consists of a successful run of the following protocol.

1. The prover sends the verifier her *personal identity information* x_k.
2. The verifier matches that information with his stored value x_k; this corresponds to asking for a log-in name (and a mismatch results in a failed log-in attempt).
3. The verifier asks for a password, which is any value x' such that $h(x') = x_k$; since the prover knows x_0, she can use h to compute x_{k-1} as such an x' and send this to the verifier.
4. The verifier can compute $h(x_{k-1})$ and match it with x_k.
5. After a successful match, the verifier grants access to the prover and then stores x_{k-1} as the current identity information of that user; the next authentication round will be done with x_{k-1} and x_{k-2} instead of x_k and x_{k-1}.

This scheme does not transmit secret information across the network. The verifier neither stores nor even knows the secret value x_0, provided he has no *trapdoor* for the hash function: an efficient algorithm for solving $h(x) = y$ for x, where $y = h(x')$ for some x'. The authority provides all provers with their initial parameters $\langle x_0, k \rangle$ and the verifier with the *initial access pair* $\langle x_k, k \rangle$. However, the authority ought to possess a trapdoor for the hash function – thus allowing it to function as an agency that can settle disputes between provers and verifiers.

The shortcomings of this scheme are that passwords can only be used once, that they must be shown before the service, and that they may be used in a *replay attack*. For example, if the verifying server crashes right after the prover supplied x_{k-1} along an unsecure channel, then another "prover" could (upon recovery of the verifier) replay x_k – provided the verifier would "remember" x_k as current personal identity information of the alleged user.

EXERCISE 4.5

1. Describe in detail a man-in-the-middle attack for Protocol 4.17, where Mallory convinces the prover that Mallory is the verifier.

4.2.0.2 The Guillou–Quisquater Protocol

Zero-knowledge proofs are protocols in which a prover can successfully demonstrate to the verifier that the prover knows a secret *without* revealing any information whatsoever about that secret to the verifier. This sounds like a paradox, but it can be realized in number theory. Using such a protocol in combination with our previous scheme, we obtain a new log-in protocol that does not expose the current user identity information x_k. This improved protocol may therefore be reused until the server requests it as an *access ticket* or *proof of usage* of the provided service.

In order to state the protocol, we must work with an explicit hash function h. Assume that $n = p \cdot q$, where p and q are two primes of about 512 bits in length such that

$$p = 2 \cdot p' + 1,$$
$$q = 2 \cdot q' + 1$$

for prime numbers p' and q'. Fix any $e \in \mathbb{N}$ with $\gcd(e, (p - 1) \cdot (q - 1)) = 1$. Then the function

$$h(x) \stackrel{\text{def}}{=} x^e \bmod n \quad (0 \le x \le n - 1) \tag{4.21}$$

is essentially the RSA-based hash function discussed in Exercise 2.19-10 (p. 61). The authority is responsible for computing p and q and keeps those parameters secret. The provers and verifiers obtain n and e so that they are able to compute h. Since the authority knows the factorization of n, it can easily derive an efficient algorithm for computing inverses of h. Indeed, it need only compute the RSA private key $\langle d, n \rangle$ for decryption, as outlined in Section 2.2. That way, the authority is able to investigate and rule on disputes between provers and verifiers.

Protocol 4.18 (Guillou–Quisquater)
In the Guillou–Quisquater protocol:

1. the prover generates a random number r between 0 and $n - 1$ and sends the verifier her *commitment*

    $$c \stackrel{\text{def}}{=} h(r)$$

    and her current *personal identity information* x_k;
2. the verifier sends a *challenge* s between 0 and e to the prover;

3. the prover computes some b with

$$b \cdot x_{k-1} = 1 \bmod n$$

using the algorithm `Extended_Euclid`, computes

$$c' \stackrel{\text{def}}{=} r \cdot b^s \bmod n,$$

and sends c' to the verifier;
4. the verifier now computes

$$x_k^s \cdot (c')^e \bmod n,$$

which should equal the prover's commitment c.

To see that a prover, who knows x_{k-1}, will be granted access under this protocol, we compute

$$
\begin{aligned}
x_k^s \cdot (c')^e \bmod n &= x_k^s \cdot (r \cdot b^s)^e \bmod n \\
&= x_k^s \cdot (b^s)^e \cdot r^e \bmod n \\
&= h(x_{k-1})^s \cdot h(b^s) \cdot h(r) \bmod n \\
&= h(x_{k-1} \cdot b)^s \cdot c \bmod n \\
&= 1^s \cdot c \bmod n \\
&= c;
\end{aligned}
\tag{4.22}
$$

this follows because (a) h is multiplicative,

$$h(x^l) = h(x)^l \bmod n \quad (x \in \mathbb{Z}, \, l \in \mathbb{N}),$$

(b) $h(1) = 1$, and (c) $b \cdot x_{k-1} = 1 \bmod n$. Any "prover" has a chance of 1 in e of guessing the challenge value s needed to construct a valid access pair $\langle c, c' \rangle$. Thus, for large enough values of e, we have a reassuring level of security that the prover is indeed the one who knows x_{k-1}. The protocol just described contains a *challenge-and-response* component, as the verifier challenges the prover with some random s. Notice that this protocol "consumes" neither the password (x_{k-1}) nor the personal identity information (x_k), since they are never revealed in any communication. Thus, a prover may reuse the same password until some verifier insists on receiving x_{k-1} as a *proof-of-usage* – after the service has been granted to the prover's satisfaction. In that case, x_{k-1} would be the next valid personal identity information and x_{k-2} the next valid password for the prover, as in the previous protocol.

EXERCISE 4.6

1. In the Guillou–Quisquater protocol, prover and verifier send various numbers to each other over (presumably) untrusted channels. The claim of this protocol is that no information about the secret password is being revealed during protocol execution. Does this mean that both parties could send their data along an open channel for anyone to observe?

4.2.0.3 Combining Identity- and Ticket-Based Log-Ins

The trusted authority can also sign the identities of users. Given another hash function f that maps text strings to values between 0 and $n - 1$, the *signed identity certificate* for user I is $S_A(f(I))$, where S_A is the authority's secret or signature key that inverts the hash function h from (4.21), the corresponding public key. If I and f are public information and are known to be used by all clients and servers, then it is possible to verify identities and tickets within the same protocol. The digital signature, along with x_0 and k, may be stored on a smartcard and rendered to the user. Indeed, once the authority has distributed the smartcards, made n and e public, and issued the pairs $\langle x_0, k \rangle$ and $\langle x_k, k \rangle$ to all provers and verifiers (respectively), the system may be *sealed* in that the authority is no longer needed unless a dispute arises.

Protocol 4.19 (Identity- and Ticket-Based Log-Ins)
In this protocol:

1. the prover with personal identity information I solves
$$b_1 \cdot S_A(f(I)) \bmod n = 1,$$
$$b_2 \cdot x_{k-1} \bmod n = 1 \tag{4.23}$$

    for b_1 and b_2 using the algorithm `Extended_Euclid`;
2. the prover picks random numbers r_1, r_2 in $\mathbb{Z}_n^*$ and computes corresponding commitments
$$c_1 = r_1^e \bmod n,$$
$$c_2 = r_2^e \bmod n; \tag{4.24}$$
3. the prover sends the verifier her identity information I and x_k as well as her commitment
$$c \stackrel{\text{def}}{=} c_1 \cdot c_2 \bmod n; \tag{4.25}$$
4. the verifier sends a random challenge s between 0 and $e - 1$;
5. the prover computes
$$c_1' = r_1 \cdot b_1^s \bmod n,$$
$$c_2' = r_2 \cdot b_2^s \bmod n \tag{4.26}$$

    and sends
$$c' \stackrel{\text{def}}{=} c_1' \cdot c_2' \bmod n$$

    to the verifier;
6. the verifier checks that
$$f(I)^s \cdot x_k^s \cdot (c')^e \bmod n = c. \tag{4.27}$$

If (4.27) holds, then the verifier knows

- that the prover knows the digital signature computed by the authority for user I and
- that the prover also knows the current access ticket x_{k-1}.

Note that this protocol retains all advantages of the previous one, since it also does not reveal any information about the digital signature.

Protocol 4.20 (Using Separate Keys for Signatures and Tickets)

One may use separate public keys for digital signatures and tickets. Let e_1 and e_2 be the public key for the ticket and signature (respectively), and set e to be $e_1 \cdot e_2$.

1. The prover solves

$$b \cdot x_{k-1} \cdot S_A(f(I)) = 1 \bmod n$$

and sends

$$c \stackrel{\text{def}}{=} r^e \bmod n$$

to the verifier as her commitment, where $r > 0$ is randomly chosen by the prover;

2. the verifier sends a challenge s between 0 and $e - 1$ to the prover;
3. the prover computes

$$c' \stackrel{\text{def}}{=} r \cdot b^s \bmod n$$

and sends it to the verifier;

4. the verifier checks that

$$f(I)^{e_1 \cdot s} \cdot x_k^{e_2 \cdot s} \cdot (c')^e = c \bmod n. \tag{4.28}$$

This protocol may also be used to establish the ownership of two independent tickets. Naturally, the security of such access protocols depends upon the security provided by the hash functions. One possible weakness of h in (4.21) is that it is *periodic*: there exist $l_0, p \in \mathbb{N}$ such that

$$x_l = x_{l+p} \quad \text{for all } l \geq l_0.$$

This is a concern because x_{l+p} may function as x_k, the current public user identity information, and then $x_{l-1} = x_{l-1+p}$ becomes a *future* password. Hence one could deduce such passwords by computing

$$x_k, x_{k+1}, x_{k+2}, \ldots$$

for the current user ID x_k until a period is found. However, in Exercise 4.7-8 we ensure that this period is "large enough".

EXERCISES 4.7

1. In the Guillou–Quisquater protocol, the prover computes a value b. Explain under what circumstances this b could *not* be computed. In that case, would there be a way to compute the trapdoor of the hash function?

2. (a) Explain how the knowledge of the factors of n for the h in (4.21) allows one to compute, for any $h(x)$, some x' such that $h(x) = h(x')$.
   (b) What property of h in (4.21) guarantees that $h(x) = h(x')$ implies $x = x' \bmod n$?

3. (a) Prove: In a legitimate run of Protocol 4.19, equation (4.27) holds.
   (b) Explain why the verifier, after checking equation (4.27), can be sure that the prover knows the signature and ticket of the client she claims to be.

4. *Mutual authentication*   Adapt Protocol 4.19 to include *mutual* authentication.

5. *Authentication shell*   Using the ideas of Protocols 4.18–4.20, sketch a protocol that authenticates *all* commands sent by a user to a server.

6. *Anonymous log-in*   Discuss to what extent the protocols of this section (or slight modifications thereof) allow for a notion of "anonymous log-in" in the sense that only the trusted authority knows the real identities of users.

7. (a) Prove: In a legitimate run of Protocol 4.20, equation (4.28) holds.

   (b) Assume that network #1 has modulus $n_1 = p_1 \cdot q_1$ and network #2 has modulus $n_2 = p_2 \cdot q_2$. Suppose that user I of network #1 has an initial access pair $\langle x_0, k \rangle$ for a server on network #2.

      (i) Why is it "safe" to assume that n_1 and n_2 satisfy $\gcd(n_1, n_2) = 1$? What could a hostile agent do otherwise?

      (ii) Adapt Protocol 4.20 to enable the server on network #2 to verify that: user I owns a valid signature from the authority for network #1; and this user has a valid access ticket for network #2.

      (iii) Can the Chinese remainder theorem be used to perform the computations in $\mathbb{Z}_{n_1 \cdot n_2}$; if so, would this be faster?

8. *Lower bound on period*   In this exercise, we prove a lower bound on the period of the hash function $x \mapsto h(x)$ from (4.21).

   (a) Let $a \in \mathbb{Z}$ and $n \in \mathbb{N}$ be given with $\gcd(a, n) = 1$. (Note that any such a has a multiplicative inverse modulo n.) Prove: For all $i, j \in \mathbb{N}$, we have

   $$a^i = a^j \bmod n \iff i = j \bmod \mathrm{ord}^{\mathbb{Z}_n^*}(a)$$

   (recall that $\mathrm{ord}^G(g)$ is described in Definition 2.37, p. 46).

   (b) Let $(x_i)_{i \geq 0}$ be the sequence of tickets generated according to (4.20). This sequence "loops" if and only if we have $x_i = x_j$ for $i \neq j$; so let us assume that this is the case for such values of i and j.

      (i) Conclude that $i = j \bmod \mathrm{ord}^{\phi(n)}(x_0^e)$.

      (ii) Use Lagrange's theorem to infer that $\mathrm{ord}^{\phi(n)}(x_0^e)$ divides $\phi(n)$.

      (iii) For $n = p \cdot q$, assume that $p = 2 \cdot p' + 1$ and $q = 2 \cdot q' + 1$ for prime numbers p' and q' and that $\gcd(e, (p-1) \cdot (q-1)) = 1$. Conclude that $\mathrm{ord}^{\mathbb{Z}_n^*}(x_0^e)$ is either p' or q'. How large would you choose p' and q' to have sufficient security against a forward computation of tickets, and how would you justify this security?

      (iv) Show that 1 is not an element of the sequence $(x_i)_{i \geq 0}$ if $\gcd(e, (p-1) \cdot (q-1)) = 1$. Could you break the entire authentication system otherwise?

4.3 AUTHENTICATION REVISITED

The traditional role of signatures is to authenticate the person, agency, or device who signed the document in question. In the digital signature standard (DSS), we use a digital signature so that the recipient/verifier V of a message M could be certain that (a) M originated from the signing agent/prover P and (b) the message had not been altered in transit.

It is less clear, however, what else we may assume about the relationship between P, V, and messages that are apparently signed by P. Protocols that use DSS as a component may vary in their interpretation of these relationships.

- For example, if the digital signature is being used to sign a legally binding contract, then authentication ought to entail *blameworthiness* in the sense that the prover P should be liable for violations of contracts that bear her signature.
- However, if the protocol administers the authenticated receipt of software engineering projects in a correspondence course, then authentication should entail that P can obtain *credit* for this course.

Although these two aspects of authentication seem quite related (a failing grade may be viewed as "blaming" the prover P with violating the course requirements for a passing grade), they may influence the correctness of a protocol design in a crucial way. That is, the design and analysis of security protocols may have to be more specific in clarifying the functional role and intent of various security mechanisms before a sound design analysis can proceed. We illustrate this matter via the two facets of *credit* and *blameworthiness* for authentication protocols. The overall lesson of this section is that designers may want to ask specific questions about the more subtle aspects of intended behavior in security protocols.

Blameworthiness may also be called *responsibility*. For example, if the verifier V is a file server, the prover P a user, and the message M a request to delete a file, then V may use P's signature as justification for P's being responsible for the removal of the file. It seems prudent that authentication protocols be clear on whether authenticity entails responsibility, credit, or both. Since responsibility and credit may be *delegated* to other agents – just as this can be done in offline financial transactions – these notions cannot be established merely by means of the nonrepudiation of message origin. For the sake of simplicity, we assume that all subsequent protocols function without a trusted third party; the agents themselves assign responsibility and credit as they deem fit.

4.3.0.4   Signatures May Not Lead to Credit

We assume that each agent A has a *long-term* pair of keys, S_A (secret) and P_A (public).

Protocol 4.21 (A Simple Protocol)
Consider a simple two-step protocol:

1. the prover P creates a short-term key pair $\langle S_{P'}, P_{P'} \rangle$ and sends the message

   $$\langle P, V, S_P(P_{P'}, P, V, N) \rangle$$

   to the verifier V, where N is a *nonce* – a randomly generated number that should ensure the uniqueness of that message;
2. the prover P then sends to V the message

   $$\langle P, V, P_V(S_{P'}(M)) \rangle;$$

   thus, P signs message M with her short-term secret key $S_{P'}$ and V's public key and then sends the resulting message to V.

If we adopt the view that authentication entails responsibility, then V could blame P for any message that is signed with $S_{P'}$.

Attack 4.22 (Authenticity as Credit)

On the other hand, if V gave P credit for any message signed with $S_{P'}$, then this protocol could be attacked as follows:

1. the first message sent in step 1 of Protocol 4.21 is intercepted by a malicious agent A with public and secret keys P_A and S_A, respectively;
2. agent A can now compute the message $\langle A, V, S_A(P_{P'}, A, V, N) \rangle$ and sends it to the verifier V;
3. the second message sent from P to V (step 2 of Protocol 4.21) is also intercepted by A;
4. agent A alters that message to $\langle A, V, P_V(S_{P'}(M)) \rangle$ and sends it to V.

It is clear that this attack results in A receiving credit for a message that actually came from P. See Exercise 4.8-1 for how this protocol could be improved.

4.3.0.5 Encryption May Not Lead to Responsibility

Protocol 4.23 (A Basic Protocol)

Consider a basic protocol in which the prover P initially sends the verifier V the message $P_V(P, K)$, where K is (say) a key for the AES cipher Rijndael. Then P sends V the encrypted messages $\text{crypt}_K(M)$ and $\text{crypt}_K(M')$ in sequence.

We assume that P and V have reliable mechanisms for recognizing and ignoring their own messages, if replayed to them. This simple protocol is adequate for applications that require responsibility for V, and it may be adequate for applications that require credit for P. You should discuss such issues in the exercises that follow. There seems to be no possible general consensus on what, precisely, authentication should achieve. Moreover, system analysis is often unclear on the exact nature of the *guarantees* that authentication provides to the protocols in which authentication mechanisms are embedded. It is curious to note that responsibility and credit may be dual notions. Responsibility sometimes comes with signatures; credit sometimes comes with encryption. Developing a better understanding of this duality should aid the design and analysis of protocols that rely on authentication mechanisms.

EXERCISES 4.8

1. For Attack 4.22:
    (a) How can agent A compute the messages he sends to V?
    (b) How can the attack result in an erroneous blame of agent A?
    (c) Modify the protocol so that agent P now signs (parts of) the message with her short-term secret key. Explain why your modification prevents Attack 4.22.
2. In Protocol 4.23:
    (a) Explain in detail why P, if she received a message encrypted with key K, can blame agent V for this message.

(b) Can V be sure that nobody other than V and P know the key K? Should V use K to encrypt and send secrets?

(c) Can V hold P responsible for any received messages that are encrypted with K?

(d) In what limited sense can P claim credit for messages encrypted under K and sent to V?

(e) Adapt this protocol so that P and V each provide half of the key (N_P and N_V, respectively); then K is the secure hash of the string obtained by concatenating N_P, N_V, and the user identities of P and V.

(f) Discuss whether the protocol from part (e) establishes *exclusive* credit to P or V.

3. **Dining Cryptographers**   Authentication can also be done *anonymously*. "The Dining Cryptographers", a protocol due to D. Chaum, is described as follows.[2] Alice, Bob, and Mallory have become friendly network agents and celebrate their friendship at the local hamburger grill. Mike, the proprietor, informs them that their bill has already been paid anonymously, either by one of them or by the NSA. Since at least one of the friends won't accept funding from the NSA, they wonder how they could determine whether the NSA paid, *without exposing the payer in case it was Alice, Bob, or Mallory who picked up the bill*. They establish a protocol that does just that. Since Alice, Bob, and Mallory sit at a round table, each has exactly one right neighbor. They each pick a fair coin and toss it; only the tosser and the tosser's right neighbor can see the outcome. Thus, each agent is able to observe two coin tosses: its own one and the one of its left neighbor. Each agent must then make only one of two statements: (i) "the two coin tosses that I see have different outcomes"; or (ii) "the two coin tosses that I see have the same outcome". All agents speak truthfully except for the agent (if any) who paid the bill, who will *not* speak truthfully. (In particular, all agents speak the truth if the NSA paid the bill.) Let n be the number of agents who reply with (i).

(a) Show that any value 0, 1, 2, or 3 is possible for n.

(b) Show that the NSA is paying if n is even.

(c) Show that the NSA is not paying if n is odd.

(d) When n is odd, assume (without loss of generality) that Mallory is paying. Argue that – after a full run of the described protocol – Bob and Alice have no information that would suggest it is most likely that Mallory has paid.

4. **Electronic voting**   Discuss the potential benefits and dangers of using authenticated electronic voting schemes in promoting and maintaining democracies. Your analysis should include technical threats as well as concerns in the realm of public policy (e.g., questions of equal access).

5. In light of events following the 2000 U.S. presidential elections, discuss the design of software products that could aid in attaining a minumum number of rejected ballots. Explore offline and online systems, systems with printouts as receipts, and so forth. Analyze potential security threats that such designs might pose to the faithful expression of the "will of the people".

---

[2] We have given the cryptographers real names and changed the setting somewhat.

4.4 SECRET-SHARING PROTOCOLS

In some applications it is desirable not to associate an entire secret to an agent but instead to have some trusted authority *distribute* the secret across n agents so that the secret can be computed only if all n agents collaborate (assuming the authority is not corrupt). For example, such a scheme would result from giving each board member of Coca Cola only part of the top-secret recipe for their soft drink; hence no executive could sell the entire recipe to a competing brand. Conceptually, one may think of such schemes as providing *distributed data structures,* where algorithms for manipulation and retrieval need to follow a precise security protocol.

In Section 3.2.2 on the AES cipher Rijndael, we used polynomials modulo 2. We now generalize this notion from 2 to n; see Definition A.9 (p. 263) for a formal definition of the general concept. We design a shared-secret protocol consisting of two parts: the *distribution* of the secret and its *recovery.*

Protocol 4.24 (Secret-Sharing Protocol)
We have n agents $A_1, A_2, \ldots, A_n$, as well as a trusted authority who knows the *entire* secret $s \in \mathbb{N}$.

In the secret *distribution* phase:

1. the authority chooses a random prime p with $s \in \mathbb{Z}_p$ such that n is "much smaller" than $\sqrt{p}$;
2. the authority then chooses $2n - 1$ random elements in $\mathbb{Z}_p$,

    $$a_1 \; a_2 \; \cdots \; a_{n-1},$$
    $$v_0 \; v_1 \; v_2 \; \cdots \; v_{n-1},$$

    where all the v_i are nonzero and pairwise distinct;
3. next, the authority defines the polynomial

    $$f(x) \stackrel{\text{def}}{=} a_{n-1} \cdot x^{n-1} + a_{n-2} \cdot x^{n-2} + \cdots + a_1 \cdot x + s \bmod p \tag{4.29}$$

    over $\mathbb{Z}_p$, where $s \in \mathbb{Z}_p$ is the secret;
4. each agent A_j obtains from the authority the pair

    $$\langle v_j, f(v_j) \rangle \in \mathbb{Z}_p \times \mathbb{Z}_p$$

    as his or her portion of the secret.

In the secret *recovery* phase: All n agents can share their individual information to construct the polynomial

$$g(x) \stackrel{\text{def}}{=} \sum_{0 \le j < n} f(v_j) \cdot \prod_{0 \le i < n,\, i \ne j} (v_j - v_i)^{-1} \cdot (x - v_i) \bmod p; \tag{4.30}$$

the secret s is then recovered by computing $g(0)$.

Example 4.25
Let us consider three agents A_1, A_2, and A_3.

- For an unrealistically small prime number $p = 1999$, the authority randomly chooses

```
evaluation point v[0]: 626
evaluation point v[1]: 674
evaluation point v[2]: 93
coefficient a[1]: 334
coefficient a[2]: 223
```

and then computes the shares $f(v_j)$, given the secret $s = 472$, as

```
share f(v[0]): 1724
share f(v[1]): 1925
share f(v[2]): 1241
```

If all three agents mean to recover s then they can exploit the fact that they need only evaluate (4.30) at zero, so this specializes to

$$s = \sum_{0 \leq j < n} f(v_j) \cdot b_j \bmod p, \tag{4.31}$$

where

$$b_j \stackrel{\text{def}}{=} \prod_{0 \leq i < n, i \neq j} v_i \cdot (v_i - v_j)^{-1} \bmod p. \tag{4.32}$$

The agents may therefore compute

```
weight b[0]: 1847
weight b[1]: 793
weight b[2]: 1359
```

and thus recover the secret 472 via (4.31).

- For a randomly generated 50-bit prime $p = 342853815608923$, we obtain:

```
evaluation point v[0]: 111350135012507
evaluation point v[1]: 207244959855905
evaluation point v[2]: 20545949133543
coefficient a[1]: 53958111706386
coefficient a[2]: 151595058245452
secret s: 151595058245452
share f(v[0]): 109351520587519
share f(v[1]): 174675701531216
share f(v[2]): 117471713218253
weight b[0]: 266921901220910
weight b[1]: 129147516050688
weight b[2]: 289638213946249
recovered secret: 151595058245452
```

Theorem 4.26 (Correctness of Shared-Secret Protocol)
The n agents of the shared-secret protocol can efficiently compute $g(0)$, and this number equals s.

Proof   Observe that g, a Lagrange interpolation of f, is a polynomial with degree less than n and that g satisfies

$$g(v_j) = f(v_j) \quad (0 \le j < n). \tag{4.33}$$

Thus $f - g$ is a polynomial over $\mathbb{Z}_p$ of degree less than n, but it has at least n different roots: numbers r with $f(r) - g(r) = 0$. It follows that $f(a) = g(a)$ for all $a \in \mathbb{Z}_p$. In particular, $g(0) = f(0)$, but the latter evaluates to s. □

One can design a variation of this shared-secret protocol, called *verifiable shared-secret protocol*, where each shareholder can verify that they hold a *valid* part of the secret without having to discover anything about the secret parts of the other shareholders. The idea of verifiable secret-sharing can be used in the design of RSA cryptosystems, where each user's private key is split among a number of trustees.

Moreover, there exist secure and efficient schemes that realize secret sharing in any *monotone access structure*. Given a finite set I of individuals, an access structure $\mathcal{A}$ over I is a set of nonempty subsets of I such that

$$A \in \mathcal{A} \ \& \ A \subseteq A' \implies A' \in \mathcal{A}.$$

A secret-sharing scheme for $\mathcal{A}$ should allow the efficient recovery of the secret for any group of individuals A if and only if $A \in \mathcal{A}$. The monotonicity requirement makes sense because then more individuals inherit the capabilities of their proper subgroups. For details on such schemes, see the bibliographic notes (Section 4.6).

EXERCISES 4.9

1. Equation (4.30) features inverses $(v_j - v_i)^{-1} \bmod p$. Explain what properties in the protocol guarantee their existence.

2. *Security of shared-secret protocol* Suppose that k players of Protocol 4.24 collaborate to gain unauthorized access to the secret s, assuming that $k < n$. Since the collaboration of more agents can only mean more of a threat, we may assume that $k = n - 1$. The protocol treats each agent the same, so we may assume that the k agents are actually $A_1, A_2, \ldots, A_{n-1}$.

   (a) How many polynomials h over $\mathbb{Z}_p$ exist that satisfy

   $$h(v_j) = f(v_j) \quad (0 \le j < n - 1) \tag{4.34}$$

   for the f from (4.29)? Note that any such h could represent the *collected knowledge* of the k agents about the secret s.

   (b) For a fixed number $c \in \mathbb{Z}_p$, how many of the h satisfying (4.34) have the property that $h(0) = c$?

   (c) Why, and to what extent, does the correct answer for part (b) suggest that the shared-secret protocol is perfectly secure against fraudulent collaborations?

   (d) Returning to Protocol 4.24, what potential security concerns could you raise regarding the implementation of this protocol? Discuss separately the distribution and the recovery phase.

3. *Generalized shared-secret protocol* We adapt Protocol 4.24 by making it depend on two parameters $\langle k, n \rangle$ with $1 \le k \le n$ such that any k players can collaborate to reconstruct the secret; the protocol is secure against attacks in which fewer than k players collaborate. The modified protocol uses the same number of values v_j but

only k values $a_1, a_2, \ldots, a_{k-1}$. The polynomial f over $\mathbb{Z}_p$ is defined as a truncated version of the original one:

$$f(x) \stackrel{\text{def}}{=} a_{k-1} \cdot x^{k-1} + a_{k-2} \cdot x^{k-2} + \cdots + a_1 \cdot x + s \bmod p. \qquad (4.35)$$

(a) Explain how *any* group of k agents can collaborate to recover the secret s.

(b) Explain in what sense this modified protocol is secure against an attack of any group of fewer than k collaborating agents.

(c) Describe this protocol when k equals 1. What do we obtain if k equals n?

4. *Implementing the distribution of the secret*   Use a pseudo-random number generator and a prime generator to implement the component used by the trusted authority for the general shared-secret protocol from Exercise 3. More specifically, the authority's program should take the parameter $\langle k, n \rangle$ as input, generate a suitable prime p, and generate a secret s.[3] The output should be the n pairs $\langle v_j, f(v_j) \rangle$.

5. *Implementing the reconstruction of the secret*   Implement the component that the group of k agents may use for the reconstruction of secret s. More specifically, the group's program should take the prime p and the k pairs $\langle v_{j_i}, f(v_{j_i}) \rangle$ as input, where the group of k agents is $A_{j_1}, A_{j_2}, \ldots, A_{j_k}$; the output should be the claimed secret s'.

6. Suppose that you and your two companions have obtained your secret shares listed below. Recover the secret s, given that

```
prime p: 386635119272011
evaluation point v[0]: 289606484363304
evaluation point v[1]: 228145533986232
evaluation point v[2]: 330844624449199
share value f(v[0]): 249291108939758
share value f(v[1]): 197249960673620
share value f(v[2]): 250460653862862
```

7. The correctness of the secret-recovery protocol depends on the fact that $f - g$ always computes 0 for all values of x. Read Proposition A.11 and its proof (p. 264) and explain how this is related to the claim about $f - g$.

4.5   MODEL CHECKING SECURITY PROTOCOL DESIGNS

The public-key encryption schemes, block ciphers, pseudo-random number generators, and other stream ciphers presented in this text are often used as components in larger systems, such as communication protocols, electronic fund transfer protocols, application programs for electronic mail, et cetera. Clearly, the security of such systems will depend on the security of each cryptographic component in isolation. We have tried to assess RSA, DES, and a variety of other cryptographic systems from such an isolated point of view, studying a mathematical idealization rather than actual implementations. Even though all cryptographic components of a complex system may attain a certain acceptable level of security, this by no means guarantees that the potential behavior of the *overall, composed*

---

[3] We assume that the secret, presumably some text, has been mapped into $\mathbb{Z}_p$.

system is secure. Compare this to having a correct (here, meaning "secure") implementation of division for floating-point arithmetic in an untyped programming language, where some program may call this implementation with ill-typed input – for example, a string "divided" by an integer. The task set out for this section is to describe in some detail a framework (due to W. Marrero, E. Clarke, and S. Jha) in which we can:

- formally specify the *possible/allowed behavior* of communication protocols that may make use of cryptographic primitives;
- model *malicious intruders,* with well-understood capabilities, as well as *unreliable communication channels*;
- abstract the preceding into a *finite-state transition system*; and
- *exhaustively check* that transition system to see whether it *violates any security property* – possibly written in some specification logic with a formal (and hence executable) semantics.

We stress that such a framework should be seen merely as a *debugger,* not as a verifier. Even if the model of a protocol does not violate its formalized security specification, this does not mean that the protocol is (say) computationally secure. Indeed, in this section we make the assumption that all cryptographic components – in isolation – are *perfectly* secure! Although this may fly in the face of concerns expressed in previous chapters, it merely reflects a shift of perspective in that we now study more complex systems and attempt to rule out security violations that are possible *even if* all cryptographic components are assumed to be secure. This kind of security violation is a major concern in realistic protocols for electronic commerce, or more generally in any security protocol that involves several agents communicating concurrently. The verification of concurrent systems – even without the consideration of security issues – is a difficult subject, and design errors (e.g. deadlocks) can be quite subtle and hard to find. Thus, it is of paramount importance to have a tool that can find these kinds of security flaws. Such a tool naturally functions as a debugger, since any *attack* (an execution trace violating the security specification) found in the protocol's idealized model is likely also to be an attack in the actual system that uses the real – and perhaps not perfectly secure – cryptographic primitives.

Definition 4.27 (Perfect Encryption Assumption)
In this section, we assume the following *perfect encryption properties* for all cryptographic components used in protocols.

1. A cipher-text cannot be decrypted into its corresponding plain-text unless one (possesses and) uses the corresponding encryption key and decryption algorithm. Conversely, a plain-text cannot be encrypted into its corresponding cipher-text unless one uses the corresponding encryption key and encryption algorithm.
2. A cipher-text can be *generated* only if one (possesses and) uses its corresponding plain-text encryption algorithm and key. A plain-text with unknown contents can be *recovered* from its corresponding cipher-text only with knowledge of the decryption algorithm and key. In particular, all encryption and decryption algorithms are *collision-free*.

The second item of this definition rules out the possibility of generating sensitive data via the composition of public data with public composition operators. For example, the bits

"0" and "1" and the concatenation operation are public, but it should still be impossible to generate a 160-bit string $\text{hash}(M)$ unless one knows the particular message M.

4.5.1 Modeling Network Messages

Let us begin by explaining the kind of messages that agents are allowed to exchange in any protocol modeled within this framework.

Definition 4.28 (Grammar for Atomic Messages)
We require five sorts of *atomic messages*, $\mathcal{A}$, generated according to the grammar

$$a ::= \text{E}_k \mid \text{D}_k \mid P \mid n \mid d, \tag{4.36}$$

where k ranges over some implicit *key space*, P over a set of *principal agents*, and n over a set of *nonces*; d is an abstraction of any *data* – whose contents or format are irrelevant to how the protocol works – that are meant to be communicated between agents.

Note that keys, if sent as atomic messages, are equipped with a mode: E_k suggests a concrete encryption algorithm with its corresponding key, whereas D_k stands for its inverse decryption procedure and key. Recall from Definition 3.1 (p. 83) that knowledge of E_k won't generally entail any knowledge about D_k unless the underlying cryptographic system is *symmetric*. Nonces n denote randomly generated numbers that, among other things, can prevent "replay" attacks. For example, the random k from Protocol 4.6 (p. 134) ensures that the same message, if signed more than once according to the Digital Signature Standard, "never" produces the same signature. With this view of atomic messages, we can define the set of all messages that may be communicated in protocols.

Definition 4.29 (Grammar for Messages)
Given the set $\mathcal{A}$ of atomic messages generated by the grammar in (4.36), we define the set $\mathcal{M}$ of all messages by the grammar

$$m ::= a \mid m \cdot m \mid \text{E}_m(m) \mid \text{D}_m(m). \tag{4.37}$$

Thus, a message is either atomic (a), a pair of two messages ($m_1 \cdot m_2$), the encryption of a message m with key k ($\text{E}_k(m)$), or the decryption of message m with key k ($\text{D}_k(m)$). Note that this framework identifies all known cryptosystems and their inherent system parameters, whether based on public or symmetric keys. We can now make precise the meaning of the perfect encryption assumptions: There are no messages a, m, m_1, m_2 and keys k such that

$$\text{E}_k(m) = a \quad \text{or} \quad \text{D}_k(m) = a;$$
$$\text{E}_k(m) = m_1 \cdot m_2 \quad \text{or} \quad \text{D}_k(m) = m_1 \cdot m_2. \tag{4.38}$$

Moreover, for all $n, n', m, m' \in \mathcal{M}$:

- $\text{D}_n(m) = \text{D}_{n'}(m')$ implies $n = n'$ and $m = m'$; and
- $\text{E}_n(m) = \text{E}_{n'}(m')$ implies $n = n'$ and $m = m'$.

We enforce these assumptions by considering (4.37) as a *free grammar*; the only valid equations of terms are trivial ones (e.g. $m = m$). Even though we "abstract away" the particular cryptosystems, we still need to ensure that they are correct – in other words, that we have the equations

$$D_k(E_k(m)) = m \tag{4.39}$$

for all keys k and messages m. Although we allow only trivial equations, we enforce (4.39) *operationally* when agents infer knowledge from other messages. The knowledge inference algorithm is discussed in Section 4.5.3.

Consider a run of some protocol, where an agent/principal A has seen the set $\mathcal{B} \subseteq \mathcal{M}$ of messages up to a certain execution point of that particular run. We must be able to model what other messages A can infer from this set $\mathcal{B}$ by means of cryptographic primitives and manipulations of pairs.

Definition 4.30 (Closure of Message Set)
Let $\mathcal{B}$ be a nonempty subset of $\mathcal{M}$. The closure of $\mathcal{B}$, denoted by $\bar{\mathcal{B}}$, is obtained as follows: $m \in \mathcal{M}$ is an element of $\bar{\mathcal{B}}$ if and only if this can be derived by means of a finite application of any of these six *knowledge inference* rules.

1. If $m \in \mathcal{B}$, then $m \in \bar{\mathcal{B}}$.
2. If $m_1 \in \bar{\mathcal{B}}$ and $m_2 \in \bar{\mathcal{B}}$, then $m_1 \cdot m_2 \in \bar{\mathcal{B}}$.
3. If $m_1 \cdot m_2 \in \bar{\mathcal{B}}$, then $m_1 \in \bar{\mathcal{B}}$ and $m_2 \in \bar{\mathcal{B}}$.
4. If $m \in \bar{\mathcal{B}}$ and $E_k \in \bar{\mathcal{B}}$, then $E_k(m) \in \bar{\mathcal{B}}$.
5. If $m \in \bar{\mathcal{B}}$ and $D_k \in \bar{\mathcal{B}}$, then $D_k(m) \in \bar{\mathcal{B}}$.
6. If $E_k(m) \in \bar{\mathcal{B}}$ and $D_k \in \bar{\mathcal{B}}$, then $m \in \bar{\mathcal{B}}$.

Rule 1 simply states that each message in $\mathcal{B}$ is in the closure of $\mathcal{B}$; it is already known to the agent/principal in question. Rules 2 and 3 state (respectively) that a principal can construct a pair of two messages provided she already knows the two messages and that she is able to extract and add the components of a pair she already knows to her stock of known messages. Rule 4 (resp., rule 5) states that a principal can encrypt (resp., decrypt) a message with a key, provided she knows the message and the key.[4] By rule 6, a principal can successfully decipher a given cipher-text of the type $E_k(m)$ if she knows that cipher-text and the corresponding key D_k.

Example 4.31 (Computation of Closure)
Let

$$\mathcal{B} \overset{\text{def}}{=} \{m_1 \cdot (E_k(m) \cdot D_k)\}$$

be a singleton set. We claim that m is in the closure of $\mathcal{B}$: by rule 3, we can access the second component of the pair $m_1 \cdot (E_k(m) \cdot D_k)$ to retrieve the message $E_k(m) \cdot D_k$. The same rule allows us to compute the messages D_k and $E_k(m)$; but then rule 6 gives us access to

---

[4] Observe that these rules are split into two modes, but in terms of knowledge we may identify E_k and D_k with k – *provided that* only symmetric-key cryptosystems are being used.

the message m. Similarly, we can deduce that $m_1 \in \bar{B}$. To see that $\bar{B}$ is an infinite set, note that we can apply our rules "forever" and so conclude that $m \cdot m_1$ and $m \cdot (m \cdot m_1)$ and so forth are all in $\bar{B}$.

A computationally problematic fact is that closures $\bar{B}$ are generally *infinite*. Fortunately, our verification framework requires only that we determine whether a certain message m (or some finite set of messages) is contained in the closure of some (finite) set of messages B – and possibly that we add m to B otherwise. In Section 4.5.3, we derive an efficient algorithm for deciding such questions.

EXERCISES 4.10

1. (a) Refine the grammar in (4.37) into a *type inference system,* where judgments have the form $\vdash m : \mathcal{M}$ (with intuitive meaning "m is a message") and $\vdash k : \mathcal{K}$ ("k is a key"). For example, we have the rule

$$\frac{\vdash m_1 : \mathcal{M} \quad \vdash m_2 : \mathcal{M}}{\vdash m_1 \cdot m_2 : \mathcal{M}} \text{ Pairing}$$

for pairing two messages and the axiom

$$\frac{}{\vdash a : \mathcal{M}} \text{ Atomic}$$

for atomic messages. Design these rules such that the encryption and decryption of messages is done only with messages of type $\mathcal{K}$. (See Figure 6.2, p. 208, for an example of a simple type inference system.)

 (b) Adapt your system, if need be, so that you can prove

$$\vdash E_{k_1}(k_2) \cdot E_{k_3}(k_1) : \mathcal{M}$$

from the assumptions $\vdash k_i : \mathcal{K}$ for $i = 1, 2, 3$.

2. (a) Write the rules of Definition 4.30 as a type inference system, where judgments are of the form $\vdash m : B$, "message m is in B", and $\vdash m : \text{closure } B$, "message m is in the closure of B". For example, the first rule is written as

$$\frac{\vdash m : B}{\vdash m : \text{closure } B} \text{ Subset.}$$

 (b) Argue that we have $m \in \bar{B}$ if and only if $\vdash m : \text{closure } B$ can be shown using only assumptions of the form $\vdash m' : B$, where $m' \in B$.

 (c) We define a function

$$\Omega : \mathcal{P}(\mathcal{M}) \to \mathcal{P}(\mathcal{M}),$$

where $\mathcal{P}(\mathcal{M})$ is the power set of $\mathcal{M}$. For any subset B of $\mathcal{M}$, we have $m \in \Omega(B)$ if and only if $m \in \bar{B}$ can be proved. For all such subsets B and B', show that:

 (i) B is a subset of $\Omega(B)$;

 (ii) $B \subseteq B'$ implies $\Omega(B) \subseteq \Omega(B')$;

 (iii) $\Omega(\Omega(B)) = \Omega(B)$;

 (iv) $\Omega(B)$ is the smallest set of messages containing B and closed under all the rules in Definition 4.30.

 Which of these arguments depend on the actual nature of the rules in Definition 4.30?

3. (a) Use the rules of Definition 4.30 (or your type inference system from Exercise 2)
to show:

(i) $k \in \bar{\mathcal{B}}$, where $\mathcal{B} \overset{\text{def}}{=} \{D_{k_1}, D_{k_2}, E_{k_2}(E_{k_1}(k) \cdot m)\}$;

(ii) $E_{k_2}(m \cdot k) \in \bar{\mathcal{B}}$, where

$$\mathcal{B} \overset{\text{def}}{=} \{D_{k_1}, E_{k_1}(D_{k_2}), E_{k_2}(E_{k_1}(E_{k_2}(k \cdot m)))\}.$$

(iii) Explain why you can (or cannot) show $k \cdot m \in \bar{\mathcal{B}}$ for the set $\mathcal{B}$ described in
part (ii).

(b) Explain why one cannot use the rules of Definition 4.30 to prove that a message
m is *not* in the closure of some set $\mathcal{B}$.

4.5.2 Modeling Network Agents

The agents that participate in a protocol have local state and do their local computations
asynchronously. For example, agent A may compute m from $E_k(m)$ and D_k while agent B
waits (= does nothing) for a response from A. In the global system, computation traces
are interleavings of:

- local internal actions, such as the generation of a nonce; and
- actions in which two agents communicate – such communication happens *synchronously* via a handshake of specific actions.

We model the local state of a *friendly agent* as a four-tuple

$$\langle A, \text{p\_A}, I_A, \rho_A \rangle,$$

where

- A is the agent's *unique name*;
- p_A is the description of the *agent's allowed behavior* given in a programming language, process algebra, or some other suitable formalism – we write p_A as

    a; p_A'

to denote that agent A may only perform action a at the current state and must then
behave according to p_A';
- I_A is a subset of $\mathcal{M}$, representing those messages (including decryption or encryption
keys) that agent A *knows* at that computational state;
- $\rho_A : \text{Var}(\text{p\_A}) \to I_A$ is a partial function that *binds messages* to some of the (free)
variables of p_A; in particular, such messages are used to denote communication channels, keys, or names of agents.

In the sequel, we are somewhat informal in our description of an agent's allowed behavior p_A. Our model assumes that all agents are *logically omniscient* as far as their
knowledge about messages is concerned. This idealization is easily modeled by insisting
that the set I_A of locally known messages be *deductively closed*:

$$I_A = \overline{I_A}.$$

For example, if agent A knows $E_k(m)$ and D_k, then she also knows message m at that same computational state. Our operational execution model of protocols needs to ensure that the dynamic set I_A remains closed under such knowledge.

4.5.2.1 Communication between Agents

Communication between two agents is modeled by a handshake established through *send* and matching *receive* actions along a variable/channel x. We write `send m along x` for sending message m across the variable/channel x and write `receive m along x` for the corresponding receive action across that same channel. For example, let

$\langle A, (\texttt{send m along x}); \texttt{p\_A'}, I_A, \rho_A \rangle,$

$\langle B, (\texttt{receive m along x}); \texttt{p\_B'}, I_B, \rho_B \rangle$

be the local states of two agents A and B, respectively. Then a message `send m along x` from agent A *matches* the corresponding message `receive m along x` of agent B if and only if there is a binding

$\rho': \mathsf{Var}(\texttt{p\_B}) \to I_B,$

extending the current binding ρ_B, such that $\rho'(\texttt{receive m along x})$ equals the corresponding binding of agent A, namely $\rho_A(\texttt{send m along x})$. In this case, communication can occur, so each agent changes his local state according to

$$\langle A, (\texttt{send m along x}); \texttt{p\_A'}, I_A, \rho_A \rangle \rightsquigarrow \langle A, \texttt{p\_A'}, I_A, \rho_A \rangle \qquad (4.40)$$

$$\langle B, (\texttt{receive m along x}); \texttt{p\_B'}, I_B, \rho_B \rangle \rightsquigarrow \langle B, \texttt{p\_B'}, I_B', \rho' \rangle. \qquad (4.41)$$

Here each agent's process description drops the synchronizing action and then lets her behave as specified after the ; keyword. Note, however, that additional state changes occur with the agent B who receives a message. First, she must respect the matching binding ρ' as its new binding information. Second, since she now is in possession of the received message $\rho'(\texttt{receive m along x})$, she updates her internal knowledge database to include anything that can be inferred from her previous knowledge, I_B, and this new message:

$$I_B' \stackrel{\text{def}}{=} \overline{I_B \cup \{\rho'(\texttt{receive m along x})\}}. \qquad (4.42)$$

4.5.2.2 Creation of Nonces and Temporary Secrets

Agents need the capability of creating *fresh nonces* and *temporary secrets*. "Freshness" here means that such data have not been generated before and that their uniqueness is guaranteed as new data are being generated.

Definition 4.32 (Secret Messages)

1. We write $\mathcal{S}_{\text{safe}}$ for the subset of *safe secrets* of $\mathcal{M}$. This set needs to be well-defined at the beginning of a protocol's execution and should remain fixed during any of its executions. Agents' long-term public keys, digital-signature keys, and any otherwise classified messages are typical examples of such secrets.

2. Similarly, we write S_{temp} for the subset of $\mathcal{M}$ consisting of *temporary secrets*. Examples are short-term session keys or other negotiation results for parameters of cryptographic systems that are redefined after each single use. Usually, the set S_{temp} evolves during the execution of a protocol.

It should be intuitively clear that S_{safe} and S_{temp} are part of a model's *global state*. Whereas a malicious agent should never be able to deduce a safe secret, temporary secrets may be exposed to an intruder. We allow the assumption of such exposure because it enables us to analyze whether it can entail the corruption of supposedly safe secrets. Syntactically, we may express the creation of nonces and secrets in the description language of agents' permitted behavior as

```
nonce(y); p_A'   and   secret(y); p_A',
```

respectively. Operationally, such process descriptions give rise to the following internal state changes:

$$\langle A, \texttt{nonce(y)}; \texttt{p\_A'}, I_A, \rho_A \rangle \rightsquigarrow \langle A, \texttt{p\_A'}, I'_A, \rho'_A \rangle, \tag{4.43}$$

$$\langle A, \texttt{secret(y)}; \texttt{p\_A'}, I_A, \rho_A \rangle \rightsquigarrow \langle A, \texttt{p\_A'}, I'_A, \rho'_A \rangle. \tag{4.44}$$

The message m, representing the temporary (`nonce(y)`) or permanent (`secret(y)`) secret, needs to be "fresh" – newly generated. If we write $\rho_A[y \mapsto m]$ for the binding that binds like ρ_A (except for y, where it assigns m as a value), we have p_A,

$$\rho'_A \stackrel{\text{def}}{=} \rho_A[y \mapsto m], \quad \text{and} \quad I'_A \stackrel{\text{def}}{=} \overline{I_A \cup \{m\}} \tag{4.45}$$

as the only components of the local state that change in (4.43) and (4.44), respectively. Note that the semantics of new nonces is the same as that for new secrets. However, they differ in their *type,* the functional role they are meant to play in a protocol. This difference is also reflected in the capabilities of the malicious intruder Z, as discussed in Section 4.5.2.3. Note that (4.43) and (4.44) don't update local states of any other friendly agents, for the generation of the nonce or secret is *internal* to the agent who generates it and can only reach other agents through subsequent communication through the channel y.

4.5.2.3 Intruders and Untrusted Channels

Our framework models any untrusted communication channels or malicious agents as a *single* intruder/adversary, the principal Z. The justification for such a radical design choice is that the intruder:

- intercepts *all* communication occurring in the protocol, thereby modeling any set of attackers or untrusted channels; and
- can send a message to any agent at any time, provided that the intruder is capable of generating that message at the given moment in time; thus, the intruder Z is a conservative abstraction of a group of adversaries and untrusted channels, as it models their full collaboration.

In this approach, all communication lines lead through the intruder's server before they reach intended receiving agents. The intruder may also impersonate friendly network agents. The intruder's *knowledge inference engine* also makes crucial use of deciding instances of "$m \in \bar{\mathcal{B}}$?", where $\mathcal{B}$ is its *knowledge base*. But since the intruder receives *all* network traffic, we need to develop a technique for a *compact* representation of the intruder's growing knowledge – the topic of Section 4.5.3. Let us now model the corruption of a temporary secret.

Definition 4.33 (Corruption of Temporary Secrets)
If the intruder's current local state is $\langle Z, \texttt{getsecret; p\_Z'}, \texttt{I}_Z, \rho_Z \rangle$,[5] then he may change his local state to

$$\langle Z, \texttt{getsecret; p\_Z'}, \texttt{I}_Z, \rho_Z \rangle \rightsquigarrow \langle Z, \texttt{p\_Z'}, \texttt{I}'_Z, \rho_Z \rangle, \tag{4.46}$$

where for some $m \in \mathcal{S}_{\text{temp}}$ we have

$$\texttt{I}'_Z \stackrel{\text{def}}{=} \overline{\texttt{I}_Z \cup \{m\}} \quad \text{and} \quad \mathcal{S}'_{\text{temp}} \stackrel{\text{def}}{=} \mathcal{S}_{\text{temp}} \setminus \{m\}. \tag{4.47}$$

Note that $\mathcal{S}'_{\text{temp}}$ in (4.47) denotes the set of temporary secrets resulting from the state change in (4.46); after the exposure of m to the intruder Z, message m is no longer a temporary secret. The latter state change could occur for *any* temporary secret; thus, our verification tool needs to model this quantification over m as an *exhaustively searched nondeterministic choice*. In (4.47), the intruder dutifully recomputes his knowledge gained from the corruption of the temporary secret m. Since the intruder models all malicious agents, no other principal is allowed to have the action $\texttt{getsecret}$ as part of their process description. Also observe that the intruder may corrupt a *temporary* secret (e.g., through the compromise of a session key) only if that secret has already been used or established in the given protocol. This is what $\mathcal{S}_{\text{temp}}$ models.

In our conservative overestimation of the intruder's capabilities, we assume that he is basically able to perform any action at any time, including $\texttt{getsecret}$. Hence there is no need for specifying the allowed behavior $\texttt{p\_Z}$ or bindings ρ_Z. However, we may put some realistic constraints on his omnipotence. For example, he may send a message through $\texttt{send m along x}$ only if the message and its format are expected by agent B at channel $\texttt{receive m along x}$ and are also in the closure of his current knowledge base $\texttt{I}_Z$.

4.5.2.4 Specifications

For now, we are interested in two kinds of properties that protocols should enjoy. First, we establish a *secrecy property* by verifying that *no computation trace of a protocol allows the intruder to infer some $m \in \mathcal{S}_{\text{safe}}$*. This is easily checked as soon as we have an efficient decision procedure for deciding "$m \in \overline{\texttt{I}_Z}$?". Second, we check certain *temporal correspondence properties*. An example would be to ask whether agent B has actually begun a protocol run with agent A if agent A believes that he has finished a run of that

---

[5] We see shortly that the local state of the intruder can be modeled in a much simpler fashion, but for now we denote his state in the manner done for friendly agents.

protocol with agent B. Generally, such properties have the form: "If event a occurs, then event b must have occurred in the past."

However, such correspondences must be *one-to-one*: if we abstract a computation trace to these two events only and omit states where none of these two events occur, then such traces should be generated by the grammar

$$S ::= SaSb \mid \varepsilon, \tag{4.48}$$

where ε is the empty string and S the only nonterminal symbol. Examples of such traces are ab, $abaabb$, and $aaaabbbbabb$. The trace $abaababab$, however, it not generated by (4.48). More specifically, we require four action types – begin_init, stop_init, begin_resp, and stop_resp – that take a principal's name as argument. For a principal A, the meaning of:

1. begin_init B is that agent A begins some protocol activity with agent B;
2. stop_init B is that agent A ends some protocol activity with agent B;
3. begin_resp B is that agent A begins to participate in (respond to) some protocol that was initiated by agent B;
4. stop_resp B is that agent A ends her participation in some protocol that was initiated by agent B.

The operational semantics of these actions, parametric in A and B, is given by

$$\langle A, \texttt{begin\_init B; p\_A'}, I_A, \rho_A \rangle \rightsquigarrow \langle A, \texttt{p\_A'}, I_A, \rho_A \rangle, \tag{4.49}$$

$$\langle B, \texttt{stop\_resp A; p\_B'}, I_B, \rho_B \rangle \rightsquigarrow \langle B, \texttt{p\_B'}, I_B, \rho_B \rangle; \tag{4.50}$$

$$\langle A, \texttt{stop\_init B; p\_A'}, I_A, \rho_A \rangle \rightsquigarrow \langle A, \texttt{p\_A'}, I_A, \rho_A \rangle, \tag{4.51}$$

$$\langle B, \texttt{begin\_resp A; p\_B'}, I_B, \rho_B \rangle \rightsquigarrow \langle B, \texttt{p\_B'}, I_B, \rho_B \rangle. \tag{4.52}$$

This is similar to the semantics we have seen for other actions, but now the only change of local state occurs in the description of allowed behavior. These rules do, however, *change global state*. For each pair of agents A and B, the model's global state has counters $C_i(A, B)$ and $C_r(A, B)$ for the initiation and response (respectively) of these agents' interaction. These counters are initially set to 0. The local state change in (4.49) is accompanied by the global state change

$$C_i(A, B) := C_i(A, B) + 1. \tag{4.53}$$

Similarly, the local state change in (4.50) results in the global state change

$$C_i(A, B) := C_i(A, B) - 1. \tag{4.54}$$

The local state change in (4.52) is accompanied by the global state change

$$C_r(A, B) := C_r(A, B) + 1. \tag{4.55}$$

Finally, the local state change in (4.51) results in the global state change

$$C_r(A, B) := C_r(A, B) - 1. \tag{4.56}$$

EXERCISE 4.11

1. Let s be any finite string over the alphabet $\{a, b\}$.

(a) Show that s is generated according to (4.48) if and only if $C(s) \geq 0$, where

$$C(\varepsilon) \overset{\text{def}}{=} 0, \tag{4.57}$$

$$C(s \cdot a) \overset{\text{def}}{=} C(s) - 1, \tag{4.58}$$

$$C(s \cdot b) \overset{\text{def}}{=} C(s) + 1. \tag{4.59}$$

(b) Which of the actions `begin_init`, `stop_init`, `begin_resp`, and `stop_resp` play the roles of a and b (and for which parameters) in the counters in part (a)?

4.5.2.5 Searching the Global State Space

As discussed previously, each friendly agent A has local state $\langle A, \texttt{p\_A}, \mathrm{I}_A, \rho_A \rangle$. The behavior of A is dictated by the description `p_A`, which specifies the permitted sequences of actions that A may engage in.

The intruder Z, however, has no such restrictions. He may communicate with any agent at any given time, he may impersonate other friendly agents, and so on. Yet our model does place one restriction on the intruder's capabilities: he may send a message m to some agent B only if m is in the set of messages I_Z known to the intruder at the time and if m matches what agent B expects at the channel advertised by Z. Although Z may generate infinitely many messages in I_Z, the number of such messages that match the input format for some agent's channel is finite at any given point in a protocol. If the sets of safe and temporary secrets are also finite, then each global state can have only finitely many immediate successor states. Thus we can implement a depth-first search over the choice of these messages and the choice of asynchronous compositions of local actions. We shall develop an efficient algorithm for deciding

$$m \in \mathrm{I}_A ? \tag{4.60}$$

for any agent A, including Z. It therefore suffices to model the state of the intruder by what he knows: the set I_Z.

A global state is the product of all local states of friendly agents with the set I_Z and all counter pairs $\mathrm{C}_i(A, B)$ and $\mathrm{C}_r(A, B)$, where A and B range over all (not necessarily friendly) agents; additionally, the global state incorporates the sets S_{temp} and S_{safe}. We have just mentioned that the resulting state transition system is *finitely-branching*: each state has only finitely many next states. Since each friendly agent A can engage in only a finite sequence of actions described in `p_A`, the asynchronous interleaving of such actions and those of Z can produce traces of only finite length. But then the entire system can have only finitely many states and contains no cycles, for agents never return to some previous local state.

In Figure 4.2, we list pseudo-code for the resulting search. The main program initializes `s` to the protocol's initial global state and returns `false` only if no compromises of temporary or permanent secrets and no violations of correspondence properties are found. The recursive procedure `found_a_bug?(s)` returns `true` only if, at state `s`, we find that

```
main(Protocol p) {
  s := initial global state of p;
  return found_a_bug?(s);
}
found_a_bug?(GlobalState s) {
    for all agents A and B {
    if (C_i(A,B) < 0 || C_r(A,B) < 0) return true;
    }
    for all m in S_temp or m in S_safe {
    if m in I_Z return true;
    }
    if (nextstate_of s) {
    return disjunction of all found_a_bug?(s'),
          s' any next state of s
    } else { return false; }
}
```

Figure 4.2. Pseudo-code for a depth-first exhaustive search of the global state space. The main program evaluates to `true` if there is a security flaw in the protocol. The call (`nextstate_of s`) returns `true` if and only if there is at least one next global state of its input state `s`.

- some correspondence property is violated (the statement `for all agents ...`), or
- some secret is compromised to the intruder (the statement `for all m ...`), or
- *some* next state `s'` of `s` returns `true` on a recursive call of the same procedure (the statement `return disjunction of ...`).

So far, we have described in almost complete detail how to compute the next possible global states for a given global state s. We basically took care of changes in the local states of agents and changes in the counters of correspondence properties, but we still owe an account of how to represent the knowledge of each agent and its possible update with messages that agents receive. Note that this is required for a complete description of local changes to friendly agents and the intruder alike; see for example (4.45) and (4.47). Incidentally, the action taken in (4.46) does not immediately or necessarily result in the detection of a flaw, for (4.47) guarantees that the compromised temporary secret is no longer a secret in any next global state.

4.5.3 Representing and Deducing Knowledge

Definition 4.34

Let $\mathcal{K}$ be a nonempty subset of our message space $\mathcal{M}$ such that $\mathcal{K}$ is *deductively closed*: $\mathcal{K} = \bar{\mathcal{K}}$. Any $\mathcal{B} \subseteq \mathcal{K}$ with $\bar{\mathcal{B}} = \mathcal{K}$ is called a *knowledge base of* $\mathcal{K}$.

Note that $\mathcal{K}$ is always a knowledge base of $\mathcal{K}$. A knowledge base $\mathcal{B}$ of $\mathcal{K}$ is useful because it represents $\mathcal{K}$ via the closure operator. In particular, if $\mathcal{B}$ is finite and has a compact representation, then we can implement tests

$$m \in \mathcal{K}\,? \tag{4.61}$$

efficiently by checking whether m is contained in the closure of the finite knowledge base $\mathcal{B}$. Careful inspection of all the operational rules for manipulating I_A and I_Z reveals that

	Introduction	Elimination
·	$\dfrac{m_1 \quad m_2}{m_1 \cdot m_2}\ \mathrm{con_i}$	$\dfrac{m_1 \cdot m_2}{m_1}\ \mathrm{con_{e1}} \qquad \dfrac{m_1 \cdot m_2}{m_2}\ \mathrm{con_{e2}}$
E_K	$\dfrac{m \quad E_k}{E_k(m)}\ \mathrm{enc_i}$	$\dfrac{E_k(m) \quad D_k}{m}\ \mathrm{enc_e}$
D_k	$\dfrac{m \quad D_k}{D_k(m)}\ \mathrm{dec_i}$	

Figure 4.3. The six knowledge inference rules from Definition 4.30 (p. 159) written as deductions.

each of these possibly infinite sets always has a *finite knowledge base*. Thus, local states need only represent and update their respective finite bases. In that case, the computation of next states involves only tests of type (4.61), so it suffices to implement these tests efficiently.

The knowledge-inference rules from Definition 4.30 can be expressed as formal inference rules, as shown in Figure 4.3. Note that these rules come in pairs of *introduction* and *elimination* rules. For example, $\mathrm{con_i}$ *introduces* the concatenation of two messages, whereas $\mathrm{con_{e1}}$ and $\mathrm{con_{e2}}$ *eliminate* such concatenations to access their respective components. Similarly, $\mathrm{enc_i}$ models the introduction of cipher-text; $\mathrm{enc_e}$ models its elimination, an activity that is usually called "decryption". The rule $\mathrm{dec_i}$ has no corresponding elimination rule unless we assume that the underlying cryptographic system is *symmetric*. We will not make this assumption and hence omit the rule $\mathrm{dec_e}$ from consideration entirely.

Example 4.35 (A Valid Derivation)
We may use these inference rules to derive some message m from a knowledge base $\mathcal{B}$. Given

$$\mathcal{B} \stackrel{\mathrm{def}}{=} \{E_{k_1}(k \cdot m),\, E_{k_2},\, D_{k_1},\, D_{k_2}\},$$

we may derive m from $\mathcal{B}$ as follows:

$$\cfrac{E_{k_1}(k \cdot m) \qquad \cfrac{\cfrac{D_{k_1} \quad E_{k_2}}{E_{k_2}(D_{k_1})}\ \mathrm{enc_i} \qquad D_{k_2}}{D_{k_1}}\ \mathrm{enc_e}}{\cfrac{k \cdot m}{m.}\ \mathrm{con_{e2}}}\ \mathrm{enc_e} \tag{4.62}$$

EXERCISES 4.12

1. Assuming that the cryptographic system for E_k and D_k is symmetric, formulate the inference rule $\mathrm{dec_e}$. In reasoning about knowledge of messages, is there then still a need to differentiate between decryption and encryption operations among these inference rules?

2. Assuming that the cryptographic system for E_k and D_k is asymmetric (= public-key cryptography), explain why the rule $\mathrm{dec_i}$ may not be needed for modeling the inference of knowledge.

Definition 4.36 (Derivations and Sequents)

1. A *derivation* is any finite tree that can be built by the application of the knowledge inference rules of Figure 4.3.
2. If $\mathcal{D}$ is a derivation with root m and leaves that are contained in $\mathcal{B} \subseteq \mathcal{M}$, then we call $\mathcal{B} \vdash m$ a *valid sequent*; $\mathcal{D}$ is the *witness* of this validity.

For example, we have just shown that the sequent

$$\{E_{k_1}(k \cdot m), E_{k_2}, D_{k_1}, D_{k_2}\} \vdash m$$

is valid and has the derivation in (4.62) as witness. Recall that we mean to decide (4.61), where $\mathcal{K}$ has a finite knowledge base $\mathcal{B}$. Thus, given $m \in \mathcal{M}$, it suffices to efficiently decide whether $\bar{\mathcal{B}} \vdash m$ is valid. In general, there are infinitely many derivations of a valid sequent, so we must somehow compute canonical derivations that are *sound* (if we can compute such a derivation for $\bar{\mathcal{B}} \vdash m$, then that sequent is valid) and *complete* (if $\bar{\mathcal{B}} \vdash m$ is valid, then we can compute such a derivation as a witness of its validity). In the end, our knowledge inference algorithm won't require the notion of a derivation at all, but it is needed to arrive at the design of an efficient algorithm and to prove its correctness. We shall demonstrate that any derivation tree for $\bar{\mathcal{B}} \vdash m$ can be replaced by one that uses no elimination rules below introduction rules.

Example 4.37 (Normal Derivation)
In (4.62) the elimination rule enc_e is used twice below the introduction rule enc_i. This derivation contains redundancy in that we could replace it with the much simpler

$$\frac{\dfrac{E_{K_1}(k \cdot m) \quad D_{k_1}}{k \cdot m}\ \text{enc}_e}{m,}\ \text{con}_{e2} \tag{4.63}$$

since D_{k_1} is already in $\mathcal{B}$.

In general, we may perform the following reductions or simplifications on any subtree of a derivation:

$$\frac{\dfrac{\dfrac{\mathcal{D}_1}{m_1} \quad \dfrac{\mathcal{D}_2}{m_2}}{m_1 \cdot m_2}\ \text{con}_i}{m_1}\ \text{con}_{e1} \implies \frac{\mathcal{D}_1}{m_1};$$

$$\frac{\dfrac{\dfrac{\mathcal{D}_1}{m_1} \quad \dfrac{\mathcal{D}_2}{m_2}}{m_1 \cdot m_2}\ \text{con}_i}{m_2}\ \text{con}_{e2} \implies \frac{\mathcal{D}_2}{m_2}; \tag{4.64}$$

$$\frac{\dfrac{\dfrac{\mathcal{D}_1}{m} \quad \dfrac{\mathcal{D}_2}{E_k}}{E_k(m)}\ \text{enc}_i \quad \dfrac{\mathcal{D}_3}{D_k}}{m}\ \text{enc}_e \implies \frac{\mathcal{D}_1}{m}.$$

Definition 4.38 (Normal Derivation)
We call a derivation *normal* if none of the reduction rules in (4.64) can be applied to it.

Lemma 4.39
Let $B \vdash m$ be a valid sequent with a derivation $\mathcal{D}$ as witness. Then we can compute a normal derivation $\mathcal{D}'$ from $\mathcal{D}$ such that $\mathcal{D}'$ is a witness for $B \vdash m$ as well.

Proof   By assumption, the derivation $\mathcal{D}$ has root m and all its leaves are contained in B. We may now apply the reduction rules in (4.64) to $\mathcal{D}$ *in any order* until we have reached a derivation for which no further reductions can be made. Notice that this computation must eventually terminate, for each reduction step reduces the height of the derivation tree that is being reduced. It is also quite clear that each reduction rule has "the current derivation has root m and all its leaves are contained in B" as an invariant.   □

The existence of normal derivations for valid sequents is not, in itself, sufficient for arriving at an efficient algorithm for knowledge inference. Fortunately, normal derivations satisfy a surprising and useful property: All introduction rules occur below elimination rules. Note that this property is violated by the derivation in (4.62), since we have the application of enc_i followed by enc_e further down that tree (where "down" means looking down the page). Yet this desirable property *is* satisfied by the tree in (4.63) – simply because that tree contains no introduction rules whatsoever.

Theorem 4.40
Let $\mathcal{D}$ be a normal derivation. Then there is no application of an introduction rule in $\mathcal{D}$ such that it is followed by the use of an elimination rule further down the tree $\mathcal{D}$.

Proof   Let $\mathcal{D}$ be a normal derivation that does *not* satisfy this property. Then it must contain the application of some introduction rule that is *immediately* followed (downward) by the use of some elimination rule. We establish a contradiction by a case analysis ranging over all possible introduction rules.

1. Suppose that the introduction rule is con_i:

$$\frac{\dfrac{\mathcal{D}_1}{m_1} \quad \dfrac{\mathcal{D}_2}{m_2}}{m_1 \cdot m_2.} \, con_i \tag{4.65}$$

   In Figure 4.3, we have three elimination rules: con_{e1}, con_{e2}, and enc_e. Since $m_1 \cdot m_1$ cannot be of the form $E_k(m)$ or D_k, we conclude that the elimination rule that immediately follows (4.65) cannot be enc_e. But any of the other two rules triggers a reduction. For example, if con_{e2} is used, we have

$$\frac{\dfrac{\dfrac{\mathcal{D}_1}{m_1} \quad \dfrac{\mathcal{D}_2}{m_2}}{m_1 \cdot m_2} \, con_i}{m_2} \, con_{e2}$$

   as a subtree of $\mathcal{D}$, contradicting the fact that $\mathcal{D}$ is normal. (Why?)

```
function member?(m,B) {
*/ m ::= a | m1 * m2 | E_k(m) | D_k(m)                    */
*/ B is a finite, nonredundant set of messages to which */
*/ no elimination rules apply                            */
if ((m == a) | (m == D_k(m'))) { return element_of(m,B);
} elseif (m == m1 * m2) { return (member?(m1,B) && member?(m2,B));
} elseif (m == E_k(m')) { return (member?(E_k,B) && member?(m',B));
} else { raise exception; }
}
```

Figure 4.4. Pseudo-code for the algorithm that decides whether m is already known or implied by a set B of basic facts. The call `member?(m,B)` returns `true` if m can be generated from messages in B. The call `element_of(m,B)` returns `true` if and only if m is already explicitly present in the list B.

2. Suppose that the introduction rule is enc_i:

$$\frac{\dfrac{\mathcal{D}_1}{m} \quad \dfrac{\mathcal{D}_2}{E_k}}{E_k(m).} \text{ enc}_i \tag{4.66}$$

Among our elimination rules con_{e1}, con_{e2}, and enc_e, the first two cannot immediately follow (4.66) because $E_k(m)$ does not have the required form $m_1 \cdot m_2$. Thus only enc_e could be used, resulting in

$$\frac{\dfrac{\dfrac{\mathcal{D}_1}{m} \quad \dfrac{\mathcal{D}_2}{E_k}}{E_k(m)} \text{ enc}_i \quad D_k}{m} \text{ enc}_e$$

as a subtree of $\mathcal{D}$, contradicting the fact that $\mathcal{D}$ is normal. $\qquad \square$

Notice that this proof crucially depends upon the perfect encryption properties postulated in Definition 4.27, which we secured by allowing only trivial equations on the message space $\mathcal{M}$. Given m and $\mathcal{B}$, Theorem 4.40 suggests that we divide the problem of deciding whether m is contained in $\bar{B}$ into two phases:

(i) apply all possible elimination rules to elements of $\mathcal{B}$, collecting all known basic facts;
(ii) do a backward search guided by the structure of m to decide whether m is implied by these basic facts.

We implement our knowledge bases as conventional lists. The resulting search algorithm is given in Figure 4.4; it performs a case analysis based on the grammar in (4.37).

- If m is atomic or a cipher-text (in which case no elimination rules can apply), then the function returns the boolean value of `element_of(m,B)` – this returns `true` if and only if m occurs in the list of basic facts B.
- Otherwise, if m is the concatenation of two messages, then the function returns `true` if and only if both function calls to its submessages return `true`.
- Similarly, we handle messages m of the form $E_k(m')$: we check whether E_k and m' are known to B; only then does the function call return `true`.
- All other cases raise an exception, as m is then not generated by the required grammar.

```
function update(m,B) {
*/ m ::= a | m1 * m2 | E_k(m) | D_k(m)                              */
*/ B is a finite, nonredundant set of messages to which */
*/ no elimination rules apply                                      */
if member?(m,B) { return B; }
if (m == D_k) {  // check whether B contains a matching cipher-text
  L := B;
  n := head(L);
  while (L != []) {
    if (n == E_k(m') {
      return update(m',B);   // ... if so, update accordingly
    }
    L := tail(L);
    n := head(L);
  }
}
// at this point, m is not a member of B
if (m == a) { return (m ::  B); }
if (m == m1 * m2) { return update(m2,update(m1,B)); }
if (m = E_k(m') && element_of(D_k,B)) {
                            // know key for cipher-text
    if (element_of(E_k,B)) {
      return update(m',B);
                  // no need to store m, storing m' suffices
    } else { return update(m',m ::  B); } // need m and possibly m'
}
return m ::  B; // at this point, m is not implicitly known
}
```

Figure 4.5. Pseudo-code for the algorithm that uses m to update the knowledge base B, if necessary.

We write [] for the empty list and write m :: l for the list whose head is m and whose tail is l. Furthermore, head(l) and tail(l) are the respective operations on lists such that l equals the result of computing head(l) :: tail(l) for lists of length ≥ 2. The boolean expression (x != []) evaluates to true if and only if variable x represents a list of length ≥ 1. With this notation, we can formulate the *knowledge update algorithm* of Figure 4.5. Observe that its strategy may be broken down as follows.

1. If m is already implied by B then we return B immediately, since no new implicit knowledge arises.
2. Otherwise, if m is a decryption key D_k then we scan all elements of B and "decrypt" all those of the form $E_k(m')$ – that is, we recursively call our knowledge update algorithm on m' and B.
3. Otherwise, if m is atomic, we add it to B and return. (By item 1, we know that m is not implied by B.)
4. Otherwise, if m equals $m_1 \cdot m_2$, we recursively update B with m_1 and m_2.
5. Otherwise, if m is of the form[6] $E_k(m')$ and D_k is already in B, we can recover m' through decryption:

---

[6] Note that m == D_k means m is of the form D_k *for some key* k. In particular, the expression (n == E_k(m')) refers to such a matching k.

```
1. A --> B : A.B.{n_a.A}E_B
2. B --> A : B.A.{n_a.n_b}E_A
3. A --> B : A.B.{n_b}E_B
```

Figure 4.6. Schematic description of the simplified Needham–Schroeder protocol. We write $\{m\}E\_k$ for $E_k(m)$; $A \rightarrow B$: m denotes that agent A sends message m to agent B; and $m.n$ denotes $m \cdot n$.

- if E_k is already in B then there is no need to update B with $E_k(m')$, as long as we update B with m';
- otherwise, we recursively update B with m and m'.

6. If no return occurs, we add m explicitly to B.

Theorem 4.41 (Soundness and Completeness)
For all finite sets

$$\mathcal{B} = \{m_1, m_2, \ldots, m_k\}$$

of messages, we have $\bar{\mathcal{B}} \vdash m$ *if and only if* `member?(m,B)` *returns* `true`, *where* B *is the list obtained from*

$$\texttt{update}(m_1, \texttt{update}(m_2, \ldots, \texttt{update}(m_k, [\,])\ldots)). \tag{4.67}$$

Proof   The proof of this theorem is relegated to the exercises.   □

EXERCISES 4.13

1. Show that there are infinitely many derivations for $\bar{\mathcal{B}} \vdash m$, where $\mathcal{B}$ and m are as in Example 4.35.
2. Prove Theorem 4.41.

4.5.4 Two Example Refutations

We now present the specification of two well-known security protocols; describe how they are modeled in our model-checking framework; feature attacks of these protocols; and discuss fixes for, or problematic aspects of, these security protocol flaws.

4.5.4.1 Needham–Schroeder Protocol

Protocol 4.42 (Simplified Needham-Schroeder Protocol)
In this simplified[7] version of the protocol, we have two principal agents, A and B. A schematic of the protocol is given in Figure 4.6.

In this protocol,

1. Agent A creates a new nonce n_a, concatenates that nonce with her unique name, and uses B's public key (E_B) to encrypt the message $n_a \cdot A$, resulting in the message $E_B(n_a \cdot A)$, which she sends to agent B along with the names of agent A and B.

---

[7] The full protocol contains three more steps in which both agents request and receive each other's public keys through an authenticating and trusted server.

2. Agent B, upon receiving a message of the form $A' \cdot B' \cdot E_B(n'_a \cdot A')$, uses her secret key D_B to compute $n'_a \cdot A'$, extracts the nonce n'_a from $n'_a \cdot A'$, creates a new nonce n_b, constructs the pair $n'_a \cdot n_b$, and uses A's public key E_A to produce the message $E_A(n'_a \cdot n_b)$, which she sends off to A with both agents' names attached.

3. Agent A, upon receiving a message of the form $B'' \cdot A'' \cdot E_A(n''_a \cdot n'_b)$, uses her secret key D_A to recover $n''_a \cdot n'_b$, extracts the nonce n'_b, uses B's public key to compute $E_B(n'_b)$, which she ships off to B as indicated.

Presumably, agent A is sure after step 2 that she is talking to B, and after step 3 agent B can be certain that she is talking to A. In the scientific literature, one even finds a "proof" that this authentication property is guaranteed by this protocol. But seventeen years after the protocol was published, it was broken by G. Lowe using the tool FDR! The attack is described shortly and can be reproduced with the framework we presented here.

Often, specifications of security protocols are not stated in such detail, leaving more freedom in the actual implementation. Although such freedom is often desirable in practice, there is a danger that security violations of the implementation cannot be detected at the specification level. This is an inherent tradeoff. More seriously, common frameworks for stating security protocols in a seemingly formal way may lack a formal semantics or may contain ambiguity of meaning; we have seen the problematic nature of such ambiguity at work in Section 4.3. Even our description here is ambiguous and incomplete. For example, what if the "second" n_a turns out to be different; and what about additional checks that agents A and B would conduct during any execution of the protocol? Figure 4.6 illustrates a popular manner of stating protocols, and it is understandable that we prefer to use these more compact ways of specifying security protocols. However, this compactness comes at the price of introducing ambiguities or flawed specifications; see Exercises 4.14 (p. 176) for some concerns along these lines.

Here we model only the allowed behavior of agent A, as described previously:[8]

```
begin_init x;
nonce(y);
compute nonce(y).A;
compute P_x(nonce(y).A);
send (P_x(nonce(y).A)) along x;
receive P_A(nonce(y).nonce(z)) along x;
compute nonce(z);
compute P_x(nonce(z));
send P_x(nonce(z)) along x;
end_init x;
```

In the exercises, you are asked to model the allowed behavior of agent B. The *initial local state* for A, B, and Z is that each agent knows

---

[8] Channel names now refer to agents.

```
1. A --> B : A.B.{n_a.A }E_B
2. B --> A : B.A.{n_a.n_b.B}E_A
3. A --> B : A.B.{n_b}E_B
```

Figure 4.7. A modified Needham–Schroeder protocol that averts Attack 4.43.

- the unique name of each agent,
- the public key associated to each unique name, and
- his or her own corresponding secret key.

Attack 4.43 (Needham–Schroeder Protocol)

We now describe an attack of the simplified Needham–Schroeder protocol that is made possible by the lack of a correspondence property. We write Z_A to denote that the malicious intruder Z impersonates agent A, either as the sender of messages to agent B or as someone who intercepts a message that agent A intends to receive; similarly, we write Z_B if the intruder impersonates agent B in this manner. A tool-based analysis of the protocol finds an attack that involves two runs (execution traces) of that protocol.[9] Steps of the second run are annotated with single primes. In the first run, agent A initiates the protocol with the intruder Z, who then initiates a second run with agent B, impersonating A and replaying A's nonce from the first run:

```
1.   A   --> Z_B : A.Z.{n_a.A}E_Z
1'.  Z_A --> B   : A.B.{n_a.A}E_B
2'.  B   --> Z_A : B.A.{n_a.n_b}E_A
2.   Z_B --> A   : Z.A.{n_a.n_b}E_A
3.   A   --> Z_B : A.Z.{n_b}E_Z
3'.  Z_A --> B   : A.B.{n_b}E_B
```

Observe that each of the six steps corresponds to allowed behavior, as specified in the protocol. Agent A initiates a protocol run with the intruder who, from the point of view of A, impersonates as B. Then the intruder initiates a protocol run with B, impersonating A. After B's response to the intruder, the intruder simply passes that message on to A. Agent A then dutifully computes the message {n_b}E_Z and sends it to the intruder, who is then able to decrypt it; finally, Z re-encrypts n_b with B's public key and sends this cipher-text to B to complete the attack. The attack exploits the fact that the intruder plays the role of A in the single-primed steps whereas, in the unprimed steps, the intruder copies the role of B in the single-primed steps. Notice the *lack of correspondence*: after successful execution of step 3', agent B believes that she has ended a protocol run with agent A, although agent A has no belief that she initiated a protocol run with agent B.

Lowe suggested the following fix to this attack. He changed the second step from the specification of Figure 4.6 to obtain the one in Figure 4.7. Observe how agent B now also includes her unique name in the message she sends to agent A. Lowe then proved that this protocol, in isolation, is correct. By hand, he could then prove that this protocol is also correct when embedded in a larger system.

---

[9] Note that we allow several instantiations of the same protocol within one run of the global state space. If the same agent instantiates the same protocol more than once, then our model would require session identity numbers.

EXERCISES 4.14

1. For the simplified Needham–Schroeder protocol:
   (a) What is its overall objective?
   (b) We notice that it has no description of the circumstances in which agent A or B decide to *abort the execution of a protocol run*. Suggest such circumstances for agents A and B, respectively.
   (c) Discuss what plausible actions agents would engage in if they detect an inconsistency between advertised agent names and corresponding keys or between other information (e.g. nonces) matched to specific agents.

2. Discuss to what extent the steps of the execution sequence in Protocol 4.42 can be performed in a different order. (Such independence can be exploited in reducing the state space of the global state transition system.)

3. (a) Relate each step of Protocol 4.42 to the more compact presentation in Figure 4.6.
   (b) What implicit assumptions are made in the presentation in Figure 4.6?

4. As we did in the text for agent A, model the allowed behavior of agent B.

5. Explain why Attack 4.43 fails for the fixed protocol from Figure 4.7.

6. Let m be a safe secret and assume that agent A means to send m to agent B via an unsecure communication channel, using Protocol 2.61 (p. 76). Model, in the style of Attack 4.43, an attack that corrupts the safe secret m.

7. *Wide-mouthed frog protocol*   Consider a protocol used to establish a shared session encryption key k_ab between agents A and B, assuming that S is a trusted server with whom A and B already share keys k_as and k_bs, respectively:

   ```
   1. A --> S : A.{t_a.B.k_ab}k_as
   2. S --> B : {t_s.A.k_ab}k_bs
   ```

   The terms t_a and t_s are time stamps generated by A and S, respectively.
   (a) Consider two runs of this protocol:

   ```
   1.  A   --> S  : A.{t_a.B.k_ab}k_as
   2.  S   --> B  : {t_s.A.k_ab}k_bs
   2'. Z_S --> B  : {t_s.A.k_ab}k_bs
   ```

   (i) Describe in detail what happens and what the state of belief is for A, B, S, and Z after these runs.
   (ii) Are all of these beliefs true? If not, in what sense does this constitute an attack of the protocol?
   (iii) Consider the modified protocol

   ```
   1. A --> S : A.{t_a.B.k_ab}k_as
   2. S --> B : {t_s.A.k_ab}k_bs
   3. B --> A : {n_b}k_ab
   4. A --> B : {n_b+1}k_ab
   ```

   Explain why the attack just described is no longer possible.
   (b) Make use of the fact that both messages in the two-step protocol are of the same form. As an intruder, replay messages to the server so that time stamps are continually updated. Can you use this to launch an attack on the protocol?

```
1. A --> B : A
2. B --> A : n_b
3. A --> B : {n_b}k_as
4. B --> S : {A.{n_b}k_as}k_bs
5. S --> B : {A.n_b}k_bs
```

Figure 4.8. An authentication protocol based on a server, S, that shares a public-key pair with network participants.

4.5.4.2 Woo–Lam Protocol

Protocol 4.44 (Woo–Lam Protocol)
In this protocol we have three friendly agents A, B, and S. Agent S is a *server* with whom network participants A and B share a secret key k_as and k_bs, respectively. The objective of the protocol's execution is to establish the authenticity of the fact that agent A is communicating with agent B. The informal specification is given in Figure 4.8.

Attack 4.45 (Woo–Lam Protocol)
One attack of Protocol 4.44 that can be re-discovered by our analysis framework portrays a very active malicious intruder Z; he impersonates not only the friendly agent A but also the server S. The attack then reads as

```
1. Z_A --> B   : A
2. B   --> Z_A : n_b
3. Z_A --> B   : n_b
4. B   --> Z_S : {A.n_b}k_bs
5. Z_S --> B   : {A.n_b}k_bs
```

Notice the ingenious twist in the third step. The intruder, impersonating the server, simply sends the nonce n_b to agent B, who is expecting a message of the form {n_b}k_as. However, agent B has no way of detecting that something went wrong because a message of that form is cipher-text and hence is indistinguishable from a nonce, unless implementations provide different data types for cipher-text and nonce – for example, if the nonce has an agreed-upon length that likely is different from the length of the cipher-text.

EXERCISES 4.15

1. Recalling Definition 4.16 (p. 143) and the objective of Protocol 4.44, explain which of the agents A, B, or S play the role of the *prover* and *verifier,* respectively.

2. As done in Protocol 4.42, provide a detailed, step-by-step account of the activities expressed in Figure 4.8. In particular, explain why agents can compute the messages that they send to other agents.

3. Explain in detail why Attack 4.45 is successful. In particular, what capabilities of the intruder do we assume when he transforms the message {A.{n_b}k_as}k_bs from step 4 to the message {A.n_b}k_bs in step 5?

4. Suggest a change in Protocol 4.44 that averts the *replay attack* of Attack 4.45.

4.6 BIBLIOGRAPHIC NOTES

The discussion of authentication in Section 4.3 is based on Abadi's (1998) paper. The threshold secret-sharing schemes of Section 4.4 were pioneered by Blakley (1979) and Shamir (1979); for more information on efficient secret-sharing schemes, refer to the textbook of Stinson (1995). Our presentation of model-checking security protocols is a customized account of the papers by Clark, Jha, and Marrero (1988, 1998) and Marrero, Clark, and Jha (1997); see also Marrero's abstract.[10] This platform is by no means the first (or only) one that allows for modeling and analyzing security protocols. It was Lowe (1996) who used the tool FDR (Failures Divergences Refinement checker) – a model checker for the process algebra CSP – to find the attack and the fix of the simplified Needham–Schroeder public-key protocol described in Section 4.5.4.1. A whole family of attacks upon authentication protocols can be found in Lowe (1997); the wide-mouthed frog protocol and its attack (Exercise 4.14-7, p. 176) are drawn from that paper. Paulson (1998) uses inductive methods to validate security protocols, circumventing the need to model beliefs or knowledge and allowing the consideration of infinite-state systems: protocols and their specifications are defined inductively as sets of traces, and a theorem prover then tries to show that the set of traces of the protocol is contained in the set of traces of its specification. Another approach – similar to the one based on FDR but with a description language (D. L. Dill's Murphi[11]) whose features are familiar from conventional programming languages – was developed by Mitchell, Mitchell, and Stern (1997). This methodology has been applied to the Secure Socket Layer 3.0 (Mitchell, Shmatikov, and Stern 1998). Meadows (1996) built a special-purpose verification tool – the NRL protocol analyzer – that is based on a logic programming language with constraints and can validate or invalidate security protocols; for an application of this tool to the Internet key-exchange protocol, see Meadows (1999). The BAN logic, a logic of authentication, was one of the first attempts to arrive at formalisms that can be used to analyze the violation of formally stated security properties of protocols (Burrows, Abadi, and Needham 1989). Example 4.13 is from R. Hofer's website[12] on elliptic curves. For a discussion of the "Dining Cryptographers" we refer to Chaum's (1988) original article. DigiCash has online demonstrations[13] that suggest how to put these ideas into practice.

---

[10] http://www.cs.cmu.edu/~marrero/abstract.html
[11] http://verify.stanford.edu/dill/murphi.html
[12] http://www.sbox.tu-graz.ac.at/home/j/jonny/projects/crypto/asymmetr/ecdlp.htm
[13] www.digicash.com/demo/

CHAPTER 5

Optimal Public-Key Encryption with RSA

So far, we have encountered various building blocks of cryptographic systems. These include:

- *pseudo-random number generators* – fundamental for the generation of random seeds and used in probabilistic algorithms that decide primality, generate a session key, output a stream cipher, et cetera;
- *hash functions* – used for digital fingerprints of passwords, messages, and so forth; and
- *public-key cryptosystems* – used in most modern cryptographic systems as an infrastructure for authentication or key exchange between participants of a local or global network.

We discussed RSA as an example of public-key cryptography in great detail in Chapter 1. Our exposition of RSA, however, focused solely on how to implement the *mathematical backbone* of RSA, the functions[1]

$$f(x) \stackrel{\text{def}}{=} x^e \bmod n, \tag{5.1}$$

$$f^{-1}(x) \stackrel{\text{def}}{=} x^d \bmod n \tag{5.2}$$

in a correct and efficient manner. Yet we reasoned about the security of these functions in isolation only.

In this chapter, we use a design and theoretical results (due to M. Bellare and P. Rogaway) to demonstrate that pseudo-random number generators, hash functions, and RSA can be skillfully combined to obtain a realistic and efficient implementation of RSA. This implementation is proven secure with *exact* security parameters; it is bit-optimal for this level of security, in that the length of the plain-text is as close to the length of cipher-text as possible without corrupting security; and it rivals heuristic methods that lack security assurance in its efficiency. However, the proven security results apply to the *random oracle model* of the cryptographic system, an idealization of the concrete hash functions it uses. The conversion of such ideal functions to implementable cryptographic functions is a heuristic leap; great care must be taken when making this step and interpreting the security results for the implemented system. We discuss the random oracle methodology and these concerns in Section 5.3.

A practitioner whose task it is to implement RSA will come up with a list that certainly contains the following demands:

---

[1] Of course, we assume as before that n is the product of large primes p and q and that $e \cdot d = 1 \bmod \phi(n)$.

- encryption of messages should require only one application of f;
- decryption of cipher-text should require only one application of f^{-1} (note that f and f^{-1} are performance bottlenecks);
- the length of the cipher-text $f(x)$ should be *exactly* k, the number of bits of n; and
- the length of the plain-text that can be encrypted should be as close as possible to k bits.

Heuristic schemes with these properties exist and operate by embedding a message x into some string r_x in a probabilistic and invertible way; the encryption of x is then defined as $f(r_x)$. Thus, proven secure systems need to accommodate these requirements if practitioners are to choose them for actual implementation. The goal of this section is therefore to provide an RSA implementation that is based on such a simple embedding scheme but is also proven secure. In fact, we present two versions, both of which can be shown to be *semantically secure*. The second one is even proven to be *plain-text aware*, a technical concept that implies the system is secure against chosen cipher-text attacks and malleability – assuming the random oracle model. Nonmalleability means that witnessing the encryption of a plain-text x is not enough for producing the encryption of a "related" plain-text x'. Examples of related plain-texts include those that differ in only one bit from x and the bitwise complement of x.

5.1   A SIMPLE SEMANTICALLY SECURE ENCRYPTION

Let k be the number of bits of the RSA modulus n. The function f in (5.1) realizes a permutation on the set of k-bit strings with inverse f^{-1} in (5.2).[2] Clearly, k is the security parameter ($k \geq 1024$ is advised).

Definition 5.1 (Attacker's Running Time and Length of Plain-Text)

1. An attacker's computational resources are modeled by $k_0 \in \mathbb{N}$ such that the attacker's running time is significantly smaller than 2^{k_0}. We assume that all queries to random oracles receive their answers in unit time.
2. We define

$$1(k) \stackrel{\text{def}}{=} k - k_0 \tag{5.3}$$

as the bit length of individual messages that can be encrypted at one time (shorter messages will have to be padded to reach this length).

Our implementation utilizes two functions that are randomly generated but deterministic: a *generator*

$$G: \{0, 1\}^{k_0} \rightarrow \{0, 1\}^{1(k)}; \tag{5.4}$$

and a *hash function*

$$H: \{0, 1\}^{1(k)} \rightarrow \{0, 1\}^{k_0}. \tag{5.5}$$

---

[2] This is not literally true; see Exercise 5.1-2.

Definition 5.2 (Simple Encryption/Decryption)

1. Given a plain-text $x \in \{0, 1\}^{\mathbb{1}(k)}$, choose a random k_0-bit string r and define the encryption of x as

$$\mathcal{E}^{(G, H)}(x) \overset{\text{def}}{=} f(x \oplus G(r) \, \| \, r \oplus H(x \oplus G(r))), \tag{5.6}$$

where $\oplus$ is the bitwise exclusive-or, $\|$ is the concatenation of bit strings, and f is the RSA function in (5.1).

2. Given a cipher-text y of bit length k, set s to be the first $\mathbb{1}(k)$ bits of the output of $f^{-1}(y)$ and let t be the last k_0 bits of $f^{-1}(y)$. We then define

$$\mathcal{D}^{(G, H)}(y) \overset{\text{def}}{=} s \oplus G(t \oplus H(s)). \tag{5.7}$$

The random oracles G, H and the function $\mathcal{E}^{(G, H)}(\cdot)$ are meant to be public, but the function $\mathcal{D}^{(G, H)}(\cdot)$ should be known only to the owner of this public-key cryptosystem.

EXERCISES 5.1

1. Prove that $\mathcal{D}^{(G, H)}(\mathcal{E}^{(G, H)}(x)) = x$ for all $\mathbb{1}(k)$-bit strings x.
2. We have identified k-bit strings with the numbers they denote in binary notation. Which numbers in $\{0, 1, \ldots, n - 1\}$ would be unwisely included as legitimate messages to be encrypted, and why?
3. In a real implementation, we require an encoding that codes source text – given in whatever format – as bit strings of the required length, and vice versa. Suppose you already have an encoding that works for the encryption function f. How can you use it to obtain an encoding for the scheme of (5.6)?
4. Implement the public-key encryption system of Definition 5.2 with some $k \geq 1024$ and $k_0 \geq 320$.
   (a) Choose G and H from appropriate calls to the secure hash function SHS, as in (5.18).
   (b) Permit only messages in $\{2, 3, \ldots, n - 1\}$ that do not have a common factor with n. Notice that this rules out (at the very least) all k-bit strings w, where $l \geq n$ for the number l that the string w represents in binary.

Evidently, (5.6) and (5.7) render a correct specification of a public-key cryptosystem that uses the RSA encryption and decryption functions *only once* per encryption or decryption task. Incidentally, in Exercise 2.7-9 (p. 34), the Blum–Goldwasser public-key cryptosystem – while also rendering a *nondeterministic* encryption – uses the RSA encryption function more than once.

Since computing with the generator G and the hash function H is presumably much more efficient than computing values of f and f^{-1}, the first three demands (p. 180) of our hypothetical practitioner are met. The last concern, that the size $\mathbb{1}(k) = k - k_0$ be as close to k as possible, will be addressed in our formal analysis of this specification. We then also prove semantic security of this encryption system. An informal, "hand-waving" manner of arguing semantic security proceeds as follows, where s and t have the same meaning as in the definition of (5.7).

- If the attacker cannot recover *all* first $1(k)$ bits (the s) of the string computed by $f^{-1}(y)$, then she should have no knowledge whatsoever about the nature of the hash value $H(s)$.
- Without any such knowledge, she should be unable to make any conclusions about the value of $t \oplus H(s)$, which equals r.
- Not knowing anything about r, the attacker knows nothing about $G(r)$.
- Therefore, she could not possibly know anything about $s \oplus G(r)$, which is uniformly distributed as a random variable in r and is equal to x.

It is obvious that this "argument" needs to be fleshed out in a formal proof. Such a proof, given in Section 5.4, is interesting not only in that it provides desired rigor but also because its structure reveals *exact security parameters that can be used to assess the security of an implementation.*

EXERCISE 5.2

1. Critically assess what assumptions are needed to establish our claim that $s \oplus G(r)$ is *uniformly* distributed as a random variable in r.

5.2 A PLAIN-TEXT–AWARE ENCRYPTION

We slightly modify the first scheme. We retain k, the bit size of the RSA modulus, and k_0, the parameter that measures the attacker's running-time constraints, but now we set the plain-text bit length to

$$1(k) \stackrel{\text{def}}{=} k - k_0 - k_1, \tag{5.8}$$

where $k_1 \in \mathbb{N}$ is another security parameter. The generator G and the hash function H change their "types" accordingly:

$$G: \{0, 1\}^{k_0} \to \{0, 1\}^{k-k_0}, \tag{5.9}$$

$$H: \{0, 1\}^{k-k_0} \to \{0, 1\}^{k_0}. \tag{5.10}$$

For the plain-text–aware implementation, we define encryption as

$$\mathcal{E}^{(G,H)}(x) \stackrel{\text{def}}{=} f((x \| 0^{k_1}) \oplus G(r) \| r \oplus H((x \| 0^{k_1}) \oplus G(r))). \tag{5.11}$$

Notice that this encryption operation works as for the previous scheme except that here the message x is padded with k_1 zeros, requiring G and H to operate over different string sizes as previously specified. In particular, the random string r is still k_0 bits long.

EXERCISES 5.3

1. Formally define the decryption operation $\mathcal{D}^{(G,H)}(y)$ for the plain-text–aware encryption system of (5.11), and prove that it recovers encrypted messages. This function should return a special value "failed" if the putative cipher-text y cannot be decrypted to a legitimate plain-text message.

2. Verify that the computation in (5.11) is "well-typed" – that is, show that all arguments have the correct number of required bits for their respective operations.
3. Consider the encryption operations

$$E_1^G(x) \stackrel{\text{def}}{=} f(r) \parallel G(r) \oplus x, \tag{5.12}$$

$$E_2^{G,H}(x) \stackrel{\text{def}}{=} f(r) \parallel G(r) \oplus x \parallel H(r \parallel x), \tag{5.13}$$

$$E_3^G(x) \stackrel{\text{def}}{=} f(r) \parallel (G(r) \oplus (x \parallel H(x))), \tag{5.14}$$

where r is a randomly generated bit string for which $f(r)$ is defined.

   (a) Describe the corresponding decryption operations and specify the input–output types of G and H. How do these types compare to the scheme of (5.6) with respect to total encryption size as a measure of efficiency?
   (b) Give an intuitive assessment of the security of these encryption functions – they all satisfy weaker *proven security* concepts than the ones presented in this chapter.

In Sections 5.4 and 5.5, we formally analyze the schemes of (5.6) and (5.11) and prove their semantic security. We also show that the second system is indeed "plain-text aware",[3] assuming *ideal* functions G and H; ideal functions and the random oracle methodology are discussed in Section 5.3. Under these assumptions, plain-text awareness implies non-malleability and also resistance against known cipher-text attacks. Although an actual implementation makes use of nonideal hash functions (e.g. SHS), this result suggests that such implementations are superior to ad hoc choices of RSA implementations.

5.2.1 Implementation of Plain-Text–Aware Encryption

A concrete instantiation of the plain-text–aware public-key encryption scheme makes use of the hash function SHS, as described in Section 3.2.3. We require a minimum size of $k = 512$ bits for the modulus n. The maximum bit length of messages that can be encrypted is set to

$$1(k) \stackrel{\text{def}}{=} k - 320; \tag{5.15}$$

that is, $k_0 + k_1$ equals 320. Thus $1(k)$ is at least 192 bits – one of the possible key sizes for the advanced encryption standard Rijndael. The message space

$$\mathcal{M} \stackrel{\text{def}}{=} \{i \in \mathbb{N} \mid 1 \leq i < n, \ \gcd(i, n) = 1, \ \gcd(f(i), n) = 1\} \tag{5.16}$$

is identified with the corresponding subset of $\{0, 1\}^k$, its representation in binary. Overall, this scheme depends on the following parameters:

- the bit length $\leq k - 320$ for the message `message` to be encrypted;
- a random string `random_coins` of *arbitrary* length;
- the security parameter k;

---

[3] We define this concept formally in Section 5.5.

- the encryption function f and its inverse, the "trapdoor" f^{-1};
- an implementation of the predicate inMessageSpace(x), which returns true if x is in the message space $\mathcal{M}$ and returns false otherwise;
- a 32-bit string key_data, which we leave unspecified;
- a string desc, containing a complete description of the function f (e.g., saying something like "we use RSA encryption with modulus n and public key e"); and
- a fixed but randomly chosen 160-bit string, str, used to make the functions G and H dependent on the instantiation of this scheme.

Inspecting the pseudo-code of SHS in Figure 3.24, we recall that the secure hash function depends on the *initial* values of the 160-bit value

$$A \parallel B \parallel C \parallel D \parallel E, \tag{5.17}$$

the concatenation of the words A to E. Given any 160-bit string σ, we can partition σ as in (5.17), thereby loading A to E with these respective words. We write $\mathrm{hash}_\sigma(M)$ for the result of running SHS on M with the initial values of A to E determined by σ in this way. This parametric version of the secure hash function can then be used to build the functions H and G.

Definition 5.3

1. For $0 \le i < 2^{32}$, we write $\langle i \rangle$ for the 32-bit binary representation of $i \in \mathbb{N}$.
2. For any binary string x and any 160-bit string σ, we define the binary string[4]

$$\mathrm{hash}_\sigma^{80}(\langle 0 \rangle \parallel x) \parallel \mathrm{hash}_\sigma^{80}(\langle 1 \rangle \parallel x) \parallel \mathrm{hash}_\sigma^{80}(\langle 2 \rangle \parallel x) \parallel \cdots, \tag{5.18}$$

where $\mathrm{hash}_\sigma^{80}(M)$ denotes the leftmost 80 bits of the 160-bit string $\mathrm{hash}_\sigma(M)$.

Of course, we cannot compute the entire infinite string; our implementation requires the computation and extraction of only an implementation-dependent number of leftmost bits. The pseudo-code for the instantiation of the plain-text–aware encryption with RSA is given in Figure 5.1. In that code, we write

HASH(sigma,l,x)

for the l leftmost bits of (5.18). Calls $\mathrm{hash}_\sigma(M)$ are denoted by hash_sigma(M). The simple probabilistic embedding is achieved by: augmenting the message with the string key_data, a word indicating the length of the message; padded zeros that turn x into a $(k-128)$-bit string; and the redundancy supplied by the 128 bits of r.

The implementation uses various useful heuristics. Inclusion of the string key_data helps shield against attacks that could be launched if the same key were to be used with different algorithms that interact somehow. For similar reasons, it uses variants of sigma. The motivation for extracting only the leftmost 80 bits of the output of our parametric secure hash function is given in the more general discussion of the random oracle methodology in Section 5.3.

---

[4] We require only the leftmost k or $k - 128$ bits of that sequence. Also, keep in mind that the secure hash standard puts a limit on the length of the message to be hashed.

```
function Plain_text_aware_encryption(bitstring message,
                                     bitstring random_coins) {
// encrypts message of less than k - 319 bits with RSA function f
// in a plain-text-aware manner
// zeros: a bit string of zeros of
//        bit length k - 192 - length_of(message)
// input:  * a bit string, message, of bit length less than k - 319
//         * a bit string, random_coins, of arbitrary length
// output: * the k bit encryption of message with function f
 sigma  = hash_str(desc);
// desc is the string describing function f
 sigma1 = hash_sigma(<1>);
// <1> is the 32-bit binary of the number 1
 sigma2 = hash_sigma(<2>);
 sigma3 = hash_sigma(<3>);
 i = 0;
 do {
   r = HASH(sigma1, 128, <i> || random_coins);
// || is concatenation
   x = key_data || < length_of(message) > || zeros || message;
   x1 = x XOR HASH(sigma2, length_of(x), r);
   r1 = r XOR HASH(sigma3, 128, x1);
   r_x = x1 || r1;
   ++i;
 } while (!inMessageSpace(r_x));
 return f(r_x);
}
```

Figure 5.1. Instantiation of the plain-text–aware encryption scheme using an encryption function f.

EXERCISES 5.4

1. The pseudo-code from Figure 5.1 manipulates various strings. Make certain that all the operations "type-check". In particular, explain why
   (a) r is 128 bits long;
   (b) x is $(k - 128)$ bits long;
   (c) x and x1 have the same length;
   (d) r and r1 have the same length;
   (e) r_x is k bits long.
2. The implementation in Figure 5.1 does not match directly the format of the functions G and H in (5.9) and (5.10).
   (a) Determine the values of k_0 and k_1.
   (b) Identify those portions of the pseudo-code that compute G and H, respectively.
3. (a) Determine how decryption works for the implementation of encryption in Figure 5.1.
   (b) Write pseudo-code for the decryption operation of the code in Figure 5.1. How do you handle messages that don't "decrypt" to something in the message space?
   (c) Suppose that f is a *symmetric* encryption function (f "equals" f^{-1}). Does your implementation still render a public-key cryptosystem?

4. Does the implementation in Figure 5.1 rely on that fact that f is an *RSA* encryption function?
5. Implement the plain-text–aware encryption system in Figure 5.1. Derive and implement its corresponding decryption scheme as well.

5.3 THE RANDOM ORACLE METHODOLOGY

Before we prove the exact security parameters of our encryption systems, we need to gain a sufficient understanding of the underlying methodology – its promises and benefits, as well as its dangers and limitations. The two encryption systems presented in this section are designed and analyzed using the *random oracle methodology* of Bellare and Rogaway. This methodology proposes to design and assess security protocols by

- formally specifying an ideal computational model for the protocol, where all agents – including any malicious attackers – have equal access to perfectly random functions (*random oracles*);
- designing a protocol within this idealized computational model;
- proving *exact* security results (thereby avoiding complexity theory or asymptotic analysis) about this ideal protocol – assuming the idealized model; and
- *heuristically* replacing the idealized random oracle functions with implementable and efficient cryptographic functions.

This approach has various benefits: it

- builds on and expands previous work (of O. Goldreich, S. Goldwasser, and S. Micali) into an actual paradigm;
- makes strong assumptions about the capabilities of attackers – they have the same opportunities of access to the random oracle;
- can prove *exact* security results for given security parameters of a protocol instantiation;
- certainly improves on methods that are purely ad hoc; and
- can come up with informal justifications for the use of several heuristics that convert random oracles into practical cryptographic functions.

Example 5.4 (Heuristic Leap)
The plain-text–aware encryption system uses functions G and H that are "ideal" in the sense that they are randomly chosen from the set of all functions of type

$$\{0, 1\}^{k_0} \to \{0, 1\}^{k-k_0} \quad \text{and}$$
$$\{0, 1\}^{k-k_0} \to \{0, 1\}^{k_0},$$

respectively. These ideal random oracles G and H are then replaced with cryptographic functions (as done, e.g., in Figure 5.1).

Despite the benefits and gains just described, this approach has its downsides as well. Its most serious drawback is that there is no formal connection between the exact security results proven in the ideal model and the actual security of the protocol, which depends on the heuristically chosen cryptographic functions. Empirical evidence exists suggesting that there is a close match between proven and actual security if care is taken in the design of a protocol and the conversion of its random oracles into practical realizations. Essentially, the heuristic step involves *trust,* based on past experience. One certainly wants to avoid cryptographic functions that are subject to known cryptanalytic attacks. But one must also ensure that these functions do not expose any "relevant structure" that may be detectable as a result of their being built from lower-level cryptographic functions.

The random oracle methodology implies the thesis that it renders secure *and* efficient protocols, if carried out "properly"; the novelty is that *and.* Practitioners usually find efficient implementations of protocols by ad hoc methods, making a formal security analysis impossible. Conversely, theoreticians formally analyze the security of ideal protocols whose primitives are unrealistic and inefficient – for example, they would typically not be willing to consider the input–output functionality of Rijndael in the ECB mode as a cryptographic primitive. The random oracle methodology is an urgently needed bridge between the gap of theory and practice.

Alas (as R. Canetti, O. Goldreich, and S. Halevi have pointed out), the universal claim of its thesis – that the formal security results derived for an ideal protocol remain valid to a significant degree in an implementation – has been refuted. Stated informally: "There exists a digital signature scheme that is proven secure in the random oracle model yet *all* of its implementations result in unsecure cryptographic systems."

We now sketch how this limitation of the approach is demonstrated. A random oracle is a *single* function O, uniformly selected from a set of possible functions of a specified type. All agents, including all attackers, access that same function whenever they query the random oracle. An attacker of the *implementation* may simulate the behavior of the attacker in the random oracle model, but she is not restricted to such behavior. She may, indeed, gain global insight into the structure of the concrete cryptographic function h that realizes O and then use that to her advantage.

A more sophisticated version of the random oracle methodology is for the concrete function h_s to be selected at random from a collection of possible cryptographic functions $\{h_s \mid s \in \Omega\}$, where Ω is a finite probability space. Real implementations first select such a function h_s and then instantiate the system with that very function: all queries to the random oracle are implemented as calls to h_s. Hence, the negative result quoted previously can be shown also for this more general interpretation of the methodology.

We now state a necessary condition for h_s to be a "good" implementation of a random oracle O. Given a relation between inputs and outputs of O, assume that it is infeasible to compute – given an "output" y – a matching input x (i.e., $O(x) = y$) such that the pair $\langle x, y \rangle$ is in the relation. In that case, a good implementation h_s of O should certainly satisfy the requirement that it be infeasible to compute such a pair, where now $h_s(x) = y$.

Definition 5.5 (Evasive Relation)

1. Let O be a random oracle. We call a relation between elements of input and output type of O *evasive for O* if it is infeasible to compute some input x such that the pair $\langle x, O(x) \rangle$ is in the relation.

2. Given a collection of concrete cryptographic functions

$$\mathcal{H} \overset{\text{def}}{=} \{h_s \mid s \in \Omega\} \tag{5.19}$$

with the same input and output type as O, we say $\mathcal{H}$ is *correlation intractable for O* if, for every evasive relation for O, it is infeasible to compute an input x such that $\langle x, h_s(x) \rangle$ is in the relation – given a random choice s and a description of the function h_s.

The first negative result can now be (informally) restated as: "There does not exist a correlation-intractable collection of cryptographic functions $\mathcal{H}$."

This result can be used to show that the implicit belief in the random oracle methodology – that validated ideal protocols can be attacked only by exposing flaws of the implementations of random oracles and not by exposing "structural flaws" of the protocol design – is false. One can show this by:

- proving that, for each collection $\mathcal{H} = \{h_s \mid s \in \Omega\}$, there exists a digital signature scheme that is secure in the random oracle model but is *not* secure when implemented via $\mathcal{H}$; and
- using a diagonalization argument to demonstrate the existence of a digital signature scheme that is proven secure in the random oracle model even though *all* of its implementations are unsecure.[5]

Although these results limit the scope and validity of the random oracle approach to designing and "validating" security protocols, we should emphasize that these negative witness protocols are completely "unnatural" – far from anything anyone would ever implement as a security protocol. It is unclear whether such negative results can be established for security protocol designs that occur in practice. Hence, this negative result does not invalidate the random oracle methodology per se but instead limits its scope of applicability and calls for a prudent evaluation of design instances.

A common way of instantiating random oracles is by means of cryptographic hash functions. The choice of such concrete functions should be guided by (a) how many queries to the random oracle are being made and (b) what the input and output lengths of these queries are. A heuristic claim is that this choice need not be concerned with the structural properties of the protocol design. However, care must be taken in following these guidelines. For example, the hash function MD5 has the curious property that, for any x, there is a y such that for any z the hash

$$\text{MD5}(x \parallel y \parallel z)$$

can be computed from the length of x, the hash of x, and z alone. Bellare and Rogaway proposed minor transformations of such hash functions to avoid such "structural" properties. Among those, we list:

- truncating a hash function's output to the l leftmost bits for an appropriate choice of l;
- finding a suitable restriction on the input length of the hash function; and
- using the hash function in a "nonstandard" way.

For an example of such heuristics at work, consider (5.18) in Definition 5.3(2).

---

[5] The technical work involves an additional step of reducing super-polynomial time algorithms to polynomial time ones, relying on CS proofs.

5.4 EXACT SECURITY FOR THE SIMPLE ENCRYPTION

For our security analysis, we assume that the functions G and H are chosen randomly among all possible functions of their type. These two choices are done independently. We use these random oracles to assess the security of the encryption schemes in Sections 5.1 and 5.2 in an exact manner.

Definition 5.6 (Capabilities of Attacker)
We model the capabilities of an attacker as a probabilistic algorithm $A^{G,H}(\cdot, \cdot)$ and assess it in terms of its

- running time t – significantly less than 2^{k_0};
- the number q_G of queries it makes to the random oracle G;
- the number q_H of queries it makes to the random oracle H; and
- the "advantage" $\varepsilon \geq 0$ she has in breaking the encryption $\mathcal{E}^{(G,H)}(\cdot)$.

Our analysis then converts $A^{G,H}(\cdot, \cdot)$ into an algorithm $U[A^{G,H}(\cdot, \cdot)]$ and determines numbers t' and $\varepsilon' \geq 0$ such that $U[A^{G,H}(\cdot, \cdot)]$ inverts the trapdoor permutation f in time t' with probability ε'. The explanatory force of this analysis comes from the explicit dependency of t' and ε' on the underlying security parameters t, q_G, q_H, ε, k, and k_0; this means that t' and ε' are functions in these parameters. As designers, we can then assess the strength of the underlying encryption function f, enabling us to arrive at formal estimates of the resources and capabilities an attacker would need to break the encryption function $\mathcal{E}^{(G,H)}(\cdot)$ used in our implementation.

We need to formalize public-key encryption systems as mathematical systems that can be analyzed rigorously in the random oracle model.

Definition 5.7 (Public-Key Encryption and Random Oracles)
An *ideal public-key encryption system in the random oracle model* is formally specified by a *probabilistic generator* $\mathcal{S}$, probabilistically mapping a natural number k to:

- two random oracles G and H – specified, for example, as in (5.4) and (5.5);
- a pair $(\mathcal{E}^{(G,H)}(\cdot), \mathcal{D}^{(G,H)}(\cdot))$, where $\mathcal{E}^{(G,H)}(\cdot)$ is a probabilistic encryption function and $\mathcal{D}^{(G,H)}(\cdot)$ its corresponding decryption function – specified, for example, as in (5.6) and (5.7), respectively;[6] and
- a *plain-text length function* $1(\cdot)$ such that $1(k)$ is the bit length of plain-text that is to be encrypted.[7]

We insist on

$$\mathcal{D}^{(G,H)}(\mathcal{E}^{(G,H)}(x)) = x$$

for all $1(k)$-bit strings x in the message space $\mathcal{M}$ and demand further that $\mathcal{D}^{(G,H)}(y)$ return the exception value "failed" if there is no x in the message space such that $\mathcal{E}^{(G,H)}(x) = y$.

---

[6] These functions can access G and H as random oracles.

[7] For our purposes, think of $1(k)$ as $k - k_0$ or $k - k_0 - k_1$, depending on which of the two encryption systems we study.

We write $T(k)$ for the time it takes to encrypt messages of bit length k with the underlying encryption function f.[8]

We formulate a notion of semantic security for algorithms that make use of random oracles. An attacker of our ideal public-key encryption system is modeled as a randomized algorithm $A^{G,H}(\cdot, \cdot)$ that has access to the random oracles G and H. We may assume that the attacker records all results of calls to the random oracles G and H during a run. Thus we may assume that the attacker never makes more than one particular query to G and H, respectively. To simplify the discussion and analysis, we further assume that the number of these queries depends only on the length of $A^{G,H}(\cdot, \cdot)$'s input, not on its internal coin tosses.

The attacker $A^{G,H}(\cdot, \cdot)$ operates in an environment where it communicates with another agent, the "system" S. Both parties engage in a computation that is being conducted in two stages.

1. In the first phase, the find-stage, the call $A^{G,H}(\mathcal{E}^{(G,H)}(\cdot), \texttt{find})$ – with a description of the encryption algorithm $\mathcal{E}^{(G,H)}(\cdot)$ as input – outputs a triple $\langle x_0, x_1, c \rangle$, where
   - x_0 and x_1 are plain-text messages, and
   - c is a string that could record $A^{G,H}(\cdot, \cdot)$'s input, execution history, and so on.

   The system S now picks x_0 or x_1; this choice is determined by a bit value b that is known only to S and is randomly chosen. That is, S picks x_b and encrypts x_b with $\mathcal{E}^{(G,H)}(\cdot)$, resulting in cipher-text y.

2. In the second phase of the run, the guess-stage, $A^{G,H}(\cdot, \texttt{guess})$ receives the triple $\langle x_0, x_1, c \rangle$ back from S and also receives the cipher-text y. In turn,

   $$A^{G,H}(\langle x_0, x_1, c, y \rangle, \texttt{guess})$$

   outputs a "guess" as to which of messages x_0 and x_1 was encrypted with $\mathcal{E}^{(G,H)}(\cdot)$. We assume that the name of that encryption algorithm is contained in c. Thus $A^{G,H}(\langle x_0, x_1, c, y \rangle, \texttt{guess})$ returns a bit that is, in effect, its "guess" of the value of the bit b that was previously chosen by the system S.

For the analysis that follows, we assume a basic understanding of probability theory and probability spaces.

Definition 5.8 (Random samples)
Given a probability space Ω of elementary events, we write $x \leftarrow \Omega$ for the random sample x from Ω.

We will not formally define the probability spaces used in the analysis; we focus instead on the analysis of probabilistic events. The reader may want to review basic probability theory before reading the remainder of this section. We are now positioned to formally define what it means to break our encryption schemes.

---

[8] Note that $T(k)$ is made to depend only on k and thus not on the instance of f; that is, $T(k)$ does not depend on the random choice of n and e.

Definition 5.9 (Breaking $\mathcal{S}(k)$)

An attacking algorithm $A^{G,H}(\cdot, \cdot)$ manages to $(t, q_G, q_H, \varepsilon)$-*break* the ideal public-key encryption system $\mathcal{S}(k)$ if and only if

$$\frac{\varepsilon + 1}{2} \leq p, \tag{5.20}$$

where p is the probability that the call $A^{G,H}(\langle x_0, x_1, c, y \rangle, \mathbf{guess})$ returns b – correctly guesses the bit b – given that (i) the probabilistic events

- $G \leftarrow \Omega$,
- $H \leftarrow \Omega$,
- $(\mathcal{E}^{(G,H)}(\cdot), \mathcal{D}^{(G,H)}(\cdot)) \leftarrow \mathcal{S}(k)$,
- $\langle x_0, x_1, c \rangle \leftarrow A^{G,H}(\mathcal{E}^{(G,H)}(\cdot), \mathtt{find})$,[9]
- $b \leftarrow \{0, 1\}$,
- $y \leftarrow \mathcal{E}^{(G,H)}(x_b)$ [10]

occurred in that order and (ii) $A^{G,H}(\cdot, \cdot)$, in its total two phases, runs for at most t steps and makes at most q_G and q_H queries to the random oracles G and H, respectively.

Observe that $\frac{1}{2} = p$ (i.e. $\varepsilon = 0$) is easily realized by an attacker who always replies with a guess that was determined by the toss of a fair random coin. Thus the $\varepsilon \geq 0$ in (5.20) is a good measure of the advantage an attacker has over this unbiased and uninformed attack. Our goal is to assess encryption systems by a method for converting $A^{G,H}(\cdot, \cdot)$ into an algorithm that can break the underlying encryption function f.

Definition 5.10 (Breaking the Encryption Function f)

The scheme $\mathcal{S}$ contains a subsystem $\mathcal{F}$, where $\mathcal{F}(k)$ probabilistically generates the pair (f, f^{-1}) for $\mathcal{S}(k)$.[11] Let $M(\cdot, \cdot)$ be an algorithm that, given a description of f and a f-cipher-text y for a f-plain-text w, returns a putative decryption of y.[12] We say that $M(\cdot, \cdot)$ is a (t, ε)-*inverse* of $\mathcal{F}(k)$ if and only if $M(f, y)$ has a probability of at least ε of recovering the f-plain-text w within t computation steps whenever the probabilistic events

- $(f, f^{-1}) \leftarrow \mathcal{F}(k)$,
- $w \leftarrow \{0, 1\}^k$

occur in that order.

EXERCISES 5.5

1. The attacker $A^{G,H}(\cdot, \cdot)$ can certainly remember the plain-texts x_0 and x_1 as well as the encryption function $\mathcal{E}^{(G,H)}(\cdot)$ from its $\mathtt{find}$-stage by coding it up in the string c. Later on, the system supplies the attacker with that string, among other things. What

---

[9] Since $A^{G,H}(\cdot, \cdot)$ is a probabilistic algorithm, its output is a random sample.
[10] Note that $\mathcal{E}^{(G,H)}(\cdot)$ is a *probabilistic* algorithm.
[11] In Chapter 1 we saw how this can be done efficiently.
[12] Recall that the encryption with f, unlike the one with $\mathcal{E}^{(G,H)}(\cdot)$, is *deterministic*.

prevents the attacker from re-encrypting x_0 and x_1 and comparing it to y, thereby determining the correct bit value b?

2. Considering (5.20), what is the possible range of the advantage ε?
3. **Semantic security** Discuss how the interaction of the system S and the attacker $A^{G,H}(\cdot, \cdot)$ in the two stages captures semantic security as a game in which the attacker is trying to deduce *any* information about a matching plain-text for a cipher-text.
4. Discuss to what extent $T(k)$ is *truly* independent from the choice of the modulus n and the public key e.

Theorem 5.11 (Exact Semantic Security)
For the ideal public-key encryption scheme S as in (5.6), there exists an oracle machine $U[\cdot]$ and a constant λ such that, for each $k \in \mathbb{N}$: If $A^{G,H}(\cdot, \cdot)$ is a $(t, q_G, q_H, \varepsilon)$-breaking $S(k)$ then $U[A^{G,H}(\cdot, \cdot)]$ is a (t', ε')-inverse of $\mathcal{F}(k)$, where

$$t' \overset{\text{def}}{=} t + q_G \cdot q_H \cdot (T(k) + \lambda \cdot k), \tag{5.21}$$

$$\varepsilon' \overset{\text{def}}{=} \varepsilon \cdot (1 - q_G \cdot 2^{-k_0} - q_H \cdot 2^{-(k-k_0)}) - q_G \cdot 2^{-k+1}. \tag{5.22}$$

This theorem suggests that, given an attack of $S(k)$ based on $A^{G,H}(\cdot, \cdot)$, we can convert this into an attack of $\mathcal{F}(k)$; the conversion is

$$A^{G,H}(\cdot, \cdot) \mapsto U[A^{G,H}(\cdot, \cdot)].$$

We think of $U[\cdot]$ as a "universal oracle machine" that can implement $U[A^{G,H}(\cdot, \cdot)]$ and has oracle access to G and H. The proof of this theorem reveals the importance of the "description" of $U[\cdot]$ being "small". The constant λ depends on the underlying computational model (Turing machines, RAM machines, Java programs, etc.).

From Attack 2.60 (p. 73) we recall that it is advisable to choose k larger than 512. For such values, we may ignore the terms $q_G \cdot 2^{-k+1}$ and $q_H \cdot 2^{-(k-k_0)}$ in (5.22) and so obtain

$$\varepsilon' \approx \varepsilon \cdot (1 - q_G \cdot 2^{-k_0}). \tag{5.23}$$

Two things can be learned from this estimate.

1. The success probability or advantage ε' for inverting $\mathcal{F}(k)$ is only slightly less than the success probability for breaking $S(k)$ and is close to its optimal value. Thus we obtain a tight correspondence between the security parameters of f and $\mathcal{E}^{(G,H)}(\cdot)$.
2. The dominant factor in the running time t' is the computation of $q_G \cdot q_H$ many encryptions with f.

EXERCISES 5.6

1. Recall that a logical implication "p implies q" is equivalent to the implication "not q implies not p". Use this to reflect on the practical significance of Theorem 5.11.
2. Inspecting (5.23), which is more advantageous for $A^{G,H}(\cdot, \cdot)$: asking more queries to G or to H?

3. Although (5.22) suggests similar success probabilities for breaking $\mathcal{F}(k)$ and $\mathcal{S}(k)$, discuss why this still means a huge win for the security of $\mathcal{S}(k)$.

5.4.1 Proof of Exact Semantic Security

Let $A^{G,H}(\cdot, \cdot)$ be $(t, q_G, q_H, \varepsilon)$-breaking $\mathcal{S}(k)$. We begin with a description of a probabilistic algorithm, $M(\cdot, \cdot)$ and then show that it is a (t', ε')-inverse of $\mathcal{F}(k)$, where t' and ε' are chosen according to (5.21) and (5.22). The input (f, y) to $M(\cdot, \cdot)$ is randomly chosen in the order

- $(f, f^{-1}) \leftarrow \mathcal{F}(k)$,
- $y \leftarrow \{0, 1\}^k$.

For all such random samples, the run $M(f, y)$ terminates; it outputs either some $w^* \in \{0, 1\}^{k-k_0}$ or "failed" – reporting a failed attempt at breaking $f(w)$.

Definition 5.12 (Execution of $M(f, y)$)

1. Using the description of f, the run $M(f, y)$ constructs a description of $\mathcal{E}^{(G,H)}(\cdot)$ that is parametric in the random oracles G and H.
2. $M(f, y)$ maintains two lists l_G and l_H, initially empty, in which it stores queries that are asked by a simulation of $A^{G,H}(\cdot, \cdot)$ that $M(f, y)$ realizes as follows.
3. $M(f, y)$ picks a bit value b at random:
   $$b \leftarrow \{0, 1\}.$$
4. Then $M(f, y)$ simulates the find stage of $A^{G,H}(\mathcal{E}^{(G,H)}(\cdot), \cdot)$ by: (a) first providing $A^{G,H}(\cdot, \text{find})$ with the description of $\mathcal{E}^{(G,H)}(\cdot)$ and fair random coins for its internal probabilistic choices; and (b) then simulating random oracles G and H for $A^{G,H}(\mathcal{E}^{(G,H)}(\cdot), \text{find})$:
   (i) if a query g to G is made, the run $M(f, y)$ provides a random $(k - k_0)$-bit string G_g as answer and adds g to its list l_G;
   (ii) if a query h to H is made, the run $M(f, y)$ produces a random k_0-bit string H_h as answer and adds h to its list l_H.
   Let $\langle x_0, x, c \rangle$ be the output of $A^{G,H}(\mathcal{E}^{(G,H)}(\cdot), \text{find})$'s simulation.
5. $M(f, y)$ now simulates the guess-stage by: (a) running $A^{G,H}(\langle x_0, x_1, c, y \rangle, \text{guess})$; and (b) simulating the queries to G and H of that simulation run as follows.
   (i) Whenever $A^{G,H}(\langle x_0, x_1, c, y \rangle, \text{guess})$ makes a query h to H, then:
   A. $M(f, y)$ computes a random $(k - k_0)$-bit string H_h as answer and adds h to the list l_H;
   B. next, for each g that is currently on the list l_G, the run $M(f, y)$ computes

   $$w_{h,g} \stackrel{\text{def}}{=} h \,\|\, g \oplus H_h, \tag{5.24}$$

   $$y_{h,g} \stackrel{\text{def}}{=} f(w_{h,g}). \tag{5.25}$$

   C. If there is some g on l_G with $y_{h,g} = y$, then $M(f, y)$ assigns

   $$w^* \stackrel{\text{def}}{=} w_{h,g}.$$

(ii) Whenever $A^{G,H}(\langle x_0, x_1, c, y \rangle, \text{guess})$ makes a query g to G, then:

    A. for each h that is currently on the list l_H, the run $M(f, y)$ computes

$$w_{h,g} \stackrel{\text{def}}{=} h \, \| \, g \oplus H_h, \tag{5.26}$$

$$y_{h,g} \stackrel{\text{def}}{=} f(w_{h,g}). \tag{5.27}$$

    B. If there is some h on l_H with $y_{h,g} = y$, then $M(f, y)$:

- assigns

$$w^* \stackrel{\text{def}}{=} w_{h,g},$$

$$G_g \stackrel{\text{def}}{=} h \oplus x_b; \tag{5.28}$$

- adds g to l_G; and
- returns G_g as the answer to query g.

    C. If there is no h on l_H with $y_{h,g} = y$, then $M(f, y)$ generates a random $(k - k_0)$-bit string G_g as answer and adds g to l_G.

If an assignment

$$w^* \stackrel{\text{def}}{=} w_{h,g}$$

is ever executed, then w^* is the output of $M(f, y)$. Otherwise, the attempt to break $f(w)$ has failed and a "failed" is reported.

We emphasize that the lists l_G and l_H maintain queries that $A^{G,H}(\cdot, \cdot)$ asks during the find-stage *and* the guess-stage.

EXERCISES 5.7

1. Given the description of a run $M(f, y)$ in Definition 5.12, prove that its running time t' is as claimed in (5.21).
2. For the simple encryption scheme and the plain-text–aware encryption scheme, which of the functions $\mathcal{E}^{(G,H)}(\cdot)$, $\mathcal{D}^{(G,H)}(\cdot)$ are deterministic and which are probabilistic?
3. Explain how $M(\cdot, \cdot)$ can be expressed as a *universal* oracle machine $U[A^{G,H}(\cdot, \cdot)]$.
4. Prove: Whenever a run $M(f, y)$ executes a statement of the form $w^* \stackrel{\text{def}}{=} w_{h,g}$, then $f(w^*)$ equals y.
5. The run $M(f, y)$ may never execute any statement of the form $w^* \stackrel{\text{def}}{=} w_{h,g}$. However, its control flow does not rule out the possibility that more than one of these statements is executed. Considering that any assigned value to w^* is a putative decrypted cipher-text, why are such multiple assignments unproblematic?
6. Inspecting the find-stage and guess-stage of the run $M(f, y)$, the same query to a random oracle evidently is likely to get a different random answer if asked more than once. What assumption about the attacker guarantees that this is not a problem?

The astute reader will have noticed that $M(f, y)$ could halt execution whenever an assignment of the form $w^* \stackrel{\text{def}}{=} w_{h,g}$ occurs. After the execution of such assignments, the algorithm continues executing and some variables – such as the bit value b – are only being used thereafter; see for example (5.28) in Definition 5.12. This activity does not alter the probability of a successful break of $f(w)$, but it does serve to provide $A^{G,H}(\cdot, \cdot)$ with a view that is as close as possible to what it would see under a run in which it is trying to break $S(k)$ – by trying to guess the bit value b.

Definition 5.13 (Game 1)

We consider the probabilistic game consisting of the random sampling

- $(f, f^{-1}) \leftarrow \mathcal{F}(k)$ and
- $y \leftarrow \{0, 1\}^k$

occurring in that order, followed by the execution of $M(f, y)$.[13] We call this experiment *game 1* and write $\Pr_1[E]$ for the probability of an event E in that game.

The f-plain-text

$$w \overset{\text{def}}{=} f^{-1}(y)$$

is k bits long, so we can write is as

$$s \parallel t \overset{\text{def}}{=} w, \tag{5.29}$$

where s and t are $(k - k_0)$-bit and k_0-bit strings, respectively. We consider

$$r \overset{\text{def}}{=} t \oplus H(s) \tag{5.30}$$

as a random variable (in the random choice of f and y). Consider two probabilistic events:

- findbad is defined to be true if and only if r was asked as a query to G in the find-stage of the run $M(f, y)$ and the oracle's answer G_r is not in the set $\{s \oplus x_0, s \oplus x_1\}$;
- guessbad is defined to be true if and only if r was asked as a query to G in the guess-stage of the run $M(f, y)$, at which time the query s to H was not in the list l_H, and the oracle's answer G_r is not in the set $\{s \oplus x_0, s \oplus x_1\}$.

Definition 5.14 (Game 2)

We define the event

$$\text{good} \overset{\text{def}}{=} \neg\text{findbad} \wedge \neg\text{guessbad}.$$

We define *game 2* as game 1 conditioned on good to be true at all times:

$$\Pr_2[E] \overset{\text{def}}{=} \Pr_1[E \mid \text{good}] \quad (E \text{ any event}). \tag{5.31}$$

We now present games that are played not by $M(\cdot, \cdot)$ but rather by the attacker $A^{G,H}(\cdot, \cdot)$. We will then relate the former games to the latter ones, giving us the promised exact security parameters.

---

[13] This is a probabilistic algorithm.

Definition 5.15 (Game 1*)

In *game 1**, we assume that the probabilistic events

- $G_* \leftarrow \Omega$,
- $H_* \leftarrow \Omega$,
- $(\mathcal{E}^{(G_*, H_*)}(\cdot), \mathcal{D}^{(G_*, H_*)}(\cdot)) \leftarrow \mathcal{S}(k)$,
- $\langle x_0^*, x_1^*, c^* \rangle \leftarrow A^{G_*, H_*}(\mathcal{E}^{(G_*, H_*)}(\cdot), \text{find})$,
- $b^* \leftarrow \{0, 1\}$,
- $y^* \leftarrow \mathcal{E}^{(G_*, H_*)}(x_{b^*})$

occurred in that order. We assume also that $A^{G_*, H_*}(\cdot, \cdot)$, in its total two phases, runs for at most t steps and makes at most q_G and q_H queries to the random oracles G_* and H_*, respectively. Let $\Pr_{1*}[E]$ be the corresponding probability of an event E.

Game 1* is, of course, just the interaction of the attacker $A^{G_*, H_*}(\cdot, \cdot)$ with the system S that defines its success probability or advantage.

Definition 5.16 (Game 2*)

Game 2* is played in the same way as game 1*, except that its *first* probabilistic event is the random choice

$$y^* \leftarrow \mathcal{E}^{(G_*, H_*)}(x_{b^*}); \tag{5.32}$$

all other events that define game 1* are then chosen according to the probability distribution that makes the outcome of game 1* and game 2* the same. Let $\Pr_{2*}[E]$ be the corresponding probability of an event E.

Since the underlying probability space is finite, we know that the probability distribution needed in Definition 5.16 exists – noting that the choice in (5.32) is made uniformly. The event good has been chosen such that the views held by the attacker in game 2 and game 2* are identical. We won't formally justify this claim, but we give an example for sake of illustration.

Example 5.17

To simplify the example, suppose the find-stage of the attacker is constant in that it always outputs the same triple $\langle x_0^*, x_1^*, c^* \rangle$. Once y^* is chosen and fixed, the distributions on G_* and H_* – conditioned on the event good in game 2 – have the following descriptions:

- choose H_* at random;
- whenever g is not equal to $t \oplus H_*(s)$, choose the answer $G_*(g)$ at random;
- the value $G_*(t \oplus H_*(s))$ can only be $s \oplus x_0^*$ or $s \oplus x_1^*$, and that choice is randomly determined.

EXERCISE 5.8

1. Verify that the probability distributions of G_* and H_* in games 2 and 2* are equal and as claimed in Example 5.17.

For the analysis of game 1, it is useful to consider the following events:

- `findask_s` is true if and only if the query s to H was made in the `find`-stage;
- `ask_r` is true if and only if r is in the list l_G at the end of the `guess`-stage;
- `ask_s` is true if and only if s is on the list l_H at the end of the `guess`-stage; and
- `win` $\stackrel{\text{def}}{=}$ `ask_r` $\wedge$ `ask_s`.

We use these events to prove that the probability of the desired event good *not* occurring is low.

Lemma 5.18
The probability of ¬good *has a low upper bound*:

$$\Pr_1[\neg\text{good}] \leq q_G \cdot 2^{-k_0} + q_H \cdot 2^{k-k_0}. \tag{5.33}$$

Proof We compute

$$
\begin{aligned}
\Pr_1[\neg\text{good}] &= \Pr_1[\neg\text{good} \mid \text{findask\_s}] \cdot \Pr_1[\text{findask\_s}] \\
&\quad + \Pr_1[\neg\text{good} \mid \neg\text{findask\_s}] \cdot \Pr_1[\neg\text{findask\_s}] \\
&\leq \Pr_1[\text{findask\_s}] + \Pr_1[\neg\text{good} \mid \neg\text{findask\_s}] \\
&\leq \Pr_1[\text{findask\_s}] + \Pr_1[\text{ask\_r} \mid \neg\text{findask\_s}].
\end{aligned}
\tag{5.34}
$$

The validity of the first equation and first inequality follows from the definition of conditional probability and the axioms of probability. The last inequality is valid since $\Pr_1[\neg\text{good} \mid \neg\text{findask\_s}] \leq \Pr_1[\text{ask\_r} \mid \neg\text{findask\_s}]$, which we can justify as follows. Whenever a query g is submitted to G, the run $M(f, y)$ adds g to the list l_G. Thus the event $\neg\text{good} = \text{findbad} \vee \text{guessbad}$ implies that r is being added to l_G, since both findbad and guessbad submit the query r to G and the run $M(f, y)$ never removes entries from the lists l_G and l_H. But then ¬good implies `ask_r`, whence the inequality.

We establish the upper bound of (5.33) by providing upper bounds for the summands $\Pr_1[\text{findask\_s}]$ and $\Pr_1[\text{ask\_r} \mid \neg\text{findask\_s}]$.

- $\Pr_1[\text{findask\_s}] \leq q_H \cdot 2^{k-k_0}$ holds because (a) the probability of asking s among all possible $(k - k_0)$-bit string queries to H during the `find`-stage is 2^{k-k_0} and (b) $M(f, y)$ is allowed to provide at most q_H many answers to queries of H.
- $\Pr_1[\text{ask\_r} \mid \neg\text{findask\_s}] \leq q_G \cdot 2^{-k_0}$ holds since $\Pr_1[\text{ask\_r} \mid \neg\text{findask\_s}]$ is the probability that r is on the list l_G at the end of the `guess`-stage, provided that the query s is not in the list l_H at the end of the `guess`-stage. But then the query r was submitted to G and s was never submitted to H during the `find`-stage. The probability of this event has $q_G \cdot 2^{k_0}$ as an upper bound, since the k_0-bit string t must be guessed at random and only q_G many queries can be made to G. $\square$

Lemma 5.19
Event win *is true if and only if the run* $M(f, y)$ *succeeds in computing* $w = f^{-1}(y)$.

Proof You are asked to show this in Exercise 5.9-2. $\square$

Next, we analyze the probability of recovering the plain-text w in game 2.

Lemma 5.20

Let E_b be the event that the attacker is successful in predicting the bit value b. Then the probability of win *in game 2 has an informative lower bound:*

$$\Pr_2[\text{win}] \geq 2 \cdot \Pr_2[E_b] - 1 - \frac{2 \cdot q_G \cdot 2^{-k}}{\Pr_1[\text{good}]}. \tag{5.35}$$

Proof We compute an upper bound for $\Pr_2[E_b]$:

$$
\begin{aligned}
\Pr_2[E_b] &= \Pr_2[E_b \mid \text{win}] \cdot \Pr_2[\text{win}] \\
&\quad + \Pr_2[E_b \mid \neg\text{ask\_r}] \cdot \Pr_2[\neg\text{ask\_r}] \\
&\quad + \Pr_2[E_b \mid \text{ask\_r} \wedge \neg\text{ask\_s}] \cdot \Pr_2[\text{ask\_r} \wedge \neg\text{ask\_s}] \tag{5.36} \\
&\leq \Pr_2[\text{win}] \\
&\quad + \Pr_2[E_b \mid \neg\text{ask\_r}] \cdot \Pr_2[\neg\text{ask\_r}] \\
&\quad + \Pr_2[\text{ask\_r} \wedge \neg\text{ask\_s}] \tag{5.37} \\
&= \Pr_2[\text{win}] \\
&\quad + \Pr_2[E_b \mid \neg\text{ask\_r}] \cdot (1 - \Pr_2[\text{win}] - \Pr_2[\text{ask\_r} \wedge \neg\text{ask\_s}]). \tag{5.38}
\end{aligned}
$$

The equality in (5.36) is justified since the events win $=$ ask_r $\wedge$ ask_s, $\neg$ask_r, and ask_r $\wedge$ $\neg$ask_s are mutually disjoint and since their union event, "true", satisfies $\Pr_2[\text{"true"}] = 1$. The inequality in (5.37) then follows from the monotonicity of probabilities applied to each of the three summands. Equation (5.38) follows from the axioms of probability.

Now if $\neg$ask_r holds, then r is not in the list l_G at the end of the guess-stage. But this gives the attacker no advantage whatsoever in predicting the correct value b. Thus

$$\Pr_2[E_b \mid \neg\text{ask\_r}] \leq \tfrac{1}{2}. \tag{5.39}$$

To compute an upper bound for $\Pr_2[\text{ask\_r} \wedge \neg\text{ask\_s}]$, let r_before_s be the event that r is on the list l_G such that s was not on the list l_H at the time that r was placed on l_G. We can then compute:

$$
\begin{aligned}
\Pr_1[\text{ask\_r} \wedge \neg\text{ask\_s} \wedge \text{good}] &= \Pr_1[\text{r\_before\_s} \wedge G_r \in \{s \oplus x_0, \, s \oplus x_1\}] \\
&= \Pr_1[\text{r\_before\_s}] \cdot \Pr_1[G_r \in \{s \oplus x_0, \, s \oplus x_1\}] \mid \text{r\_before\_s}] \\
&\leq (q_G \cdot 2^{-k_0}) \cdot (2 \cdot 2^{k-k_0}) \\
&= 2 \cdot q_G \cdot 2^{-k}. \tag{5.40}
\end{aligned}
$$

From (5.40), we have

$$
\begin{aligned}
\Pr_2[\text{ask\_r} \wedge \neg\text{ask\_s}] &= \frac{\Pr_1[\text{ask\_r} \wedge \neg\text{ask\_s} \wedge \text{good}]}{\Pr_1[\text{good}]} \\
&\leq \frac{2 \cdot q_G \cdot 2^{-k}}{\Pr_1[\text{good}]}. \tag{5.41}
\end{aligned}
$$

Given the inequalities from (5.39) and (5.41), we use them in (5.38) to obtain

$$\Pr_2[E_b] \leq \frac{1}{2} \cdot \Pr_2[\text{win}] + \frac{1}{2} + \frac{q_G \cdot 2^{-k}}{\Pr_1[\text{good}]}, \tag{5.42}$$

which renders the claimed upper bound. But (5.42) can easily be converted into (5.35).

□

We have remarked that game 2 and game 2* are equivalent from the point of view of the attacker. Thus

$$\Pr_2[E_b] \geq \frac{\varepsilon + 1}{2}$$

follows from (5.20). Using this in the inequality of Lemma 5.20 yields

$$\Pr_1[\text{win} \mid \text{good}] = \Pr_2[\text{win}]$$

$$\geq 2 \cdot \Pr_2[E_b] - 1 - \frac{2 \cdot q_G \cdot 2^{-k}}{\Pr_1[\text{good}]}$$

$$\geq 2 \cdot \frac{\varepsilon + 1}{2} - 1 - \frac{2 \cdot q_G \cdot 2^{-k}}{\Pr_1[\text{good}]}$$

$$= \varepsilon - \frac{2 \cdot q_G \cdot 2^{-k}}{\Pr_1[\text{good}]}. \tag{5.43}$$

We then use (5.43) and Lemma 5.18 to obtain

$$\Pr_1[\text{win}] \geq \Pr_1[\text{win} \mid \text{good}] \cdot \Pr_1[\text{good}]$$

$$\geq \left(\varepsilon - \frac{2 \cdot q_G \cdot 2^{-k}}{\Pr_1[\text{good}]} \right) \cdot \Pr_1[\text{good}]$$

$$= \varepsilon \cdot \Pr_1[\text{good}] - 2 \cdot q_G \cdot 2^{-k}$$

$$\geq \varepsilon \cdot (1 - q_G \cdot 2^{-k_0} - q_H \cdot 2^{k-k_0}) - 2 \cdot q_G \cdot 2^{-k}. \tag{5.44}$$

By Lemma 5.19, we must have $\varepsilon' \geq \Pr_1[\text{win}]$, giving us the desired

$$\varepsilon' \geq \varepsilon \cdot (1 - q_G \cdot 2^{-k_0} - q_H \cdot 2^{k-k_0}) - 2 \cdot q_G \cdot 2^{-k}. \tag{5.45}$$

EXERCISES 5.9

1. In the proof of Lemma 5.18, explain in detail why all equations and inequalities hold; make use of the definition of conditional probabilities and the axioms of probability.
2. Prove Lemma 5.19.
3. Explain in detail why (5.39) holds.
4. Justify all equations and inequalities in (5.40).

5.5 EXACT SECURITY FOR THE PLAIN-TEXT–AWARE ENCRYPTION

In formalizing our notion of a "plain-text–aware" encryption system, we assume an adversary B($\cdot$) who takes an encryption algorithm $\mathcal{E}^{(G,H)}(\cdot)$ as input and outputs a string y – a putative cipher-text. We rely on an algorithm K($\cdot, \cdot, \cdot, \cdot$), which (all things being equal) can decrypt cipher-texts that B($\cdot$) may output simply by observing B($\cdot$)'s interaction with the random oracles G and H.

Definition 5.21 (Plain-Text Extractor)

1. We write

$$\langle y, 1_G, 1_H \rangle \leftarrow \text{run } B(\mathcal{E}^{(G,H)}(\cdot)) \tag{5.46}$$

to denote that:

- the run $B(\mathcal{E}^{(G,H)}(\cdot))$ outputs the string y; and
- a record of this run's interaction with its random oracles G and H has been made, where $G(g)$ (resp., $H(h)$) is the reply of the random oracle G (H) to query g (h).[14] The record is

$$1_G \overset{\text{def}}{=} [\langle g_1, G(g_1) \rangle, \langle g_2, G(g_2) \rangle, \ldots, \langle g_{q_G}, G(g_{q_G}) \rangle], \tag{5.47}$$

$$1_H \overset{\text{def}}{=} [\langle h_1, H(h_1) \rangle, \langle h_2, H(h_2) \rangle, \ldots, \langle h_{q_H}, H(h_{q_H}) \rangle]. \tag{5.48}$$

2. A (t, ε)-*plain-text extractor for* $B(\cdot)$ *and* $\mathcal{S}(k)$ is an algorithm $K(\cdot, \cdot, \cdot, \cdot)$ such that the probability of

$$K(\mathcal{E}^{(G,H)}(\cdot), y, 1_G, 1_H) \neq \mathcal{D}^{(G,H)}(y)$$

is less than or equal to ε, provided that the algorithm ran in at most t steps and that the probabilistic events

- $G \leftarrow \Omega(k)$,
- $H \leftarrow \Omega(k)$,
- $(\mathcal{E}^{(G,H)}(\cdot), \mathcal{D}^{(G,H)}(\cdot)) \leftarrow \mathcal{S}(k)$, and
- $\langle y, 1_G, 1_H \rangle \leftarrow \text{run } B(\mathcal{E}^{(G,H)}(\cdot))$

occurred in that order.

Notice the kind of information that is being supplied to the plain-text extractor. It obtains only the encryption algorithm $\mathcal{E}^{(G,H)}(\cdot)$, the output of run $B(\mathcal{E}^{(G,H)}(\cdot))$, and the list of interactions that this run had with the random oracles G and H. The plain-text extractor has no access to the random oracles themselves, only to their "view" as determined by this single run. In particular, the plain-text extractor has no access to the random coin tosses of the run $B(\mathcal{E}^{(G,H)}(\cdot))$. As mentioned earlier, one can prove – in the random oracle model – that the plain-text–aware encryption scheme is nonmalleable and secure against chosen cipher-text attacks. The latter is intuitively clear: if an attacker has temporary access to the decryption function $\mathcal{D}^{(G,H)}(\cdot)$, then no additional power is gained because the knowledge extractor can typically decrypt cipher-text based on $\langle y, 1_G, 1_H \rangle \leftarrow \text{run } B(\mathcal{E}^{(G,H)}(\cdot))$.

We reuse Theorem 5.11 to prove the semantic security of the plain-text–aware encryption scheme.

Theorem 5.22 (Exact Semantic Security)
Each plain-text–aware public-key encryption scheme S' has an oracle machine $U[\cdot]$ and a constant λ such that, for each $k \in \mathbb{N}$: If $A^{G,H}(\cdot, \cdot)$ is a $(t, q_G, q_H, \varepsilon)$-breaking $S'(k)$ then $U[A^{G,H}(\cdot, \cdot)]$ is a (t', ε')-inverse of $\mathcal{F}(k)$, where

$$t' \overset{\text{def}}{=} t + q_G \cdot q_H \cdot (T(k) + \lambda \cdot k), \tag{5.49}$$

$$\varepsilon' \overset{\text{def}}{=} \varepsilon \cdot (1 - q_G \cdot 2^{-k_0} - q_H \cdot 2^{-[(k+k_1)-k_0]}) - q_G \cdot 2^{-k+1}. \tag{5.50}$$

---

[14] Note that $G(g)$ is different from G_g, the "answer" provided by $M(f, y)$.

Proof Let S^* be the simple encryption scheme of (5.6) with subsystem $\mathcal{F}$ and security parameter $k + k_1$. We define an adversary $A_*^{G,H}(\cdot, \cdot)$ from $A^{G,H}(\cdot, \cdot)$ as follows: first, it simulates the find-stage of $A^{G,H}(\cdot, \cdot)$, thereby obtaining $\langle x_0, x_1, c \rangle$, and outputs $\langle x_0 0^{k_1}, x_1 0^{k_1}, c \rangle$. Second, it receives cipher-text y from the system S', removes the padded k_1 rightmost zeros from $x_0 0^{k_1}$ and $x_1 0^{k_1}$, and simulates the guess-stage of $A^{G,H}(\cdot, \cdot)$ with input $\langle x_0, x_1, c, y \rangle$. The rest follows immediately from Theorem 5.11. $\square$

An intuitive account of this semantic security for plain-text–aware encryption may be summarized as follows.

- Let y be the output of $B(\mathcal{E}^{(G,H)}(\cdot))$.
- If r has not been submitted to G, then – with very high probability – the first $k - k_0 + k_1$ bits of $w = f^{-1}(y)$ won't end in 0^{k_1} for its k_1 rightmost bits.
- If s has not been submitted to H, then the attacker cannot know r.
- However, if the attacker knows s, then she evidently knows its $k - k_0$ leftmost bits (which constitute w).

Finally, we address the exact security of the plain-text–aware encryption scheme.

Definition 5.23
Let S be the plain-text–aware encryption scheme. We call $B(\cdot)$ a (t, q_G, q_H)-*adversary* for an instance $S(k)$ if and only if, for all $k \in \mathbb{N}$ and all $\mathcal{E}^{(G,H)}(\cdot) \leftarrow S(k)$, we have that $B(\mathcal{E}^{(G,H)}(\cdot))$:

- runs in at most t time steps;
- makes at most q_G queries to G; and
- makes at most q_H queries to H.

Theorem 5.24 (Exact Plain-Text–Aware Security)
Let S be the plain-text–aware encryption scheme with subsystem $\mathcal{F}$ and with parameters k_0 and k_1. Then there exists an oracle machine $K[\cdot]$ and a constant λ such that, for each $k \in \mathbb{N}$: If $B(\cdot)$ is a (t, q_G, q_H)-adversary for $S(k)$ then $K[B(\cdot)]$ is a (t', ε')-plain-text extractor for $B(\cdot)$ and $S(k)$, where

$$t' \overset{\text{def}}{=} t + q_G \cdot q_H \cdot (T(k) + \lambda \cdot k), \tag{5.51}$$

$$\varepsilon' \overset{\text{def}}{=} q_G \cdot 2^{-k_0} + 2^{-k_1}. \tag{5.52}$$

5.5.1 Proof of Exact Security for Plain-Text–Aware Encryption

First, we define the behavior of the plain-text extractor K. Suppose that $\mathcal{F}(k)$ chooses (f, f^{-1}), $\mathcal{E}^{(G,H)}(\cdot)$ is the corresponding plain-text–aware encryption system, and

$$1_G \overset{\text{def}}{=} [\langle g_1, G(g_1) \rangle, \langle g_2, G(g_2) \rangle, \ldots, \langle g_{q_G}, G(g_{q_G}) \rangle],$$

$$1_H \overset{\text{def}}{=} [\langle h_1, H(h_1) \rangle, \langle h_2, H(h_2) \rangle, \ldots, \langle h_{q_H}, H(h_{q_H}) \rangle]$$

are the interactions of the run $B(\mathcal{E}^{(G,H)}(\cdot))$ with the random oracles G and H, respectively. We record the queries into separate lists

$$l_G \stackrel{\text{def}}{=} [g_1, g_2, \ldots, g_{q_G}],$$

$$l_H \stackrel{\text{def}}{=} [h_1, h_2, \ldots, h_{q_H}].$$

The algorithm K receives input $\langle \mathcal{E}^{(G,H)}(\cdot), y, l_G, l_H \rangle$. The algorithm has variables $x_{i,j}$, $y_{i,j}$, and $z_{i,j}$ for each $1 \le i \le q_G$ and $1 \le j \le q_H$.

1. For each combination of i and j, the run $K\langle \mathcal{E}^{(G,H)}(\cdot), y, l_G, l_H \rangle$:
   (a) assigns to $x_{i,j}$ the leftmost m bits of $h_i \oplus G(g_j)$;
   (b) assigns to $z_{i,j}$ the (remaining) rightmost k_1 bits of $h_i \oplus G(g_j)$;
   (c) assigns

   $$w_{i,j} \stackrel{\text{def}}{=} h_i \| g_j \oplus H(h_i);$$

   and
   (d) computes

   $$y_{i,j} \stackrel{\text{def}}{=} f(w_{i,j}).$$

2. If there is a choice of i and j such that

$$y_{i,j} = y \quad \text{and} \quad z_{i,j} = 0^{k_1}, \tag{5.53}$$

then the run $K\langle \mathcal{E}^{(G,H)}(\cdot), y, l_G, l_H \rangle$ outputs $x_{i,j}$; otherwise, it returns "failed" – indicating failure.

As for the analysis part, we define

$$w \stackrel{\text{def}}{=} f^{-1}(y) \quad \text{and}$$

$$s \| t \stackrel{\text{def}}{=} w,$$

where s and t are $(k - k_0 + k_1)$-bit and k_1-bit strings, respectively. Next, we define three random variables r, x, z by

$$r \stackrel{\text{def}}{=} t \oplus H(s),$$

$$x \| z \stackrel{\text{def}}{=} s \oplus G(r),$$

where x is $k - k_0$ bits long and y is a k_1-bit string. Consider three probabilistic events:

- `failure` is true if and only if the output of the run $K\langle \mathcal{E}^{(G,H)}(\cdot), y, l_G, l_H \rangle$ is different from $\mathcal{D}^{(G,H)}(y)$;
- `ask_r` is true if and only if r is in the list l_G;
- `ask_s` is true if and only if s is on the list l_H.

Given these events, we manage to prove a first upper bound for the probability of failure:

$$\begin{aligned}
\Pr[\text{failure}] = {} & \Pr[\text{failure} \mid \neg\text{ask\_r}] \cdot \Pr[\neg\text{ask\_r}] \\
& + \Pr[\text{failure} \mid \text{ask\_r} \wedge \text{ask\_s}] \cdot \Pr[\text{ask\_r} \wedge \text{ask\_s}] \\
& + \Pr[\text{failure} \mid \text{ask\_r} \wedge \neg\text{ask\_s}] \cdot \Pr[\text{ask\_r} \wedge \neg\text{ask\_s}] \\
\le {} & \Pr[\text{failure} \mid \neg\text{ask\_r}] \\
& + \Pr[\text{failure} \mid \text{ask\_r} \wedge \text{ask\_s}] \\
& + \Pr[\text{ask\_r} \wedge \neg\text{ask\_s}]. \tag{5.54}
\end{aligned}$$

1. If r is not on the list l_G, then the probability that z equals 0^{k_1} is at most 2^{-k_1}. If z does not equal 0^{k_1}, then the run reports "failed" – which in this case is *not* representing the event failure. Therefore, we conclude that

$$\Pr[\texttt{failure} \mid \neg\texttt{ask\_r}] \leq 2^{-k_1}. \tag{5.55}$$

2. If r is on the list l_G and s is on the list l_H, then there exist i and j such that $w = w_{i,j}$. Thus K will decrypt y correctly, whence $\Pr[\texttt{failure} \mid \texttt{ask\_r} \wedge \texttt{ask\_s}] = 0$.

3. Finally, if s is not on the list l_G, then the answer $H(s)$ is uniformly distributed and thus r is uniformly distributed as an exclusive-or of t and $H(s)$. But then we have

$$\Pr[\texttt{ask\_r} \wedge \neg\texttt{ask\_s}] \leq \Pr[\texttt{ask\_r} \mid \neg\texttt{ask\_s}] \leq q_G \cdot 2^{-k_0}.$$

These three items and the upper bound of (5.54) establish the upper bound of Theorem 5.24.

EXERCISES 5.10

1. Explain why (5.55) holds.
2. For item 2 (following (5.55)), explain in detail why K will succeed in decrypting y correctly.
3. Justify the reasoning involved in (5.54).

5.6 BIBLIOGRAPHIC NOTES

The core of this chapter presents work done by Bellare and Rogaway (1995); our description of the random oracle methodology is based on Bellare and Rogaway (1993). The ideas that underlie this approach go back to work done by Goldreich, Goldwasser, and Micali (1984, 1986). A general website[15] on the random oracle methodology is maintained by the MIT Cryptography and Information Security Group Research Project. For a paper on the use of the random oracle methodology for deriving perfectly one-way probabilistic hash functions, see Canetti, Micciancio, and Reingold (1998). The sketch that shows the limitation of the random oracle methodology is from Canetti, Goldreich, and Halevi (1998), which contains a more detailed and technical treatment. A representative text on elementary probability theory is Feller (1968).

---

[15] http://theory.lcs.mit.edu/~cis/rom/rom.html

CHAPTER 6

Analysis of Secure Information Flow

6.1 MOTIVATION

Information is meaningful only if it *flows* from one location to another. Such flow can take on many forms. Information may flow from a filing cabinet into somebody's brain; it may pass through various departments of a commercial or military organization; it may be input into – and transformed by – computer programs. In any event, it is of paramount importance that sensitive information not be leaked to unauthorized agents during its flow through a network or program that processes information.

In Chapter 1, we encountered public-key cryptography as a technique for guaranteeing secure flow of confidential messages (e.g., a key for the Rijndael cipher) from one agent to another through an unsecure communication channel. However, such secure information flow may be corrupted when implementing cryptographic algorithms – for example, the RSA and DES encryption modules shown in Figure 6.1 and Figure 3.4 (respectively). Clearly, it is quite straightforward and reasonably simple to write programs that provide the specified input–output functionality. Yet program variables, other programs, or other users of the operating system in which these programs run may be able to deduce information about the secret key for those public-key or symmetric cryptographic systems, either by observing run-time behavior of these implementations or by analyzing their concrete syntax.

For example, putting the RSA encryption algorithm from Figure 6.1 onto a smartcard *as is* may allow a timing attack, noting that the for-statement may take less time to execute whenever the ith bit of the secret key is 0. We may think of this program as a *covert timing channel*. Similarly, a program that assigns secret information to identifiers cannot be considered secure if those identifiers can be read by unauthorized processes: if you need to enter your Rijndael key with a secure smartcard into an encryption module, then this security measure is of no use if that module not only encrypts messages with that key but also copies your key and passes it on to some unauthorized process.

Access control mechanisms are a more abstract but equally important application of reasoning about information flow. Historically, such systems were designed to control the *immediate* physical access to information, and little (if any) attention was paid to the implicit or implied information flow made possible by a particular access policy. Our approach assumes that each object or agent is bound to a security class (e.g., a security clearing) *statically*, meaning that its class won't change *dynamically* during the flow of information through some access structure. Dynamic bindings are inherently problematic. The dynamic increase of an object's security class may "remove" that object from the view of some agent whose security clearance is not sufficient for accessing data of that higher class. Nonetheless, this change of an agent's capability may be used as a covert channel

```
RSA_encryption(BigInteger m, BigInteger n) {
    // returns m ** d mod n, where d is the secret RSA key and
    // n is the RSA modulus
    // the array b stores the binary representation of d
    // and has been ''entered'' into the program via a
    // ''secure'' mechanism;
    // b[k] is the most significant bit of d
    int[] b;
    BigInteger c = 1; // identifier for cipher-text
    for (int i = k; i >= 0; --i) {
      c = (c * c) mod n;
    if (b[i] == 1) c = (c * m) mod n;
    }
    return c;
}
```

Figure 6.1. RSA encryption with iterative squaring.

of communication. An agent with top security clearance can send a secret message to an agent with lower security class by increasing and decreasing two object's security status (the two objects representing the bits 0 and 1, respectively) in a certain pattern to generate a desired bit string – assuming both agents agree that these actions have those meanings. However, we can sometimes model such dynamic capabilities by creating state variables that record and monitor system parameters such as "disk space full", "number of files in a folder", and so forth. Naturally, such parameters are a potential security concern, for if d is a secret "small" natural number then we may leak the value of d by creating d many files in a certain folder or by creating a file of length d. If an agent knows what and where to look for, and if that agent has access to this kind of information, then the secret is being exposed through what is generally called a *covert storage channel*. Such channels can be subsumed by our analysis only to the extent that we may be able to adequately model them with informative state variables. This may be difficult if not impossible for some channels. Moreover, there is an infinity of possible covert channels out there yet we can (attempt to) model only a bounded number of them.

Before we formalize the notion of secure information flow and its analyses, let us begin with an overview of *principal ways in which secure information flow is violated in programs*.

1. A *direct* violation of secure information flow occurs in an assignment

    ```
    x = y;
    ```

    where y stores secret information and x can be read by someone who is not authorized to know the secret stored in y.

2. More subtly, secret information may flow to unsecure program variables in an *indirect* way. This is achieved by *control structures* of programming languages. For example, we may use an if-statement as in

    ```
    if ((y % 2) == 0) { x = 0; } else { x = 1; }
    ```

    to leak the least significant bit of the secret y into x. This example also illustrates that information flow is unsecure already even if only a small part (here: a single bit) of secret information is being exposed.

3. One may use the *termination behavior* of a program as a covert channel for leaking secret information. The program

```
x = y;
while (x != 0) {
    x = x * x;
}
```

terminates only when the value stored in y is 0. Otherwise, the program "loops", meaning in practical terms that some overflow exception will occur at run time. An observer can simply run the program and deduce whether y equals 0.

4. If a program contains *probabilistic choice,* then one may sometimes succeed in a *probabilistic analysis* of the program's behavior that reveals sensitive information. Let us assume that we have a programming language construct

```
(com_1 por com_2)
```

whose effect is the execution of com_1 or com_2 (resp.) with probability 0.5; see Exercise 6.1-1 for how to implement such a construct. Consider the program

```
y = y mod 2;
( x = y por (x = 0 por x = 1) );
```

It should be apparent that the final value of x reveals the least significant bit of y with probability

$$0.5 + 0.5 \cdot 0.5 = 0.75.$$

Such examples are disturbing, since we are unable to detect this kind of violation if we reason only about the *possible* behavior of programs; a probabilistic analysis may then be called for.

5. Assume that our programming language has a real-time construct

```
sleep n;
```

with the effect of making the program be idle for *n* milliseconds. The program

```
if (y = 1) { sleep 1000; } else { sleep 1; }
```

allows an *external observer* to infer information about y by measuring the program's timing behavior. Such a timing analysis is also possible in a nondeterministic setting. Assume that we have a construct

```
(com_1 ++ com_2)
```

whose effect is to execute com_1 or com_2, where the choice is resolved by some (not necessarily deterministic) scheduler. In the program

```
( {if (y = 1) { sleep 1000
        } else { sleep 1;
        }
    x = 1;
}
    or
    x = 0;
)
```

the nature of timing leaks naturally depends on the specific scheduler of nondeterministic choices, but for this program many schedulers determine a *distribution* of final values of x. Note that this example combines timing aspects with potentially probabilistic flows.

6. *Nondeterminism* may also expose secret flow information without timing aspects. The program

> (x = y - 3; ++ x = y + 5;)

has the effect that the final value x stored in x is one of the numbers $y - 3$ or $y + 5$, where y is the initial value stored in y. In particular, $y - 3 \leq x \leq y - 5$. In most circumstances, such a *proximity of values* is considered to be unsecure.

Obviously, one analysis alone cannot certify realistic mobile code, such as multi-threaded Java programs, but each analysis ought to rule out certain kinds of violations of secure information flow. In this chapter, we set out the limited tasks of:

- providing formal criteria that rule out a certain kind of leakage of any secret information (no "write down" and no "read up"), thus giving a sound *definition* of secure information flow;
- coming up with fully automatic (or semi-automatic but efficient) analyses that investigate whether programs allow only secure information flow; and
- proving that these analyzes are *sound* – that programs *certified* to be secure by an analysis actually *satisfy* the formal definition of security.

EXERCISES 6.1

1. Given a programming language that has if-statements and a "good" pseudo-random number generator, show how you can implement the program construct com_1 por com_2.

2. (a) Reevaluate the examples of unsecure programs listed in the text with respect to the following notion of security: x is considered a low-security variable and y a high-security variable. We call a program "secure" if the outcomes of any observations that can be made about final values of low-level security variables are independent from the initial values of any high-security variables.

   (b) For this notion of security, explain to what extent program nontermination may affect the security of programs.

6.2 A TYPE SYSTEM FOR ANALYSIS OF SECURE INFORMATION FLOW

In our first approach, we use the notion of *types* and *type systems* to define and certify secure information flow in programs. Types are a mechanism for guaranteeing a minimal form of security for the execution of program expressions. For example, if an expression has type

```
int * int --> bool
```

then it "assumes" two inputs of type int before its execution and "guarantees" to return some output of type bool; this promise is conditional on the inputs having the advertised

$$\frac{x : \tau \in \Gamma}{\Gamma \rhd x : \tau} \ \text{Id} \qquad\qquad\qquad \frac{}{\Gamma \rhd \text{true} : \text{bool}} \ \text{Tr}$$

$$\frac{}{\Gamma \rhd n : \text{int}} \ \text{Lit} \qquad\qquad \frac{\Gamma \rhd E1 : \text{bool}, \quad \Gamma \rhd E2 : \text{bool}}{\Gamma \rhd E1 \ \&\& \ E2 : \text{bool}} \ \text{And}$$

$$\frac{\Gamma \rhd E : \text{bool}}{\Gamma \rhd !E : \text{bool}} \ \text{Neg} \qquad\quad \frac{\Gamma \rhd E1 : \text{int}, \quad \Gamma \rhd E2 : \text{int}}{\Gamma \rhd E1 \ < \ E2 : \text{bool}} \ \text{LT}$$

$$\frac{\Gamma \rhd E1 : \text{int}, \quad \Gamma \rhd E2 : \text{int}}{\Gamma \rhd E1 \ + \ E2 : \text{int}} \ \text{Add} \qquad \frac{\Gamma \rhd E : \text{int}}{\Gamma \rhd -E : \text{int}} \ \text{Min}$$

Figure 6.2. A type system for the expressions defined in (6.1).

types at run time. Program expressions are typed in this manner within, for example, Java (an object-oriented programming language) and Standard ML of New Jersey (a functional language).

Definition 6.1 (Type System)

1. A set of rules for inferring *types* of program expressions from types of subexpressions or other program expressions is called a *type system*.
2. *Type inference* is the activity of computing a type, if possible, for a given program expression.
3. *Type checking* is the task of verifying that, given an expression and a type, the expression actually has that type – according to a given set of type inference rules.

6.2.1 Type System for Boolean and Integer Expressions

Definition 6.2 (Context and Typing Rules)

1. Consider the syntactic category E of expressions defined by the grammar

$$E ::= \text{true} \ | \ n \ | \ x \ | \ E \ \&\& \ E \ | \ !E \ | \ E < E \ | \ E + E \ | \ -E \qquad (6.1)$$

where n and x are metavariables ranging over integer literals (5, 127, -53, etc.) and identifiers (e.g., x1, y_init, average), respectively. We choose two types, int and bool, and design a type system for proving judgments of the form

$$\Gamma \rhd E : \tau, \qquad\qquad\qquad\qquad\qquad\qquad\qquad\qquad\qquad (6.2)$$

where τ is either int or bool and Γ is a *context* that binds identifiers to types. Contexts are generated by

$$\Gamma ::= \text{empty} \ | \ \Gamma, x : \tau; \qquad\qquad\qquad\qquad\qquad\qquad\qquad (6.3)$$

here empty is the context with no bindings, and $\Gamma, x : \tau$ binds x to τ and honors all bindings of Γ as well. We restrict contexts in (6.3) to those Γ that list identifiers x at most once. We also identify contexts that merely permute pairs $x : \tau$ and write

$$x : \tau \in \Gamma$$

to say that the pair $x : \tau$ occurs in Γ. In that case, we often write $\Gamma(x)$ for this τ.
2. The type system is given in Figure 6.2. We call a judgment *valid* if it can be proved by means of the system's inference rules.

$$\dfrac{\dfrac{\dfrac{\overline{\texttt{x : int} \triangleright \texttt{53 : int}}\ \text{Lit}}{\texttt{x : int} \triangleright \texttt{-53 : int}}\ \text{Min} \quad \overline{\texttt{x : int} \triangleright \texttt{x : int}}\ \text{Id}}{\texttt{x : int} \triangleright (\texttt{-53)} + \texttt{x : int}}\ \text{Add} \quad \overline{\texttt{x : int} \triangleright \texttt{x : int}}\ \text{Id}}{\texttt{x : int} \triangleright (\texttt{-53)} + \texttt{x} < \texttt{x : bool}}\ \text{LT}$$

$$\dfrac{\dfrac{\overline{\texttt{x : int} \triangleright \texttt{true : bool}}\ \text{Tr}}{\texttt{x : int} \triangleright \texttt{!true : bool}}\ \text{Neg} \qquad \cdots}{\texttt{x : int} \triangleright (\texttt{!true)} \ \&\& \ ((\texttt{-53)} + \texttt{x} < \texttt{x)} : \texttt{bool}}\ \text{And}$$

Figure 6.3. Certificate for x : bool ▷ !true && (((-53) + x) < x) : bool (complete proof).

The rule And states: in order to prove that E1 && E2 has type bool in context Γ, we must prove that E1 and E2 both have type bool in that same context. The rule LT means that we can prove E1 < E2 to have type bool in context Γ if E1 and E2 both can be proven to have type int in that context, and so forth. A complete proof for the judgment

$$\texttt{x : bool} \triangleright \texttt{!true \&\& (((-53) + x) < x) : bool}$$

is given in Figure 6.3. Not every judgment Γ ▷ E : τ has a proof. For any context Γ, the judgment

$$\Gamma \triangleright \texttt{!((-x) < true)} : \tau$$

cannot be proven for τ being int or bool. Obviously, a type system should allow us to prove judgments only if they imply safe program executions.

The verification task of type checking is quite simple if the verifier receives not only the expression and type but also the details of a type inference proof demonstrating that some expression E has type τ. It is easier to check the correctness of the proof in Figure 6.3 than it is to produce it in the first place. This discrepancy of difficulty is generally more pronounced the more expressive the type system is. But even for the most complex type systems, one need merely verify that all the inference rules of the proof have been used correctly. However, we need *both* – type inference and type checking – for a viable framework for validating secure information flow in mobile code.

- Type inference is used to prove that a program is secure in this sense. This can be a complex and time-consuming task, and clearly it is not a due burden on all users of mobile code to perform this analysis prior to the local execution of a program.
- Rather, the verification (i.e. type inference) is done centrally, presumably by the producer of that code, and this mobile code together with its *certificate* (the type inference proof) is shipped to a remote code consumer who can instantly verify the certificate, through type checking, before she uses that code as often as she wishes.

It is worth stressing that such *a framework for trusted mobile code cannot be implemented with cryptographic techniques alone.* We can use cryptography to authenticate the origin of mobile code, or to ensure the fact that this code has not been tampered with in transit. But even if all of that has been established, we know nothing about the actual behavior of the program when it is being executed locally, although there do exist circumstances under which we may decide to trust mobile code that comes from certain sources (e.g., your IT contractor – just kidding!).

EXERCISES 6.2

1. Explain in detail why there cannot exist proofs for the judgments

    $\Gamma \triangleright !((-x) < \text{true}) : \text{int}$ and $\Gamma \triangleright !((-x) < \text{true}) : \text{bool}$.

2. Show that the judgment

    $x : \text{int}, y : \text{int} \triangleright !((!\text{true}) \&\& ((-12) + (x + (-y)))) < y) : \text{bool}$.

    is valid.

3. The advantage of program certification is that a user need only verify that the certificate of a program is valid. Investigate in detail what kind of trust or knowledge of the user is implied by this.

6.2.2 Specifying Secure Information Flow

Any analysis of secure information flow has to be carried out against a *specification* that states which kind of information flow is considered to be secure. We express such specifications as extensions of the classical Bell and La Padula model of security classes.

Definition 6.3 (Information Flow Policy)

1. An *information flow policy* is a finite set SCLs, whose members are *security classes*, together with $\leq$, a subset of SCLs $\times$ SCLs.
2. We call $\leq$ a *permissible flow relation*, where $\tau \leq \tau'$ means that information of security class τ is permitted to flow to security class τ'.
3. We further demand that $\leq$ be
   * reflexive ($\tau \leq \tau$ for all $\tau \in$ SCLs),
   * transitive (for all $\tau, \sigma, \nu: \tau \leq \sigma$ and $\sigma \leq \nu$ imply $\tau \leq \nu$), and
   * antisymmetric (for all τ and $\sigma: \tau \leq \sigma$ and $\sigma \leq \tau$ imply $\tau = \sigma$).
4. Moreover, for each τ and τ' in SCLs, there exist elements $\tau \wedge \tau'$ and $\tau \vee \tau'$ in SCLs that satisfy:
   (inf) • $\tau \wedge \tau' \leq \tau$,
         • $\tau \wedge \tau' \leq \tau'$, and
         • for all $\sigma \in$ SCLs that satisfy $\sigma \leq \tau$ and $\sigma \leq \tau'$, we have $\sigma \leq \tau \wedge \tau'$;
   (sup) • $\tau \leq \tau \vee \tau'$,
         • $\tau' \leq \tau \vee \tau'$, and
         • for all $\sigma \in$ SCLs that satisfy $\tau \leq \sigma$ and $\tau' \leq \sigma$, we have $\tau \vee \tau' \leq \sigma$.

The structure

   (SCLs, $\leq, \wedge, \vee$)

is an example of a finite *lattice*. We call $\tau \wedge \tau'$ and $\tau \vee \tau'$ the *infimum* and *supremum* of τ and τ', respectively.

Remark 6.4

In a finite lattice, we always have a least and a largest element L and H, respectively. The element L is the infimum of all lattice elements, whereas H is the supremum of all lattice elements.

Observe the operational meaning of infima: checking whether the flows $\tau \leq \sigma$ and $\tau' \leq \sigma$ both are permissible amounts to verifying whether the *single* flow $\tau \vee \tau' \leq \sigma$ is so. Dually, checking whether both flows $\sigma \leq \tau$ and $\sigma \leq \tau'$ are permissible reduces to verifying the permissibility of the single flow $\sigma \leq \tau \wedge \tau'$.

Proposition 6.5 (Justification of Lattice Structure)
The assumption that (SCLs, $\leq, \wedge, \vee,$ L, H) *is a finite lattice with least* (L) *and largest* (H) *element is justified.*

Proof

1. SCLs finite: Clearly, we have no need for modeling infinitely many security classes.
2. $\leq$ reflexive: The relation $\tau \leq \tau$ must hold for all $\tau \in$ SCLs to ensure consistency; information that one process or agent of class τ is permitted to access should be allowed to flow to some process or agent of that same security class.
3. $\leq$ transitive: If $\tau \leq \sigma$ and $\sigma \leq \nu$ in SCLs then we argue that information can flow from τ to ν, since it is first permitted to flow to σ (via $\tau \leq \sigma$) and then to ν (via $\sigma \leq \nu$). Thus, $\tau \leq \nu$ should hold as well.
4. $\leq$ antisymmetric: If $\tau \leq \sigma$ and $\sigma \leq \tau$ hold, then any information is allowed to flow between the security classes τ and σ in any direction. Thus there is no need to differentiate between these security classes; that is, τ should be equal to σ.
5. Existence of L: Programming constants and any publicly available data should be able to flow into *any* security class. Since a least element L of SCLs satisfies $L \leq \tau$ for all $\tau \in$ SCLs, the class L is an ideal model for the security class of such data.
6. Existence of H: This follows from the existence of L; see Exercise 6.3-2(b).
7. $\leq$ has suprema: Let ν be a security class such that information can flow to ν from τ and σ; for example, ν could be H. It is generally more efficient to assume the existence of some $\tau \vee \sigma$, for then we can express the former two permissible flows via a single permissible flow $\tau \vee \sigma \leq \nu$.
8. $\leq$ has infima: This follows from the existence of suprema; see Exercise 6.3-2(a).　□

Example 6.6 (Information Flow Policies)

1. There may be no other security classes except L and H. The only permissible nontrivial information flow is given by

   $L \leq H.$

   All our program examples will be considered with respect to this simple information flow policy.
2. We may represent a strictly hierarchical system of information flow as a linear chain (we write $\tau < \tau'$ for $\tau \leq \tau'$ and $\tau \neq \tau'$)

   $L < \tau_1 < \tau_2 < \cdots < \tau_n < H,$

   where information can flow (if at all) from τ_i to τ_j through only one path. What are $\tau_i \wedge \tau_j$ and $\tau_i \vee \tau_j$ in this case? One such example is the chain

   unclassified $<$ confidential $<$ secret $<$ top secret. 　　　　　　　　(6.4)
3. *Monotone access structures* can also be modeled in this way. Given a set A of access privileges or agents, a monotone access structure is a family $\mathcal{A}$ of sets such that $A \in \mathcal{A}$

and $A \subseteq B$ imply $B \in \mathcal{A}$. The information flow policy is modeled by subset inclusion: information may flow from A to B in $\mathcal{A}$ if and only if $A \subseteq B$. For example, if B equals

$$\{\text{soc.sec.nr, medical\_record, financial\_record, criminal\_record}\} \quad (6.5)$$

for Bob, then Alice has access to Bob's medical record only if Alice's security class A contains B. Note that this structure does not model implicit or implied flow. For example, any one with access to Bob's medical record presumably has access also to his social security number.

EXERCISES 6.3

1. We extend the definition of infima and suprema to finite subsets of SCLs. For $\{\tau_1, \tau_2, \ldots, \tau_n\}$, we define the supremum of that set recursively as the supremum of τ_1 and the supremum of the smaller set $\{\tau_2, \ldots, \tau_n\}$. Infima are defined in a similar way. Argue that these definitions are independent of the order in which we listed these elements, so these notions are well-defined.

2. (a) Prove: If suprema $\tau \vee \tau'$ exist for all τ and τ' in SCLs, then their infima $\tau \wedge \tau'$ exist as well. (*Hint:* Call $\nu \in$ SCLs a *lower bound* of τ and τ' if and only if $\nu \leq \tau$ and $\nu \leq \tau'$ hold; consider the supremum of all these lower bounds.)

   (b) Use part (a) (for the general versions of suprema and infima from Exercise 1) to show that the existence of L implies the existence of H.

3. Let SCLs be a finite set of security classes with a flow relation $\leq$ that is reflexive, transitive, and antisymmetric. Although SCLs may not have suprema, infima, L, or H, we can always embed SCLs into a finite lattice such that the given flow relation $\leq$ is preserved. Let $\mathcal{L}$ be the set of subsets L of SCLs that are *downwards closed*:

   $$\sigma \leq \tau \ \& \ \tau \in L \implies \sigma \in L.$$

   The information flow relation on $\mathcal{L}$ is given by *subset inclusion*: information may flow from $L_1 \in \mathcal{L}$ to $L_2 \in \mathcal{L}$ if and only if $L_1 \subseteq L_2$.

   (a) Show that the map $f : \text{SCLs} \to \mathcal{L}$, specified by

   $$f(\tau) \stackrel{\text{def}}{=} \{\sigma \in \text{SCLs} \mid \sigma \leq \tau\}, \quad (6.6)$$

   is well-defined (i.e., $f(\tau)$ is downwards closed for all $\tau \in$ SCLs).

   (b) Show that $\tau \leq \tau'$ holds if and only if $f(\tau)$ is a subset of $f(\tau')$.

   (c) Show that $f(\tau) = f(\tau')$ implies $\tau = \tau'$ (i.e., f is injective).

   (d) Show that $(\mathcal{L}, \subseteq, \cap, \cup)$ is a finite lattice.

   (e) Which subsets function as L and H, respectively?

6.2.3 A Core Programming Language

We study a core imperative programming language with simple block structures but without procedures, records, arrays, or other data structures. Our analysis of secure information flow must therefore be adapted to each additional language construct that is added to this core. Some of these language extensions (e.g. arrays) result in rather straightforward adaptations of our secure information flow analysis and are included as exercises. Other additions, such as nondeterminism or parallelism, make our analysis more difficult and will not be discussed in this section.

Definition 6.7 (Core Programming Language)
We specify our core programming language by the grammar

$$p ::= e \mid c, \tag{6.7}$$

$$e ::= n \mid x \mid \text{true} \mid e + e \mid e - e \mid e == e \mid !e \mid e < e, \tag{6.8}$$

$$c ::= e = e \mid c; c \mid \text{if } (e) \{c\} \text{ else } \{c\}$$
$$\quad \text{while } e \{c\} \mid \text{letvar } x = e \text{ in } \{c\}.$$

The syntactic category p of *program phrases* consists of *expressions* e and *commands* c. The syntactic category e of expressions ranges over metavariables denoting integer literals (n) and identifiers (x). Further, expressions formed via addition, subtraction, and boolean expressions are formed through the constant `true`, negation (`!e`), equality (e1 == e2), and the strictly-less-than relation (e1 < e2) on integer expressions. Finally, commands c are built from assignments

```
x = e;
```

by means of sequencing

```
c1 ; c2
```

the if-statements

```
if (e) {c1} else {c2}
```

and while-statements

```
while e {c}
```

and a local declaration

```
letvar x = e in {c}
```

whose intuitive meaning is that expression e is evaluated, its value *bound* to x, and then command c executed with that binding. Moreover, this binding is ineffective outside of command c or within those portions of c that may rebind x.

You may have noticed that this grammar allows for the formation of phrases that won't execute safely. For example,

```
x = !5 + 3
```

makes no sense because addition expects two integer expressions but `!5` is a boolean expression. This is precisely where the conventional application of types and type systems, such as the toy example from Figure 6.2, steps in. A language designer encodes such constraints as typing rules, which may be explicit or implicit in the syntax of a programming language, and a compiler then performs type inference based on that type system. In Exercise 6.4-1, you are asked to design such a type system. Our analysis of secure information flow already assumes that language expressions are analyzed only if they have been proven to be well-typed in the conventional sense. Thus we design a *separate* type system that merely reasons about information flow.

A realistic core language would also include the boolean constant `false`, numerical constants such as 0, as well as multiplication, division, and modulo operations on integer expressions. In example programs, we feel free to write code that is not strictly contained in the core as defined in (6.7); our analysis easily extends to such a larger core language. Note that the absence of input–output facilities is not a real restriction, since this can easily be modeled by identifiers (x): input is "read" by accessing designated "input" identifiers; output is "written" by assigning it to designated "output" identifiers.

EXERCISE 6.4

1. We sketch a conventional type system for the core programming language of (6.7). Contexts Γ are generated by

$$\Gamma ::= \texttt{empty} \mid \Gamma, x : \tau, \tag{6.9}$$

where τ is `int` or `bool`. We have two kinds of judgments[1]

$$\Gamma \rhd p : \tau, \tag{6.10}$$

$$\Gamma \rhd p : \texttt{comm}, \tag{6.11}$$

where p is a program phrase of our core language. We give four typing rules as examples:

$$\frac{x : \tau \in \Gamma}{\Gamma \rhd x : \tau,} \; \text{Id}$$

$$\frac{\Gamma \rhd x : \tau, \quad \Gamma \rhd e : \tau}{\Gamma \rhd x \; \texttt{=} \; e : \texttt{comm},} \; \text{Ass}$$

$$\frac{\Gamma \rhd e : \texttt{bool}, \quad \Gamma \rhd c : \texttt{comm}}{\Gamma \rhd \texttt{while} \; e \; \{c\} : \texttt{comm},} \; \text{Wh}$$

$$\frac{\Gamma \rhd x \; \texttt{=} \; e : \texttt{comm}, \quad \Gamma \rhd c : \texttt{comm}}{\Gamma \rhd \texttt{letvar} \; x \; \texttt{=} \; e \; \texttt{in} \; \{c\} : \texttt{comm}.} \; \text{Let}$$

(a) Complete this type system for the entire core language of (6.7).
(b) Explain how and why the typing rule Let is intuitively "correct".
(c) Prove that your type system is "sound" with respect to the grammar (6.7):
    (i) if (6.10) holds, then p is an expression e;
    (ii) if (6.11) holds, then p is a command c.
(d) In the previous item, are the converses valid as well?

---

[1] Recall that we write τ for `int` or `bool`.

6.2.4 Formal Semantics of Core Language

Before we design a type system for reasoning about information flow in programs, we need a precise operational model of program executions. Such a formal semantics not only clarifies the meaning of programs written in the core language, it also provides the designer of the type system for secure information flow with a rigorous framework against which it is then possible to verify that the designed type system is *sound* – in other words, that programs it certifies as being secure *are* secure with respect to their formal execution semantics.

Definition 6.8 (Model of Stores)
We formalize the evaluation of program phrases as judgments, one for each kind of program phrase: expressions e and commands c. These judgments are all relative to a model ρ of the store, or memory, that program phrases operate on. A simple but sufficiently expressive model of stores are functions ρ that associate integer values n to finitely many identifiers x. We write $\rho[x \mapsto n]$ for the store that behaves like ρ except that it maps x to n.

An example store is a function ρ that maps x1 to -7, maps x2 to 3456, and is undefined for all other identifiers.

Definition 6.9 (Judgments for Evaluation)

1. The judgments for the evaluation of expressions e have the form

$$\rho \vdash e \Rightarrow v, \tag{6.12}$$

   meaning that *expression e evaluates to integer or boolean value v in store ρ*.
2. Similarly, the judgment for the evaluation of a command is

$$\rho \vdash c \Rightarrow \rho', \tag{6.13}$$

   meaning that the *execution of command c transforms the store ρ into the store ρ'* (provided that this execution terminates).

The inference system for these judgments is given in Figure 6.4. The rules Lit and Tr say that literals and `true` are already values. The rule Id allows us to inspect the contents of stores. The typing rules Sub, Add, Eq, Neg, and LT all follow the same pattern: first compute the values for all arguments, then use these to compute the composed value. For example, plus(4, -7) denotes the literal -3 and equal?(*true, false*) denotes *false*. The rules Seq, IfT, and IfF encode the familiar semantics of these constructs. Note, however, that we reduced the evaluation of while-statements to the repeated evaluation of an if-statement in Wh. This is justified because `while e {c}` is operationally equivalent to `if (e) {c; while e {c}} else {}`. The rule Let is the most complex one, but it matches exactly the intuitive meaning of `letvar x = e in {c}`: we evaluate the expression e in the current store ρ to some value n; then we evaluate the command c in the *updated* store $\rho[x \mapsto n]$, in which x is now bound to the current value of e, to obtain a resulting store ρ' that is the net effect of `letvar x = e in {c}`.

$$\frac{}{\rho \vdash \mathtt{n} \Rightarrow n} \ \text{Lit} \qquad\qquad \frac{\rho(\mathtt{x}) \text{ defined}}{\rho \vdash \mathtt{x} \Rightarrow \rho(\mathtt{x})} \ \text{Id}$$

$$\frac{}{\rho \vdash \mathtt{true} \Rightarrow true} \ \text{Tr} \qquad\qquad \frac{\rho \vdash \mathtt{e1} \Rightarrow n_1, \quad \rho \vdash \mathtt{e2} \Rightarrow n_2}{\rho \vdash \mathtt{e1} + \mathtt{e2} \Rightarrow \mathrm{plus}(n_1, n_2)} \ \text{Add}$$

$$\frac{\rho \vdash \mathtt{e1} \Rightarrow n_1, \quad \rho \vdash \mathtt{e2} \Rightarrow n_2}{\rho \vdash \mathtt{e1} - \mathtt{e2} \Rightarrow \mathrm{subtr}(n_1, n_2)} \ \text{Sub} \qquad \frac{\rho \vdash \mathtt{e1} \Rightarrow b_1, \quad \rho \vdash \mathtt{e2} \Rightarrow b_2}{\rho \vdash \mathtt{e1}\ \mathtt{==}\ \mathtt{e2} \Rightarrow \mathrm{equal?}(b_1, b_2)} \ \text{Eq}$$

$$\frac{\rho \vdash \mathtt{e} \Rightarrow b}{\rho \vdash \mathtt{!e} \Rightarrow \mathrm{not}(b)} \ \text{Neg} \qquad\qquad \frac{\rho \vdash \mathtt{e1} \Rightarrow n_1, \quad \rho \vdash \mathtt{e2} \Rightarrow n_2}{\rho \vdash \mathtt{e1} < \mathtt{e2} \Rightarrow \mathrm{less\_than?}(n_1, n_2)} \ \text{LT}$$

$$\frac{\rho \vdash \mathtt{e} \Rightarrow n}{\rho \vdash \mathtt{x = e} \Rightarrow \rho[\mathtt{x} \mapsto n]} \ \text{Ass} \qquad\qquad \frac{\rho \vdash \mathtt{c1} \Rightarrow \rho', \quad \rho' \vdash \mathtt{c2} \Rightarrow \rho''}{\rho \vdash \mathtt{c1;\ c2} \Rightarrow \rho''} \ \text{Seq}$$

$$\frac{\rho \vdash \mathtt{e} \Rightarrow true, \quad \rho \vdash \mathtt{c1} \Rightarrow \rho'}{\rho \vdash \mathtt{if\ (e)\ \{c1\}\ else\ \{c2\}} \Rightarrow \rho'} \ \text{IfT} \qquad \frac{\rho \vdash \mathtt{e} \Rightarrow false, \quad \rho \vdash \mathtt{c2} \Rightarrow \rho'}{\rho \vdash \mathtt{if\ (e)\ \{c1\}\ else\ \{c2\}} \Rightarrow \rho'} \ \text{IfF}$$

$$\frac{\rho \vdash \mathtt{if\ (e)\ \{c;\ while\ e\ \{c\}\}\ else\ \{\}} \Rightarrow \rho'}{\rho \vdash \mathtt{while\ e\ \{c\}} \Rightarrow \rho'} \ \text{Wh} \qquad \frac{\rho \vdash \mathtt{e} \Rightarrow n, \quad \rho[\mathtt{x} \mapsto n] \vdash \mathtt{c} \Rightarrow \rho'}{\rho \vdash \mathtt{letvar\ x = e\ in\ \{c\}} \Rightarrow \rho'} \ \text{Let}$$

Figure 6.4. An inference system for the evaluation of expressions and commands.

Example 6.10 (Formal Program Evaluation)

Consider the command phrase c given by

```
x = 0;
while (0 < y) {
    x = x + y;
    y = y - 1;
}
```

For any store ρ with $\rho(y) = 2$, we can use the typing rules just described to establish the judgment

$$\rho \vdash c \Rightarrow \rho[\mathtt{x} \mapsto 3][\mathtt{y} \mapsto 0]. \tag{6.14}$$

Since this is a sequential composition, we need to apply Seq as the last typing rule. Thus it suffices to show that

$$\rho[\mathtt{x} \mapsto 0] \vdash \mathtt{while}\ \ldots \Rightarrow \rho[\mathtt{x} \mapsto 3][\mathtt{y} \mapsto 0]$$

holds. Since this is a while-statement, we can only apply the typing rule Wh, so it suffices to show that

$$\rho[\mathtt{x} \mapsto 0] \vdash \mathtt{if}\ (0 < \mathtt{y})\{\ \mathtt{x = x + y};\ \mathtt{y = y - 1};\ \mathtt{while}\ \ldots\ \}\ \mathtt{else}\ \{\}$$
$$\Rightarrow \rho[\mathtt{x} \mapsto 3][\mathtt{y} \mapsto 0]$$

holds, and so on. Please complete the proof.

Remark 6.11 (Inversion Principle)

In Example 6.10, we said that we can apply "only" one typing rule at each point of the argument. This is actually a blessing since it means that we won't obtain a search space that grows exponentially. We put this to good use later on when we prove the soundness of our secure information flow analysis with respect to our formal semantics of program evaluation.

EXERCISES 6.5

1. Let $\rho(z) = 15$, $\rho(x) = 17$, and $\rho(y) = 39$. Prove

$$\rho \vdash !((z - (x + (25 - y))) == 12) \Rightarrow true.$$

2. Consider the command c, given by

```
x = 2;
letvar x = 3 + z in {
  z = x + y;
  letvar x = 4 + z in {
    z = x + y;
  }
}
```

   (a) Let ρ be a store such that $\rho(x) = 0$, $\rho(y) = 0$, and $\rho(z) = 5$. For which ρ' do we have $\rho \vdash c \Rightarrow \rho'$? Prove your claim.
   (b) Explain which parts of the command c are under the scope of the first letvar construct of the second line of code.
3. (a) Prove

$$\rho \vdash \text{if } (x < y + 2) \; \{x = y;\} \text{ else } \{y = x;\} \Rightarrow \rho[x \mapsto -3],$$

   where $\rho(x) = -2$ and $\rho(y) = -3$.
   (b) Complete the proof sketched in Example 6.10.
4. Prove that the operational semantics in Figure 6.4 is *deterministic*: "Let c be any command phrase and let ρ, ρ', ρ'' be program stores such that the judgments $\rho \vdash c \Rightarrow \rho'$ and $\rho \vdash c \Rightarrow \rho''$ are valid; then ρ' equals ρ''. You may first have to prove a corresponding statement about judgments of the form $\rho \vdash e \Rightarrow v$.

6.2.5 Analysis of Secure Information Flow

In Exercise 6.4-1 (p. 214) we sketched a conventional type system that establishes data type compatibility for our core language from (6.7). We now assume that program phrases are well-typed in that sense and introduce a different type system that validates the secure information flow of programs. Then we prove that programs that are well-typed with respect to this new type system satisfy a certain noninterference property, thereby establishing the correctness of this type system. We work with an arbitrary finite lattice of security classes,

$$(\text{SCLs}, \leq, \wedge, \vee),$$

with least and greatest elements L and H, respectively.

Definition 6.12 (Types for Secure Information Flow)

1. The types of our system are generated by the following grammar:

$$\sigma ::= \tau \mid \text{var}\,\tau \mid \text{com}\,\tau, \tag{6.15}$$

where τ ranges over elements of the set SCLs of security classes. The judgments of our type system are of the form

$$\Gamma \triangleright p : \sigma, \tag{6.16}$$

where contexts Γ are defined by

$$\Gamma ::= \text{empty} \mid \Gamma, x : \text{var}\,\tau. \tag{6.17}$$

2. We extend the permissible flow relation $\leq$ (a subset of SCLs $\times$ SCLs) to all types σ.
   - We define
   $$\text{var}\,\tau \leq \text{var}\,\tau' \iff \tau \leq \tau'; \tag{6.18}$$
   - but for command types we set
   $$\text{com}\,\tau \leq \text{com}\,\tau' \iff \tau' \leq \tau. \tag{6.19}$$

3. We call σ a *subtype* of σ' if and only if $\sigma \leq \sigma'$.
4. We write $\Gamma[x : \tau]$ for the context that behaves the same as Γ – except for x, which it binds to type τ.

We mean to design a type system for the judgments in (6.16) such that expressions e only have types τ or var τ and commands only have type com τ.

Remark 6.13 (Intuitive Meaning of Judgments)

The intuitive meaning of $\Gamma \triangleright p : \sigma$ is that σ *is the security class of program phrase* p *in context* Γ. More specifically:

- $\Gamma \triangleright e : \tau$ means that no subexpression of e has a security class *higher* than τ in context Γ;
- $\Gamma \triangleright x : \text{var}\,\tau$ means that identifier x may store values computed from expressions of security class τ or *lower*;
- $\Gamma \triangleright c : \text{com}\,\tau$ means that every identifier x updated in the command c has security class τ or *higher*.

Note the dual interpretation of var τ and com τ, justifying (6.19). The type inference system for these judgments is given in Figure 6.5. The rules Lit and Tr say that literals and the constant `true` are in the lowest security class (since they are public information). The rule Id allows us to access the type information provided in contexts. The rule SubI enables us to increase the security class associated with identifiers x when viewed as expressions. The rules Add, Sub, Neg, Eq, and LT all work on the same principle: compute the security class of each argument and form their supremum as the security class representing the entire expression.

Example 6.14 (No Read Up)

If $x : \text{var}\,H$ and $y : \text{var}\,L$, then the rule Add says that $x + y$ should have type $L \vee H = H$. Indeed, this makes sense, for x is public and so one could recover y from public knowledge of $x + y$. Thus the latter should have security class H, which is exactly what is inferred by our type inference system.

$$\frac{x : \text{var}\,\tau \in \Gamma}{\Gamma \triangleright x : \text{var}\,\tau} \; \text{Id} \qquad\qquad \frac{\Gamma \triangleright x : \text{var}\,\tau \quad \tau \leq \tau'}{\Gamma \triangleright x : \tau'} \; \text{SubI}$$

$$\frac{}{\Gamma \triangleright \texttt{true} : L} \; \text{Tr} \qquad\qquad \frac{\Gamma \triangleright e1 : \tau_1 \quad \Gamma \triangleright e2 : \tau_2}{\Gamma \triangleright e1\ \texttt{+}\ e2 : \tau_1 \vee \tau_2} \; \text{Add}$$

$$\frac{\Gamma \triangleright e1 : \tau_1 \quad \Gamma \triangleright e2 : \tau_2}{\Gamma \triangleright e1\ \texttt{-}\ e2 : \tau_1 \vee \tau_2} \; \text{Sub} \qquad\qquad \frac{\Gamma \triangleright e1 : \tau_1 \quad \Gamma \triangleright e2 : \tau_2}{\Gamma \triangleright e1\ \texttt{==}\ e2 : \tau_1 \vee \tau_2} \; \text{Eq}$$

$$\frac{\Gamma \triangleright e : \tau}{\Gamma \triangleright \texttt{!}e : \tau} \; \text{Neg} \qquad\qquad \frac{\Gamma \triangleright e1 : \tau_1 \quad \Gamma \triangleright e2 : \tau_2}{\Gamma \triangleright e1\ \texttt{<}\ e2 : \tau_1 \vee \tau_2} \; \text{LT}$$

$$\frac{\Gamma \triangleright x : \text{var}\,\tau, \quad \Gamma \triangleright e : \tau, \quad \tau' \leq \tau}{\Gamma \triangleright x\ \texttt{=}\ e : \text{com}\,\tau'} \; \text{Ass} \qquad\qquad \frac{\Gamma \triangleright c1 : \sigma \quad \Gamma \triangleright c2 : \sigma}{\Gamma \triangleright c1;\ c2 : \sigma} \; \text{Seq}$$

$$\frac{}{\Gamma \triangleright n : L} \; \text{Lit} \qquad\qquad \frac{\Gamma \triangleright e : \tau, \quad \Gamma \triangleright c1 : \text{com}\,\tau, \quad \Gamma \triangleright c2 : \text{com}\,\tau, \quad \tau' \leq \tau}{\Gamma \triangleright \texttt{if (e) \{c1\} else \{c2\}} : \text{com}\,\tau'} \; \text{If}$$

$$\frac{\Gamma \triangleright e : \tau, \quad \Gamma \triangleright c : \text{com}\,\tau, \quad \tau' \leq \tau}{\Gamma \triangleright \texttt{while e \{c\}} : \text{com}\,\tau'} \; \text{Wh} \qquad\qquad \frac{\Gamma \triangleright e : \tau \quad \Gamma[x : \text{var}\,\tau] \triangleright c : \text{com}\,\tau'}{\Gamma \triangleright \texttt{letvar x = e in \{c\}} : \text{com}\,\tau'} \; \text{Let}$$

Figure 6.5. A type inference system for the analysis of secure information flow in program phrases.

The rule Ass says that if x and e have security level τ, then the assignment x = e may have any security level that is less than or equal to τ. In particular, a "write up" is possible.

Example 6.15 (Write Up)
We prove

$$x : \text{var}\,H, \; y : \text{var}\,L \triangleright x\ \texttt{=}\ y : \text{com}\,H,$$

meaning that the information contained in y is permitted to flow into x:

$$\frac{\dfrac{}{x : \text{var}\,H, \; y : \text{var}\,L \triangleright x : \text{var}\,H} \; \text{Id} \quad \dfrac{\dfrac{}{x : \text{var}\,H, \; y : \text{var}\,L \triangleright y : \text{var}\,L \quad L \leq H} \; \text{Id}}{x : \text{var}\,H, \; y : \text{var}\,L \triangleright y : H} \; \text{SubI} \quad H \leq H}{x : \text{var}\,H, \; y : \text{var}\,L \triangleright x\ \texttt{=}\ y : \text{com}\,H.} \; \text{Ass}$$

The rule Seq expresses that a composition has a certain security level only if its two commands already have that security level. The rule If is similar to the one for assignments: if we establish that the boolean guard e has security level τ and that the two branches c1 and c2 have security level com τ, then the if-statement may have any security level that is less than or equal to τ. The rule While functions in the same way, only the two branches are reduced to the body c.

The rule Let is the most complex one. To prove that `letvar x = e in {c}` has security class com τ' in context Γ, we need to:

(i) prove that e has security class τ in that same context; and
(ii) use the updated context $\Gamma[x : \tau]$ to prove that the body c has security class com τ'.

EXERCISE 6.6

1. Informally justify the proof rules of Figure 6.5 based on the intuitive meaning of judgments from Remark 6.13.

6.2.6 Correctness of Analysis

In Example 6.14 we discussed a simple notion of security – namely, that it should not be possible to assign a security class to some expression e such that this expression contains an identifier with a higher security class. We prove this as a property of our type inference system.

Proposition 6.16 (No Read Up)
Let e *be any expression that has security class* τ *in context* Γ. *Then* $\Gamma(x) \leq \tau$ *holds*[2] *for all identifiers* x *occurring in* e.

Proof We proceed by mathematical induction on the number of proof rules that are used to derive

$$\Gamma \rhd e : \tau \tag{6.20}$$

and argue by a case analysis on the rule that was applied last in the proof of (6.20). Since our type inference system is *syntax-directed*, this amounts to doing an induction on the structure of expression e.

1. If e is n or true, there is nothing to show as e then contains no identifiers.
2. If e equals e1 + e2, then the last rule used in the proof of (6.20) must have been Add. Thus
   (a) τ equals $\tau_1 \vee \tau_2$,
   (b) $\Gamma \rhd e1 : \tau_1$ is valid, and
   (c) $\Gamma \rhd e2 : \tau_2$ is valid.
   Let x be an identifier occurring in e.
   (a) If x occurs in e1, then $\Gamma \rhd e1 : \tau_1$ and induction render $\Gamma(x) \leq \tau_1 \leq \tau$.
   (b) Otherwise: x occurs in e2, and $\Gamma \rhd e2 : \tau_2$ together with induction gives us that $\Gamma(x) \leq \tau_2 \leq \tau$.
   In any event, $\Gamma(x) \leq \tau$ as desired.
3. If e equals e1 - e2, e1 == e2, or e1 < e2, then we reason in the same manner as in part 2.
4. If e equals !e1, then the last rule in the proof of (6.20) must have been Neg. Thus $\Gamma \rhd e1 : \tau$ is valid. If x occurs in e, then x occurs in e1 and so $\Gamma(x) \leq \tau$ follows by induction.
5. If e equals x, then the last rule in the proof of (6.20) could not have been Id, for τ is not of the form var τ'. Thus this last rule must have been SubI. Hence there exists some τ' such that $\Gamma(x) = \tau'$ and $\tau' \leq \tau$. Therefore, $\Gamma(x) \leq \tau$. $\square$

We can also show that our type inference system validates the intuition behind judgments for command phrases.

---

[2] Recall that $\Gamma(x)$ denotes the unique σ with $x : \sigma \in \Gamma$.

Proposition 6.17 (No Write Down)

Let c *be any command that has security class* com τ. *Then* $\tau \leq \Gamma(x)$ *holds for all identifiers* x *updated in command* c.

Proof   As in the case of expressions, we may proceed by induction on the structure of the command c in the valid judgment

$$\Gamma \rhd c : \text{com } \tau, \tag{6.21}$$

exploiting that our type system is syntax-directed.

1. If c equals x = e, then the last rule in the proof of (6.21) must have been Ass. Hence there exists some τ' such that
   (i) $\tau \leq \tau'$,
   (ii) $\Gamma \rhd x : \text{var } \tau'$ is valid, and
   (iii) $\Gamma \rhd e : \tau'$ is valid.
   But then $\tau \leq \tau' = \Gamma(x)$, and x is the only identifier updated in c.
2. If c equals c1 ; c2, then the last rule in the proof of (6.21) must have been Seq, so
   (i) $\Gamma \rhd c1 : \text{com } \tau$ is valid and
   (ii) $\Gamma \rhd c2 : \text{com } \tau$ is valid.
   If x is updated in c, then it is updated in c1 or c2. In any event, (i) and (ii), together with induction, ensure that $\tau \leq \tau' = \Gamma(x)$.
3. If c equals if (e) {c1} else {c2}, then the last rule in the proof of (6.21) must have been If. Thus there exists some τ' such that
   (i) $\tau \leq \tau'$,
   (ii) $\Gamma \rhd e : \tau'$,
   (iii) $\Gamma \rhd c1 : \text{com } \tau'$ is valid, and
   (iv) $\Gamma \rhd c2 : \text{com } \tau'$ is valid.
   If x is updated in c, then it is updated in c1 or c2. By (iii), (iv), and induction, we get $\tau \leq \tau' = \Gamma(x)$ in any event.
4. If c equals while e {c1} then the last proof rule of (6.21) must have been Wh, so there exists some τ' such that
   (i) $\tau \leq \tau'$,
   (ii) $\Gamma \rhd e : \tau'$ is valid, and
   (iii) $\Gamma \rhd c1 : \text{com } \tau'$ is valid.
   If x is updated in c, then x is updated in c1. By (iii), we may use induction to infer that $\tau \leq \tau' = \Gamma(x)$.
5. If c equals letvar x = e in {c1} then the last proof rule of (6.21) must have been Let, so there exists some τ' such that
   (i) $\Gamma \rhd e : \tau'$ and
   (ii) $\Gamma[x : \text{var } \tau'] \rhd c1 : \text{com } \tau$
   are all valid. If y is an identifier updated in the program letvar x = e in {c1}, then y is updated in c1. By (i), (ii), and induction, we obtain $\Gamma(y) \leq \tau$. $\square$

Example 6.18

Consider the command c given by

```
if (x == 1) {
  letvar y = 1 in {
    c1; }
} else {
  letvar y = 0 in {
    c2; }
}
```

where c1 and c2 are arbitrary commands that possibly assign to x or y. We can prove that this command has security class com H, even if the context is x : var H, y : var L. This may seem surprising, since there is an implicit flow from x to y. But the rule Let ensures that no information leakage occurs. (Why?)

We are finally in a position to formulate the correctness criterion for our type system that reasons about secure information flow; it is a *noninterference property*.

Noninterference Property

Identifiers in a well-typed program cannot interfere with identifiers that have a lower security level: no program execution that modifies the initial values of the former identifiers influences the final values of the latter ones, *assuming program termination*.

We may also think of this as a *confinement property*: a service process can be prevented from an unauthorized leaking of confidential information about a customer process. This model also applies to flow of data in databases if we think of tables as processes. For example, one may want to prevent the flow of information from a table of pairs (name, salary) to tables that list these attributes separately. The next theorem formalizes and proves this noninterference property. Recall that a store ρ is a function that associates integer or boolean values n to a finite set of identifiers; we denote this set of identifiers as

$$\text{dom}(\rho) \stackrel{\text{def}}{=} \{x \mid \rho(x) \text{ is defined}\}. \tag{6.22}$$

Similarly, we write

$$\text{dom}(\Gamma) \stackrel{\text{def}}{=} \{x \mid \Gamma(x) \text{ is defined}\}. \tag{6.23}$$

Theorem 6.19 (Correctness of Information Flow Analysis)
Suppose that

(1) $\Gamma \triangleright c : \text{com } \tau$,
(2) $\rho \vdash c \Rightarrow \rho'$,
(3) $\nu \vdash c \Rightarrow \nu'$,
(4) $\text{dom}(\rho) = \text{dom}(\nu) \subseteq \text{dom}(\Gamma)$, *and*
(5) $\rho(x) = \nu(x)$ *for all* $x \in \text{dom}(\rho)$ *such that* $\Gamma(x) \leq \tau$.

Then $\rho'(x) = \nu'(x)$ *for all* $x \in \text{dom}(\rho')$ *such that* $\Gamma(x) \leq \tau$.

Proof   We proceed by induction on the "height" of the proof of (2); this allows us to use induction on all subtrees of the tree that proves (2). This boils down to a case analysis on the last rule applied in the proof of (2). We prove only three cases for the sake of illustration and delegate the remaining cases to the exercises.

1. The last rule applied in the proof of (2) is Ass. Therefore,
   (i) c equals x = e,
   (ii) $\rho \vdash e \Rightarrow n$ is valid, and
   (iii) ρ' equals $\rho[x \mapsto n]$
   for some value n, identifier x, and expression e. The last rule applied in the proof of (3) can only be Ass as well. Thus we have
   (ii') $v \vdash e \Rightarrow n'$ is valid and
   (iii') v' equals $v[x \mapsto n']$
   for some value n'. From (1), we obtain the existence of some τ' such that
   (a) $\tau \leq \tau'$,
   (b) $\Gamma \rhd x : \text{var } \tau'$ is valid, and
   (c) $\Gamma \rhd e : \tau'$ is valid.
   Let y be any identifier in $\text{dom}(\rho')$ such that $\Gamma(y) \leq \tau$.
   • If y is different from x, then $y \in \text{dom}(\rho)$ is clear. But then

   $$\begin{aligned} \rho'(y) &= \rho[x \mapsto n](y) \\ &= \rho(y) \\ &= v(y) \quad \text{(by (5))} \\ &= v[x \mapsto n'](y) \\ &= v'(y). \end{aligned}$$ (6.24)

   • Otherwise, y equals x, so $\Gamma(x) \leq \tau$ holds by assumption. From (a) and (b) we have $\tau' = \Gamma(x) \leq \tau \leq \tau'$, so τ equals τ'. Therefore, Proposition 6.16 and (c) imply that $\Gamma(z) \leq \tau$ for all z occurring in e. But then (5) certainly implies that n equals n'. Thus $\rho'(x)$ must equal $v'(x)$.

2. The last rule applied in the proof of (2) is Wh. Hence
   (i) c equals while e {c1}, and
   (ii) $\rho \vdash$ if (e) {c1; while e {c1}} else {} $\Rightarrow \rho'$ is valid
   for some expression e and command c1. The last rule applied in the proof of (3) also can only be Wh. Thus we also have
   (ii') $v \vdash$ if (e) {c1; while e {c1}} else {} $\Rightarrow v'$ is valid.
   From (1), we obtain the existence of some τ' such that
   (a) $\tau \leq \tau'$,
   (b) $\Gamma \rhd e : \tau'$ is valid, and
   (c) $\Gamma \rhd c1 : \text{com } \tau'$ is valid.
   Let x be in $\text{dom}(\rho')$ such that $\Gamma(x) \leq \tau$. Since the proof of (ii) has less height than the proof of (2), we may use induction to infer $\rho'(x) = v'(x)$, *provided* that

   $$\Gamma \rhd \text{if (e) \{c1; while e \{c1\}\} else \{\}} : \text{com } \tau$$ (6.25)

   is valid. But this readily follows from (a), (b), and (c).

3. The last rule applied in the proof of (2) is Let. Thus we have that
   (i) c equals letvar x = e in {c1},
   (ii) $\rho \vdash e \Rightarrow n$, and
   (2') $\rho[x \mapsto n] \vdash c1 \Rightarrow \rho'$

are valid for some value n, expression e, and command c1. The last rule applied in the proof of (3) can therefore only be Let as well. Hence,

(ii') $\nu \vdash e \Rightarrow n'$ and

(3') $\nu[x \mapsto n'] \vdash c1 \Rightarrow \nu'$

are valid for some value n'. From (1), we obtain the existence of some τ' such that

(a) $\Gamma \rhd e : \tau'$ and

(1') $\Gamma[x : \mathrm{var}\, \tau'] \rhd c1 : \mathrm{com}\, \tau$

are valid. Since the height of the proof for (2') is less than the height of the proof for (2), we may use induction, *provided* that we can establish (1')–(5'). Note that we already have secured (1'), (2'), and (3'). Since $\mathrm{dom}(\rho) = \mathrm{dom}(\nu) \subseteq \mathrm{dom}(\Gamma)$, we have

$$\mathrm{dom}(\rho[x \mapsto n]) = \mathrm{dom}(\nu[x \mapsto n']) \subseteq \mathrm{dom}(\Gamma[x : \mathrm{var}\, \tau']),$$

which is (4'). Let y be different from x with $y \in \mathrm{dom}(\rho[x \mapsto n])$ such that $\Gamma[x : \mathrm{var}\, \tau'](y) \le \tau$. Then $\Gamma(y) \le \tau$ and $y \in \mathrm{dom}(\rho)$ follow. By (5), we thus conclude that $\rho(y) = \nu(y)$ and therefore

$$\rho[x \mapsto n](y) = \nu[x \mapsto n'](y).$$

Hence we can show (5') by proving

$$\Gamma[x : \mathrm{var}\, \tau'](x) \not\le \tau \quad \text{or} \quad n \text{ equals } n'.$$

But since $\Gamma[x : \mathrm{var}\, \tau'](x)$ equals τ', it suffices to show that $\tau' \le \tau$ implies that n equals n'. From $\tau' \le \tau$, (a), and Proposition 6.16, we obtain $\Gamma(y) \le \tau' \le \tau$ for all identifiers y occurring in e. But then $y \in \mathrm{dom}(\rho)$ and (5) imply that $\rho(y) = \nu(y)$. Therefore, n must equal n'.   □

Thus, if c has security class com τ and if c is executed in two stores whose values for identifiers of security classes $\le \tau$ are identical, then (assuming these executions terminate) the final values of all identifiers with security class $< \tau$ are identical in both executions. We can recover the noninterference property (p. 222) from this theorem; see Exercise 6.7-2.

EXERCISES 6.7

1. Formally prove the claim from Example 6.18.
2. Consider the noninterference property (p. 222) for the lattice SCLs $= \{L < H\}$. How can we use Theorem 6.19 to ensure this property?
3. Show: If one can prove $\rho \vdash c \Rightarrow \rho'$ and if $x \in \mathrm{dom}(\rho)$ is not updated in c, then $\rho(x) = \rho'(x)$.
4. Determine the remaining cases required for completion of Theorem 6.19 and then prove them.
5. *Secrecy and integrity* Discuss to what extent our type system and the lattice of security classes treat *secrecy* and *integrity* uniformly. Consider the concrete setting, where the secrecy lattice SCLs is

   unclassified < classified

and the integrity lattice is

trusted < untrusted;

explain what Propositions 6.16 and 6.17 and Theorem 6.19 mean in this context.

6.2.7 Analyses for Extensions of Core Language

Extending our programming language with *locations* (1) allows us to read and write directly to locations in memory. Identifiers (x) allow read and write operations as well, but they are symbolic names representing actual memory locations. For low-level programming or implementations of higher-level source languages, it is desirable to have both syntactic categories at our disposal. In Exercise 6.8-1, you are asked to extend our core language with locations and adapt our secure information flow analysis. The extension of our analysis to *arrays* and *records* is also discussed in the exercises.

We already pointed out that an analysis of secure information flow is quite difficult in the presence of nondeterminism. For example, if x has security class L and our language has a pseudo-random number generator rand(), then the assignment

    x = rand()

should be permissible. But this makes our type inference system incorrect, since the execution of this assignment in the same memory may result in different final values of x. This is a problem not so much of our type system as of the fact that our noninterference property (p. 222) is not suitable for *all* security concerns in program executions. We return to the issue of nondeterminism in the next section.

The degree of difficulty in extending our secure information flow analysis to programs with *procedures* varies with the semantics of procedure invocation mechanisms. Typically, procedures may have parameter identifiers that are

read-only (RO), *read-and-write* (RW), or *write-only* (WO).

The latter, for example, is usually adopted for statements of the form

    return x.

Read-only parameters merely provide input to the procedure without changing the value of the input expression; this typically makes it easier to reason about the overall effect of procedure calls. None of these restrictions apply for read-and-write parameters. An artificial (but very general) syntax for declaring a procedure with the name xpro is

    proc xpro (RO x1, RW x2, WO x3) {c}

where c is a command that can mention the identifiers x1, x2, and x3 only in the sense indicated in the procedure head. We need to extend our system of types from (6.15) to include those of the form

$$\sigma ::= \ldots \mid \text{acc } \tau \mid \text{pro}(\tau_1, \text{var } \tau_2, \text{acc } \tau_3)\tau, \tag{6.26}$$

where acc τ behaves the same as com τ in (6.19) and where τ is the type for which the command c has type com τ – *assuming*[3] that the parameters x1, x2, and x3 have types τ_1, var τ_2, and acc τ_3 (respectively). The invocation of a procedure with name xpro is achieved by

```
xpro(e1,e2,e3);
```

EXERCISES 6.8

1. (a) Extend the core language with a category of memory locations (1) and define a proof rule for
   (i) the evaluation of locations in expressions and
   (ii) the assignment 1 = e.
   For the latter, stores should now bind identifiers (x) to locations, and locations should be bound to values.
   (b) If ρ is a store for this extended core language, note that $\rho(x) = 1$ must imply that ρ is defined for 1. Prove that this extended type inference system for evaluation leaves this property invariant – that is, if ρ is such a store and $\rho \vdash c \Rightarrow \rho'$ is valid, then ρ' has this property as well.
   (c) Extend the type inference system for $\Gamma \triangleright p : \sigma$ to include locations as well.
   (d) Prove that this extended secure information flow analysis is still correct.
2. (a) Extend the core language with a category of arrays (a[1..n]) and define suitable proof rules for the evaluation of array fields a[e] and assignments of the form a[e] = e1. (Your extended core needs syntax that can declare such arrays.) What problems can arise in evaluating a[e], and how do you choose to handle them? Are these problems mitigated if programs can determine the size of an array at run time?
   (b) Extend the type inference system for $\Gamma \triangleright p : \sigma$ to include arrays. Assume that the fields of an array a[1..n] all have the same security class. Why might this be desirable?
   (c) Prove that this extended secure information flow analysis is still correct.
3. (a) Extend the core language with a category of records

   (r,{x1,x2,..,xn})

   where r is the name of the record structure and the xi are the names of the records' components. Define suitable proof rules for the evaluation of record components r.xi and assignments of the form r.xi = e. (Your extended core needs syntax that can declare such records.)
   (b) Extend the type inference system for $\Gamma \triangleright p : \sigma$ to include records as well. Assume that the components of records may have different security classes. Why might this be desirable?
   (c) Prove that this extended secure information flow analysis is still correct.

---

[3] This assumption is realized in a similar way as the assumption that x has security class τ in the inference rule Let of Figure 6.5.

4. Extend the type inference system for judgments $\Gamma \rhd p : \sigma$, where the core language contains procedure declarations and invocations.

6.3 A SEMANTIC APPROACH TO ANALYSIS OF SECURE INFORMATION FLOW

6.3.1 Motivation

The noninterference property defined on page 222 is an informal description of a kind of program security. D. Denning's subsequent work on uncertainty modeled by entropy was an attempt to formalize and justify this notion of secure information flow in programs. However, it is unclear how such a characterization can be proved with respect to a standard programming language semantics, such as a structural operational, axiomatic, or denotational semantics. A major challenge of such characterizations and accompanying certification mechanisms is that they should smoothly scale if applied to nontrivial language extensions (nondeterminism, higher-order functions, exceptions, etc.).

In this section, we demonstrate that the ideas behind the definition of entropy can indeed be used *within* a programming language semantics not only to express noninterference formally but also to verify that programs are secure. The latter aspect can largely be realized as a (relatively standard) task in automated theorem proving. The advantages of such a semantic approach are

- a precise semantic definition of security,
- a *uniform* treatment of language constructs based on the formal semantics of the respective programming constructs, and
- the fact that this analysis of information leakage *includes* termination behavior.[4]

Note that the second point allows us to carry out this program for more realistic languages that feature nondeterminism, exceptions, and other modern language constructs – as long as they have a clear and efficiently modeled semantics. The third point turns out to be a nonissue when the core language itself (without the construct H?? to be defined shortly) is deterministic.

Before we present this approach (due to R. Joshi and K. R. M. Leino), let us point out that a *precise* flow analysis of programs – which considers *all* possible program executions – is generally undecidable. Thus our secure information flow analysis of Section 6.2 cannot be modified to exactly capture this precision; nonetheless, it conservatively abstracts all possible program executions. We say that this analysis is *sound,* since all certified programs are actually secure; this is the content of Theorem 6.19. We call this analysis *incomplete* because it won't certify some programs that really are secure. In this section we work exclusively with the lattice

$$L < H$$

of security classes.

---

[4] That is to say, an attacker is assumed to have the capacity of "observing" nonterminating program executions.

Definition 6.20 (Secure Programs)

1. A command phrase c is *secure in security context* Γ if the initial and final values of those variables x of c with $\Gamma(x) = L$ reveal no information whatsoever about the *initial* values of those variables y in c with $\Gamma(y) = H$.
2. We write ∞ for a special store that assigns a novel value (also denoted by ∞) to variables x. The store and value ∞ simply denote nontermination.

Note that this notion of security is different from the noninterference property (p. 222). For one thing, the latter notion only ensures secure program behavior *provided* that the program terminates. The notion above does include termination information, as we shall see.

Example 6.21 (Secure but Rejected Program)
Consider the program

```
if (x == 0) {
    if (x != 0) {
        y = z;
    }
}
```

where no flow of information from z to y is permitted: $\Gamma(z) = H$ and $\Gamma(y) = L$. Clearly, this program satisfies the noninterference property, for no program execution can reach the assignment y = z. Nonetheless, the type inference system of Section 6.2 classifies this program as being unsecure.

In Section 6.1 we discussed principal ways in which secure information flow is violated in programs. Our program certification based on the type inference system from Figure 6.5 is *compositional*. Compositionality may be a good or a bad thing. Compositionality is good in that it often allows our analyses to scale up to *very large programs*; it implies that a program is classified as being unsecure if one of its subprograms is classified in this manner. This may be desirable, for an attacker could attempt to isolate the effect of that subprogram (e.g., by means of interrupts). However, compositionality may restrict programmers too much or a lot of precision in the analysis may be lost, so more flexibility may be required.

Example 6.22 (Unsecure Subprograms in Secure Programs)
For the security context y : H and x : L, consider the programs

- x = y; x = -53;
- y = x; x = y;
- x = y; x = x - y; and
- if false {x = y;} else {}.

All of these programs are rejected by our type inference system for secure information flow, based on the compositional reasoning of that system. Each of these programs contains an unsecure subprogram. But each of these programs is secure as a unit in the formal sense of Definition 6.20.

We now use a little trick (due to R. Joshi and K. R. M. Leino) to encode a *nondeterministic* version of entropy[5] as an actual programming construct, thereby allowing for a more precise analysis of secure information flow. This trick depends on the fact that we abstract our lattice of security classes, SCLs, to contain only the elements L < H; we may regain the original precision of SCLs by using such abstractions successively with varying sets of classes that are identified with L.

Definition 6.23 (Nondeterministic Uncertainty)

1. We equip our programming language with a command

   H??

   that, if considered in security context Γ, has the following effect: to each identifier x with Γ(x) = H, it assigns a *nondeterministically chosen* value.[6] We also include {} as a legitimate command.[7] For the sake of simplicity, we drop the command phrase

   letvar x = e in { c; }

   from this language.
2. Given a notion of equivalence on program phrases, we say that command phrase c is *noninterfering* if and only if the command phrases c and H??; c; H?? are equivalent.

Of course, the operational definition of H?? can be implemented in only a very approximative sense. But we are actually more interested in its ideal property of encoding perfect nondeterministic uncertainty about the value of any identifier of security type H in a given security context. Note how the program H??; c; H?? behaves. The leftmost H?? erases any knowledge about initial values of any identifiers of type H; then program c is executed in the updated store; finally, the rightmost H?? erases any knowledge about final values of any identifiers of type H. We see intuitively that, if H??; c; H?? is equivalent to program c, then c must satisfy the noninterference property (p. 222).[8] Given a formal semantics of our original core programming language, we merely have to extend this semantics to express the formal meaning of H??. Then we can establish noninterference of programs with as much ease (or difficulty) as we can prove that programs are equivalent. In general, this task – just as the precise analysis of secure information flow – is undecidable. But quite often programs can be proven to be equivalent, and efficiently so, with the support of automated tools.

EXERCISES 6.9

1. For the program in Example 6.21:
   (a) Explain in detail why it satisfies the noninterference property.
   (b) We formalize our discussion by assuming y : L and z : H. Thus, no information may flow from z to y. Assume further that x : τ for an unspecified type τ and

---

[5] A probabilistic notion.

[6] That is to say, if x points to a memory location that stores integers, then any integer allowed by the language implementation may occur as that choice.

[7] It was not part of our grammer in (6.7).

[8] Observe that this claim depends on a sound notion of program equivalence that we still have to define.

attempt to prove that the overall program has security class L. Why does such an
attempt fail for all choices of τ?

2. Explain why none of the programs in Example 6.22 are provably secure – based on
the type system of Figure 6.5. For each program, identify an unsecure subprogram.

3. The nondeterministic choice of the overwriting values in H?? is different from a similar construct, where the overwriting value is chosen probabilistically according to
a (uniform) distribution. Explain why that is so by studying the termination behavior of

```
do { H??; } while (x != 5);
```

under the nondeterministic and probabilistic interpretation, where $\Gamma(x) = H.$[9]

6.3.2 Relational Semantics

For the core language of (6.7), we defined an operational semantics using judgments of
the form

$$\rho \vdash c \Rightarrow \rho'$$

in Figure 6.4, meaning that command phrase c, if evaluated in store ρ, terminates and results in store ρ' upon termination. We can use this formal inference system to derive a
relational semantics of command phrases.

We extend the operational semantics for judgments $\rho \vdash c \Rightarrow \rho'$ in Figure 6.4 to the
extended language that contains H?? as a command phrase as well. Since H?? nondeterministically updates all "high-security" variables, such judgments need to depend on a
security context Γ. We make this dependency explicit by writing judgments of the form
$\rho \vdash_\Gamma c \Rightarrow \rho'$. Throughout, we assume $\mathrm{dom}(\Gamma) \subseteq \mathrm{dom}(\rho)$.

Definition 6.24 (Relational Semantics)

1. The operational semantics for judgments of the form $\rho \vdash_\Gamma c \Rightarrow \rho'$ is defined in Figure 6.6.

2. The *relational semantics of a command phrase* c *in security context* Γ is the set

$$[\![c]\!]_\Gamma \overset{\mathrm{def}}{=} \{\langle \rho, \rho' \rangle \mid \rho \vdash_\Gamma c \Rightarrow \rho' \text{ is valid}\}$$
$$\cup \{\langle \rho, \infty \rangle \mid \text{for no } \rho' \text{ is } \rho \vdash_\Gamma c \Rightarrow \rho' \text{ valid}\}$$
$$\cup \{\langle \infty, \infty \rangle\}$$

of pairs that either relate start stores ρ to termination stores ρ' of c or record nontermination in security context Γ.

3. We call programs c1 and c2 *relationally equivalent in security context* Γ if and only if

$$[\![c1]\!]_\Gamma = [\![c2]\!]_\Gamma.$$

Notice how we build nonterminating behavior into these relational semantics. From the
operational nature of rule New in Figure 6.6 we conclude that, for any security context Γ,

---

[9] This exercise courtesy of K. R. M. Leino.

$$\frac{}{\rho \vdash_\Gamma n \Rightarrow n} \text{ Lit}$$

$$\frac{\rho(x) \text{ defined}}{\rho \vdash_\Gamma x \Rightarrow \rho(x)} \text{ Id}$$

$$\frac{}{\rho \vdash_\Gamma \text{ true} \Rightarrow true} \text{ Tr}$$

$$\frac{\rho \vdash_\Gamma \text{ e1} \Rightarrow n_1, \quad \rho \vdash_\Gamma \text{ e2} \Rightarrow n_2}{\rho \vdash_\Gamma \text{ e1} + \text{ e2} \Rightarrow \text{plus}(n_1, n_2)} \text{ Add}$$

$$\frac{\rho \vdash_\Gamma \text{ e1} \Rightarrow n_1 \quad \rho \vdash_\Gamma \text{ e2} \Rightarrow n_2}{\rho \vdash_\Gamma \text{ e1} - \text{ e2} \Rightarrow \text{subtr}(n_1, n_2)} \text{ Sub}$$

$$\frac{\rho \vdash_\Gamma \text{ e1} \Rightarrow b_1 \quad \rho \vdash_\Gamma \text{ e2} \Rightarrow b_2}{\rho \vdash_\Gamma \text{ e1} == \text{ e2} \Rightarrow \text{equal?}(b_1, b_2)} \text{ Eq}$$

$$\frac{\rho \vdash_\Gamma \text{ e} \Rightarrow b}{\rho \vdash_\Gamma \text{ !e} \Rightarrow \text{not}(b)} \text{ Neg}$$

$$\frac{\rho \vdash_\Gamma \text{ e1} \Rightarrow n_1, \quad \rho \vdash_\Gamma \text{ e2} \Rightarrow n_2}{\rho \vdash_\Gamma \text{ e1} < \text{ e2} \Rightarrow \text{less\_than?}(n_1, n_2)} \text{ LT}$$

$$\frac{\rho \vdash_\Gamma \text{ e} \Rightarrow n}{\rho \vdash_\Gamma \text{ x} = \text{ e} \Rightarrow \rho[x \mapsto n]} \text{ Ass}$$

$$\frac{\rho \vdash_\Gamma \text{ c1} \Rightarrow \rho', \quad \rho' \vdash_\Gamma \text{ c2} \Rightarrow \rho''}{\rho \vdash_\Gamma \text{ c1; c2} \Rightarrow \rho''} \text{ Seq}$$

$$\frac{\rho \vdash_\Gamma \text{ e} \Rightarrow true, \quad \rho \vdash_\Gamma \text{ c1} \Rightarrow \rho'}{\rho \vdash_\Gamma \text{ if (e) \{c1\} else \{c2\}} \Rightarrow \rho'} \text{ IfT}$$

$$\frac{\rho \vdash_\Gamma \text{ e} \Rightarrow false, \quad \rho \vdash_\Gamma \text{ c2} \Rightarrow \rho'}{\rho \vdash_\Gamma \text{ if (e) \{c1\} else \{c2\}} \Rightarrow \rho'} \text{ IfF}$$

$$\frac{\rho \vdash_\Gamma \text{ if (e) \{c; while e \{c\}\} else \{\}} \Rightarrow \rho'}{\rho \vdash_\Gamma \text{ while e \{c\}} \Rightarrow \rho'} \text{ Wh}$$

$$\frac{\rho(x) = \rho'(x) \text{ for all x with } \Gamma(x) = L}{\rho \vdash_\Gamma \text{ H??} \Rightarrow \rho'} \text{ New}$$

Figure 6.6. A context-dependent type inference system for the evaluation of expressions and commands with possible nondeterministic overwrites of "high-security" variables. The store ∞ is not allowed in these rules.

the set $[\![H??]\!]_\Gamma$ consists of those store pairs that have identical values for all identifiers of security class L. We stress that our relational semantics, characterization of formal noninterference, and formal analysis of programs *depends on, and varies with, such a security context* Γ.

Example 6.25 (Programs and Their Relational Semantics)
In a security context Γ:

- The meaning of composition c1; c2 is the relational composition of the meanings of c1 and c2, taking note of termination behavior: $\langle \rho, \rho'' \rangle \in [\![\text{c1; c2}]\!]_\Gamma$ if and only if there is some ρ' with $\langle \rho, \rho' \rangle \in [\![\text{c1}]\!]_\Gamma$ and $\langle \rho', \rho'' \rangle \in [\![\text{c2}]\!]_\Gamma$.

- The program c; H?? first executes command c in some store ρ. If that execution terminates in store ρ' then command H?? is executed in ρ', effectively destroying any information about values $\rho'(x)$ whenever $\Gamma(x) = H$. Thus, programs of this form erase any knowledge of final values of "high-security" variables. Observe how this erasure is prevented by relational composition if c does not terminate.

- The program H??; c, on the other hand, first erases any knowledge about the initial values of "high-security" variables. Then it executes c.

- The program $\{\}$, which terminates but does not manipulate any store, has as meaning all store pairs of the form $\langle \rho, \rho \rangle$.

EXERCISES 6.10

1. In Exercise 6.5-4 (p. 217), we proved that the operational semantics in Figure 6.4 is *deterministic*. Show that this is not the case for the operational semantics in Figure 6.6.

2. Figure 6.6 does not have an operational rule for the command phrase $\{\}$. Formulate such a rule.

3. In the rule New, what if $\rho(x)$ or $\rho'(x)$ is undefined when $\Gamma(x) = L$? What implicit assumption are we making about all stores in context Γ?

4. In this exercise, we identify programs c with their relational meaning $[\![c]\!]_\Gamma$. In that way, we can also think of *any* relation of that type as a "program". For example, let T be the "program" that relates *all* stores:

$$T \overset{\text{def}}{=} \{\langle \rho, \rho' \rangle \mid \rho, \rho' \text{ are any stores}\}.$$

We write $S, S_1, S_2, \ldots$ for other "programs" and write $S_1; S_2$ for "program composition", and so on.[10]

(a) Show that

$$T \subseteq S; T$$

holds if and only if S is *left-total*: for all stores ρ, there is some store ρ' such that $\langle \rho, \rho' \rangle \in S$.

(b) Show that "program composition" is *monotone*: $S_1 \subseteq S_1'$ and $S_2 \subseteq S_2'$ imply $S_1; S_2 \subseteq S_1'; S_2'$. (State what this means for real programs.)

(c) Show that the programs

  (i) c,

  (ii) {}; c, and

  (iii) c; {}

are all equivalent for any security context Γ.[11]

We can use the relational characterizations of these example programs to arrive at a more applicable characterization of formal program security.

Proposition 6.26

Let Γ be a security context.

1. *The relational semantics of program* H?? *is reflexive and transitive.*

2. *The relational semantics of composition is monotone*:

$$[\![c1]\!]_\Gamma \subseteq [\![c1']\!]_\Gamma \ \& \ [\![c2]\!]_\Gamma \subseteq [\![c2']\!]_\Gamma \implies [\![c1; c2]\!]_\Gamma \subseteq [\![c1'; c2']\!]_\Gamma.$$

3. *Any command phrase c is secure (in the sense of Definition 6.20) if and only if it is noninterfering*:

$$[\![c; H??]\!]_\Gamma = [\![H??; c; H??]\!]_\Gamma. \tag{6.27}$$

4. *Any command phrase c is secure (in the sense of Definition 6.20) if and only if*

$$[\![H??; c]\!]_\Gamma \subseteq [\![c; H??]\!]_\Gamma. \tag{6.28}$$

Proof

1. By definition, $\langle \infty, \infty \rangle \in [\![H??]\!]_\Gamma$. From the proof rule New in Figure 6.6, it is then immediate that any state pair of the form $\langle \rho, \rho \rangle$ is in $[\![H??]\!]_\Gamma$, so this relation is reflexive. For its transitivity, assume that $\langle \rho, \rho' \rangle$ and $\langle \rho', \rho'' \rangle$ are in $[\![H??]\!]_\Gamma$. We need to establish that $\langle \rho, \rho'' \rangle \in [\![H??]\!]_\Gamma$.

---

[10] Keep in mind that real programs are a special case of such "programs".

[11] Don't forget to reason about the state ∞.

(a) If ρ' equals ∞, then ρ'' must equal ∞ and we are done.

(b) Otherwise, let $\Gamma(x) = L$. From $\langle \rho, \rho' \rangle \in [\![H??]\!]_\Gamma$ we infer that $\rho(x) = \rho'(x)$, but from $\langle \rho', \rho'' \rangle \in [\![H??]\!]_\Gamma$ we get $\rho'(x) = \rho''(x)$. Thus $\rho(x) = \rho''(x)$ and $\langle \rho, \rho'' \rangle \in [\![H??]\!]_\Gamma$ follow.

2. The proof that relational composition is monotone was the subject of Exercise 6.10-4 (p. 232).

3. The proof that (6.27) captures the security notion of Definition 6.20 is Exercise 6.12-1 (p. 237).

4. (a) Let c be secure as in Definition 6.20. The set $[\![H??; c]\!]_\Gamma$ equals $[\![H??; c; \{\}]\!]_\Gamma$ because the program $\{\}$ terminates without affecting any store. But the latter set is contained in $[\![H??; c; H??]\!]_\Gamma$, since $[\![H??]\!]_\Gamma$ is reflexive and relational composition is monotone. Therefore, $[\![H??; c]\!]_\Gamma$ is contained in $[\![c; H??]\!]_\Gamma$ by (6.27).

(b) Conversely, let $[\![H??; c]\!]_\Gamma \subseteq [\![c; H??]\!]_\Gamma$. We need to verify (6.27). Since $[\![H??]\!]_\Gamma$ is reflexive and since $\{\}$ terminates without affecting any store, we infer that $[\![c; H??]\!]_\Gamma$ equals $[\![\{\}; c; H??]\!]_\Gamma$, which is a subset of $[\![H??; c; H??]\!]_\Gamma$. For the other inclusion, we use (6.28) and the monotonicity of the relational composition of programs to ensure that $[\![H??; c; H??]\!]_\Gamma$ is contained in $[\![c; H??; H??]\!]_\Gamma$. But the latter set is contained in $[\![c; H??]\!]_\Gamma$ – again, because relational composition is monotone and using that the meaning of H?? is transitive. $\square$

Remark 6.27 (Left-Total Programs)

For the remainder of this section, we assume that all programs c are *left-total* for all security contexts Γ:

For every ρ, there is some η with $\langle \rho, \eta \rangle \in [\![c]\!]_\Gamma$.

Notice that this is *not* saying that all programs terminate, for we might be able to choose ∞ as η.

6.3.3 Safe Abstractions of Security

Alternative characterizations of our security definition are useful if they make proving security easier in some applications. In practice, we may not prove security directly. Instead, we try to prove the security of a program c by:

- finding a property Φ and a proof that all programs (of a certain kind) are secure whenever they satisfy Φ; and
- proving that program c (of that kind) does indeed satisfy that Φ.

We think of such a Φ as an *overapproximation* of the precise definition of security. The approach of Section 6.2 is an example of such an overapproximation. In this section, however, we develop more precise approximations that still have relatively simple certification mechanisms. We also provide additional characterizations of precise security, to which we turn first.

Definition 6.28 (Low-Security Equivalent Stores)

1. Let Σ be the set of stores ρ for programs of our core programming language, including ∞.

2. Given stores ρ, $\rho' \in \Sigma$, we say that ρ and ρ' are *low-security equivalent under security context* Γ, denoted by $\rho \equiv_\Gamma \rho'$, if and only if $\rho(x) = \rho'(x)$ whenever $\Gamma(x) = L$.

Example 6.29

We may use $\equiv_\Gamma$ to rewrite the rule New from Figure 6.6:

$$\frac{\rho \equiv_\Gamma \rho'}{\rho \vdash_\Gamma \text{H??} \Rightarrow \rho'.} \text{ New} \tag{6.29}$$

Theorem 6.30

Let c *be a program and* Γ *a security context. Then the following statements are equivalent.*

1. *The program* c *is secure in security context* Γ.
2. *We have*

$$[\![\text{H??}; \text{c}]\!]_\Gamma \subseteq [\![\text{c}; \text{H??}]\!]_\Gamma. \tag{6.30}$$

3. *For all stores* $\rho_1, \rho_2 \in \Sigma$ *and* $\eta \in \Sigma$: *if* $\rho_1 \equiv_\Gamma \rho_2$ *and* $\langle \rho_1, \eta \rangle \in [\![\text{c}]\!]_\Gamma$, *then there exists some* $\eta' \in \Sigma$ *such that* $\langle \rho_2, \eta' \rangle \in [\![\text{c}]\!]_\Gamma$ *and* $\eta \equiv_\Gamma \eta'$.

Proof

- We have already shown that item 1 implies item 2.
- To see that item 2 implies item 3, let $\rho_1, \rho_2, \eta \in \Sigma$ with $\rho_1 \equiv_\Gamma \rho_2$ and $\langle \rho_1, \eta \rangle \in [\![\text{c}]\!]_\Gamma$. We need to find some η' with $\langle \rho_2, \eta \rangle \in [\![\text{c}]\!]_\Gamma$ and $\eta \equiv_\Gamma \eta'$. Since $\rho_1 \equiv_\Gamma \rho_2$, we have $\rho_2 \equiv_\Gamma \rho_1$. By (6.29), we infer that $\langle \rho_2, \rho_1 \rangle \in [\![\text{H??}]\!]_\Gamma$. By the relational semantics of composition, we conclude that $\langle \rho_2, \eta \rangle \in [\![\text{H??}; \text{c}]\!]_\Gamma$, which is a subset of $[\![\text{c}; \text{H??}]\!]_\Gamma$ by item 2. Therefore $\langle \rho_2, \eta \rangle \in [\![\text{c}; \text{H??}]\!]_\Gamma$ implies the existence of some η' such that $\langle \rho_2, \eta' \rangle \in [\![\text{c}]\!]_\Gamma$ and $\langle \eta', \eta \rangle \in [\![\text{H??}]\!]_\Gamma$. But the latter implies $\eta \equiv_\Gamma \eta'$.
- Since we already showed that item 1 and item 2 are equivalent, it suffices to show that item 3 implies item 2. So let $\langle \rho_1, \eta \rangle \in [\![\text{H??}; \text{c}]\!]_\Gamma$. By the relational semantics of composition, there exists some $\rho_2 \in \Sigma$ such that $\langle \rho_1, \rho_2 \rangle \in [\![\text{H??}]\!]_\Gamma$ (i.e., $\rho_1 \equiv_\Gamma \rho_2$) and $\langle \rho_2, \eta \rangle \in [\![\text{c}]\!]_\Gamma$. By item 3, there exists some $\eta' \in \Sigma$ such that $\langle \rho_1, \eta' \rangle \in [\![\text{c}]\!]_\Gamma$ and $\eta' \equiv_\Gamma \eta$. But then $\langle \eta', \eta \rangle \in [\![\text{H??}]\!]_\Gamma$ follows. Since $\langle \rho_1, \eta' \rangle \in [\![\text{c}]\!]_\Gamma$, we obtain $\langle \rho_1, \eta \rangle \in [\![\text{c}; \text{H??}]\!]_\Gamma$. $\qquad \square$

We emphasize that these results retain their validity if the core programming language without H?? already contains nondeterminism.

EXERCISES 6.11

1. Let Γ be a security context. Show that $\equiv_\Gamma$ is an equivalence relation on the set of stores Σ:
   (a) for all $\rho \in \Sigma$, $\rho \equiv_\Gamma \rho$;
   (b) for all $\rho, \rho' \in \Sigma$, $\rho \equiv_\Gamma \rho'$ implies $\rho' \equiv_\Gamma \rho$;
   (c) for all $\rho, \rho', \rho'' \in \Sigma$, $\rho \equiv_\Gamma \rho'$ and $\rho' \equiv_\Gamma \rho''$ imply $\rho \equiv_\Gamma \rho''$.
2. Prove that each program of Example 6.22 satisfies the property of Theorem 6.30(3) *as stated.*

3. Item 3 of Theorem 6.30 is of interest in its own right. For a program c and security context Γ, the semantics $[\![c]\!]_\Gamma$ defines a directed graph, where the nodes are all elements of Σ and we have an edge from ρ to η (denoted $\rho \to \eta$) if and only if $\langle \rho, \eta \rangle \in [\![c]\!]_\Gamma$. For such a directed graph, a binary relation $R \subseteq \Sigma \times \Sigma$ is called a *bisimulation* if and only if, whenever $\langle \rho, \rho' \rangle \in R$, then:

- for all $\eta \in \Sigma$, if $\rho \to \eta$ then there exists some $\eta' \in \Sigma$ such that $\rho' \to \eta'$ and $\langle \eta, \eta' \rangle \in R$;
- for all $\eta' \in \Sigma$, if $\rho' \to \eta'$ then there exists some $\eta \in \Sigma$ such that $\rho \to \eta$ and $\langle \eta, \eta' \rangle \in R$.

(a) Prove that c is secure in security context Γ if and only if $\equiv_\Gamma$ is a bisimulation.

(b) We define a function

$$F : \Sigma \times \Sigma \to \Sigma \times \Sigma$$

by $\langle \rho, \rho' \rangle \in F(R)$ if and only if $\langle \rho, \rho' \rangle$ satisfies the foregoing two bulleted items *as stated*.

(i) Prove that F is monotone:

$$R \subseteq R' \implies F(R) \subseteq F(R').$$

(ii) Show that there is a greatest bisimulation R.

6.3.4 Weakest Preconditions

We now characterize security by means of predicate transformers.

Definition 6.31 (Predicate Transformers)

1. We call subsets P of Σ *predicates*. We write $\mathcal{P}(\Sigma)$ for the set of all predicates.
2. *Predicate transformers* are functions

$$F : \mathcal{P}(\Sigma) \to \mathcal{P}(\Sigma)$$

that map predicates to predicates.

Example 6.32

Example predicates are:

- $\emptyset$, satisfied by no state;
- Σ, satisfied by all states; and
- $\{\rho \in \Sigma \mid \rho(x) = -5, \rho(y) < 11\}$, satisfied by all states ρ whose value for x is -5 and whose value for y is less than 11.

The last example indicates that we may view formulas as such predicates; for this case, such a formula is

$$(x = -5) \wedge (y < 11).$$

However, not all predicates can be expressed by formulas; see Exercise 6.12-3.

Definition 6.33 (Formulas as Predicates)

Given a formula ϕ, we write $(\!|\phi|\!)$ for the set of all stores $\rho \in \Sigma$ that satisfy ϕ.[12]

For example,

$$(\!| x \bmod 2 = 0 |\!)$$

is the set of all $\rho \in \Sigma$ such that $\rho(\mathrm{x})$ is even. We define two famous predicate transformers (due to E. W. Dijkstra) adapted to our semantics, which is parametric in a security context Γ.

Definition 6.34 (Weakest Precondition)

Let Γ be a security context. We define the *weakest liberal precondition for* Γ, $\mathrm{wlp}_\Gamma(\cdot, \cdot)$, and the *weakest precondition for* Γ, $\mathrm{wp}_\Gamma(\cdot, \cdot)$, by

$$\mathrm{wlp}_\Gamma(c, P) \overset{\mathrm{def}}{=} \{\rho \in \Sigma \mid \forall \rho' \in \Sigma : \langle \rho, \rho' \rangle \in [\![c]\!]_\Gamma \text{ implies } \rho' = \infty \text{ or } \rho' \in P)\},$$

$$\mathrm{wp}_\Gamma(c, P) \overset{\mathrm{def}}{=} \{\rho \in \Sigma \mid \forall \rho' \in \Sigma : \langle \rho, \rho' \rangle \in [\![c]\!]_\Gamma \text{ implies } \rho' \neq \infty \text{ and } \rho' \in P)\}.$$

Let us explain these definitions in plain English as follows.

- The predicate $\mathrm{wlp}_\Gamma(c, P)$ consists of all stores ρ such that any program run of c from such an initial store ρ either does not terminate ($\rho' = \infty$) or terminates in a store contained in P.
- The predicate $\mathrm{wp}_\Gamma(c, P)$ consists of all stores ρ such that any program run of c from such an initial store ρ results in a store ρ' contained in P such that ρ' is different from ∞ (i.e., that run terminates). Thus, executions of c beginning in any store in $\mathrm{wp}_\Gamma(c, P)$ *invariably terminate* and do so in a state from P.

Example 6.35

Consider the program c defined by

```
y = 1;
z = 0;
while (z != x) {
    z = z + 1;
    y = y * z;
}
```

whose intent is to compute the factorial $x!$ of x and store that result in y. Recall that

$$0! \overset{\mathrm{def}}{=} 1,$$

$$(n+1)! \overset{\mathrm{def}}{=} (n+1) \cdot n! \quad (n \geq 0).$$

For example, $5! = 1 \cdot 1 \cdot 2 \cdot 3 \cdot 4 \cdot 5 = 120$. We choose the predicate

---

[12] We will not specify formally what it means to satisfy ϕ, but we hope that the underlying intuition is quite clear.

$$P \stackrel{\text{def}}{=} (y = x!).$$

Then $\text{wlp}_\Gamma(c, P)$ and $\text{wp}_\Gamma(c, P)$ turn out to be different. The former is the entire set of possible stores Σ; the latter consists of only those stores ρ that satisfy $\rho(x) \geq 0$.

We may express $\text{wp}_\Gamma(\cdot, \cdot)$ in terms of $\text{wlp}_\Gamma(\cdot, \cdot)$ and $\text{wp}_\Gamma(\cdot, \Sigma)$.

Lemma 6.36
For all predicates P and all programs c, we have

$$\text{wp}_\Gamma(c, P) = \text{wlp}_\Gamma(c, P) \cap \text{wp}_\Gamma(c, \Sigma). \tag{6.31}$$

By definition, $\text{wp}_\Gamma(c, \Sigma)$ is the set of initial states for which runs of c are guaranteed to terminate. This is the key to proving (6.31). We use this insight to define program equivalence formally.

Definition 6.37 (Program Equivalence)
Let c and c' be programs. We say that c are c' are *equivalent* if and only if

$$\text{wp}_\Gamma(c, \Sigma) = \text{wp}_\Gamma(c', \Sigma) \tag{6.32}$$

and, for all predicates P,

$$\text{wlp}_\Gamma(c, P) = \text{wlp}_\Gamma(c', P). \tag{6.33}$$

From (6.32), it follows that equivalent programs have the same termination behavior. But (6.33) ensures that equivalent programs have the same "input–output" behavior.

Example 6.38 (Equivalence of Programs)
The programs

- `if (B) { c; while (B) { c;} }` and
- `while (B) { c;}`

are equivalent for any boolean expression B and command c.

EXERCISES 6.12

1. Prove that (6.27) holds if and only if c is secure in security context Γ, as in Definition 6.20.
2. Prove that all programs from Example 6.22 satisfy (6.28).
3. Assume that our programming language allows for countably many identifiers x1, x2, ... that can take on any integer as a value.
   (a) Show that the set of predicates $\mathcal{P}(\Sigma)$ is not countable.
   (b) Show informally that the set of formulas of predicate logic whose variables refer to countably many program identifiers and that makes use of standard constant and function symbols of arithmetic is countable.

(c) Conclude that there must exist predicates P that cannot be expressed as formulas of that logic – and plenty of them.

(d) In what sense is part (c) independent from the choice of logic?

4. Prove the claims about $\text{wlp}_\Gamma(c, (y = x!))$ and $\text{wp}_\Gamma(c, (y = x!))$ in Example 6.35.

5. Prove (6.31).

6. Show that the two programs in Example 6.38 are equivalent.

7. Let c and c' be relationally equivalent. Are they necessarily equivalent in the sense of Definition 6.37?

8. Let c and c' be equivalent in the sense of Definition 6.37. Are they necessarily relationally equivalent?

We shall now provide more compact characterizations of security that ultimately allow an efficient and mechanical check of security, provided that all while-statements are annotated with informative invariants (more on that later). Predicates that are invariant under the execution of H?? are instrumental in this.

Definition 6.39 (Γ-Invariant)

Let Γ be a security context and P a predicate. We call P a Γ-*invariant* if and only if

$$\text{wlp}_\Gamma(\text{H??}, P) = P. \tag{6.34}$$

Example 6.40

Given the security context $\Gamma(x) = L$ and $\Gamma(y) = H$, the predicate

$$P \stackrel{\text{def}}{=} (x > 5)$$

is a Γ-invariant, but

$$P \stackrel{\text{def}}{=} ((x > 5) \wedge (y < x))$$

is not.

These Γ-invariants have a very elegant characterization.

Proposition 6.41 (Characterization of Γ-invariants)

Let Γ be a security context and P a predicate. Then P is a Γ-invariant if and only if, for all $\rho_1, \rho_2 \in \Sigma$,

$$\rho_1 \in P \ \& \ \rho_1 \equiv_\Gamma \rho_2 \implies \rho_2 \in P. \tag{6.35}$$

Proof

1. Let P be a Γ-invariant. Given $\rho_1 \in P$ and $\rho_1 \equiv_\Gamma \rho_2$, we need to show that $\rho_2 \in P$. Since P is a Γ-invariant, we infer that

$$\rho_1 \in P = \text{wlp}_\Gamma(\text{H??}, P).$$

But $\rho_1 \equiv_\Gamma \rho_2$ means $\langle \rho_1, \rho_2 \rangle \in [\![H??]\!]_\Gamma$, so $\rho_1 \in \mathrm{wlp}_\Gamma(H??, P)$ yields $\rho_2 \in P$ or $\rho_2 = \infty$. But the latter would imply $\rho_1 = \infty$ by (6.29). In any case, $\rho_2 \in P$.

2. Let P satisfy (6.35). We need to show that P is a Γ-invariant.
   - Let $\rho_1 \in P$. Given $\rho_2 \in \Sigma$ with $\langle \rho_1, \rho_2 \rangle \in [\![H??]\!]_\Gamma$, the latter means $\rho_1 \equiv_\Gamma \rho_2$ and so $\rho_2 \in P$ follows from (6.35). But then we have $\rho_1 \in \mathrm{wlp}_\Gamma(H??, P)$ by definition.
   - Conversely, let $\rho_2 \in \mathrm{wlp}_\Gamma(H??, P)$. Because H?? is left-total,[13] there exists some $\rho_1 \in \Sigma$ with $\langle \rho_2, \rho_1 \rangle \in [\![H??]\!]_\Gamma$. But the latter means $\rho_2 \equiv_\Gamma \rho_1$, and since $\rho_2 \in \mathrm{wlp}_\Gamma(H??, P)$ it also tells us that $\rho_1 \in P$. But $\rho_2 \equiv_\Gamma \rho_1$ is equivalent to $\rho_1 \equiv_\Gamma \rho_2$, so (6.35) entails $\rho_2 \in P$. □

We make good use of this characterization of Γ-invariants to prove a useful characterization of program security.

Proposition 6.42
A program c *is secure in security context* Γ *if and only if*

1. $\mathrm{wp}_\Gamma(c, \Sigma)$ *is a* Γ-*invariant and*
2. $\mathrm{wlp}_\Gamma(c, P)$ *is a* Γ-*invariant for all* Γ-*invariants* P.

Proof
- Assume that c is secure in security context Γ.
   1. $Q \stackrel{\mathrm{def}}{=} \mathrm{wp}_\Gamma(c, \Sigma)$ is a Γ-invariant: Let $\rho_1 \in Q$ and $\rho_1 \equiv_\Gamma \rho_2$. By Proposition 6.41, we are done if $\rho_2 \in Q$, meaning that $\eta \neq \infty$ for all η with $\langle \rho_2, \eta \rangle \in [\![c]\!]_\Gamma$. But given $\langle \rho_2, \eta \rangle \in [\![c]\!]_\Gamma$, there exists some $\eta' \in \Sigma$ such that $\langle \rho_1, \eta' \rangle \in [\![c]\!]_\Gamma$ and $\eta \equiv_\Gamma \eta'$, since c is secure (Theorem 6.30). Now $\rho_1 \in Q$ implies $\eta' \neq \infty$, which in conjunction with $\eta \equiv_\Gamma \eta'$ implies $\eta \neq \infty$. Thus $\rho_2 \in Q$.
   2. Let P be a Γ-invariant. Then we claim that $R \stackrel{\mathrm{def}}{=} \mathrm{wlp}_\Gamma(c, P)$ is a Γ-invariant as well: Let $\rho_1 \in R$ and $\rho_1 \equiv_\Gamma \rho_2$. By Proposition 6.41, we are done if $\rho_2 \in R$. But given $\langle \rho_2, \eta \rangle \in [\![c]\!]_\Gamma$, there exists some $\eta' \in \Sigma$ such that $\langle \rho_1, \eta' \rangle \in [\![c]\!]_\Gamma$ and $\eta \equiv_\Gamma \eta'$, since c is secure. Now $\rho_1 \in R$ implies $\eta' \in P$, which in conjunction with $\eta \equiv_\Gamma \eta'$ implies $\eta \in P$, since P is a Γ-invariant. Thus $\rho_2 \in R$.
- Conversely, we assume the two conditions just listed and show that c is secure.

Proof by contradiction: If c is not secure, then (6.30) does not hold. So there exist $\rho_1 \equiv_\Gamma \rho_2$ and $\langle \rho_2, \eta \rangle \in [\![c]\!]_\Gamma$ such that $\langle \rho_1, \eta \rangle \notin [\![c ; H??]\!]_\Gamma$. The latter implies that, for all $\eta' \in \Sigma$,

$$\langle \rho_1, \eta' \rangle \in [\![c]\!]_\Gamma \text{ entails } \eta' \not\equiv_\Gamma \eta. \tag{6.36}$$

For η fixed as before, the set

$$P \stackrel{\mathrm{def}}{=} \{\eta^* \in \Sigma \mid \eta^* \not\equiv_\Gamma \eta\} \tag{6.37}$$

is a Γ-invariant. By our second assumption,

---

[13] The program H?? is left-total since $\equiv_\Gamma$ is reflexive: $\eta \equiv_\Gamma \eta$ for all $\eta \in \Sigma$.

$$Q \stackrel{\text{def}}{=} \text{wlp}_\Gamma(c, P)$$

is also a Γ-invariant. Let $\langle \rho_1, \eta' \rangle \in [\![c]\!]_\Gamma$ be given. By (6.36) we have $\eta' \not\equiv_\Gamma \eta$. Thus $\eta' \in P$ shows $\rho_1 \in Q$. But Q is a Γ-invariant, so $\rho_1 \equiv_\Gamma \rho_2$ implies $\rho_2 \in Q$. But then $\langle \rho_2, \eta \rangle \in [\![c]\!]_\Gamma$ and (6.36) yield $\eta \not\equiv_\Gamma \eta$, a contradiction.[14]   □

Remark 6.43 (H?? Not Needed Anymore)
Recalling that our ultimate objective is to find efficient ways of proving that programs c are secure, the combination of Proposition 6.41 and Proposition 6.42 entail that there is no need to have the program H?? in our language, nor to use it in our analysis. In fact, this "program" is merely a metaphor that was useful in developing the aforementioned results. In the sequel, we make Proposition 6.41 into a "definition" of Γ-invariants and then provide tools for verifying the two items in Proposition 6.42.

Unfortunately, Proposition 6.42 as such cannot be put into practice, for its second item quantifies over infinitely many predicates (see Exercise 6.13-3). We need to address this next. Let i be an integer expression and x an identifier. It is easy to see that all sets of the form

$$(\!(x \neq i)\!)$$

are Γ-invariants if $\Gamma(x) = L$. We consider these sets only in terms of integers, for the sake of simplicity. These sets and the following results can be secured for any data domain.

Proposition 6.44
Let c be a program and Γ a security context. Then c is secure for that context if and only if:

1. $\text{wp}_\Gamma(c, \Sigma)$ *is a Γ-invariant; and*
2. $\text{wlp}_\Gamma(c, (\!(x \neq i)\!))$ *is a Γ-invariant for all integers $i \in \mathbb{Z}$ and all program identifiers x with $\Gamma(x) = L$.*

Proof By Exercise 6.13-3, $(\!(x \neq i)\!)$ is a Γ-invariant whenever $\Gamma(x) = L$. Therefore, the security of c in security context Γ implies the two listed conditions.

Conversely, assume that conditions 1 and 2 hold. Inspecting the second part of the proof of Proposition 6.42, it clearly suffices to show that $\text{wlp}_\Gamma(c, P)$ is a Γ-invariant for the P in (6.37). A moment's thought reveals that

$$P = \bigcup_{\text{x} \in \text{dom}(\eta)} (\!(x \neq \eta(\text{x}))\!). \tag{6.38}$$

---

[14] The reader may wonder what happened to the first assumption about sets of the form $\text{wp}_\Gamma(c, \Sigma)$. The definition of P subsumes this termination analysis: if $\eta = \infty$, then one can easily see that $Q = \text{wlp}_\Gamma(c, P)$ is indeed $\text{wp}_\Gamma(c, \Sigma)$.

By assumption, all the sets $\text{wlp}_\Gamma(c, (\!| x \neq \eta(x) |\!))$ are Γ-invariants. Hence their union

$$U \stackrel{\text{def}}{=} \bigcup_{x \in \text{dom}(\eta)} \text{wlp}_\Gamma(c, (\!| x \neq \eta(x) |\!)) \tag{6.39}$$

is also a Γ-invariant, because such sets are closed under arbitrary unions. But U equals $\text{wlp}_\Gamma(c, P)$, since the predicate transformer

$$S \mapsto \text{wlp}_\Gamma(c, S) \colon \mathcal{P}(\Sigma) \to \mathcal{P}(\Sigma)$$

preserves arbitrary unions:

$$\text{wlp}_\Gamma\left(c, \bigcup_{i \in I} S_i\right) = \bigcup_{i \in I} \text{wlp}_\Gamma(c, S_i). \tag{6.40}$$

$\square$

EXERCISES 6.13

1. Verify the two claims of Example 6.40.
2. Find necessary and sufficient conditions on a security context Γ such that there are infinitely many Γ-invariants.
3. For any set $(\!| x \neq i |\!)$, show that it is a Γ-invariant whenever $\Gamma(x) = \mathsf{L}$.
4. Explain in detail why (6.38) holds.
5. Prove that U in (6.39) is a Γ-invariant. More generally, prove that the union of any collection of Γ-invariants is a Γ-invariant.
6. Prove that (6.40) holds.

6.3.5 Deterministic Programs

After all this preparatory work, we can now cash in by making special assumptions about our programming language. In this section, we assume that all programs c are deterministic (i.e., $\langle \rho, \eta \rangle \in [\![c]\!]_\Gamma$ and $\langle \rho, \eta' \rangle \in [\![c]\!]_\Gamma$ imply $\eta = \eta'$) and left-total – meaning that they either terminate, or don't terminate; they don't "get stuck" or "disappear".[15]

Lemma 6.45

Let c be a left-total and deterministic program, Γ a security context, and P any predicate. Then

$$\text{wp}_\Gamma(c, P) = \Sigma \setminus \text{wlp}_\Gamma(c, \Sigma \setminus P). \tag{6.41}$$

Proof Since c is left-total and deterministic, each $\rho \in \Sigma$ has a unique η such that $\langle \rho, \eta \rangle \in [\![c]\!]_\Gamma$. For that η, we have $\rho \in \text{wp}_\Gamma(c, P)$ if and only if $\eta \neq \infty$ and $\eta \in P$. But

---

[15] For example, the former could happen at a lower level of implementation when a virtual machine executes the "byte code" of c and reaches a configuration that has no next computational state.

we also have $\rho \in \Sigma \setminus \text{wlp}_\Gamma(c, \Sigma \setminus P)$ if and only if $\eta \notin \Sigma \setminus P$ and $\eta \neq \infty$. These conditions are obviously equivalent. $\qquad\qquad\square$

We can use this insight to get rid of the requirement of checking that $\text{wp}_\Gamma(c, \Sigma)$ is a Γ-invariant.

Theorem 6.46 (Safe to Ignore Termination)

Let c be a left-total and deterministic program. Then c is secure in security context Γ if and only if $\text{wlp}_\Gamma(c, \emptyset)$ and $\text{wlp}_\Gamma(c, (\!| x \neq i |\!))$ are Γ-invariants for all integers $i \in \mathbb{Z}$ and all program identifiers x with $\Gamma(\text{x}) = \text{L}$.

Proof   By Proposition 6.44, it suffices to realize that $\text{wp}_\Gamma(c, \Sigma)$ is a Γ-invariant provided that $\text{wlp}_\Gamma(c, \emptyset)$ is also one. In that case, the argument for Exercise 6.14-1 informs us that $\Sigma \setminus \text{wlp}_\Gamma(c, \emptyset)$ is a Γ-invariant as well. But this set is just $\Sigma \setminus \text{wlp}_\Gamma(c, \Sigma \setminus \Sigma)$, which equals $\text{wp}_\Gamma(c, \Sigma)$ by (6.41). $\qquad\qquad\square$

From Exercise 6.14-1, we readily derive a corollary.

Corollary 6.47

Let c be a left-total and deterministic program. Then c is secure in security context Γ if and only if $\text{wlp}_\Gamma(c, \emptyset)$ and

$$\text{wlp}_\Gamma(c, (\!| x = i |\!)) \tag{6.42}$$

are Γ-invariants for all integers $i \in \mathbb{Z}$ and all program identifiers x with $\Gamma(\text{x}) = \text{L}$.

Let us comment on the practical significance of Theorem 6.46. We began with the very conservative assumption that an attacker is somehow able to "observe" the entire termination behavior of programs, represented by the set $\text{wp}_\Gamma(c, \Sigma)$. Our proof of security for a program c then requires showing that $\text{wp}_\Gamma(c, \Sigma)$ is a Γ-invariant. Since this predicate consists of all those initial stores ρ for runs of c that guarantee termination, our security proof needs to take such termination information into account. However, Theorem 6.46 states that we may ignore termination altogether for deterministic left-total programs. That is to say, the termination analysis is carried out by computing the set $\Sigma \setminus \text{wlp}_\Gamma(c, \emptyset)$.

EXERCISE 6.14

1. Show that $\Sigma \setminus P$ is a Γ-invariant if and only if P is a Γ-invariant.

6.3.6   Partial Correctness Proofs

So how can we compute the predicates $\text{wlp}_\Gamma(c, (\!| x \neq i |\!))$ and $\text{wlp}_\Gamma(c, \emptyset)$ for a given program c? It turns out that there is a beautiful calculus, due to R. Floyd and C. A. R. Hoare that can do just that. We have already pointed out that many important predicates P can be represented as formulas. This holds also for the predicates under consideration here. The predicate $\emptyset$ is faithfully represented by `false`, which is satisfied ($=$ true) by no store $\rho \in \Sigma$. Conversely, `true` represents Σ.

Definition 6.48 (Hoare Triples)

Let ϕ and ψ be formulas and c a program. We call

$$(\!|\phi|\!)\, c \,(\!|\psi|\!)$$

a *Hoare triple*; ϕ is its *precondition* and ψ its *postcondition*. Such a triple is *valid under partial correctness* if and only if: Whenever program c begins execution in a state ρ satisfying ϕ such that this run terminates in a state $\eta \neq \infty$, then η satisfies ψ.

Since we won't have to study validity under *total correctness* – which additionally enforces termination – we simply refer to such Hoare triples as being *valid* (or invalid, as the case may be).

Example 6.49 (Valid and Invalid Hoare Triples)

- The Hoare triple

  $$(\!|y > 5|\!)\, \mathtt{x = y} \,(\!|x > 5|\!)$$

  is valid because, if we execute the assignment `x = y` in any store ρ with $\rho(\mathtt{y}) > 5$, then that run terminates in a store η with $\eta(\mathtt{x}) > 5$.
- The Hoare triple

  $$(\!|x > 5|\!)\, \mathtt{x = y} \,(\!|y > 5|\!),$$

  however, is invalid: there is an initial store ρ with $\rho(\mathtt{x}) = 7$ and $\rho(\mathtt{y}) = 2$ that satisfies $x > 5$ such that the execution of `x = y` terminates, resulting in a store η with $\eta(\mathtt{y}) = 2$, in violation of the desired $y > 5$.
- The Hoare triple

  $$(\!|x \cdot y > 1|\!)\, \mathtt{x = y * x;\ y = x - 2 * y;\ x = x + y} \,(\!|x > y + 1|\!)$$

  is valid, but its proof is somewhat more complex as we must reason about the effect of the three assignments in sequence. The calculus that we shall present deals with such programs in a purely mechanical and efficient way.
- The Hoare triple

  $$(\!|\mathtt{true}|\!)\, \mathtt{if\ (x - 2 == 0)\ \{y = 4;\}\ else\ \{y = x+1;\}} \,(\!|y - x \leq 2|\!)$$

  is valid, where `true` denotes the formulas satisfied by all states, representing Σ.
- The Hoare triple $(\!|\mathtt{true}|\!)\, c \,(\!|y = x!|\!)$ is valid for program c of Example 6.35.[16]
- The Hoare triple

  $$(\!|x = 1|\!)\, \mathtt{while\ (true)\ \{x = x + 1;\}} \,(\!|x = 2|\!)$$

  is also valid, for none of the program's executions terminate.

---

[16] It is not valid regarding total program correctness. In that case, `true` must be replaced by $x \geq n$ for some $n \geq 0$.

$$\frac{(\!(\phi)\!)\, c1\, (\!(\eta)\!)\quad (\!(\eta)\!)\, c2\, (\!(\psi)\!)}{(\!(\phi)\!)\, c1;\ c2\, (\!(\psi)\!)}\ \text{Composition}$$

$$\frac{}{(\!(\psi[E/x])\!)\, x\ =\ E\, (\!(\psi)\!)}\ \text{Assignment}$$

$$\frac{(\!(\phi_1)\!)\, c1\, (\!(\psi)\!)\quad (\!(\phi_2)\!)\, c2\, (\!(\psi)\!)}{(\!((B \rightarrow \phi_1) \wedge (\neg B \rightarrow \phi_2))\!)\, \texttt{if (B) \{c1\} else \{c2\}}\, (\!(\psi)\!)}\ \text{If-statement}$$

$$\frac{(\!(\psi \wedge B)\!)\, c\, (\!(\psi)\!)}{(\!(\psi)\!)\, \texttt{while (B) \{c\}}\, (\!(\psi \wedge \neg B)\!)}\ \text{Partial-while}$$

$$\frac{\vdash \phi' \rightarrow \phi\quad (\!(\phi)\!)\, c\, (\!(\psi)\!)\quad \vdash \psi \rightarrow \psi'}{(\!(\phi')\!)\, c\, (\!(\psi')\!)}\ \text{Implied}$$

Figure 6.7. Proof rules for valid Hoare triples (partial correctness).

We can verify or refute the validity of such triples $(\!(\phi)\!)\, c\, (\!(\psi)\!)$ in a mechanical way. In Figure 6.7, we list proof rules that allow us to infer a valid triple (the one under the bar of a rule) from one or several valid triples (the ones above the bar of a rule), where those triples involve subprograms of the program c. We represent the repeated use of these rules by taking the postcondition ψ and "pushing" it upwards through the code of c, arriving at a condition that had better be implied by the precondition ϕ; otherwise, validity may be violated.

Example 6.50 (Correctness of While-Statements)
To see this at work, consider the program c:

```
a = 0;
z = 0;
while (a != y) {
    z = z + x;
    a = a + 1;
}
```

We show that

$$(\!(y \geq 0)\!)\, c\, (\!(z = x \cdot y)\!)$$

is a valid Hoare triple. The proof is as follows:

$$(\!(y \geq 0)\!)$$
$$(\!(0 = x \cdot 0)\!)\qquad\qquad \text{(Implied)}$$
  a = 0;
$$(\!(0 = x \cdot a)\!)\qquad\qquad \text{(Assignment)}$$
  z = 0;
$$(\!(z = x \cdot a)\!)\qquad\qquad \text{(Assignment)}$$
  while (a != y) {
$$\qquad(\!((z = x \cdot a) \wedge (a \neq y))\!)\quad \text{(Invariant Hyp. } \wedge \text{ guard)}$$

$$(\!|z + x = x \cdot (a + 1)|\!) \qquad \text{(Implied)}$$

```
z = z + x;
```

$$(\!|z = x \cdot (a + 1)|\!) \qquad \text{(Assignment)}$$

```
a = a + 1;
```

$$(\!|z = x \cdot a|\!) \qquad \text{(Assignment)}$$

```
}
```

$$(\!|(z = x \cdot a) \wedge \neg(a \neq y)|\!) \qquad \text{(Partial-while)}$$

$$(\!|z = x \cdot y|\!) \qquad \text{(Implied).}$$

Notice that the condition we computed for the initial store, $0 = x \cdot 0$, is equivalent to `true`, so it is stronger than the actual precondition $y \geq 0$. If we were to take termination into account, however, then $y \geq 0$ would become instrumental. Several comments are in order concerning the use of these rules.

1. To push a formula ϕ through an assignment `x = E`, we simply replace all occurrences of x in ϕ with E, denoted by $\phi[E/x]$. For example, $z = x \cdot a$ changes to $z = x \cdot (a + 1)$ when pushed through the assignment `a = a + 1`:

   $$(\!|z = x \cdot (a + 1)|\!)$$

   ```
   a = a + 1;
   ```

   $$(\!|z = x \cdot a|\!) \qquad \text{(Assignment).}$$

2. The proof rule Implied can be invoked any time, as long as the formula immediately above the occurrence of Implied logically implies the formula that is tagged with Implied. For example,

   $$(\!|(z = x \cdot a) \wedge (a \neq y)|\!)$$

   $$(\!|z + x = x \cdot (a + 1)|\!) \qquad \text{(Implied)}$$

   is a legitimate use of that rule because $(z = x \cdot a) \wedge (a \neq y)$ implies $z + x = x \cdot (a + 1)$ by general arithmetic – the truth of the boolean guard (`a != y`) is not material here.

3. Last, but definitely not least, the portion

   $$(\!|z = x \cdot a|\!)$$

   ```
   while (a != y) {
   ```

   $$(\!|(z = x \cdot a) \wedge (a \neq y)|\!) \qquad \text{(Invariant Hyp. } \wedge \text{ guard)}$$

   $$(\!|z + x = x \cdot (a + 1)|\!) \qquad \text{(Implied)}$$

   ```
       z = z + x;
   ```

   $$(\!|z = x \cdot (a + 1)|\!) \qquad \text{(Assignment)}$$

   ```
       a = a + 1;
   ```

   $$(\!|z = x \cdot a|\!) \qquad \text{(Assignment)}$$

   ```
   }
   ```

   $$(\!|(z = x \cdot a) \wedge \neg(a \neq y)|\!) \qquad \text{(Partial-while)}$$

reasons about the behavior of the while-statement in isolation. The formula $z = x \cdot a$ plays the role of ψ in proof rule Partial-while of Figure 6.7. Such a formula is called an *invariant* for this while-statement, because if it is true before the execution of that while-statement then it will be true when that execution has terminated. This is formally shown in the portion

$$(\!(z = x \cdot a) \wedge (a \neq y))\!)$$
$$(\!(z + x = x \cdot (a + 1))\!) \qquad \text{(Implied)}$$
```
z = z + x;
```
$$(\!(z = x \cdot (a + 1))\!) \qquad \text{(Assignment)}$$
```
a = a + 1;
```
$$(\!(z = x \cdot a)\!) \qquad \text{(Assignment)},$$

where the invariant is pushed upward through the body of the while-statement, hoping that the formula thus found (here, $z + x = x \cdot (a + 1)$) is implied by the invariant and the truth of the boolean guard. An invariant is "good" if it:

- implies – in conjunction with the falsity of the boolean guard – the desired postcondition, as in

$$(\!(z = x \cdot a) \wedge \neg(a \neq y))\!)$$
$$(\!(z = x \cdot y)\!) \qquad \text{(Implied)};$$

and

- if it can be made true immediately before the while-statement begins, as in

$$(\!(y \geq 0)\!)$$
$$(\!(0 = x \cdot 0)\!) \quad \text{(Implied)}$$
```
a = 0;
```
$$(\!(0 = x \cdot a)\!) \quad \text{(Assignment)}$$
```
z = 0;
```
$$(\!(z = x \cdot a)\!) \quad \text{(Assignment)}.$$

These two concerns are like conflicting forces ("implied" versus "being implied"), and this need for "good" invariants is the sole reason – apart from proving logical implications cited in Implied – why validation of Hoare triples is not entirely a mechanical endeavor.

Things are much easier when it comes to if-statements.

Example 6.51 (Correctness of If-Statements)
Consider the program c:

```
if (x > 5) {
y = x - 2;
} else {
y = x * x + 4;
}
```

We prove that the Hoare triple

$$(\!|\text{true}|\!)\ c\ (\!|y > 3|\!)$$

is valid:

$(\!|\text{true}|\!)$

$(\!|(((x > 5) \to (x - 2 > 3)) \land (\neg(x > 5) \to (x^2 + 4 > 3)))|\!)$ (Implied)

```
if (x > 5) {
```

    $(\!|x - 2 > 3|\!)$ (If-statement)

```
    y = x - 2;
```

    $(\!|y > 3|\!)$ (Assignment)

```
} else {
```

    $(\!|x^2 + 4 > 3|\!)$ (If-statement)

```
    y = x * x + 4;
```

    $(\!|y > 3|\!)$ (Assignment)

```
}
```

$(\!|y > 3|\!)$ (If-statement).

Example 6.52 $(3n + 1$ Collatz$)$
Finding "good" invariants is a nontrivial task, and reasoning about termination of programs can be much harder still. Consider the program

```
c = x;
while (c != 1) {
  if (c % 2 == 0) { c = c / 2;
  } else {          c = 3 * c + 1;
  }
}
```

Despite its compactness and seeming simplicity, this is a rather famous program. It stores the current value of x in c and then executes a while-statement where the value of c is halved if it is even; otherwise, the value of c is increased to $3 \cdot c + 1$. This activity occurs and repeats until this value reaches 1. To ensure termination, it is clear that $x \geq 1$ is needed. But nobody has been able to prove that this program terminates for all initial values of x with $x \geq 1$.

We still owe an example of how the computation of $\text{wlp}_\Gamma(c, \emptyset)$ can reveal all about program c's termination behavior.

Example 6.53 (Computing Termination Behavior)
Consider the program c:

```
while (true) {
  y = y + 1;
  y = y - 1;
}
```

Clearly, this program never terminates. We can compute the exact set $\text{wlp}_\Gamma(\text{c}, \emptyset)$ by using the invariant `true`:

```
(true)                    (Assignment)
while (true) {
    ((true ∧ ¬true))      (Invariant Hyp. ∧ guard)
    (true)                (Implied)
  y = y + 1;
    (true)                (Assignment)
  y = y - 1;
    (true)                (Assignment)
}
  ((true ∧ ¬true)         (Partial-while)
  (false)                 (Implied).
```

Thus the Hoare triple

$$(\text{true})\; c\; (\text{false})$$

is valid, from which we infer that

$$[\![c]\!]_\Gamma = \{\langle \rho, \infty \rangle \mid \rho \in \Sigma\},$$

meaning that no program run terminates. Notice that this set is a Γ-invariant for $\Gamma(\text{y}) = H$. In fact, it is quite easy to prove that this program is secure in context Γ.

EXERCISES 6.15

1. Use the proof rules of Figure 6.7, as discussed in the text, to prove that all triples of Example 6.49 (except the second one) are valid.

2. Explain informally why all proof rules in Figure 6.7 are *sound* – that is, explain why their conclusion (the triple below the bar of a rule) is valid if all its premises (the triple(s) above the bar of a rule) are valid.

3. Verify that the following instance of the rule Implied,

$$(\text{true})$$
$$(((x > 5) \to (x - 2 > 3)) \wedge (\neg(x > 5) \to (x^2 + 4 > 3)))\quad \text{(Implied)}$$

(from Example 6.51), is valid.

4. Implement the program of Example 6.52 for BigInteger values of x and observe how many iterations, on average, the while-statement performs in the bit length of x.

6.3.7 Verifying and Refuting Program Security

Example 6.54 (Refutation of Security)

Given a security context $\Gamma(x) = L$ and $\Gamma(y) = H$, consider the program c:

```
if (y % 2 == 0)
  { x = 0;
} else {
    x = 1;
}
```

where y % 0 denotes the remainder of y modulo 2. We investigate whether c is secure in that security context. We may put Theorem 6.46 into use because c is deterministic and left-total. For the Γ-invariant $(\!|x \neq 0|\!)$, we know that c is unsecure if $\mathrm{wlp}_\Gamma(c, (\!|x \neq 0|\!))$ is not a Γ-invariant. We compute $\mathrm{wlp}_\Gamma(c, (\!|x \neq 0|\!))$:

$$(\!|((y \bmod 2 = 0) \to (0 \neq 0)) \wedge (\neg(y \bmod 2 = 0) \to (1 \neq 0))|\!)$$

```
if (y % 2 == 0) {
```
$$(\!|0 \neq 0|\!) \hspace{8cm} \text{(If-statement)}$$
```
    x = 0;
```
$$(\!|x \neq 0|\!) \hspace{8cm} \text{(Assignment)}$$
```
} else {
```
$$(\!|1 \neq 0|\!) \hspace{8cm} \text{(If-statement)}$$
```
    x = 1;
```
$$(\!|x \neq 0|\!) \hspace{8cm} \text{(Assignment)}$$
```
}
```
$$(\!|x \neq 0|\!) \hspace{8cm} \text{(If-statement)},$$

concluding that $\mathrm{wlp}_\Gamma(c, (\!|x \neq 0|\!))$ equals

$$(\!|(y \bmod 2 = 0) \to (0 \neq 0)) \wedge (\neg(y \bmod 2 = 0) \to (1 \neq 0))|\!). \tag{6.43}$$

It is immediate that this is the set of all $\rho \in \Sigma$ satisfying "$\rho(y)$ is odd". This set is not a Γ-invariant: For $\rho_1, \rho_2 \in \Sigma$ with

$$\rho_1(y) \overset{\text{def}}{=} 5, \quad \rho_1(x) \overset{\text{def}}{=} 2,$$
$$\rho_2(y) \overset{\text{def}}{=} 6, \quad \rho_2(x) \overset{\text{def}}{=} 2,$$

we have $\rho_1 \in \mathrm{wlp}_\Gamma(c, (\!|x \neq 0|\!))$ (since $\rho_1(y) = 5$ is odd) and $\rho_1 \equiv_\Gamma \rho_2$ (since $\rho_1(x) = \rho_2(x)$), but $\rho_2 \notin \mathrm{wlp}_\Gamma(c, (\!|x \neq 0|\!))$ (since $\rho_2(y) = 6$ is even). Therefore, program c is not secure in security context Γ.

This example illustrated how simple it can be to prove that a program is unsecure. We have only to find a value i such that $\mathrm{wlp}_\Gamma(c, x \neq i)$ is not a Γ-invariant. In Example 6.54, the value $i \overset{\text{def}}{=} 0$ made this attempt succeed; the value $i \overset{\text{def}}{=} 1$ would have succeeded as well.

EXERCISES 6.16

1. For $\rho \in \Sigma$, show that ρ is in the set in (6.43) if and only if $\rho(y)$ is an odd number.
2. For Example 6.54:
    (a) adapt its argument to the case where $i \overset{\text{def}}{=} 1$ to prove that the program is unsecure;
    (b) investigate whether any choice of i other than 0 or 1 reveals that the program is unsecure.

Some of the example programs of this chapter also contain nondeterministic choice. The proof rules for valid Hoare triples can be extended to this programming construct:

$$\frac{(\!(\phi_1)\!)\ c1\ (\!(\psi)\!)\quad (\!(\phi_2)\!)\ c2\ (\!(\psi)\!)}{(\!(\phi_1 \wedge \phi_2)\!)\ c1\ \texttt{++}\ c2\ (\!(\psi)\!).}\ \text{Choice} \tag{6.44}$$

Its operational nature is similar to that for if-statements, only that ϕ_1 and ϕ_2 are not conditioned on the truth of a boolean guard. Since the programmer has no control over this choice, she must unconditionally ensure each of the preconditions computed for any of the chosen branches.

Example 6.55 (Insecure Nondeterministic Program)
Recall the program c,

```
( x = y - 3 ++ x = y + 5 );
```

from Section 6.1 (p. 207). We deemed this program unsecure for $\Gamma(x) = L$ and $\Gamma(y) = H$ because the final value stored in x is "close" to the value initially stored in y. We won't specify the value of i, but push it up through the two commands. For the first command, we get

$$(\!(y - 3 \neq i)\!)$$
$$\quad \texttt{x = y - 3;}$$
$$(\!(x \neq i)\!) \qquad \text{(Assignment)};$$

for the second command, we obtain

$$(\!(y + 5 \neq i)\!)$$
$$\quad \texttt{x = y + 5;}$$
$$(\!(x \neq i)\!) \qquad \text{(Assignment)}.$$

Applying the proof rule Choice of (6.44) to these two proofs, we infer that

$$(\!((y - 3 \neq i) \wedge (y + 5 \neq i))\!) = \text{wlp}_\Gamma(c, (\!(x \neq i)\!)).$$

However,

$$(\!((y - 3 \neq i) \wedge (y + 5 \neq i))\!)$$

is not a Γ-invariant. For example, when $i \stackrel{\text{def}}{=} 2$, we can set

$$\rho_1(\mathbf{x}) \stackrel{\text{def}}{=} 11, \quad \rho_1(\mathbf{y}) \stackrel{\text{def}}{=} 0,$$
$$\rho_2(\mathbf{x}) \stackrel{\text{def}}{=} 11, \quad \rho_2(\mathbf{y}) \stackrel{\text{def}}{=} -3.$$

It then follows that $\rho_1 \equiv_\Gamma \rho_2$ and $\rho_1 \in (\!((y - 3 \neq i) \wedge (y + 5 \neq i))\!)$; however, ρ_2 is not in $(\!((y - 3 \neq i) \wedge (y + 5 \neq i))\!)$, since $\rho_2(\mathbf{y}) + 5$ equals i.

Example 6.56 (Unsecure Program Termination)
Let $\Gamma(\mathbf{x}) = \mathsf{L}$ and $\Gamma(\mathbf{y}) = \mathsf{H}$. We prove that the program c,

```
if (y == 0) {
  while (true) { };
} else {
  y = y + 1;
}
```

is unsecure:

$$(\!(((y = 0) \rightarrow \texttt{true}) \wedge ((y \neq 0) \rightarrow (x \neq i)))\!)$$

```
if (y == 0) {
```
    $(\!(\texttt{true})\!)$ (If-statement)
```
  while (true) { };
```
    $(\!(x \neq i)\!)$ (*Justification*)
```
} else {
```
    $(\!(x \neq i)\!)$ (If-statement)
```
  y = y + 1;
```
    $(\!(x \neq i)\!)$ (Assignment)
```
}
```
$(\!(x \neq i)\!)$ (If-statement).

The argument for *Justification* is similar to that in Example 6.53. Because this step computes the exact precondition, we infer that

$$(\!(((y = 0) \rightarrow \texttt{true}) \wedge ((y \neq 0) \rightarrow (x \neq i)))\!) \tag{6.45}$$

is the exact precondition of program c for the postcondition $x \neq i$. However, the set in (6.45) is not a Γ-invariant. Thus c is unsecure in security context Γ.

These examples suggest that we found an elegant and efficient way of refuting or proving the security of programs, but there are some problems with putting this into practice.

1. Although it seems intuitively easy to check (even automatically) whether a formula ϕ defines a Γ-invariant $(\!(\phi)\!)$, there are at least two potential problems.

- That ϕ mentions "high-security" variables does not automatically mean that $(\!|\phi|\!)$ is not a Γ-invariant. Given $\Gamma(x) = L$ and $\Gamma(y) = H$, the formula $y = x + 1$ mentions y but determines a Γ-invariant $(\!|y = x + 1|\!)$ nonetheless, noting that y is a function of x. Determining such functional dependencies can be tricky, and these dependencies are not the only ones that can make $(\!|\phi|\!)$ a Γ-invariant.

- Showing that $\text{wlp}_\Gamma(c, (\!|x \neq i|\!))$ is a Γ-invariant requires that we compute the *entire* set $\text{wlp}_\Gamma(c, (\!|x \neq i|\!))$. Any smaller subset thereof won't due in general, leading to possibly flawed refutations or validations of program security. Inspecting the proof rules in Figure 6.7, we immediately see that rule Implied is suspect in that it may lose a lot of precision – an extreme example is

    $(\!|\texttt{false}|\!)$

    $(\!|\texttt{true}|\!)$ (Implied),

    where $\Sigma = (\!|\texttt{true}|\!)$ is turned into $\emptyset = (\!|\texttt{false}|\!)$. However, applying this rule when proving invariants is usually less of a problem. Indeed, if a program is annotated with "good" invariants for all its while-statements, then the exact computation of sets $\text{wlp}_\Gamma(c, (\!|x \neq i|\!))$ can be achieved in most practical cases. The idea of annotating proofs with such information is one important approach to "proof-carrying code" that we will briefly discuss in Section 6.4.

2. In trying to verify the security of a program, we need to compute $n + 1$ many sets of the form $\text{wlp}_\Gamma(c, P)$, where n is the number of possible distinct data values that x can take on. Clearly, this is unacceptable for all but the smallest domains, such as booleans. We therefore require methods that safely abstract the value i in $\text{wlp}_\Gamma(c, (\!|x \neq i|\!))$. Also, this analysis must be done for each x with $\Gamma(x) = L$. We return to the issue of abstraction in the next section.

3. In an ideal world of program development for sequential programs that contain nondeterminism, we would begin with a specification written in the same "language" and then refine that specification step by step until an implementation is reached that faithfully reflects the intent of the specification *and* resolves all nondeterminism. Also, one would hope for refinement to be a formal notion that can be validated. Moving from specifications to implementations typically means that predicates P grow or shrink. Unfortunately, a predicate $(\!|\phi|\!)$ that is a Γ-invariant for one program may not be a Γ-invariant for a refined program. Note, though, that this is of no concern for programs whose specifications are already deterministic.

EXERCISES 6.17

1. Show that the proof rule in (6.44) is *sound* – that is, its conclusion (the triple below the bar of the rule) is valid if its two premises (the two triples above the bar of the rule) are valid.

2. In this exercise, assume that all proof rules of Figure 6.7 are such that all their premises compute *exact* weakest liberal preconditions. For example, for the proof rule If-statement, assume that

    $\phi_1 = \text{wlp}_\Gamma(c1, \psi)$,

    $\phi_2 = \text{wlp}_\Gamma(c2, \psi)$.

Determine for which rules it is then the case that the precondition of their conclusion is also an exact weakest precondition. For the proof rule If-statement, the claim would be that

$$(B \to \phi_1) \wedge (\neg B \to \phi_2) = \text{wlp}_\Gamma(\text{if } (B) \{c1\} \text{ else } \{c2\}, \psi).$$

Justify your findings in each case.

3. Prove that the set in (6.45) is not a Γ-invariant for $\Gamma(x) = L$ and $\Gamma(y) = H$.

6.3.8 A Safe Abstraction

We conclude this discussion of a semantic approach to secure information flow by presenting a safe abstraction of security as outlined in Section 6.3.3 (p. 233). We prove that programs are secure whenever their final values for "low-security" identifiers are a function of their initial values.

Definition 6.57 (Programs That Are Functional in Γ)
Let Γ be a security context and c a program. We call c *functional in security context* Γ if and only if, for all $\rho, \rho', \eta, \eta' \in \Sigma$, we have that

$$\rho \equiv_\Gamma \rho' \ \& \ \langle \rho, \eta \rangle \in \llbracket c \rrbracket_\Gamma \ \& \ \langle \rho', \eta' \rangle \in \llbracket c \rrbracket_\Gamma \implies \eta \equiv_\Gamma \eta'.$$

Proposition 6.58 (Functional Programs Are Secure)
Let c be left-total [17] and functional in security context Γ. *Then c is secure in security context* Γ.

Proof It suffices to establish Theorem 6.30(3). Let $\rho \equiv_\Gamma \rho'$ and $\langle \rho, \eta \rangle \in \llbracket c \rrbracket_\Gamma$. Since c is left-total, there exists some $\eta' \in \Sigma$ with $\langle \rho', \eta' \rangle \in \llbracket c \rrbracket_\Gamma$. Since c is functional in Γ, we conclude that $\eta \equiv_\Gamma \eta'$. □

We now bridge the gap between this safe abstraction result and its applicability via proving valid Hoare triples.

Proposition 6.59
Let c be a left-total program, Γ *a security context, and f a function from integers to integers. Suppose we can prove that the Hoare triples*

$$(\!| x = i |\!) \ c \ (\!| x = f(i) |\!) \tag{6.46}$$

are valid for all x with $\Gamma(x) = L$ *and all integers i that identifiers can take on as values. If additionally* $\text{wp}_\Gamma(c, \emptyset)$ *is a* Γ-invariant, then c is secure in security context Γ.

Proof Again, we merely show item 3 of Theorem 6.30. Let $\rho \equiv_\Gamma \rho'$ and $\langle \rho, \eta \rangle \in \llbracket c \rrbracket_\Gamma$. Since c is left-total, there exists some $\eta' \in \Sigma$ with $\langle \rho', \eta' \rangle \in \llbracket c \rrbracket_\Gamma$. Since $\text{wp}_\Gamma(c, \emptyset)$ is a Γ-invariant, we have $\eta = \infty$ if and only if $\eta' = \infty$, in which case we obtain $\eta \equiv_\Gamma \eta'$.

---

[17] We need not assume that c is deterministic.

Otherwise, both η and η' are different from ∞. Since $\eta \neq \infty$, we may invoke (6.46) for all x with $\Gamma(x) = L$ and $i \stackrel{\text{def}}{=} \rho(x)$, securing that

$$\eta(x) = f(\rho(x)).$$

But since $\eta' \neq \infty$, we again invoke (6.46) for all x with $\Gamma(x) = L$, this time with $i \stackrel{\text{def}}{=} \rho'(x)$, and secure that

$$\eta'(x) = f(\rho'(x)).$$

But $\rho \equiv_\Gamma \rho'$ implies $\rho(x) = \rho'(x)$ for all x with $\Gamma(x) = L$. Therefore,

$$\eta(x) = f(\rho(x)) = f(\rho'(x)) = \eta'(x)$$

holds for all x with $\Gamma(x) = L$, since f is a function. This means that $\eta \equiv_\Gamma \eta'$.   □

Example 6.60 (Functional in Γ)
We use this insight to prove the security of the program c,

```
y = abs(h);
while (0 < y) {
    y = y - 1;
    x = x + 1;
}
x = y;
```

by using the function

$$f(i) \stackrel{\text{def}}{=} 0$$

for all integers i. We verify the Hoare triple

$$(\!| x = i |\!) \; c \; (\!| x = 0 |\!).$$

Note that abs(y) denotes the *absolute value* of y:

$$\text{abs}(y) \stackrel{\text{def}}{=} \max(y, -y).   \tag{6.47}$$

For example, abs(-2) = 2 and abs(0) = 0. The verification of the Hoare triple requires a "good" invariant and proceeds as follows:

```
    (| 0 ≤ abs(y) |)
y = abs(y);
    (| 0 ≤ y |)                    (Assignment)
while (0 < y) {
        (| (0 ≤ y) ∧ (0 < y) |)    (Invariant Hyp. ∧ guard)
        (| 0 ≤ y − 1 |)            (Implied)
```

```
y = y - 1;
```
$$(\!|0 \le y|\!) \qquad\qquad \text{(Assignment)}$$
```
x = x + 1;
```
$$(\!|0 \le y|\!) \qquad\qquad \text{(Assignment)}$$
```
}
```
$$(\!|(0 \le y) \wedge \neg(0 < y)|\!) \qquad \text{(Partial-while)}$$
$$(\!|y = 0|\!) \qquad\qquad \text{(Implied)}$$
```
x = y;
```
$$(\!|x = 0|\!) \qquad\qquad \text{(Assignment)}.$$

Note that

$$(\!|0 \le \mathrm{abs}(y)|\!) = \Sigma$$

is implied by (contains) $(\!|x = i|\!)$. Since the program can also be shown to always terminate, we conclude that it is secure in security context Γ.

EXERCISES 6.18

1. Compute $\mathrm{wp}_\Gamma(c, \emptyset)$, noting that $\emptyset = (\!|\mathtt{false}|\!)$, for the program c from Example 6.60.
2. Explain why $\mathrm{wp}_\Gamma(c, (\!|x = 0|\!))$ equals Σ for the program c from Example 6.60.
3. Is every program that is functional in Γ also deterministic?
4. Is every deterministic program functional in Γ?

6.4 PROGRAM CERTIFICATION

We encountered one form of program certification in Section 6.2. In that case, certificates were proofs of judgments

$$\Gamma \triangleright c : \tau,$$

where c is a program (phrase). If such a program is to be installed on a system, then this program can be shipped with its certificate, the certificate can be verified, and the user then knows that every identifier x assigned to in the program c has security class τ or *higher*.

The proof and the verification are both done *statically,* meaning that they simply compute over the syntax of c without ever executing c on a machine. This has important advantages. For one, we may validate the security of c *before* we execute it on our system, so we can find out whether c is able to do damage without actually giving it a chance to do so. Second, the verification of a certificate is usually much faster than the generation of its proof and, once verified, program c may be executed time and again without any slowdown of performance (caused e.g. by alternative certification checks at run time). Third, casting our security analysis in a type system for a higher-level programming language provides for an easily understandable and unambiguous formal specification of what it really means to certify and verify. This formal approach also enables the use of different verification algorithms, since we need merely show that each one satisfies the specification.[18] Such flexibility may well be required in a heterogeneous place such as the Internet.

Unfortunately, focusing on a higher-level language has its downside as well; one may use hardware malfunctions at a lower level to make "secure" programs unsecure. Moreover, a programming language such as Java has both static and dynamic types. Verifying only the static features of a program is typically insufficient. For example, one may force array bounds to go beyond a declared range. Handling such events with exceptions and including these exceptions in our analysis can mitigate – but not completely eliminate – such disastrous effects. Further, programs often access files or "foreign" code, so the linker may be forced to verify that the composition of such code does not violate the information flow policy of each code participant. The semantic approach to secure information flow analysis suggests a similar framework for proof-carrying code, where while-statements are annotated with "precise" invariants and then security verification can be achieved through the methods developed in Section 6.3.

All of these approaches face challenges in realistic settings, however. For example, what is one to do with programs that generate random session keys for encryption (recall the comment on page 225)? Identifying and verifying formal descriptions of security properties for the execution and dynamic linking of mobile code is an important area of research in computer security. Conventional theoretical properties – such as noninterference, separability, and restrictiveness – are not sufficient for reasoning about the privacy, integrity, and availability of a client's machine during and after the execution of mobile code (e.g., an applet downloaded from some untrusted web server). Such frameworks are needed to ensure the unhindered growth and economic success of the Internet, extensible operating system kernels, and active networks. Although these challenges may appear to be insurmountable, they do suggest a strategy for the design of secure web programming languages: define a small core language and then incrementally extend this language to include new language constructs, each one specified by a formal semantics; this formal semantics is used, in turn, to verify that the extended language satisfies all security properties that have been formally modeled. See Exercises 6.8 (p. 226) for this methodology at work.

6.5 COVERT CHANNELS

Covert channels are lines of communication between two processes that allow these processes to exchange information (at a rate ranging from a few bits to a few thousand bits each second) by modifying shared resources; the point is that these two processes are not permitted to communicate at all! Complex hardware and modern embedded and/or multi-user systems unavoidably provide the capacity for such covert channels. Although it is highly nontrivial to implement an attack exploiting this capacity without being exposed by a regular audit of a "secure" operating system, successful attempts have demonstrated that such channels can be realized. In a digital picture, one can change the lower-order two bits of each pixel to encode a message without anybody noticing a decline in the picture's quality. One may hide a bit of information in the choice of a "random" session key

---

[18] Moreover, certifying a program on the basis of some certification program says nothing unless the certification program can be proved to be correct, requiring a formal specification of correctness in the first place.

for encryption; one may make use of disk arm movements to convey secret information, and so on. Research activities on covert channels focus primarily on their *explanation, discovery, measurement,* and *mitigation.* The latter, for example, may be achieved by "fuzzifying" the underlying real-time operating system by adding random time delays to all atomic operating system tasks.

6.6 BIBLIOGRAPHIC NOTES

The discussion of secure information flow is based on various research papers. All of these papers draw from the classical work of Denning (1976, 1977), which builds on the Bell and La Padula (1973) security model. Volpano, Smith, and Irvine (1996; see also Volpano 1996, Volpano and Smith 1997) present Denning's work in a typed setting and give a formal and rigorous soundness proof of the secure information flow analysis. We followed that exposition for the most part, but we changed the core programming language slightly and simplified the presentation of the type system. The material on the semantic approach to secure information flow is taken from Leino and Joshi (1997; see also Leino 1998, Joshi and Leino 2000) but adapted to our notational and conceptual setting. Some program examples are taken from the paper by Sabelfeld and Sands (2000), which contains another semantic approach to secure information flow in programs. The text by Dijkstra (1976) is an authoritative source on weakest preconditions. For approaches that make use of data flow analysis techniques, see Andrews and Reitman (1980), Banâtre, Bryce, and Le Métayer (1994), and Mizuno and Schmidt (1992). The exposition of partial correctness proofs is based on the account in Huth and Ryan (2000); Figure 6.7 is taken from that text. We also mention Backhouse (1986), which contains numerous examples and exercises. A text that focuses on correctness proofs of concurrent programs is Apt and Olderog (1991). A text that discusses the issue of writing to arrays and the problem of array cell aliasing is Francez (1992). We recommend the monograph by Milner (1989) on bisimulation and its use in concurrency theory.

One may characterize noninterference in terms of the observations that "low-security" tests can make about "high-security" processes. Within a process algebraic framework, such approaches can lead to a high degree of compositionality, as is the case in Schneider's work using CSP (Schneider 2000). Some thoughts on the security of mobile code are taken from Volpano (1996) and McGraw and Felten (1997). The brief discussion of covert channels is taken from Millen (1999). For an introduction to the methodology of proof-carrying code – promoted by G. Necula, P. Lee, F. Pfenning, and others – we recommend Crary, Harper, Lee, and Pfenning (2000) and Lee's online overview[19] of proof-carrying code.

---

[19] http://www.cs.cmu.edu/~petel/papers/pcc/pcc.html

APPENDIX

Primitive Roots

A.1 EXISTENCE OF PRIMITIVE ROOTS

The existence of a primitive root for $\mathbb{Z}_p^*$, when $p > 1$ is prime, is one of the central results in number theory whose importance cannot be underestimated. In our context of RSA public-key encryption, it provides the last missing link to the guarantee of correctness for the program Witness(a,n) with respect to all its returns with value true. Our proof of the probabilistic upper bound for "false positives" of the Miller–Rabin algorithm required the stronger claim that prime powers p^k with $p > 2$ and $k \geq 1$ have primitive roots. This section proves the existence of such roots.

For $[m]_p \in \mathbb{Z}_p^*$, Lagrange's and Fermat's theorems together tell us that the size of the subgroup $\langle [m]_p \rangle$ in $\mathbb{Z}_p^*$ is a divisor of $p - 1$, the size of the group $\mathbb{Z}_p^*$. Thus, for $[m]_p$ to be a primitive root, we need

$$\operatorname{ord}^{\mathbb{Z}_p^*}([m]_p) = p - 1.$$

Conversely, if $\operatorname{ord}([m]_p) = p - 1$ then the $p - 1$ elements

$$[m]_p, [m^2]_p, \ldots, [m_p^{p-1}]$$

are all different, so $[m]_p$ generates $\mathbb{Z}_p^*$. In summary, we "only" have to show the existence of some $[g]_p \in \mathbb{Z}_p^*$ such that

$$\operatorname{ord}([g]_p) = p - 1.$$

This requires a concept dual to that of a greatest common divisor.

Definition A.1 (Least Common Multiple)
Let $a, b \in \mathbb{Z}$. We define

$$\operatorname{lcm}(a, b) \stackrel{\text{def}}{=} \begin{cases} \dfrac{a \cdot b}{\gcd(a, b)} & \text{if } \gcd(a, b) \neq 0, \\ 0 & \text{otherwise.} \end{cases} \tag{A.1}$$

We define inductively

$$\operatorname{lcm}(a_1, a_2, a_3, \ldots, a_{n+1}) \stackrel{\text{def}}{=} \operatorname{lcm}(a_1, \operatorname{lcm}(a_2, a_3, \ldots, a_{n+1})) \tag{A.2}$$

for all $n \geq 2$ in $\mathbb{N}$. We call $\operatorname{lcm}(a, b)$ the *least common multiple* of a and b. If $S = \{a_1, a_2, \ldots, a_{n+1}\}$, we sometimes write $\operatorname{lcm}(S)$ for the expression computed in equation (A.2).

For example, we compute

$$\operatorname{lcm}(770, 42) = (770 \cdot 42)/\operatorname{gcd}(770, 42)$$
$$= 32340/14$$
$$= 2310 \tag{A.3}$$

for $\operatorname{gcd}(770, 42) \neq 0$.

Definition A.2
Let $\langle G, \circ, e \rangle$ be a finite commutative group. We define

$$\Lambda(G) \stackrel{\text{def}}{=} \operatorname{lcm}(\{\operatorname{ord}^G(g) \mid g \in G\}). \tag{A.4}$$

Thus $\Lambda(G)$ is the least common multiple of orders of all group elements in G.

We show the existence of a primitive root for $\mathbb{Z}_p^*$ in two steps:

1. we first prove that
   $$\Lambda(\mathbb{Z}_p^*) = \operatorname{ord}([m]_p)$$
   for some $[m]_p \in \mathbb{Z}_p^*$; then,
2. we show that $\Lambda(\mathbb{Z}_p^*)$ equals $p - 1$.

Only the second step makes use of the primeness of p. It is best to divide the first step into a few technical lemmas. These lemmas are valid for finite commutative groups in general and are also easier to read if stated, and proved, in this generality. Recall that we write g^t in a group G to denote the tth power of $g \in G$.

Lemma A.3
Let $\operatorname{ord}^G(g) = \alpha \cdot \beta$ in a finite group G. Then $\operatorname{ord}^G(g^\alpha) = \beta$.

Proof Since $\operatorname{ord}^G(g) = \alpha \cdot \beta$, we know that the elements in the sequence $g^1, g^2, \ldots, g^{\alpha \cdot \beta}$ are all different. Since the sequence $g^\alpha, g^{2 \cdot \alpha}, \ldots, g^{\beta \cdot \alpha}$ is a subsequence of the former, it follows that all its elements are different as well. Since its last element $g^{\beta \cdot \alpha}$ equals the group's two-sided identity, we deduce that $\operatorname{ord}^G(g^\alpha) = \beta$. □

Lemma A.4
Let $g^\alpha = e$ and $g^\beta = e$ in a finite group $\langle G, \circ, e \rangle$. Then $g^{\operatorname{gcd}(\alpha, \beta)} = e$ as well.

Proof From Proposition 2.23 (p. 39), we know that $\operatorname{gcd}(\alpha, \beta) = r \cdot \alpha + s \cdot \beta$ for some $r, s \in \mathbb{Z}$. Thus

$$g^{\operatorname{gcd}(\alpha, \beta)} = g^{r \cdot \alpha + s \cdot \beta} = g^{r \cdot \alpha} \circ g^{s \cdot \beta} = (g^\alpha)^r \circ (g^\beta)^s = e^r \circ e^s = e,$$

since $\langle g \rangle$ is commutative (by Exercise 2.11-8, p. 42). □

Lemma A.5
Let $\langle G, \circ, e \rangle$ be a finite commutative group and let $a, b \in G$. Let $\operatorname{ord}^G(a) = \alpha$ and $\operatorname{ord}^G(b) = \beta$ such that $\operatorname{gcd}(\alpha, \beta) = 1$. Then $\operatorname{ord}^G(a \circ b) = \alpha \cdot \beta$.

Proof   We have

$$e = e \circ e = (a^\alpha)^\beta \circ (b^\beta)^\alpha = a^{\alpha \cdot \beta} \circ b^{\alpha \cdot \beta} = (a \circ b)^{\alpha \cdot \beta};$$

the last equality holds because G is commutative. So let

$$(a \circ b)^\gamma = e$$

for some $1 \le \gamma \le \alpha \cdot \beta$. It suffices to show that γ equals $\alpha \cdot \beta$. By Lagrange's theorem, $\gamma \mid \alpha \cdot \beta$. In Exercise 2.11-5 we saw that every natural number has a unique factorization into powers of prime numbers. Therefore, it is possible to write γ as a product of two natural numbers γ_1 and γ_2 such that $\gamma_1 \mid \alpha$ and $\gamma_2 \mid \beta$. Since $\gamma_1 \cdot \gamma_2 \mid \gamma_1 \cdot \beta$ and since $(a \circ b)^\gamma = e$, we conclude

$$e = (a \circ b)^{\gamma_1 \cdot \beta} = a^{\gamma_1 \cdot \beta} \circ b^{\gamma_1 \cdot \beta} = a^{\gamma_1 \cdot \beta},$$

because $\beta \mid \gamma_1 \cdot \beta$ and $b^\beta = e$. Therefore, $a^\alpha = e$ and $a^{\gamma_1 \cdot \beta} = e$ imply, by Lemma A.4, that $a^{\gcd(\alpha, \gamma_1 \cdot \beta)} = e$. But $\gcd(\alpha, \beta) = 1$ and $\gamma_1 \mid \alpha$ imply $\gcd(\alpha, \gamma_1 \cdot \beta) = \gamma_1$. So we have $a^{\gamma_1} = e$ and therefore $\gamma_1 \mid \operatorname{ord}^G(a)$, since the order of a in G is α; hence we obtain $\gamma_1 = \alpha$. We may argue in a symmetric manner that $\gamma_2 = \beta$, and so $\gamma = \gamma_1 \cdot \gamma_2 = \alpha \cdot \beta$ follows. $\square$

Proposition A.6
Let $\langle G, \circ, e \rangle$ be a finite commutative group with $a, b \in G$ such that $\operatorname{ord}^G(a) = \alpha$ and $\operatorname{ord}^G(b) = \beta$. Then there exist numbers $i, j \in \mathbb{N} \cup \{0\}$ such that

$$\operatorname{ord}^G(a^i \circ b^j) = \operatorname{lcm}(\alpha, \beta).$$

Proof   Let $\gamma \stackrel{\text{def}}{=} \operatorname{lcm}(\alpha, \beta)$ and $\delta \stackrel{\text{def}}{=} \gcd(\alpha, \beta)$; note that $\alpha \cdot \beta = \gamma \cdot \delta$. But δ cannot be zero because the order of group elements cannot be zero either. Thus we may define

$$\alpha_1 \stackrel{\text{def}}{=} \alpha/\delta, \qquad \beta_1 \stackrel{\text{def}}{=} \beta/\delta.$$

Then $\gcd(\alpha_1, \beta_1) = 1$ by construction. By the definition of least common multiple, we have $\gamma = \alpha_1 \cdot \beta_1 \cdot \delta$. The magic trick resides in an ingenious partitioning of δ. Let

$$\delta = \delta_{\alpha_1} \cdot \delta_{\beta_1} \cdot \delta_r, \tag{A.5}$$

where

- δ_{α_1} is the product of all prime factors occurring in δ and α_1;
- the number δ_{β_1} is similarly the product of all prime factors that occur in δ and β_1; and
- δ_r is the product of all those prime factors of δ that occur neither in α_1 nor in β_1.

In these products, the prime factors retain their powers according to δ. Note that this definition makes sense only because $\gcd(\alpha_1, \beta_1) = 1$; otherwise, prime factors of δ may occur in α_1 and β_1, causing equation (A.5) to fail. But $\gcd(\alpha_1, \beta_1) = 1$ also guarantees that each pair from $\{\delta_{\alpha_1}, \delta_{\beta_1}, \delta_r\}$ has $\gcd = 1$. Therefore, we succeed in factoring γ into two factors whose gcd equals 1:

$$\gamma = (\alpha_1 \cdot \delta_{\alpha_1} \cdot \delta_r) \cdot (\beta_1 \cdot \delta_{\beta_1}). \tag{A.6}$$

Since

$$\operatorname{ord}^G(a) = \alpha = \alpha_1 \cdot \delta = \alpha_1 \cdot \delta_{\alpha_1} \cdot \delta_{\beta_1} \cdot \delta_r,$$

we use Lemma A.3 to infer that $\operatorname{ord}^G(a^{\delta_{\beta_1}})$ equals $\alpha_1 \cdot \delta_{\alpha_1} \cdot \delta_r$. Similarly, since

$$\operatorname{ord}^G(b) = \beta = \beta_1 \cdot \delta = \beta_1 \cdot \delta_{\alpha_1} \cdot \delta_{\beta_1} \cdot \delta_r,$$

we use the same lemma to conclude that $\operatorname{ord}^G(b^{\delta_{\alpha_1} \cdot \delta_r}) = \beta_1 \cdot \delta_{\beta_1}$. By construction, we have $\gcd(\alpha_1 \cdot \delta_{\alpha_1} \cdot \delta_r, \beta_1 \cdot \delta_{\beta_1}) = 1$. Thus we may use Lemma A.5 to obtain

$$
\begin{aligned}
\operatorname{ord}^G(a^{\delta_{\beta_1}} \circ b^{\delta_{\alpha_1} \cdot \delta_r}) &= (\alpha_1 \cdot \delta_{\alpha_1} \cdot \delta_r) \cdot (\beta_1 \cdot \delta_{\beta_1}) \\
&= \alpha_1 \cdot \beta_1 \cdot \delta_{\alpha_1} \cdot \delta_{\beta_1} \cdot \delta_r \\
&= \alpha_1 \cdot \beta_1 \cdot \delta \\
&= \gamma. \tag{A.7}
\end{aligned}
$$

$\square$

EXERCISE A.1

1. Let p be 31. We take a closer look at the proof of Proposition A.6 with $G = \mathbb{Z}_p^*$, $a = [15]_p$, and $b = [10]_p$.
   (a) Determine $\operatorname{ord}^{\mathbb{Z}_p^*}([15]_p)$ and $\operatorname{ord}^{\mathbb{Z}_p^*}([10]_p)$ (i.e. α and β, respectively).
   (b) Compute $\operatorname{lcm}(\alpha, \beta)$ (i.e. γ).
   (c) Show that the order of the product $[15]_p *_p [10]_p$ is different from γ. Thus, the numbers i and j of Proposition A.6 cannot always be 1.
   (d) Determine δ, δ_{α_1}, δ_{β_1}, and δ_r.
   (e) What are i and j? Verify the correctness of that choice.

Theorem A.7
Let $p > 2$ be prime. Then there exists an element $[m]_p$ such that

$$\operatorname{ord}^{\mathbb{Z}_p^*}([m]_p) = \Lambda(\mathbb{Z}_p^*).$$

Proof We construct this element m inductively. Initially, let the set S be $\mathbb{Z}_p^*$. Choose any two elements $[a]_p$ and $[b]_p$ from S.[1] By Proposition A.6, there exists an element $[m_1]_p$ whose order is the least common multiple of the orders for $[a]_p$ and $[b]_p$. Remove $[a]_p$ and $[b]_p$ from S. Assume that we have constructed $[m_1]_p$ up to $[m_k]_p$ in the manner to be described. As long as S is nonempty, pick an element $[c]_p$ from it. By Proposition A.6, there exists an element $[m_{k+1}]_p$ whose order is the least common multiple of the order for $[m_k]_p$ and $[c]_p$. Clearly, this process terminates (i.e., S will be empty) for some value of l, and then $[m_l]_p$ has $\Lambda(\mathbb{Z}_p^*)$ as its order, which is what we had to show. Of course, this proof works in any finite commutative group. $\square$

---

[1] This can be done because $p > 2$, so the initial S has $p - 1$ elements.

Thus, to show the existence of a primitive root for $\mathbb{Z}_p^*$, it suffices to prove that $\Lambda(\mathbb{Z}_p^*)$ equals $p - 1$ if $p > 2$ is prime. This requires a little excursion into the elementary algebra of polynomials "modulo p". From basic calculus or linear algebra, you may be familiar with polynomials in one unknown x. For example, $4 \cdot x^3 - 6 \cdot x + 5$ is a polynomial, and so is $-x$. We already encountered polynomials modulo 2 in our discussion of the cipher Rijndael.

Definition A.8 (Polynomial over $\mathbb{Z}$)

A *polynomial in one unknown* x is any expression of the form $a_n \cdot x^n + a_{n-1} \cdot x^{n-1} + \cdots + a_1 \cdot x + a_0$, where all coefficients $a_0, a_1, \ldots, a_n$ are in $\mathbb{Z}$ and $n \in \mathbb{N} \cup \{0\}$. The *zeros* of

$$f(x) \stackrel{\text{def}}{=} a_n \cdot x^n + a_{n-1} \cdot x^{n-1} + \cdots + a_1 \cdot x + a_0$$

are those integers $z \in \mathbb{Z}$ that satisfy $f(z) = 0$.

Every polynomial over $\mathbb{Z}$ induces a function of type $\mathbb{Z} \to \mathbb{Z}$. For example, for $f(x) = 4 \cdot x^3 - 6 \cdot x + 5$ we have $f(1) = 3$, $f(-1) = 7$, et cetera. Some expressions that are not polynomials may easily be transformed into one. For example, $(x - 5) \cdot 3 \cdot (x^2 - 4 \cdot x)$ can be rewritten as a polynomial by applying the usual distributivity laws. The only zeros of the resulting polynomial are 5, 0, and 4. Our reason for discussing polynomials at all is that we are interested in the polynomial

$$x^{\Lambda(\mathbb{Z}_p^*)} - 1,$$

where $p > 2$ is prime. We show that this polynomial cannot have more zeros modulo p than its degree modulo p. We define these notions shortly. This insight then implies

$$p - 1 \leq \Lambda(\mathbb{Z}_p^*),$$

noting that

$$z^{\Lambda(\mathbb{Z}_p^*)} = 1 \bmod p \quad \text{for all } z \in \{1, 2, \ldots, p - 1\},$$

since $\Lambda(\mathbb{Z}_p^*)$ is the lcm of all $\mathrm{ord}^{\mathbb{Z}_p^*}(z)$. Observe that the reverse inequality

$$\Lambda(\mathbb{Z}_p^*) \leq p - 1$$

holds by Lagrange's theorem, for $\Lambda(\mathbb{Z}_p^*)$ is the order of a subgroup of $\mathbb{Z}_p^*$ by Theorem A.7.

Definition A.9 (Polynomial over $\mathbb{Z}_l$)

Let $l \in \mathbb{N}$. We extend the equivalence relation $=_l$ (see Exercise 2.8-1, p. 36) from $\mathbb{Z}$ to polynomials. Let

$$f(x) \stackrel{\text{def}}{=} a_n \cdot x^n + a_{n-1} \cdot x^{n-1} + \cdots + a_1 \cdot x + a_0,$$
$$g(x) \stackrel{\text{def}}{=} b_m \cdot x^m + b_{m-1} \cdot x^{m-1} + \cdots + b_1 \cdot x + b_0$$

be two polynomials over $\mathbb{Z}$ with $n, m \in \mathbb{N} \cup \{0\}$. Then $f(x) =_l g(x)$ holds if and only if

$$a_i - b_i = 0 \bmod l \quad \text{for all } i = 0, 1, \ldots, \max(n, m),$$

where we define a_i and b_i to be 0 if they are not explicitly defined in the representations of f and g, respectively.

Thus two polynomials are equivalent modulo l if and only if "all their coefficients" of the same power are equivalent modulo l. For example, $x^3 - 4 \cdot x^2 + x$ and $x^3 + x$ are equivalent modulo 4, but $x^3 - 4 \cdot x^2 + x$ and $x^3 + x^2 + x$ are not.

EXERCISES A.2

1. In the proof of Theorem A.7, could we also remove $[m_1]_p$ from S before we compute $[m_2]_p$?
2. Show that $=_l$ is an equivalence relation for polynomials over $\mathbb{Z}$.
3. Show that $x^3 + x + 1$ has no zeros z satisfying $z = 0 \bmod 5$.
4. Show that $x^2 + x + 1$ has no zero over $\mathbb{Z}$ at all. (*Hint:* Show that there are no zeros z with $z = 0 \bmod 2$ or $z = 1 \bmod 2$. Why does this suffice?)
5. Compute all zeros of

$$x^6 + 2 \cdot x^4 + 4 \cdot x^3 - 3 \cdot x + 4$$

   modulo 7 – that is, all zeros of this polynomial that are in $\{0, 1, 2, \ldots, 6\}$.
6. Implement an efficient algorithm that takes as input the representation of a polynomial $f(x)$ over $\mathbb{Z}$ and a natural number l, and outputs all zeros of $f(x)$ modulo l.

Definition A.10 (Degree of a Polynomial)
The *degree* of a polynomial $a_n \cdot x^n + a_{n-1} \cdot x^{n-1} + \cdots + a_1 \cdot x + a_0$ is the maximal i such that $a_i \neq 0$; its *degree modulo l* is the maximal i such that $a_i \neq 0 \bmod l$.

Note that the degree of a polynomial is its degree modulo 1. The degree of $6 \cdot x^3 + x + 1$ is 3; its degree modulo 7 is also 3. However, its degree modulo 2 is only 1.

Proposition A.11
Let $f(x) \stackrel{\text{def}}{=} a_n \cdot x^n + a_{n-1} \cdot x^{n-1} + \cdots + a_1 \cdot x + a_0$ *be a polynomial over* $\mathbb{Z}$ *and let* $p > 2$ *be prime. Then* $f(x)$ *cannot have more zeros in* $\{0, 1, 2, \ldots, p-1\}$ *than the degree of* $f(x)$ *modulo* p. *In particular, the polynomial*

$$x^{\Lambda(\mathbb{Z}_p^*)} - 1 \tag{A.8}$$

cannot have more than $\Lambda(\mathbb{Z}_p^*)$ *many zeros modulo* p.

Proof Without loss of generality, we may assume that $a_n \neq 0 \bmod p$ – that is, the degree of $f(x)$ modulo p equals n. Since p is prime, all elements in $\{1, 2, \ldots, p-1\}$ have multiplicative inverses modulo p, so we may assume that $a_n = 1$ without changing the set of zeros of $f(x)$ modulo p. Let l be the number of zeros of $f(x)$ modulo p. We need to show that $l \leq n$. For that, we construct a finite family of polynomials $f_k(x)$ with $k = n, n-1, \ldots$ ($k \in \mathbb{N} \cup \{0\}$) in the following manner. First,

$$f_n(x) \stackrel{\text{def}}{=} f(x)$$

is the original polynomial. If $f(x)$ does not have a zero modulo p at all, then $l = 0 \le n$ and we are done. Otherwise, let $r_n \in \{0, 1, \ldots, p-1\}$ be a zero of $f_n(x)$ modulo p. Since $a_n = 1$, it is elementary to see that

$$f_n(x) =_p (x - r_n) \cdot f_{n-1}(x)$$

for some polynomial $f_{n-1}(x)$ of degree $n-1$ modulo p. Assume that the family $f_n(x)$, $f_{n-1}(x), \ldots$ has already been constructed in this way. Because the degree of $f_k(x)$ modulo p decreases with k, this process terminates at some $n - k_0 \in \mathbb{N}$. By construction, $f_{n-k_0}(x)$ has no zeros modulo p and

$$f(x) =_p (x - r_n) \cdot (x - r_{n-1}) \cdots (x - r_{n-k_0+1}) \cdot f_{n-k_0}(x).$$

The construction made no use of the fact that p is prime (except for securing $a_n = 1$). However, the primeness of p ensures that the zeros of $f(x)$ modulo p can only be among

$$\{r_n, r_{n-1}, r_{n-2}, \ldots, r_{n-k_0+1}\},$$

for $f(z) = 0 \bmod p$ implies that p is a divisor of

$$(z - r_n) \cdot (z - r_{n-1}) \cdots (z - r_{n-k_0+1}) \cdot f_{n-k_0}(z).$$

But a prime number divides a product of integers if and only if it divides at least one of its factors (see Exercise A.3-1). Since $f_{n-k_0}(z) \ne 0 \bmod p$, this can only mean $p \mid z - r_{n-k'}$ for some $k' \in \{1, 2, \ldots, k_0 - 1\}$. Thus $z = r_{n-k'} \bmod p$ shows that l equals k_0, which is less than or equal to n. $\qquad \square$

Corollary A.12
Theorem 2.32 (p. 43) is valid.

Proof By Theorem A.7, there exists some element in $\mathbb{Z}_p^*$ whose order is $\Lambda(\mathbb{Z}_p^*)$. Thus we may invoke Lagrange's theorem and infer that $\Lambda(\mathbb{Z}_p^*) \mid p - 1$, so $\Lambda(\mathbb{Z}_p^*) \le p - 1$ follows since $p - 1$ is positive. By Proposition A.11, the polynomial $x^{\Lambda(\mathbb{Z}_p^*)} - 1$ has at most as many zeros modulo p as its degree modulo p, which is $\Lambda(\mathbb{Z}_p^*)$ since $\Lambda(\mathbb{Z}_p^*) < p$. But since $\Lambda(\mathbb{Z}_p^*)$ is the lcm of all $\mathrm{ord}^{\mathbb{Z}_p^*}(z)$ with $z \in \{1, 2, \ldots, p - 1\}$, we infer that $\{1, 2, \ldots, p-1\}$ is the set of zeros of $x^{\Lambda(\mathbb{Z}_p^*)} - 1$ modulo p. Thus $p - 1 \le \Lambda(\mathbb{Z}_p^*)$ follows. But then $\Lambda(\mathbb{Z}_p^*) = p - 1$, so $\mathbb{Z}_p^*$ has a primitive root; this is all we still had to show to ensure the validity of Theorem 2.32. $\qquad \square$

Corollary A.13
Let p be prime. Then $\mathbb{Z}_p^*$ has a primitive root.

Corollary A.14
If the call `Witness(a,n)` *returns with* `true`, *then n is not a prime number.*

EXERCISES A.3

1. Prove: If p is prime and $a, b \in \mathbb{Z}$, then $p \mid a \cdot b$ if and only if $p \mid a$ or $p \mid b$.
2. It is instructive to consider the proof construction of Proposition A.11 with a concrete example.

   (a) Let $f(x) \stackrel{\text{def}}{=} x^5 + x^2 + x - 5$ and $p = 11$. Verify that 2 is a zero of $f(x)$ modulo 11.

   (b) Let z_5 be 2 and verify that $f_4(x)$ equals $x^4 + 2 \cdot x^3 + 4 \cdot x^2 + 9 \cdot x + 19$ modulo 11.

   (c) Verify that -3 is a zero of $f_4(x)$ modulo 11.

   (d) Choose z_4 to be -3 and verify that $f_3(x)$ equals $x^3 - x^2 - 4 \cdot x - 1$ modulo 11.

   (e) Prove that $f_3(x)$ has no zeros modulo 11.

   (f) Show that if $z \in \mathbb{Z}$ is a zero of $f(x)$ with $0 \leq z \leq 10$, then z equals 2 or 8.

3. Prove Corollary A.14.

4. For $n \in \mathbb{N}$, we define

$$\binom{n}{0} \stackrel{\text{def}}{=} 1,$$

$$\binom{n+1}{k+1} \stackrel{\text{def}}{=} \binom{n}{k} \cdot \frac{n+1}{k+1}$$

for all $k, n \in \mathbb{N}$ with $n \geq k$.

   (a) Compute $\binom{13}{5}$.

   (b) Prove: If $0 < k < p$ and p is prime, then $p \mid \binom{p}{k}$.

   (c) Use part (b) to prove that

$$(x + y)^p = x^p + y^p \bmod p \quad (p \text{ prime}). \tag{A.9}$$

   (d) Use part (c) to prove that

$$a^p = a \bmod p$$

for all $a \in \mathbb{N}$; use mathematical induction on a.

   (e) Why, and how, does part (d) imply Fermat's theorem?

The existence of a primitive root for $\mathbb{Z}_p^*$ suffices to demonstrate that `true` replies of calls `Witness(a,n)` are always correct, but we need to strengthen this existence proof to the group $\mathbb{Z}_{p^n}^*$, where $p > 2$ is prime and $n \in \mathbb{N}$. This stronger version is required for proving upper bounds on the probability of the algorithm `Miller-Rabin(a,s)` wrongly classifying a number as prime – a "false positive". It is advantageous to first consider the case $n = 2$. For that, we need to know $\phi(p^n)$ explicitly.

Lemma A.15 (Totient for Prime Powers)
For $p, n \in \mathbb{N}$ we have

$$\phi(p^n) = p^{n-1} \cdot (p - 1).$$

Proof Recall that $\phi(p^n)$ is the number of elements in $\mathbb{Z}_{p^n}$ that have a multiplicative inverse, so we may identify them with the elements x in $\{1, 2, \ldots, p^n - 1\}$ with $\gcd(x, p^n) = 1$. Since p is prime, the last condition is equivalent to $p \nmid x$. Since exactly every pth number in $\{1, 2, \ldots, p^n - 1\}$ is divided by p, we obtain $\phi(p^n) = p^n - p^n/p = p^{n-1} \cdot (p-1)$.   □

We now stage our argument for primitive roots in $\mathbb{Z}_{p^n}^*$, beginning with the case where n equals 2.

Theorem A.16

Let $p > 1$ be prime. Then $\mathbb{Z}_{p^2}^*$ has a primitive root.

Proof　By Corollary A.13, we know that $\mathbb{Z}_p^*$ has a primitive root g. Consider $\mathrm{ord}([g]_{p^2})$. Since $z = 1 \bmod p^2$ implies $z = 1 \bmod p$, we know that $\mathrm{ord}([g]_{p^2})$ must be an integral multiple of $\phi(p) = p - 1$, because $[g]_p$ is a primitive root for $\mathbb{Z}_p^*$. Thus

$$\mathrm{ord}([g]_{p^2}) = k \cdot (p - 1)$$

for some $k \in \mathbb{N}$. By Lagrange's theorem, we know that $\mathrm{ord}([g]_{p^2})$ divides $\phi(p^2)$, which is $p \cdot (p - 1)$ by Lemma A.15. But the only divisors $k \cdot (p - 1)$ of $p \cdot (p - 1)$ are $p - 1$ and $p \cdot (p - 1)$, so k is either 1 or p. In the latter case, $\mathrm{ord}([g]_{p^2})$ equals the size of the group $\mathbb{Z}_{p^2}^*$ and so g is a primitive root for $\mathbb{Z}_{p^2}^*$. In the former case, we have

$$g^{p-1} = 1 \bmod p^2 \tag{A.10}$$

and claim that $g + p$ is a primitive root for $\mathbb{Z}_{p^2}^*$. Toward that end, we compute

$$(g + p)^{p-1} = g^{p-1} + (p - 1) \cdot g^{p-2} \cdot p \bmod p^2,$$

since all other summands have at least a factor of p^2 by a variation of Exercise A.3-4(c) (when y equals p). If $(g + p)^{p-1} = 1 \bmod p^2$, then

$$g^{p-1} + (p - 1) \cdot g^{p-2} \cdot p = 1 \bmod p^2$$

and

$$g^{p-1} = 1 \bmod p^2$$

imply that

$$(p - 1) \cdot g^{p-2} \cdot p = 0 \bmod p^2;$$

that is, $(p - 1) \cdot g^{p-1} = 0 \bmod p$, which means that $p \,|\, g^{p-1}$ as $p > 1$ and p prime, contradicting Fermat's theorem because $g \neq 0 \bmod p$. (Why?) Therefore, $(g + p)^{p-1} \neq 1 \bmod p^2$. Now we may argue with $g + p$ as we did before with g, implying that $\mathrm{ord}([g + p]_{p^2})$ equals $k \cdot (p - 1)$ for k either 1 or p. But $(g + p)^{p-1} \neq 1 \bmod p^2$ excludes the case $k = 1$ and so $\mathrm{ord}([g + p]_{p^2}) = p \cdot (p - 1)$ ensures that $g + p$ is a primitive root for $\mathbb{Z}_{p^2}^*$. $\qquad\square$

Corollary A.17

Let $p > 1$ be prime and let g be a primitive root of $\mathbb{Z}_p^*$. Then g or $g + p$ is a primitive root of $\mathbb{Z}_{p^2}^*$.

Theorem A.16 can be lifted to arbitrary powers p^n with $n \in \mathbb{N}$, provided we can demonstrate that a primitive root g for $\mathbb{Z}_{p^2}^*$ is also a primitive root g for $\mathbb{Z}_{p^n}^*$ for all $n \in \mathbb{N}$ with $n > 2$. This can indeed be done, but we need the concept of a degree of a factor.

Definition A.18 (Degree of a in b)

The unique number $k \in \mathbb{N} \cup \{0\}$ that satisfies $a^k \mid b$ and $a^{k+1} \nmid b$ is called the *degree of a in b*. We write $a^k \| b$ in that case.

Note that for all $a, b \in \mathbb{Z}$ we have $a^0 \mid b$ and there is some $l \in \mathbb{N}$ such that $a^l \nmid b$. Hence the number k in $a^k \| b$ is indeed uniquely defined, since $a^{k+k_0} \mid b$ implies $a^k \mid b$ for all $k_0 \in \mathbb{N}$. For example, $2^3 \| 40$ and $5^2 \| 100$ hold, but $2^3 \| 12$ does not. The transfer of Theorem A.16 to the more general case of p^n necessitates an understanding of whether (and how) $p^n \| x - 1$ determines the degree of p in $x^p - 1$.

Lemma A.19

Let $p \in \mathbb{N}$ be prime, $p > 1$, and $k \in \mathbb{N}$. For any $x \in \mathbb{Z}$, if $p > 2$ or $k > 1$ then $p^k \| x - 1$ implies $p^{k+1} \| x^p - 1$.

Proof Since $p^k \| x - 1$, we have

$$x = 1 + p^k \cdot u$$

for some $u \in \mathbb{Z}$ with $p \nmid u$. Then $x^p - 1$ equals

$$(1 + p^k \cdot u)^p - 1$$

$$= \left(1^p + \binom{p}{1} \cdot p^k \cdot u + \binom{p}{2} \cdot p^{2k} \cdot u^2 + \cdots + p^{pk} \cdot u^p \right) - 1$$

$$= \binom{p}{1} \cdot p^k \cdot u + \binom{p}{2} \cdot p^{2k} \cdot u^2 + \binom{p}{3} \cdot p^{3k} \cdot u^3 + \cdots + p^{pk} \cdot u^p. \qquad \text{(A.11)}$$

In trying to determine whether $p^{k+1} \mid x^p - 1$, it suffices to show that all summands in (A.11) are divisible by p^{k+1}. Obviously, this is the case if $p > 2$ or if $k > 1$. In order to see that $p^{k+2} \nmid x^p - 1$, observe that $p^{k+2} \mid x^p - 1$ implies $p \mid u + \binom{p}{2} \cdot p^{k-1} \cdot u^2 + \binom{p}{3} \cdot p^{2k-1} \cdot u^3 + \cdots + p^{pk-(k+1)} \cdot u^p$ yet all summands except the first are divisible by p – a contradiction. $\square$

The constraint "$p > 2$ or $k > 1$" is no accident. For example, $p = 2$ is prime, but $\mathbb{Z}_{2^3}^*$ has no primitive root.

Theorem A.20

Let $p > 2$ be prime and let $n \in \mathbb{N}$ with $n > 1$. If $g \in \mathbb{Z}$ is a primitive root for $\mathbb{Z}_{p^2}^*$, then g is also a primitive root for $\mathbb{Z}_{p^n}^*$. In particular, $\mathbb{Z}_{p^n}^*$ has a primitive root for all such n.

Proof By Fermat's theorem, we have $p \mid g^{p-1} - 1$. Since g is a primitive root for $\mathbb{Z}_{p^2}^*$, whose group size is $p \cdot (p - 1)$, we cannot have $p^2 \mid g^{p-1} - 1$ for $p > 1$ and so $p^1 \| g^{p-1} - 1$ follows. Since $p > 2$, we may invoke Lemma A.19 repeatedly to infer

$$p^2 \| g^{p \cdot (p-1)} - 1,$$

$$p^3 \| g^{p^2 \cdot (p-1)} - 1,$$

$$\vdots$$

$$p^n \| g^{p^{(n-1)} \cdot (p-1)} - 1. \qquad \text{(A.12)}$$

These relations ensure that $p^n \nmid g^{p^{(i-1)} \cdot (p-1)} - 1$ for any $i \in \mathbb{N}$ with $i < n$. $\square$

A.2 COMPUTING PRIMITIVE ROOTS

We already saw that $\mathbb{Z}_n^*$ has a primitive root for all $n = p^k$ with $p > 2$ prime and $k \in \mathbb{N}$. Indeed, these are almost all the cases where such primitive roots exist.

Remark A.21 (Existence of Primitive Roots)
For $n \in \mathbb{N}$, the group $\mathbb{Z}_n^*$ has a primitive root if and only if n equals 2, 4, p^k, or $2 \cdot p^k$, where p is an odd prime and $k \in \mathbb{N}$.

Knowing the existence of a primitive root is often extremely useful in proving properties about $\mathbb{Z}_n^*$. However, some key-exchange protocols work with an explicit primitive root g, so one must be able to *compute* a primitive root. If it proves to be too difficult to find a primitive root, or if no primitive root exists for a given value of n, then one would like to compute an element g that generates a very large subgroup. We saw one technique for this at work when discussing the digital signature standard in Section 4.1.1; see Exercise 4.7-8 (p. 149) for details.

EXERCISES A.4

1. Show that $\mathbb{Z}_{2^3}^*$ has no primitive root by computing, for each element of $\mathbb{Z}_{2^3}^*$, its generating subgroup and then showing that it is smaller than $\mathbb{Z}_{2^3}^*$.
2. Explain *in detail* why the proof of Lemma A.19 does not work if $p = 2$ and $k = 1$.
3. Explain why the proof of Theorem A.20 guarantees that g is a primitive root of $\mathbb{Z}_{p^n}^*$.
4. Write a program `Prim_root?(g,n,e)` that decides whether g is a primitive root for $\mathbb{Z}_n^*$ for "small" values of n. The program *assumes* (and does not verify) that the value e equals $\phi(n)$. First, check whether $[g]_n \in \mathbb{Z}_n^*$. If so, generate its subgroup and compare its size to $\phi(n)$. (Does your program have to maintain the history of values being computed?)
5. Use the algorithm `Prim_root?(g,n,e)` to find a primitive root for 1999^{23}. You should do this in two different ways.
   (a) Compute a primitive root g for 1999 and then test whether g or $g + 1999$ is a primitive root for 1999^2. (One of them has to be – why?) Conclude that the respective root for 1999^2 is also one for 1999^{23}.
   (b) Compute a primitive root for 1999^2 by making calls to `Prim_root?(g,n,e)` for $n = 1999^2$. What is the correct value of e?
6. Find a primitive root for $\mathbb{Z}_{3^3}^*$.
7. Find a primitive root for $\mathbb{Z}_n^*$, where n equals 2476099.

Bibliography

Abadi, M. (1998). Two facets of authentication. Technical report SRC-TR-1998-007, Systems Research Center, Palo Alto, CA.

Andrews, G. R., and R. P. Reitman (1980). An axiomatic approach to information flow in programs. *ACM Transactions on Programming Languages and Systems* 2: 56–76.

Apt, K. R., and E.-R. Olderog (1991). *Verification of Sequential and Concurrent Programs.* Berlin: Springer-Verlag.

Bach, E., and J. Shallit (1996). *Algorithmic Number Theory.* Cambridge, MA: MIT Press.

Backhouse, R. C. (1986). *Program Construction and Verification.* Englewood Cliffs, NJ: Prentice-Hall.

Banâtre, J.-P., C. Bryce, and D. Le Métayer (1994). Compile-time detection of information flow in sequential programs. In *Proceedings of the European Symposium on Research in Computer Systems* (Lecture Notes in Computer Science, vol. 875), pp. 55–73. Berlin: Springer-Verlag.

Bell, D. E., and L. J. La Padula (1973). Secure computer systems: Mathematical foundations and model. Technical report M74-244, MITRE Corp., Bedford, MA.

Bellare, M., and P. Rogaway (1993). Random oracles are practical: A paradigm for designing efficient protocols. In *Proceedings of the First Annual Conference on Computer and Communications Security.* Perugia, Italy: ACM Press.

Bellare, M., and P. Rogaway (1995). Optimal asymmetric encryption – How to encrypt with RSA. In A. De Santis (Ed.), *Advances in Cryptology – Eurocrypt 94 Proceedings* (Lecture Notes in Computer Science, vol. 950). Berlin: Springer-Verlag.

Blake, I., G. Seroussi, and N. Smart (1999). *Elliptic Curves in Cryptography* (London Mathematical Society Lecture Note Series, vol. 265). Cambridge University Press.

Blakely, G. R. (1979). Safeguarding cryptographic keys. *AFIPS Conference Proceedings* 48: 313–17.

Blum, L., M. Blum, and M. Shub (1986). A simple unpredictable random number generator. *SIAM Journal of Computing* 15: 364–83.

Boneh, D. (1999). Twenty years of attacks on the RSA cryptosystem. *NAMS* 46: 203–13.

Burrows, M., M. Abadi, and R. Needham (1989). A logic of authentication. Technical report 39, DEC Systems Research Center, Palo Alto, CA.

Canetti, R., O. Goldreich, and S. Halevi (1998). The random oracle methodology, revisited (preliminary version). In *Proceedings of the Thirtieth Annual ACM Symposium on Theory of Computing,* pp. 209–18. Perugia, Italy: ACM Press.

Canetti, R., D. Micciancio, and O. Reingold (1998). Perfectly one-way probabilistic hash functions. In *Proceedings of the Thirtieth Annual ACM Symposium on Theory of Computing,* pp. 131–40. Perugia, Italy: ACM Press.

Chaum, D. (1988). The dining cryptographers probem: Unconditional sender and recipient untraceability. *Journal of Cryptology* 1: 65–75.

Clarke, E. M., S. Jha, and W. Marrero (1988). A machine checkable logic of knowledge for specifying security properties of electronic commerce protocols. In *Workshop on Formal Methods and Security Protocols* (June, Indianapolis, IN).

Clarke, E. M., S. Jha, and W. Marrero (1998). Using state space exploration and a natural deduction style message derivation engine to verify security protocols. In D. Gries and

W.-P. de Roever (Eds.), *Proceedings of the IFIP Working Conference on Programming Concepts and Methods* (Shelter Island, NY), pp. 87–106. Boston: Chapman & Hall.

Cormen, T. H., C. E. Leiserson, and R. L. Rivest (1990). *Introduction to Algorithms*. Cambridge, MA: MIT Press.

Crary, K., R. Harper, P. Lee, and F. Pfenning (2000). Automated techniques for provably safe mobile code. In *Proceedings of the DARPA Information Survivability Conference and Exposition, 2000* (Hilton Head, SC), vol. 1, pp. 406–19.

Denning, D. (1976). A lattice model of secure information flow. *Communications of the ACM* 19: 236–43.

Denning, D. (1977). Certification of programs for secure information flow. *Communications of the ACM* 20: 504–13.

Denning, D. (1999). *Information Warfare and Security*. Perugia, Italy: ACM Press.

Denning, D., and H. S. Lin (Eds.) (1994). *Rights and Responsibilities of Participants in Networked Communities*. Computer Science and Telecommunications Board, National Research Council. Washington, DC: National Academy Press.

Diffie, W., and M. E. Hellmann (1976). New directions in cryptography. *IEEE Transactions on Information Theory* 22: 644–54.

Dijkstra, E. W. (1976). *A Discipline of Programming*. Englewood Cliffs, NJ: Prentice-Hall.

ElGamal, T. (1985). A public-key cryptosystem and a signature scheme based on discrete logarithms. In *Advances in Cryptology: Proceedings of the CRYPTO '84*, pp. 10–18. Berlin: Springer-Verlag.

Feller, W. (1968). *An Introduction to Probability Theory and Its Applications*. New York: Wiley.

Francez, N. (1992). *Program Verification*. Reading, MA: Addison-Wesley.

Goldreich, O. (1997). The foundations of modern cryptography. In *Proceedings of Crypto '97* (Lecture Notes in Computer Science, vol. 1294). Berlin: Springer-Verlag.

Goldreich, O., S. Goldwasser, and S. Micali (1984). On the cryptographic applications of random functions. In R. Blakely (Ed.), *Advances in Cryptology – Crypto '84 Proceedings* (Lecture Notes in Computer Science, vol. 196). Berlin: Springer-Verlag.

Goldreich, O., S. Goldwasser, and S. Micali (1986). How to construct random functions. *Journal of the ACM* 33: 210–17.

Huth, M., and M. Ryan (2000). *Logic in Computer Science: Reasoning and Modelling about Systems*. Cambridge University Press.

Joshi, R., and K. R. M. Leino (2000). A semantic approach to secure information flow. *Science of Computer Programming* 37: 113–38.

Kahn, D. (1967). *The Code Breakers: The Story of Secret Writing*. New York: Macmillan.

Leino, K. R. M. (1998). A semantic approach to secure information flow. In Johan Jeurig (Ed.), *Proceedings of the Fourth International Conference on Mathematics of Program Construction* (Lecture Notes in Computer Science, vol. 1422), pp. 254–71. Berlin: Springer-Verlag.

Leino, K. R. M., and R. Joshi (1997). A semantic approach to secure information flow. Technical report SRC-TN-1997-032, Systems Research Center, Palo Alto, CA.

Lowe, G. (1996). Breaking and fixing the Needham–Schroeder public-key protocol using FDR. In *Tools and Algorithms for the Construction and Analysis of Systems* (Lecture Notes in Computer Science, vol. 1055), pp. 144–66. Berlin: Springer-Verlag.

Lowe, G. (1997). A family of attacks upon authentication protocols. Technical report TR-1997/5, Department of Mathematics and Computer Science, University of Leicester, U.K.

Marrero, W., E. M. Clarke, and S. Jha (1997). Model checking for security protocols. Technical report CMU-SCS-97-139, Carnegie Mellon University, Pittsburgh, PA.

McGraw, G., and E. W. Felten (1997). *Securing Java*. New York: Wiley.

Meadows, C. (1996). The NRL protocol analyzer. *Journal of Logic Programming* 26: 113–31.

Meadows, C. (1999). Analysis of the internet key exchange protocol using the NRL protocol analyzer. In *IEEE Symposium on Security and Privacy*. New York: IEEE.

Millen, J. (1999). 20 years of covert channel analysis. In *Proceedings of the 1999 IEEE Symposium on Security and Privacy*. New York: IEEE.

Milner, R. (1989). *Communication and Concurrency*. Englewood Cliffs, NJ: Prentice-Hall.

Mitchell, J. C., M. Mitchell, and U. Stern (1997). Automated analysis of cryptograhpic protocols using Murφ. In *IEEE Symposium on Security and Privacy*. New York: IEEE.

Mitchell, J. C., V. Shmatikov, and U. Stern (1998). Finite-state analysis of SSL 3.0. In *7th USENIX Security Symposium* (San Antonio, TX).

Mizuno, M., and D. A. Schmidt (1992). A security flow control algorithm and its denotational semantics correctness proof. *Formal Aspects of Computing* 4: 722–54.

Motvani, R., and P. Raghavan (1995). *Randomized Algorithms*. Cambridge University Press.

Negroponte, N. *Being Digital*. New York: Vintage.

Oldyzko, A. (1994). Discrete logarithms in finite fields and their cryptographic significance. In *Advances in Cryptology – EUROCRYPT '94* (Lecture Notes in Computer Science, vol. 314), pp. 224–314. Berlin: Springer-Verlag.

Paulson, L. (1998). The inductive approach to verifying cryptographic protocols. *Journal of Computer Security* 6: 85–128.

Rifkin, J. (2000). *The Age of Access*. New York: Putnam.

Rivest, R. L., A. Shamir, and L. Adleman (1978). A method for obtaining digital signatures and public-key cryptosystems. *Communications of the ACM* 21: 120–6.

Roszak, T. (1994). *The Cult of Information*. Berkeley: University of California Press.

Rueppel, R. A. (1986). *Analysis and Design of Stream Ciphers*. Berlin: Springer-Verlag.

Sabelfeld, A., and D. Sands (2000). Probabilistic noninterference for multi-threaded programs. In *Proceedings of the 13th IEEE Computer Security Foundations Workshop* (July). New York: IEEE.

Schneider, S. (2000). May testing, non-interference, and compositionality. Technical report, Department of Computer Science, Royal Holloway, University of London. Presented at the Workshop on Foundations in Computer Security (July, Cork, Ireland).

Schneier, B. (2000). *Secrets and Lies: Digital Security in a Networked World*. New York: Wiley.

Shamir, A. (1979). How to share a secret. *Communications of the ACM* 22: 612–13.

Singh, S. (2000). *The Code Book*. New York: Anchor Books.

Stinson, D. R. (1995). *Cryptography: Theory and Practice*. Boca Raton, FL: CRC Press.

Volpano, D. (1996). Provably secure programming languages for remote evaluation. *ACM Computing Surveys* 28A(2): electronic.

Volpano, D., and G. Smith (1997). A type-based approach to program security. In *Theory and Practice of Software Development: Proceedings of TAPSOFT '97, Seventh Internat. Conference CAAP/FASE* (Lecture Notes in Computer Science, vol. 1214), pp. 607–21. Berlin: Springer-Verlag.

Volpano, D., G. Smith, and C. Irvine (1996). A sound type system for secure information flow. *Journal of Computer Security* 4: 1–21.

von zur Gathen, J., and J. Gerhard (1999). *Modern Computer Algebra*. Cambridge University Press.

Index

Printed in the United States
By Bookmasters